INSIDE CHRISTIE'S

John Herbert

Hodder & Stoughton

LONDON SYDNEY AUCKLAND TORONTO

The author and the publisher are grateful to Design and Artists Copyright Society Limited for permission to reproduce *Jeune Arlequine* by Pablo Picasso and to John Murray (Publishers) Ltd for permission to reproduce the cartoon by Osbert Lancaster on page 112.

British Library Cataloguing in Publication Data

Herbert, John, *1924–*
Inside Christie's.
1. Auctioneering firms. Christies International Group
I. Title
381′.1

ISBN 0-340-43043-5

Published by Hodder & Stoughton,
a division of Hodder and Stoughton Ltd,
Mill Road, Dunton Green, Sevenoaks, Kent TN13 2YA.
Editorial Office: 47 Bedford Square, London WC1B 3DP.

Photoset by Rowland Phototypesetting Ltd,
Bury St Edmunds, Suffolk

Printed in Great Britain by
St Edmundsbury Press Ltd,
Bury St Edmunds, Suffolk

Contents

Illustrations

———❦———

Author's Note

This is an autobiographical account of the recovery of Christie's, the fine art auctioneers, from a perilously weak position in 1958 to one of strength and success in 1988. I was privileged to be one of the team selected by Peter Chance, whose leadership as chairman, ably followed by that of Jo Floyd, was responsible for the firm's regaining a position worthy of its historic past. Although I was public relations director from September 1959 to July 1985, I must emphasise that this is in no way an official history. I think this will become clear to the reader quite quickly.

In order fully to understand Christie's achievement, it is necessary to know the differences in 1958 between Christie's and their main rivals Sotheby's; and to appreciate the totally divergent personalities of the two chairmen, Peter Chance and Peter Wilson, which were responsible in the end for the success of Christie's and the downfall of Sotheby's as a British-owned company. Sotheby's story is dealt with in considerable detail up to the time it was taken over by Mr Alfred Taubman, the American real estate magnate. Lastly my book concerns the whole of the London and New York art markets, how they have grown and changed in the last thirty years and their possible future.

Acknowledgments and Bibliography

This book could not possibly have been written without the help of a large number of people to whom I am deeply grateful; many of them were willing to grant me long tape-recorded interviews. Without these it would not be possible to present what I claim to be an accurate picture of Christie's in the late '50s to the mid-'60s when the firm was fighting to survive. I am particularly grateful to Arthur Grimwade, who is the firm's elder statesman although long-since retired. Having joined the firm in 1932 he was able to give me invaluable information regarding Christie's in the '20s, '30s and immediate post-war years, and why in 1958 it was *in extremis*.

Although this book is titled *Inside Christie's* I realised as I dug deeper that it was impossible not to make a comparison with Sotheby's whose management during the '20s and '30s was extraordinarily enlightened for those times. I may be wrong but I think a comparison of the styles of management of the two firms and the main personalities makes a more interesting story. I am extremely grateful therefore to Frank Herrmann for permission to draw on his *Sotheby's: Portrait of an Auction House*, the firm's official history which was published by Chatto and Windus in 1980.

For the time following the formation of Christie's new Board in 1958, I have relied on those who joined about the same time as me or later, some of whom lasted a comparatively short time. Ex-colleagues from Christie's in chronological order: Anthony du Boulay; Richard Falkiner; Brian Sewell; Ian Lowe; David Barclay; Huon Mallalieu; Ray Perman; Christopher Wood; David Bathurst; Colin Anson; David Messum; John Harding: Johnnie van Haeften; Sara and Bill Ward. All of them with the exception of Ian Lowe who went to the Ashmolean and was assistant Keeper until recently became dealers. Brian Sewell, rather ironically when I remember his disgust when he heard I was going to be responsible for dealing with the Press, has for some years like Huon Mallalieu been a journalist and in 1989 was awarded the Critic of the Year prize. In addition there is John Critchley who retired after many years cataloguing furniture.

Of equal importance were my interviews with the following, some of whom are still on Sotheby's Board while others left to become dealers or follow other pursuits: Peregrine Pollen; Marcus Linell; Howard Ricketts; Richard Day; Michel Strauss; Peter Spira and Sir Gordon Brunton. I also had conversations with Lord Westmorland; Graham Llewellyn and Julian Thompson.

Then there is the Press. There are so many saleroom correspondents – foreign as well as British – that there is not space to mention them by name. I am grateful to all of them, not only because their reports and comments formed useful source material, but because with very few exceptions we achieved together a friendly as well as professional working relationship.

Museum directors and members of the Fine Art Trade have also been very helpful: Christopher White, Director of the Ashmolean Museum; Seymour Slive, Gleason Professor of Fine Arts and former Director of the Harvard University Art Museums, and Burton Fredericksen, Director Provenance Index and Senior Curator of Research, The Getty Art History Information Program. Jack Baer, managing director of Hazlitt, Gooden and Fox; Evelyn Joll, chairman of Agnew's; Sir Hugh Leggatt and John Partridge – their firms need no mention; Martin Summers of the Lefevre Gallery.

Sir Anthony Lousada who advised – if not nursed – Christie's for many years, and till recently was chairman of the British Art Market Standing Committee; the late Nigel Hollis; the Russell Partnership; Dr Christian Carritt, the twin sister of David; Walter Goetz; Lady Amabel Lindsay; Mrs Mark Wyndham; Mrs Simon Fraser; the Countess Bobrinskoy; John Young; Teather and Greenwood, members of the Stock Exchange, and G. Cawley, senior manager of the St James's branch of Lloyds Bank and his economic staff.

Lastly I cannot express my gratitude adequately to Jane Osborn, my long-suffering editor. Being responsible for a "first-book" author must be a trying experience, particularly when his original manuscript lands with a thud 60,000 words too long. I am eternally grateful for her advice and patience.

John Herbert

Bibliography

H. C. Marillier: *Christie's, 1766–1925*, Constable/Houghton, 1926.

Jeremy Cooper: *Under the Hammer*, Constable, 1977.

Frank Herrmann: *Sotheby's: Portrait of an Auction House*, Chatto and Windus, 1980.

Nicholas Faith: *SOLD: The Revolution in the Art Market*, Hamish Hamilton, 1985.

1

A Bad Day for El Greco

"Oh Brian, could you join us please?" It was May 7th, 1958, and for Brian Sewell and me our first day at Christie's, fine art auctioneers since 1766. The summons had come from Bill Martin, then Christie's picture director, and the Hon. Patrick Lindsay, his assistant, who were standing at the top of the stairs by the entrance to the anteroom. "It appears that I'm wanted," said Brian, and hurried off, with me tagging along out of a mixture of curiosity to know what Bill wanted Brian for and keenness to learn anything I could about how Christie's was run, having never set foot in the place before.

Bill led the way into the Big Room, as the main saleroom is called, where pictures and furniture were on view prior to being sold. Bill was holding a thin white catalogue. Pointing to a picture with it Bill asked, "Who do you think that's by, Brian?" Without much hesitation Brian replied, "I should think El Greco. Probably his *Christ Healing the Blind*. Why?" There was an embarrassed pause. Bill then said, "Well, it's catalogued here as Veronese School." "Oh," said Brian, "what a pity. Perhaps John here can give it some publicity?"

Brian and I had been on the gallery floor overlooking the great staircase leading up from Christie's Front Hall to the salerooms when Bill had called for Brian's help. We'd agreed to meet after lunch to get to know each other and, like new boys at school who are not quite sure what to make of each other, were making desultory conversation. "So you're going to deal with the Press," Brian had just said in his rather plummy and somewhat deprecating tone of voice, giving me the impression that he thought it a most distasteful prospect. I had been told on arrival that morning that I would be meeting Brian. "He was one of Anthony Blunt's prize pupils at the Courtauld," "Peter" Chance had told me. (Peter Chance, chairman only since April, was christened Ivan Oswald but all his life was called Peter by his parents and many friends.) Peter had evidently asked Blunt's advice about any promising recruits for the firm's picture department. Blunt was then still Keeper of the Queen's Pictures – many years later Brian organised his successful flight from the Press when his wartime activities became public. Bill told Brian he was the second person that day to have told him the picture was by El Greco. Bill's father, Sir Alec Martin, who had been unseated from his post as managing director in April, had apparently catalogued the picture as Veronese School after having seen it "up a back passage of some great house".

Missing an El Greco may nowadays seem incredible. However, in 1958 it wasn't so strange, as Brian told me. During the last thirty years there has been a tremendous growth in knowledge not only by art historians and dealers but also among the general public, because of art education in schools and a plethora of books and programmes on TV. In 1958 there was still astonishingly little known about such works as the one Brian had just identified. A considerable amount of research had been done on Dutch and Flemish pictures, and there were consequently reference books on those schools, but little on Spanish and Italian works.

It was quite understandable that Sir Alec did not recognise the painting as an El Greco, Brian explained to me after the somewhat traumatic scene in the Big Room, but it was unforgivable for him not to recognise the quality of the work. "He was obviously wholly inadequate in connoisseurship. I'd done a seventeenth-century course at the Courtauld and I specialised in Spanish painting. I take no pride in recognising the picture as by El Greco. It was easy for me. It couldn't have been by anyone else."

An erratum slip was duly typed out and pinned underneath the picture, much to the dealers' interest, while Bill prepared a short Press release which I sent down by taxi to the quality Press, but I think it was only Denys Sutton, then art critic of the *Financial Times*, who made something of it. To take this action so late in the day was quite wrong – it would never be done now. Not only is it highly unlikely that there would be such a crass piece of cataloguing, but a painting of that quality would be withdrawn, kept for a special sale, illustrated in the catalogue and advertised world-wide.

Years later Brian said that Bill would not have known it was by El Greco, even though he'd been to the Courtauld as well, but he did have an unerring eye for quality. If he'd seen it a week before, he would have thought to himself he must ask someone like Professor

Ellis Waterhouse. He would then have been able to persuade his father to withdraw the picture before it went on view. In the years to come there were quite a number of similar cases of pictures being recognised at the last moment, and they were all withdrawn.

However, in 1958, even if Bill was picture director, he didn't have the self-confidence to go against his father, whose authority still lingered on although he was no longer a managing director. It wasn't till July that Sir Alec actually left the firm and became a consultant. When he was managing director he had insisted on Bill's desk being in Sir Alec's own office. With his autocratic ways he had brainwashed Bill and never given him any real responsibility. Bill was respected by such people as Ellis Waterhouse and John Pope-Hennessy, later Director of the Victoria and Albert Museum and the Metropolitan Museum, New York, but he'd been emasculated so far as taking difficult decisions went.

As I walked back to the Bruton Street offices of Patrick Dolan and Associates, public relations consultants, I reflected on all that had happened in the year since I'd left Fleet Street. After ten years in journalism, most of them as a reporter on the *Daily Telegraph*, I decided like many others that the future might be brighter in PR. One night while on the 5 p.m. to midnight shift, I was kicking the furniture from boredom when a colleague told me there was a job going at "PDA", as it was known in the media world. I applied for it the next day; saw Patrick Dolan, the cherubic-looking but tough and intelligent chairman, and got the job, virtually doubling my salary in the process. The National Union of Journalists was very weak in those days and pay was in inverse proportion to the quality of the paper, irrespective of initiative and extra work such as writing features.

Working for Patrick Dolan certainly was never boring. At a moment's notice one had to become spokesman, image-builder and self-appointed expert on widely different subjects. My first client was the Western Region of Nigeria which had been granted regional independence and had engaged PDA mainly to encourage foreign investment. This involved my learning almost overnight the tribal, economic and political problems of the region, and within a month taking the Premier and his cabinet on a trade mission all over Scandinavia. On my return a few months later I was saddled with looking after the interests of butter producers in New Zealand, Australia, Holland, the United Kingdom and Eire, and in particular trying to persuade people to buy butter rather than margarine.

The first mention of Christie's had come a few days before. I'd been having lunch with my managing director, Noel Newsome, and as we went up in the lift afterwards, he said, "If we get this Christie's account I think I'll give it to you." "God, I don't know anything about antiques. I don't even know where the place is," I replied, thinking that three different accounts in one year was too much.

"There's been a bit of a power struggle at Christie's," Noel said later. "A new company has been formed under the chairmanship of Mr I. O. Chance. I've just finished speaking to him and he has asked us to open a Press Office on their premises and advise on public relations generally. I have told him that you will be reporting to him tomorrow." I had read in the papers about the new company being formed, but wondered whether my being given the account was quite as simple a matter as Noel said.

Among my new colleagues at PDA was an amusing and very young Old Etonian, Richard Berens, who had told me that he had written to Peter Chance (his godfather) suggesting that in view of the publicity Sotheby's was getting, Christie's needed some PR advice and general help with Press matters. Richard in fact was the office dogsbody, and Dolan had agreed to employ him only as a favour to Jocelyn Hambro and Richard's father, the great "C." Berens, for many years one of the most respected figures in the City. Hambro's were Christie's bankers – Jocelyn Hambro till 1987 was on the Board of Christies International – so Peter Chance probably asked Jocelyn about Dolan and PDA.

Another thought struck me. One of my brothers-in-law was Anthony Lousada, Christie's solicitor. That evening I rang him and asked him if Chance had said anything to him about PDA. Sure enough he had done. "Yes, first he asked me what I thought about the principle of employing a public relations firm – 'I suppose one has to have someone to deal with these bloody journalists. Some firm called Patrick Dolan and Associates, I think they're called – actually work for Jocelyn Hambro – have written in, or rather my godson Richard Berens has suggested they could be helpful.'" Anthony had remarked on the coincidence, explaining, "That's the firm my brother-in-law works in." I presume after that Peter asked for the professional equivalent of my vital statistics: a Wykehamist (that must have made him happy for he was an Old Etonian and when I covered the Fourth of June for the *Daily Telegraph* I remember boys saying quite seriously, "Of course Winchester is the only other school we recognise"), four years in the

RNVR, studied PPE at Oxford followed by ten years in journalism.

In spite of Peter's dislike of the Press, he did realise – some months before Sotheby's took similar action, in spite of their more progressive image – that professional PR was a necessary part of his "new broom".

So it was that I made my way for the first time to 8 King Street, St James's, where Christie's has been since 1823. I remember thinking as I approached it that it was a somewhat austere and anonymous building. Judy Cleave, my excellent secretary from PDA, was with me as we entered Christie's; that, I gathered, was part of the deal worked out with Christie's for a fee of £3,000, which was considerably less than the combined salaries of myself and Judy. When I queried this with Noel, he just winked and said something about "a sprat to catch a mackerel", but it didn't work out that way.

I had been told to report to Guy Hannen, one of the directors. He handed Judy over to a senior secretary and told her to take Judy round and introduce her to the other secretaries and see she had everything she needed. This was after showing us a small room to the left of the front door which was to be our office. Guy, whom I guessed correctly to be about my age – thirty-four – then took me to see Peter Chance, the chairman. After a perfunctory chat, Chance told me I would be meeting Brian Sewell. Guy then showed me round the building introducing me to the other directors and also Anthony du Boulay, who was not a director but had joined the firm in 1949 and after four years on the Front Counter was in charge of the porcelain department, a comparatively new development as previously porcelain had been sold with furniture.

The sight of the salerooms ended Guy's tour. He never showed me where the pictures were catalogued, took me down to the vaults in the basement or explained the procedure for receiving works of art over the Front Counter. I went back to our office where Judy was getting things organised. Suddenly somebody said, "Excuse me, sir, but are you joining us?" There stood a silver-haired, black-suited, stiff-collared man with a rose in his buttonhole and a delightful welcoming smile. "Yes," I said, "we're feeling a little lost, but we've been asked to handle the Press for Christie's and this is to be our office. Perhaps you could tell us how Christie's works?" And he did. His full name was Ridley Cromwell Leadbeater and he had been Front Counter manager for many years. I could see immediately that he had exactly the right personality for this most important post. First impressions count and it was quickly obvious that Ridley would treat an old lady with a shopping bag full of optimism but little value, with the same courtesy as someone he recognised as being an important collector or dealer. All the young girls and men under him were new recruits; some of them had arts degrees and others no qualifications at all save that they were the sons or daughters of collectors with whom Christie's hoped to do business in the future – or that's what I read into Ridley's description of them.

"Mind you, all the directors started behind the Front Counter, including the chairman Mr Chance, but that was before my time. My young men and girls learn by listening to the experts whom we ask down to answer the queries of those who bring their property in for sale or just valuation. You'd be amazed what I've seen dragged out from scruffy shopping baskets. Equally others are disappointed. When any of my team appear bright and there's a vacancy they're moved on to a department and gradually help with the cataloguing."

Ridley explained how everything was registered in through the "daybook" which gave each property, regardless of whether it was a dozen or two items, a number which would stay with it until it was sold. The daybook number – a series of letters and numbers – was stuck on or put on a label or in the case of a picture stencilled on the back of the stretcher. The stencilled numbers were highly important not only to keep track of the picture for the future sale, so it could be traced when wanted; also if it already had a stencilled number that would mean it had been sold by Christie's before. By referring to the old daybook ledgers the stencilled number would reveal what collection it had come from years back, which would certainly make the catalogue entry more interesting and could affect the price paid for it this time.

Ridley then took us to the next door office which he said was the clerical section of the picture department. Two people were at work in veritable Black Hole of Calcutta conditions. One of them was John Hancock, a member of the picture department although he had no academic training. He told me he had joined Christie's as a catalogue boy, and had been promoted from that "department" – a midden of an office near the back door – by what seems a natural process even to this day. No doubt it was while working in this little office that John developed the very good eye he has for pictures. I was to learn quite quickly this could apply to anyone in any department, even the Press Office, which is what makes working in a fine art auctioneer's so interesting. The second man in the room was Brian Sewell who, as Peter had told me, had joined that morning, but was already hard at work. We arranged to meet after lunch for a chat – which is where I began.

The following Friday morning the saleroom was abuzz with dealers discussing the El Greco, the highlight of what was otherwise an uninteresting sale. For Judy and me it was our first experience of the drama of a fine art auction. It was only when the El Greco was handed to the porter standing on the table (to display pictures so that they could be seen by everyone) that there were murmurs of interest and a feeling of tension; I felt that excitement and physical increase in the heartbeat which still occur when I go back for a big sale. The El Greco was bought by Agnew's for 35,000 gns, and there were suitable headlines in the *Daily Telegraph* and elsewhere. That was quite a lot of money in those days; however, if properly promoted the picture would probably have fetched over twice that amount. Evelyn Joll, the present chairman of Agnew's, told me many years later: "The picture was sold to Mr and Mrs Charles Wrightsman for a good profit, although for very considerably less than the reported sale figure of £178,000 which was published in the *Daily Telegraph* on May 16th, 1960." Mr and Mrs Wrightsman, well-known New York collectors, put the picture on indefinite loan to the Metropolitan Museum.

In spite of the headlines "35,000 gns for El Greco", the sale and the way it had been handled did great harm to Christie's because it gave substance to an impression among collectors and solicitors that all was not well at Christie's, particularly in the picture department. Some clients not altogether surprisingly decided to go "up the road" to Sotheby's. For Peter Chance the El Greco fiasco must have been a most depressing start to his reign as chairman.

Worse, however, was to come for on October 15th the cream of the late Jakob Goldschmidt's Impressionist and Post-Impressionist pictures were sold at Sotheby's on behalf of his son Erwin. It was this sale which sent Sotheby's into orbit. There were seven pictures: Cézanne's *Le Garçon au Gilet Rouge* and a *Still Life of Apples* by the same artist; Van Gogh's *Le Jardin du Poète, Arles*; Renoir's *La Pensée* and three Manets, *La Rue de Berne*, *La Promenade* and a *Self-Portrait*. Some of these pictures had been seized by the Nazis and auctioned by their Ministry of Finance in 1941. Erwin Goldschmidt got them back only after years of legal battles.

Sotheby's produced a special catalogue with every picture illustrated in colour which had never been done before. The final irony was that the catalogue still bore Sotheby's original title: "Auctioneers

of Literary Property and Works of Art Illustrative of the Fine Arts",
which is how they began in 1744. It was not only the first sale to have
a catalogue fully illustrated in colour, but the first sale to be a black
tie affair. The seven pictures sold for £781,000, outstripping the
previous record for a one-day sale of the Holford pictures easily. No
picture before had fetched £100,000, yet Cézanne's *Le Garçon au Gilet
Rouge* sold for £220,000; the Van Gogh went for £132,000 and Renoir's
delicious *La Pensée* was bought by Edward Speelman, a leading dealer
(now retired), for the property tycoon Jack Cotton for £72,000. In one
night the balance of power between the two auction houses shifted to
New Bond Street. Almost more important than the financial result of
the sale was the psychological effect it had on collectors, particularly
in the USA where there were attractive tax advantages for those
who bought important works of art. From then on many collectors
approached Sotheby's direct, instead of through a dealer as had been
the custom before. The resulting publicity gave Sotheby's, and Peter
Wilson, the image of super-salesmen.

Sotheby's had made a lot of money from the sale by backing their
judgment and agreeing to terms under which their commission would
be minimal until a certain figure was reached, after which their
commission was much greater than the normal 10 per cent. Not
everything had gone absolutely according to plan; it seldom does. A
few moments before the sale was due to start, Erwin Goldschmidt
heard a man making an anti-Semitic remark about him. He threatened
to cancel the sale, but calmed down when he was told that the man
had been ejected.

Not surprisingly there was dejection next day at Christie's. No one
in the firm would have believed that in 1980 Christie's New York
office would sell the Van Gogh for $5.2 million (just over £2.2 million).
The irony was that if Sir Alec Martin had recognised the importance
of agreeing to Erwin Goldschmidt's terms two years before, when he
first tried out the London market, Christie's might well have got the
sale in 1958.

"Come to the Savoy, Sir Alec"

"Die hier gefallen mir viel besser" – "I like this lot much better." This pronouncement was probably the most fateful to be made in the turbulent post-war history of the London art market. Spoken by Erwin Goldschmidt, a New York insurance broker, in 1956 to his lawyer Jesse D. Wolff, it unleashed the series of sales at Sotheby's which brought Christie's, the Establishment firm of fine art auctioneers, to their knees.

In the sumptuous setting of the Savoy Hotel it was a moment of drama and irony. Erwin's father, Jakob, a Berlin banker and owner of a great picture collection, had fled from Berlin to Switzerland and thence to New York just in time to avoid arrest by the Nazis. He had died in 1955, and under the terms of his will his picture collection was to be sold and the proceeds divided between Erwin and his two grandsons.

Following the lifting of exchange controls on foreign currency in 1955, Erwin had decided that London was the best place to sell. What is more, he instructed Christie's to clear the pictures through Customs at Southampton – there were fourteen of them, a mixture of Old Masters and Impressionists. He had instructed Christie's because his father had used the firm to sell his great collection of eighteenth-century Chinese porcelain in 1938. However, Jakob Goldschmidt had only gone to Christie's then because he had had a blazing row with Geoffrey Hobson, then Sotheby's chairman, who refused to bargain with him over terms. History was about to reverse itself.

Erwin decided to see both Christie's and Sotheby's. Having installed himself in the Savoy Hotel, he summoned Sir Alec Martin, who had been Christie's managing director since 1940, and Peter Wilson, who was in charge of Sotheby's picture department but was to become chairman the following year. Sir Alec for some reason asked

"Jo" Floyd, a young director but future chairman, to accompany him although he was not a picture expert, and also Roy Davidge who had already been in touch with Customs at Southampton. Before Sir Alec left Christie's, Peter Chance, then a senior director, implored him to agree to whatever Goldschmidt wanted in the way of terms.

Goldschmidt had reserved two adjoining suites so that unknown to both parties he could interview them virtually simultaneously. He first saw Peter Wilson and Carmen Gronau, Sotheby's Old Master expert, handing them a list of the pictures and the minimum prices he wanted. The list included Corot's *Vénus au Bain*; a *View of the Maas* by Cuyp; two works by Delacroix; *Two Heads of Negroes* by Van Dyck; *A Young Girl Lifting Her Veil* by Murillo, which had sold for £5,880 at Christie's in the famous Holford sale in 1928; a street scene by Camille Pissarro; a head of a woman by Renoir and a Daumier of a blacksmith at work. Goldschmidt gave Peter Wilson and Carmen Gronau "a very rough ride". He then left them and went to see Sir Alec in the suite next door.

To be fair, Sir Alec may have been under the impression that Christie's had the sale in their pocket because they had been told to clear the pictures through Customs. However, when he was handed the list of pictures and prices by Goldschmidt he entirely forgot Peter Chance's advice. It is unlikely that Sir Alec had ever been face to face with a client like Goldschmidt who was virtually stipulating reserve prices. Sir Alec was used to advising the owners of collections from some of the greatest houses in Britain and regarded the setting of reserve prices as his prerogative. The Murillo was a particular stumbling block. Whereas Peter Wilson realised that Goldschmidt was a tough American Jew who expected to get his way, Sir Alec refused to budge. Goldschmidt bid him good day and added ominously, "I must see your rivals."

It was then that he said, "Die hier gefallen mir viel besser," outside the suite in which Peter Wilson and Carmen Gronau were waiting anxiously. They heard him – and Carmen, the widow of the art historian Hans Gronau who had worked for Sotheby's for some years, understood German. They realised that Sir Alec had been in the adjoining room, but that Sotheby's appeared to have won the day.

The Goldschmidt pictures were included in an Old Masters sale in November and raised £135,850 – a minute sum by today's prices, and lower than those of the late 1920s. The Corot was bought by Frank Partridge for £27,000 on behalf of the Maharanee of Baroda who is said to have hung it in her bathroom, while the Murillo was bought by a Greek shipowner for £25,000. Although three of the pictures had been bought in, Erwin Goldschmidt was well pleased; so pleased that the following year he drew Peter Wilson's attention to the possibility of Sotheby's selling the Weinberg collection, for the insurance of which he was responsible.

Sotheby's had not made a great deal of money from this first Goldschmidt sale, but, more important, they had made a friend of Goldschmidt. He did indeed write to one of the executors of William Weinberg, outlining his experience in selling his father's pictures and advising him to go to Sotheby's.

Leaving aside the publicity which Sotheby's received for the sale – the first one for many years of pictures sent to London from New York – Goldschmidt's letter was an unexpected bonus. This unsolicited testimonial soon reached the ears of other executors and when it came to advising their clients they did not forget it. (In America executors have far greater responsibility thrust upon their shoulders, and can be sued by beneficiaries if there is any suggestion that they have not acted wisely.)

The Weinberg collection of fifty-six Impressionists fell into Sotheby's lap like a ripe plum. William Weinberg was a German financier who had settled in Holland soon after the First World War. In 1940 he was on a business trip to Paris when the Germans invaded Holland. He had already dispatched his possessions to America, including his pictures. Unable to return to Holland, he never saw his wife and three children again as they were arrested and died in a concentration camp. Weinberg, like Goldschmidt, emigrated to America, where he tried to console himself for his loss by collecting pictures, particularly those by Van Gogh.

Having no family left, Weinberg gave instructions in his will that his collection should be sold and the proceeds given to charity. This background fuelled the pre-sale publicity for Sotheby's which was tremendous – thanks to careful orchestration of the arrangements by a public relations firm, such as the use for the first time of closed circuit television (at the insistence of Weinberg's lawyer).

After the sale, which totalled £326,520, the *Christian Science Monitor* stated: "London has become the centre of the art market." This was echoed in the report of the sale by Frank Davis, saleroom correspondent of *The Times* (who at the time of writing is still contributing his elegant weekly articles for *Country Life* at the age of over ninety):

"It was a memorable occasion, not merely because it made auction history . . . but also because it would appear to provide overwhelming evidence that London has fully regained its position as a highly efficient centre for the disposal of works of art from either side of the Atlantic." To many readers of *The Times* and other newspapers and magazines all over the world, it seemed that when Frank Davis described London as being the "centre of the art world", he meant Sotheby's in New Bond Street.

In retrospect the prices at the Weinberg sale were by no means exceptional, and in many cases did not match up to those Christie's got for similar works in the 1920s, allowing for the fact that the pound was worth much more in those years. Yet the Weinberg sale achieved the highest total for a one-day sale since the Dutch and Flemish pictures in the Holford collection fetched £364,095 at Christie's in 1928. But for the Press and the public, 1928 was a long time ago and most people, including myself, had never even heard of the Holford collection.

In Christie's, amazing though it may seem, it was business as usual. There were no emergency meetings to discuss ways of getting Impressionists or generally how to counter Sotheby's challenge. I am told that Bill Martin was appalled at the way his father had handled the 1956 negotiations with Goldschmidt and had said, "We're sunk." His father's refusal even after the success of the Weinberg sale to acknowledge the importance of the Impressionist market made Bill realise that Sir Alec had been at Christie's too long. Arthur Grimwade, the firm's elder statesman, long since retired but still one of the greatest silver experts in the world, explained to me: "Alec treated Sotheby's as a fly to be brushed aside. It was part of his arrogance which he became a prisoner of because of the pre-war sales, and we were all inculcated with the same attitude. In any case Jo Floyd, Guy Hannen and myself were far too junior to question Alec's running of the picture department." I am sure, however, that Peter Chance must have been worried.

To understand fully Sir Alec's not only disastrous but in some ways paradoxical attitude towards Impressionists it is necessary to know something about him. Alec Martin had had an amazing career. He first came to Christie's in 1897 at the age of twelve as an office boy and was told that he might become a porter if he "gave satisfaction". His capacity for hard work was recognised by Lance Hannen, senior partner for many years. However, it was W. B. Anderson (Peter's uncle by marriage) who was really responsible for giving the boy a chance; he had a close connection with St Columba's Church, Pont Street, and used the church boys' club as a source for recruits. Alec had been born in the area and eventually became Anderson's assistant.

During the summer break – the sales season ran as it does today, from October to the end of July – all the porters and clerical staff were laid off unpaid. This sounds appalling these days, but fortunately it does not appear to have resulted in any hardship. Most of the porters had been "gentlemen's gentlemen", I am told, and were able to get jobs as valets, footmen, gunbearers and the like; it was a very different world. Alec on the other hand was determined to learn about pictures and went to Paris even though it meant earning his keep by washing dishes in a Montmartre café.

Back in London, Alec would get in early to Christie's and browse around the salerooms looking at the pictures on view. It was in this way that he caught the eye of Sir Hugh Lane, whose extraordinary flair for pictures, modern and old, had earned him the respect of the whole art world. Lane and Alec soon became close friends, and as Lane never bid for pictures himself Alec very often acted for him. Over many years Lane put his vast knowledge at Alec's disposal. From 1906 to 1908 Lane was buying Impressionists for himself and was influential in forming other people's Impressionist collections, his prime interest indeed being Impressionist and Post-Impressionist pictures. For all his contact with Lane, however, none of that awareness, none of that connoisseurship rubbed off on Alec.

There was also ample evidence that Impressionism was destined to become a great force from the sales of such pictures which Christie's had held since 1889. That was the first year any Impressionist pictures were auctioned in Britain. In 1892 one of Christie's sales included Degas's haunting masterpiece *L'Absinthe*, catalogued at the time merely as *Figures at a Café*. This was bought by the Société des Beaux Arts for £180 and later acquired by the Louvre through a bequest – today of course it is one of the museum's greatest possessions. Other sales followed with higher prices; in 1918 Degas's *Deux Blanchisseuses Portant du Linge* sold for what was then the huge price of 2,300 gns, while in 1927 Degas's *Deux Danseuses en Scène*, now in the Courtauld Collection, fetched £7,200.

One would have thought it impossible for Alec Martin not to be aware of the market for such pictures, particularly in the 1920s when the art market was more buoyant than it had ever been. In 1924 Samuel

Courtauld, whom Alec knew well – because by then he himself was a figure in the art world – began to supplement his own collection of Impressionists and Post-Impressionists. What is more he endowed the National Gallery with £50,000, the income from which was enough to buy *La Grande Jatte*, one of Seurat's masterpieces, and other works by Degas and Van Gogh.

Brian Sewell had first-hand experience of Alec's attitude to Impressionism. "One of Alec's closest friends of his own generation was Oliver Brown who ran the Leicester Gallery," Sewell told me. "Now Oliver was the prime source of French Impressionists and Post-Impressionists in this country from the very moment the market began to exist. When I went to work at Christie's, who was the expert who was called in when any French Impressionist pictures were to be catalogued? It was Oliver, and whatever he said went because we were instructed by Alec to accept his opinion.

"Now you can't maintain that someone who had spent hours talking to Hugh Lane, who knew Samuel Courtauld and whose closest friend was the leading dealer in Impressionists was a victim of a change in the market in the 1950s. It was simply that Alec hated them. He could see no quality in them and the reason why the Goldschmidt pictures went was because he wouldn't give way."

Anthony Lousada, of Stephenson, Harwood and Tatham, Christie's lawyers since the late 1920s (now Stephenson, Harwood), who took over the legal reins of Christie's on his father's death in 1944, naturally saw a lot of Alec and confirmed what Sewell said, even if in more moderate tones: "His whole taste was really towards Old Masters and as modern art became more modern, he became more and more out of touch." I asked if Alec had ever expressed his thoughts to him on Impressionism. "Yes, I do remember one particular occasion," Lousada said. "My personal recollection is of going up to Christie's one day and walking round the rooms with him when there was a considerable number of important works by Picasso, Braque and others on the walls and Alec referring to them as we went past as 'this 'ere filth'."

However, by the mid-1920s, as I have already said, Alec had become one of the art world's most illustrious figures. How else could he have become a Trustee of the Wallace Collection, Hon. Secretary of the National Art Collections Fund and been made a KBE? Nor should we forget the valiant way Alec kept the firm ticking over during the Second World War, even after a stick of incendiaries had totally destroyed Christie's premises on the night of April 16th, 1941. Everything went up in flames except the bound catalogues of sales since James Christie's first one on December 5th, 1766, and, almost as important, some splendid jewels which Alec was to auction on behalf of the Red Cross. These had been placed in a steel vault and survived the blaze and the firemen's attempts to extinguish it.

Not to be defeated by Hitler, Alec approached Lord Derby who kindly agreed to lend the firm his newly acquired Derby House, off Oxford Street. Here sales continued, though obviously on a much reduced scale, for six years until Sir Walter Hutchinson bought the house. Lord Spencer then came to Christie's aid and rented them his splendid eighteenth-century house overlooking Green Park until the rebuilding of the firm's King Street premises was finished in 1953.

However, by 1956 Alec was seventy-two. Like many great men before him he refused to see the necessity for change within the firm; for more scholarly catalogues, specialisation and a more professional approach to clients' needs. Shortly after joining Christie's in 1958, I was told by George Howard, a personal friend and later to become Governor and then Chairman of the BBC, how he had asked Alec after the war to arrange for a revaluation of the contents of Castle Howard, the great house designed by Inigo Jones near York with grounds laid out by Capability Brown. Christie's had "naturally" been called in to do one before the war. No great house would have thought of asking Sotheby's. Now Howard wanted a new appraisal. Alec went up to Castle Howard by himself and implied that he could do the whole job in one day. Howard not surprisingly dispensed with his services and sent for Sotheby's. Peter Wilson and a team stayed a week.

Alec's problem was not just that he was out of touch, as Lousada described it, with modern art, but that he had been in the job too long and didn't know when it was time for him to go.

3

Goodbye to the Old Guard

Sir Alec Martin was not the only problem. In 1940 Christie's had become a private limited company. As all the other partners were on active service or otherwise engaged in the war effort, Alec had brought in Mr R. W. Lloyd, a close friend of his, as chairman. Lloyd was a tough, hard-headed businessman who treated Christie's like any other business in which he had money. He expected it to show a profit. With this in mind he bought a large number of shares, thus providing the firm with much needed capital to keep it running in such difficult times. Lloyd's policy was low pay, no expansion and no experiments. By 1958 he was ninety and not at all well. Apart from Alec, there was another managing director, Brigadier-General Sir Harry Floyd, who had been made a partner in 1928 and had returned to King Street after a distinguished war. These, then, were the Old Guard.

The need for younger management and more enlightened policies was obvious, at least to Peter Chance. Even in the early 1950s when still at Spencer House he had drawn attention to Sotheby's more scholarly catalogues and other signs that they were on the attack. However, in spite of the post-Weinberg alarm, there does not seem to have been any real attempt to oust the Old Guard until Peter found out that Alec was trying to sell his shares to Brian Mountain (later Sir Brian and chairman of Eagle Star Insurance). According to Arthur Grimwade, "That's what triggered things off." Anthony Lousada told me about that time. "Fortunately, through my having been proved right about some complicated advice I gave Christie's immediately I took over acting for them, Lloyd formed a reasonable opinion of me. In fact the dramatic change of feeling was demonstrated by him inviting me to dinner in his 'set' in Albany and giving me some excellent wine and showing me some remarkable things." This was a reference to Lloyd's magnificent collection of Turner drawings (long since in

28

the British Museum) and, somewhat oddly, an equally important collection of beetles which is now in the Natural History Museum.

"In any event," Lousada continued, "Alec had got into a situation very, very normal in older men of being sure that he was right and not realising that the younger people had grown up. In fact it had become pretty intolerable for the people younger than himself, but Harry Floyd gave absolutely invaluable service to the younger members. He was a very fair man and realised that things were quite impossible as they were. And so the time came when someone had to tell Alec that the firm was going to be reorganised and that although he might possibly be a consultant he was no longer going to be managing director and the lot fell on me.

"Well, it was not agreeable. I had known him since I was a child and he was a close friend of my father, which didn't make it any easier, but I told him, and shortly afterwards there was a dinner at Brooks's which was more or less a 'Goodbye and thank you' party. I remember it very clearly. I knew nearly everybody there, but not quite everybody. I had just had an inoculation and had a very sore arm. After dinner Alec marched me round the table clutching my bad arm and saying to those people I didn't know, ''Ere's the fellow who pushed me out of Christie's.' However, in spite of that gibe I continued to be on reasonable terms with him for the rest of his life."

In fact it must have been a month or two before the farewell dinner could be held, because the immediate reaction of Lloyd and Alec to Lousada's news was to ask what price they were going to get for their shares. Alec's excuse to Peter regarding his offer to Brian Mountain was that he didn't think the rest of the Board could raise sufficient money for his shares, and he was quite right. More serious still, Lloyd had nearly 24 per cent of the equity which would have given him a controlling interest in decisions. I think it was Guy Hannen, or a friend of his, who suggested a solution to the impasse. This was to sell the Crown Lease of 8 King Street to the Commercial Union Assurance Co. Ltd, realising £486,000, and to lease back the premises until mid-1992 at an annual rent of £29,500 and then for a further twenty-five years until mid-2017 at a rental to be agreed.

On Wednesday, April 2nd, Christie's announced the liquidation of the company formed in 1958 and the formation of Christie, Manson and Woods Ltd under the chairmanship of Mr I. O. Chance: "There will be no change of policy and as the new Christie's will be composed of the younger directors of its predecessor, the essentially family nature of the business will be preserved." The new company's issued capital was £60,000. At the time of writing (January 1989), Christie's Stock Exchange valuation is around £225.5 million.

The reference in the statement given to the Press to the "family nature of the business" was obviously made to reassure Christie's oldest clients that the character of the firm would not change. In my opinion, in order to satisfy those who had lost confidence in Christie's ability to adapt to the art market of the day, it should have been tempered with the acknowledgment that certain changes were necessary. Changes were in fact made, but they were not far-reaching enough and the firm was soon in difficulties.

Three factors were responsible: the pre-war system of recruiting partners was Christie's Achilles' heel; secondly, the firm had had a 150-year-old monopoly in auctioning works of art; and lastly, there was the psychological effect this had on those responsible for running the firm, which was one of complacency. Fine art auctioneering is a very personal business and prior to the war Christie's were mainly concerned with the property of the titled, the gentry and the wealthy. Most people become creatures of the environment they work in, so Christie's pre-war partners and even the post-war directors would have been less than human if some of the grandness of their clients had not rubbed off on them. Many dukes carry their titles lightly and are remarkably unassuming. Not so some of those who work for them.

Today anything verging on nepotism has been discredited as not likely to produce enlightened and dynamic management. After the war it was still natural for sons to be automatically considered for their father's firms and this applied even to membership of certain trade unions. Tracing the relationship of the members of the 1958 Board shows that the roots of the majority of the directors were deeply embedded in Christie's past, to an unhealthy extent.

Walter Agnew, of the famous firm of picture dealers, was a great-uncle of Peter's and a partner from 1889 till his death in 1915; his son Charles was already on the Board by then and with two other partners interviewed Peter over lunch at the Berkeley in 1927. Peter was due to leave Eton the following year and was told to come back in two years' time. He spent it fruitfully in France learning the language, and duly joined the firm in February 1930, at the age of nineteen. In addition to the Agnew connection, W. B. Anderson, Peter's uncle by marriage, had been a partner since 1896, though he had retired in 1927.

The year 1889 had also seen the retirement of James Christie IV, the last member of the family to have a connection with the firm. This left Christie's in the hands of the legendary Thomas Woods, who had become a partner in 1859. (The firm since that date has always been Christie, Manson and Woods.) Looking for new colleagues, Woods found one in Lance Hannen, the young son of a partner in Holland, Hannen and Cubitt. That firm had just undertaken the re-facing of the exterior of the old King Street premises to the plans of H. MacVicar Anderson, the father of W. B. Anderson – even renovations to the building were kept in the family or used as a source of partners.

Thomas Woods, of course, was the exception to beat all exceptions, being originally the gamekeeper's son from Stowe House. When Christie's in 1848 were asked to sell the contents of Stowe House – which took forty days – the housekeeper was asked if there was anyone who knew anything about the paintings, and replied, "Young Woods the gamekeeper's son knows all about the pictures." He made such an impression that he was asked to join the firm.

Lance Hannen proved an excellent choice. His athletic prowess at Cambridge – stroking his university's boat to victory in the Boat Races of 1888 and 1889 – preceded his great achievements at Christie's. He was senior partner from 1903 to 1936, taking all the great picture sales in the 1920s. In addition he negotiated many private sales with Duveen, such as the Duke of Westminster's two famous pictures, Reynolds's *The Tragic Muse* and Gainsborough's *Blue Boy*, which went for a huge sum. In Peter's opinion he was the greatest auctioneer of his time.

Gordon Hannen, Lance's son, was a good organiser and became in fact if not in name managing director – a position in which Guy, his son, was to distinguish himself for many years. In 1930 Gordon had an idea which was most enlightened for those days, particularly as it involved extra expense, and that was "foreign study leave". Many of the young men on the technical side, even if they were earmarked to be partners, were hard up. Those selected were allowed three weeks off every year and given not only their travelling expenses but £75 as well, which was remarkably generous. Peter Chance and Arthur Grimwade were two of the first to benefit from this opportunity. In 1958 Gordon was in charge of the book department, although all the cataloguing was done by the erudite and delightful Dudley Massey, acting as a consultant; he was senior partner of Pickering and Chatto, antiquarian book dealers, now owned by Lord Rees-Mogg, ex-editor of *The Times*.

Guy, Gordon's son, came straight to the Front Counter after being demobbed from the Army. He had been in the 9th Lancers and had won a very good MC at the age of twenty when his troop of tanks was ordered to hold a vital bridgehead in Italy against vastly superior forces, an order which led even to hand-to-hand fighting. Guy, who was responsible for Objects of Art and Vertu, also took sales of coins and medals. Some years after I had joined the firm, he was auctioning a medal from his old regiment. Looking as always for a news peg, I rang up the Ministry of Defence and asked for a copy of Guy's citation to be sent round. Having read it with admiration, I said to him jokingly after the sale, "I suppose you lost your temper again." Guy did in fact have a "short fuse", although curiously his rage seldom touched me. When angry he would go quite white and his hands would begin to shake. Whether this was due to the war, I don't know. Contemporaries of his at Eton told me he was "as thick as two planks"; well, he may have been slow, like many of us, at school but he was to prove in the years to come that, while not academic, he had a very good managerial and financial mind.

John Floyd, always known as Jo, was a cousin of Sir Harry Floyd, Sir Harry being the regular soldier who before becoming a partner in 1928 had been ADC to Prince Henry, later Duke of Gloucester. "Touting for business" was frowned upon in those days, but it was thought quite rightly that Harry would introduce business in a gentlemanly way by just being himself.

Jo Floyd, six foot three and good-looking, was a man of considerable charm, save when occasionally something displeased him and he then took up a giraffe-like posture, looking down his nose as if he had become aware of some obnoxious smell. During the war he had been with the 60th Rifles. Unlike Peter, whose military asperity could at times make the bravest cringe, and Guy, Jo seldom lost his cool and proved in later years to be a shrewd negotiator. This was because he not only exuded charm but also had a reliable, businesslike manner which gave clients and their advisers confidence. In 1958 he was responsible for the furniture department and became quite an expert, but like Guy he was not an academic, least of all an intellectual, and would have hated to be considered one. He was happiest when playing golf, a sport at which he excelled. However, as with Peter but in a different way, when his time came to be chairman his contribution was considerable. Jo and Guy had been contemporaries at Eton, which must have been of mutual comfort when in 1954 Lloyd grudgingly agreed to make them partners.

Arthur Grimwade, who by 1958 had already made a name for himself as a silver expert, joined the Board the same year as Jo and Guy. He was the only partner whose views, which he would quite often state with some vehemence, could not be said to have been influenced by having had grandfathers, fathers, uncles or cousins on the Board before him. He joined Peter on the Front Counter one morning in January 1932, after having had an interview with Alec. He was not yet nineteen and was told that he could come for two years' trial at £1 a week "to make himself useful in the silver department", which had recently been created.

Arthur was a little younger than Peter, and like Bill Martin, Alec's son, he was an Old Pauline. His immediate impression of Peter, his mentor, was that he had an enviably self-assured manner, which is the mark of so many young Old Etonians. Arthur came from an entirely different social background and did not live Peter's sophisticated life. As often as not it was white tie and tails in the evening for Peter, for even in the aftermath of the slump following the Wall Street crash there were many balls and eligible bachelors were in short supply. Arthur, on the other hand, came to Christie's with fragments of the classics ringing in his ears. At the weekends he could be found leading one of the Fulham troops of boy scouts; a rather charming contrast. When he joined he had no knowledge of silver and just wanted a job. By sheer industry and a natural application he became a world authority on the subject.

I have already mentioned that Bill Martin, picture director, had just such an eye for the quality of a picture but owing to his father's autocratic ways had never been given any real responsibility. Bill never developed any strength of character or sufficient drive to put into force the new policies which he agreed were necessary. Far from being stiff-necked with newcomers such as myself he was a most generous lunchtime host; he was in many ways, probably because of his frustration while under his father's thumb, a *bon vivant* and this certainly in time affected or prevented any decisions being made by him in the afternoon.

Lastly there was the Hon. Patrick Lindsay. Patrick was the second son of the 28th Earl of Crawford and 11th Earl of Balcarres, and became not only a great auctioneer but a larger than life individualist, as many aristocrats do. After leaving Eton he served with the Scots

Guards in Malaya and then went to Magdalen College, Oxford, but a skiing accident prevented him from sitting for his degree. He studied for a short time at I Tatti, Bernard Berenson's famous villa in Tuscany, a period which he described as "easily the most stimulating time in my life". But in 1958 he was assistant to Bill Martin, having become a partner in 1955. It must have been difficult for him. His father, a man with a magnificent leonine head, was an art historian of distinction with a great collection of pictures and a world famous library who had made a huge contribution to the arts. However, being brought up surrounded by works of art to the extent of having a Duccio metaphorically, if not literally, above your bed, is no substitute for a course at the Courtauld and an art historian's eye.

In 1962 Patrick had to take over the picture department when Bill Martin was forced to retire owing to ill-health. This was a position of considerable responsibility for which he was hardly ready, not only due to lack of knowledge – in time, like everyone at Christie's with a real interest in their subject, he did develop an eye – but also because he was very resistant to new policies which were vitally needed in the picture department at that time. Because he was strong-willed and very assertive there were many clashes of temperament. Even his best friends have gone on record as saying he was "not always an easy man to work with", but, as one who had many disagreements with him, I can say that there was never any rancour; sometimes even an apology – the mark of a man – and often an invitation to have lunch at White's. Such occasions were always enjoyable because of his splendid sense of humour, even if it was directed against oneself. Apart from his charisma on the racing circuits or when flying his beloved Spitfire, it was in the auction box that he came into his own.

This was the Christie Board in 1958. With the exception of Arthur Grimwade it was an inbred team when compared with the opposition, and one more suited to the easy-going ways of the 1920s and 1930s than the highly competitive years that quite evidently lay ahead. With the exception of Peter and Arthur, the Board was also short on expertise. Peter was very well read, and through his long apprenticeship on the Front Counter, and having been sent on valuations and trips abroad, had acquired a considerable knowledge of eighteenth-century art and was completely at ease on the Continent, as Jo and Guy never were. Silver sales were assured, thanks to Arthur. It was the picture department, the most important from a business point of view, which was so vulnerable and in need of reinforcement.

The casual approach to expertise was a hangover from the 1920s and 1930s, when apart from Alec none of the partners would have dreamed of calling themselves experts. In the morning they wrote the necessary letters replying to those who wanted valuations or a sale, or saw owners and their advisers, and took the occasional sale. At the weekend it was metaphorically or literally "off to the grouse moors". Alec was responsible for cataloguing pictures, but as regards furniture, tapestries, carpets, porcelain, silver and objects of art, the remarkable Arthur Abbey catalogued all these sales for nearly thirty years. He rarely referred to a book; quite obviously the descriptions were not so fulsome as today, but he had a remarkable eye, and basically what he catalogued had to be "right". When he joined the firm in the 1890s, the then cataloguer told him in answer to a query over French furniture: "My boy, it's quite easy; if it's curly you call it Louis XV; if it's straight it's Louis XVI, and if it's Boulle it's Boulle."

When Abbey retired in 1932 his place was taken by John Critchley who is still with us. John told me how, when he joined the firm in 1928 at a salary of £120 a year, he worked first in the Instructions Office helping to prepare the auctioneer's catalogue. "When I took over Abbey's job, I had no knowledge at all of works of art," he said. "I just had to learn from books and go round the museums." It was really thanks to John that Christie's sold the Jakob Goldschmidt collection of eighteenth-century Chinese porcelain in 1938. Goldschmidt saw him rather than Alec, as John was responsible for porcelain among other things. Goldschmidt, fortunately perhaps, didn't insist on seeing a partner. Goldschmidt asked John if he would go to Amsterdam and value his collection, which John did. It took him five days. When Alec and Harry Floyd heard about his trip they were appalled at the idea of having to pay John's expenses. Nothing like this had ever happened before. However, owing to John's helpful attitude, Christie's had got the sale and it was a great success. By 1958 Critchley had acquired considerable knowledge of English and French furniture and was rightly much respected by the fine art trade. When Jo Floyd joined the department from the Front Counter he was Critchley's assistant and had to take down his descriptions of pieces of furniture in his notebook "till his fingers ached", John told me.

Today it is unbelievable that what was assumed to be a professional business was run in such a casual manner, that such responsibility was given to staff who had had no art education of any sort. It was not as if the inherent economic dangers of fine art auctioneering – rising costs and falling prices – had not been made abundantly clear to Sotheby's, Phillips and Bonham's as well as Christie's, so much so that in 1934 as a result of the slump, in 1940 because of the outbreak of war and in 1947 because of lack of business there had been serious talks about amalgamation. In 1933 Christie's had made a substantial loss compared with Sotheby's profit of £13,000. In spite of this there was little confidence among the partners in New Bond Street. Curiously, what worried them most was the cost of advertising; it was the saving which would result from joint advertising, although very small, which sparked off the merger suggestion.

Lengthy talks developed, but came to nothing as it was virtually impossible to work out a fair valuation of the two businesses. In 1947 Christie's made another approach to Sotheby's, but by this time Peter Wilson already had his eyes on Parke-Bernet so although Sotheby's Board was by no means unanimous, the talks once again broke down. However, this did not worry Alec who least of all saw any need to change the system.

Even after the Second World War the magic name of Christie's drew such great works as Constable's *Young Waltonians* from the Swaythling collection which had sold in 1946 for £43,000 to Walter Hutchinson. In 1951 there was the sale of the Hutchinson Collection of Sporting Pictures, which included Stubbs's superb *Gimcrack*, but after that Christie's apparent assumption that pictures and works of art would come to their rooms as naturally as driftwood floating up the Thames was rudely shattered. This was because their rivals in New Bond Street were at last catching up with them. The sales total for the 1954-5 season at Sotheby's was £1.7 million compared with £1.5 million at Christie's (both figures include works of art which failed to reach their reserve price); but from that year the gap widened annually for a long time. This was even before the impetus given by the Goldschmidt and Weinberg sales and the many others that followed them.

Sotheby's are often said to be the oldest fine art auctioneers in Britain. This is not so – although the matter is academic as age is no guarantee of efficiency. Sotheby's was founded in 1744 in Wellington Street, off the Strand, as "Auctioneers of Literary Property and Works Illustrative of the Fine Arts". Christie's was founded by James Christie in December 1766, and the firm has sold pictures and works of art of all kinds ever since. In 1917 Sotheby's moved to 34/35 New Bond Street and began to hold regular sales of pictures and the full range of works of art. Pictures had been abandoned half a century earlier, although even before that they had not formed an important part of Sotheby's business. Any pictures of real quality were passed on to Christie's, who reciprocated by passing over their clients' books and manuscripts. Books, it seems, were regarded as a nuisance by Christie's because they took up valuable space and required a real expert to catalogue them (Sotheran's the book dealers did this for Christie's in the 1920s and 1930s). However, the great houses of Britain, Christie's traditional clients, were likely to have large libraries if they had a collection of Old Masters; so, unwittingly, Christie's gave strength to the opposition. Walter Buccleuch, the father of the present Duke, told Peter once how his family had always been to Christie's "but when you gave up having book sales we had no choice but to go to Sotheby's and they have done us very well".

The three men primarily responsible for the rise of Sotheby's all had a basis of academic brilliance. More significant still, each one of them had had valuable experience in other professions before joining Sotheby's in 1910. Montague Barlow, who had achieved a First in law at Cambridge and had been called to the Bar, also lectured at the London School of Economics and became Conservative MP for South Salford in 1910. Felix Warre, the fifth son of a distinguished head-master of Eton, was like Lance Hannen a great oarsman, but unlike him had been a banker in Hong Kong for six years before going to Sotheby's; and the youngest member of the new triumvirate was Geoffrey Dudley Hobson, who was destined to be the most brilliant of the "new men". Hobson had been at Harrow, got a First in modern history at University College, Oxford and passed the Foreign Office exam with distinction. He was a very good classical scholar, spoke French, German and Italian fluently and had a working knowledge of Spanish, Portuguese and Dutch. This was altogether a very different team from that at 8 King Street, just prior to the First World War, because their minds had been broadened not only by successful aca-demic careers but by experience in professions completely different from fine art auctioneering.

In 1913 the business was reorganised on more modern lines. There was a partners' meeting every Monday where divisions of responsibility were laid down regarding the sale programme – regular sales of pictures and works of art becoming the policy while the firm was still at Wellington Street. A significant innovation was the decision to charge clients for illustrations, which resulted in more impressive catalogues at lower cost. However, it wasn't until the early 1920s, after the move to New Bond Street in 1917, that significant changes were made in the technical staff.

After the war business had increased considerably. The book department was the first to get a new recruit, who in time became chairman. This was Charles des Graz, who having been Captain of the Oppidans at Eton and a scholar of Trinity College, Cambridge, went on to be Director of the British Library, Washington. Eventually, after much unexplained delay, which naturally annoyed Barlow, des Graz arrived and became immersed in books. However, it was not all plain sailing. Barlow found himself forced to reprimand des Graz about his dress, indifference and even haughtiness:

> . . . generally the impression that you do not find the business
> of interest . . . We have a great deal of capital locked up in the
> business, we have spent a great many years in building it up
> and in the years to come the safety of our capital and the future
> of the business will depend very largely on the new blood we
> take in. In the rival business of Messrs C. undoubtedly the business
> is already beginning to suffer from the fact that the juniors they
> took in a year or two ago are proving to be of very little use.

That letter was written in 1922 and showed Barlow's attitude towards the business: that clients' first impressions were of vital importance and that a casual approach could not be tolerated; equally that even then he thought Christie's administration was vulnerable. Des Graz took the hint and, working under Hobson, recruited an expert team of cataloguers for the book department during the 1920s which assured Sotheby's the continuation of the supremacy they have always held in that field.

Works of art was the next department to receive help, from someone who became a legendary and much-loved figure in the art world. A. J. B. Kiddell came from the unlikely background of the Ministry of Pensions. Jim Kiddell joined in 1921 admitting that he knew "less than nothing about the auction business or what was sold". Pottery and porcelain were the subjects for which he became renowned, but he also made himself an expert in Oriental art, furniture and even antiquities during his fifty-eight years at Sotheby's.

Most important of all perhaps in view of the decision to challenge Christie's strength in the picture field was Tancred Borenius, a Finnish art historian who had won a considerable reputation for himself as an

Old Master authority. Apart from being highly knowledgeable, he had a superb visual memory, could speak nine languages and had a wide circle of acquaintances among art historians and artists. Christie's would not have considered such a man, if they knew of him, even in 1958. Thanks to Borenius the volume of picture sales rose from £33,000 in 1924–5 to £186,000 by 1928–9; this was nothing compared with Christie's picture sales total, but significant when we come to the 1950s. Borenius was Sotheby's part-time adviser from 1924 till the end of the war.

An important addition to Sotheby's in 1926 was Tom Lumley who at the age of nineteen was taken on at £4 a week as silver cataloguer. Tom was not only a hard worker but even when he was a young man he did not hesitate to question the firm's procedures. This is never popular in any firm, as in due course I was to learn, but Barlow and his colleagues had to admit that Tom was often right.

It was Tom, for instance, who suggested that the obituaries of people known to the firm should be circulated every day among directors. Without knowing anything about Sotheby's policies, this was one of my recommendations to Christie's in 1959 in a report I wrote on behalf of PDA. To some people this practice may seem callous, but it can in fact be helpful to the people concerned with the winding up of an estate provided that the letter is tactfully worded.

It was Tom also who was responsible for sales on the premises of semi-stately homes being undertaken far more frequently. These not only brought in extra revenue but generated valuable publicity in the provinces and resulted in new clients. Christie's had of course carried out the sales of the contents of Stowe House and Clumber, but had not pursued such sales in the same enterprising way. Tom left Sotheby's in 1936 and became a much respected silver dealer.

Montague Barlow's most enlightened action probably was over staff relations. Each year in August following the last sale of the season he summoned the staff and told them how the firm was progressing. In 1924, apart from paying the bonus – a scheme introduced in 1919 – he asked the staff whether they wanted a Works Council. It's true it took two years to organise, but in comparison with the attitude towards the staff at Christie's, even in the 1960s, it was a remarkable development.

It was not until Jo Floyd became chairman that there were similar staff meetings at the end of the season at Christie's. Jo spoke very well without notes, but he had to be pushed by Guy Hannen into doing it, and there was seldom any mention of increased wages; those who had been with the firm for twenty-five years got a cheque for £100, but I can only remember this happening on three occasions. A staff bonus was introduced by Peter, to be paid if the profits allowed it, but the idea of a Works Council would have been anathema to him. Many years later I remember a Board meeting when Hugo Morley-Fletcher, the porcelain director, was bold enough to suggest that the opinion of the staff should be sought on a certain matter. Peter said to Jo, out of the corner of his mouth, as he was wont to do in moments of stress, "What's that fellah think this is, a bloody commune?"

Another difference between the two firms was Sotheby's determination to stretch out into Europe for business. Christie's had acted for many distinguished foreigners from the days of the founder, but Lance Hannen and Alec had never thought of making regular forays in search of works of art on the Continent. Tancred Borenius had strong links with Paris, and French collections came to Sotheby's right up until 1939. Geoffrey Hobson and Jim Kiddell were determined to spread the Sotheby net as widely as possible. A German-speaking English ex-Army officer was engaged to act as Sotheby's representative in Germany. By the autumn of 1931 he had assembled twenty possible clients and Hobson accompanied by Tom Lumley went to see them. Among them was the German banker Jakob Goldschmidt whose eighteenth-century Chinese porcelain was much admired.

Christie's were taking no initiatives in Europe. Worse still, the majority of letters in French or German and other foreign languages went straight into the waste-paper basket, until it was discovered that Peter and another colleague on the Front Counter could speak some European languages. From then on every letter in a foreign tongue was handed to them, and one of the sales which resulted from their linguistic talents was that of the Wittelsbach Crown Jewels in 1931. Alec just ignored such problems in his normal egotistical way.

Sotheby's main problem after the war was finding a successor to Tancred Borenius. Unlike Christie's who took years to realise that they had to look outside the firm if the picture department was to regain any credibility, Sotheby's looked for the best and by a stroke of luck found Hans Gronau. Vere Pilkington, who had become a partner of Sotheby's in 1927, had been invalided out of the Army in 1945. Going out to lunch one day he bumped into Sir Kenneth Clark, former director of the National Gallery and later of *Civilisation* fame, who suggested Hans Gronau. He was an art historian to his fingertips and he leaped at the chance. However, his health deteriorated, so that his wife, Carmen, came in to help carry some of the load. Having considerable energy and also an art training, she not only took to the work but absorbed a great deal of Hans's knowledge. In 1948 it was suggested that Carmen should join the department part-time. Her husband was against it, but Hobson and Peter Wilson insisted.

Peter Wilson now enters our story. Prior to joining Sotheby's, Wilson had been a lowly advertising representative on *The Connoisseur* magazine. This had been as a result of an introduction from Marion Davies, the mistress of Randolph Hearst. Hearst's empire included amongst other things the National Magazine Company of which *The Connoisseur* is still a part. Following a chance meeting with Vere Pilkington, Wilson was granted an interview and in 1936 he was taken on as a trainee in the furniture department – altogether a somewhat haphazard start for someone who within thirty years was described as wielding "the fastest gavel in the West". Wilson quickly made a name for himself, not only because of his social connections, which the senior partners were well aware of – his father was Sir Mathew "Scatters" Wilson, an eccentric Yorkshire baronet – but also by hard work. In 1938 he became a director and partner, buying 5,000 shares with his wife's money.

Shortly after the end of the war Wilson took over Sotheby's picture department and with Hans and Carmen Gronau made a most effective team. In 1951 Gronau died and Carmen took over the general administration of the department. She soon realised that there was a need to establish a separate department for Impressionist works, something which Christie's did not do until 1964.

In a little over thirty years Sotheby's had developed from being just book auctioneers to fine art auctioneers in every sense; Peter Wilson, for instance, won his spurs by cataloguing the highly specialist collection of Guilhou rings – dating from the Pharaohs to the France of the French Empire. Imaginative management in many spheres, apart from a far more professional approach to art expertise and getting business, had brought about this change. Above all there was none of the complacency and inertia which virtually paralysed Christie's until early in 1958.

Peter and his younger colleagues knew it was time for Lloyd and Alec to go, but they cannot have realised how desperate the situation was because the second Goldschmidt sale was yet to come. Mr Lloyd died on April 29th, 1958, and the *on dit* was that his last words were,

"What did I get for my Christie shares?" At a Board meeting of Christie's on May 7th proper tribute was paid to him. Among other decisions at the same meeting was "The appointment of Patrick Dolan and Associates as public relations advisers provided they agree to John Herbert being their representative". I naturally knew nothing of this, until ordered to go and see Noel Newsome.

Fighting to Survive

The Goldschmidt sale resulted in a cornucopia of works of art for Sotheby's. In few other businesses is it so true that success breeds success. From now on it was going to be a fight for survival for Christie's. Peter Chance had realised that action had to be taken – that was why Brian Sewell and PDA had been employed – but in May when we joined he could not have known how desperate the situation was to become. Business-getting, expertise, the specialisation of sales, and finally marketing were the prime considerations. Peter also knew that Christie's must look towards America, and Europe as well, for works of art. After the Wall Street crash several collections had come Christie's way, but there was no systematic drive to attract American collectors until as late as 1954. That year Peter and "Paddy", his wife, were invited to stay for three weeks in New York with an old friend, Harry Morgan, son of the great banker J. P. Morgan. However, because of the financial state even of Christie's partners, or because of Alec's unimaginative attitude or jealousy, the Board only grudgingly agreed to pay Peter's third-class fare for such an obviously worthwhile trip; Peter had to pay for Paddy.

While in America Peter realised that the sooner Christie's had a representative there the better. At his suggestion W. G. Constable, the first Director of the Courtauld Institute and later curator of paintings at Boston, was appointed Christie's representative in America. Although he did his best, Constable never produced much business. This was mainly Christie's fault. He could not give single-minded service from his home in Cambridge, Massachusetts, and as the Board refused to pay for a secretary for him there was not really much incentive to make a systematic approach to collectors. Constable did, however, manage to convince Alec of the need for Peter to make annual or even biannual trips. America for the moment was covered even if it was not a perfect arrangement.

In the early 1950s there was still no thought of venturing forth into Europe in search of business, as Sotheby's had done in the 1930s, until Peter became chairman. On October 10th, 1958, five days before the Goldschmidt sale, Christie's announced that Hans Backer would be their European representative, the first to be appointed by a British auction house. Hans Backer was sixty-seven and a world authority on Meissen porcelain. Born in Dresden and belonging to the fourth generation of a family of antique dealers – his great-grandfather was appointed to the court of the last King of Hanover – Hans had been closely connected with works of art since his youth. Before the war he had transferred his business to London and Queen Mary often called on him. On her last visit, when she was eighty-one, Hans told me, "We talked china for three hours and she insisted on standing the whole time."

In spite of Backer's family background, a lifetime's experience and contacts among collectors all over the Continent, Peter had the greatest difficulty in getting agreement to his appointment. "We can't have a dealer," said Jo. "Nor a foreigner," said Guy. However, in the end the Board grudgingly accepted that the firm needed someone in Europe and that Hans, who was naturalised British, had good credentials. Just to prove Peter's point and the blindness of his colleagues, Hans told him shortly after he joined that he had been approached by Jim Kiddell of Sotheby's. Hans was based in Rome, which was not ideal for visiting collectors all over Europe, but he was very energetic in spite of his age and business soon began to flow. The establishment of the Rome office was a most important step, as from it other offices with representatives were appointed in virtually every country in Europe in due course. Sotheby's were certainly ahead of us in the United States, but Peter's vision had got Christie's into Europe ahead of them.

Hans and Tony du Boulay became firm friends. "He taught me a tremendous lot," Tony told me. "I only became a porcelain specialist because Jo Floyd and John Critchley were bored with porcelain and having it in furniture sales. I had wanted to join the furniture depart-ment but instead I was made to cut my teeth on the famous Baroness von Zuylen van Nyeveldt collection of Nymphenburg Commedia dell'Arte figures modelled by Franz Anton Bustelli." This was in 1956. Bustelli's figures were one of the most famous Nymphenburg groups ever made. The figures sold for £35,000, then a very good price, although in 1977 a complete set of sixteen similar figures sold at Christie's for £230,800 ($394,668).

How Anthony took over the porcelain department was yet another example of how ill-prepared Christie's was to meet Sotheby's expertise and specialisation. It was all very well taking on Jim Kiddell in the 1920s when he knew nothing, but the ad hoc way Christie's set about getting a porcelain specialist in the 1950s was amateurish beyond belief. Amazingly it worked and Anthony's judgment became acknowledged in spite of his youth. One of the exciting things that soon struck me about the art auction world was that it was possible for young men (and women) to acquire a considerable amount of expertise simply by being in a specialist department for a year or so; by seeing a seemingly unending flow of pictures or works of art come before their eyes; and by hearing what the general consensus of opinion of those senior to them was they could learn what was "right" from what was "wrong".

Apart from Tony and Brian, another bright young man was Richard Falkiner. Richard, who had joined a month before Brian and myself, was already a numismatist, having been given a two-anna piece when he was six which inspired him to collect coins as a hobby. After two years at Glendinnings, the coin auctioneers, he decided he would like to join Christie's. A remote cousin, the late Lady Exeter, wrote to Harry Floyd who with Peter interviewed him and decided to take him on.

Unlike most recruits, Richard spent only three months on the Front Counter before Guy recognised his talents and that he could help him catalogue Objects of Art and Vertu – which covers everything from miniatures, gold snuff boxes and Fabergé to Russian icons and medieval and Renaissance jewellery. "I think it was basically because of my numismatic background that I was given a chance to specialise so soon. I was used to looking things up in books which helps enormously in cataloguing anything," Richard said to me with a disarming smile nearly thirty years later. On my wanderings round the departments I often heard Guy busily checking the catalogue proofs with Richard. I remember in particular a catalogue of medieval and Renaissance jewels and works of art belonging to the Duke of Norfolk and an important Swiss collector. This was the first complete sale of its type held in England since the war, so Richard produced a catalogue with many colour illustrations. Unfortunately it had one unforgettable literal which referred to "Pontius Pilot" and naturally aroused Peter's wrath; luckily a second one which spoke of "the Profit Isaiah" had been corrected.

In spite of having an undoubtedly iconoclastic sense of humour Richard was a highly intelligent young man. In 1960 Guy was asked by Peter to reorganise the picture department, which considering that he had no pretensions about knowing anything about pictures, speaks volumes about its administration or the lack of it. Guy asked Richard if he thought he could cope with running the objects of art department by himself: "I gulped once," he told me, "and said 'Yes'." So at the age of twenty-two he became the youngest head of a department not only in Christie's but probably in any auctioneering firm in the world, responsible for the following: objects of art and vertu, coins (the last coin sale Christie's had had was the Fitzwilliam Coin Collection in 1949 so he was breaking new ground to a certain extent), antiquities, watches, ethnographica, medieval and Renaissance jewels, works of art and icons. Sotheby's had twelve people covering the subjects Richard was responsible for, each one of which now is a separate department in Christie's.

Unfortunately the Board in the years to come did not fully recognise the importance of the talent that it was spawning on its own premises, and that the young men and women needed not only encouragement in the form of more pay, but that if they were to get business, particularly from abroad, some form of title such as "associate director" was essential. As a result Christie's lost a large number of promising recruits who decided their talents would be appreciated more elsewhere, as well as those who decided they wouldn't learn much in the picture department as it then was. Sotheby's did not make this mistake.

Turning to marketing, although that word wasn't in vogue then as it is now, Peter instructed all the Board and technical staff such as Anthony and Brian to report back to him with notes of people they had met or stayed with for the weekend who had collections. This was the beginning of an intelligence system of "who had what and who would get it when the present owner died". To begin with it was very amateurish, compared with the comprehensive system that exists today, but it was a step in the right direction. Links with collectors who were already friends of Christie's were strengthened. George Spencer-Churchill – or, to give him his full title, Captain E. G. Spencer-Churchill, MC – was a case in point, the owner of the world famous Northwick Park Collection, near Moreton-in-Marsh,

Gloucestershire. Peter, Patrick, Anthony and Richard Falkiner, whose home was nearby, were frequent weekend guests.

Another decision was that special collections needed better presentation and if necessary cataloguing by an outside expert. In November 1958 there was the two-day sale of the Skippe collection of Old Master drawings, the largest of its kind to come on to the market for twenty-five years. The drawings, over 700 in number and the work of Italian artists for the most part, belonged to Edward Holland-Martin, a director of the Bank of London and South America, whose family had inherited them. The collection had been formed by John Skippe who is believed to have bought them from a monastery near Venice in the eighteenth century. In view of their importance it was decided to get Mr A. E. Popham, Keeper of Prints and Drawings at the British Museum from 1945 to 1954, to catalogue them.

The finished product complete with illustrations and hard cover was as thick as a 300-page book. The two-day sale totalled £91,000, the top price being 15,000 gns for two pen and ink studies of *Christ at the Column* which Popham attributed to Giovanni Bellini, one of the Italian Renaissance's rarest masters; the work is now believed to be by Andrea Mantegna. The sale was a success but being so academic had had little public impact.

Peter was constantly looking for new ways of getting business or improving the firm's "image" – although he would never have used such a word. As chairman he was a somewhat lonely figure. With the exception of Arthur – who was really only interested in "tin", as he mockingly described his beloved silver – all the rest of the Board were of a younger generation; although they were concerned about the firm's problems he did not, I think, feel that the directors could provide the answers. He tended therefore to lean heavily on his contemporaries for advice when discussing Christie's future; or, when he had made decisions, to announce them to the Board in peremptory tones like the adjutant of a battalion. Sitting at the head of the Board Room table, in his black suit with his black hand-made tie of heavy silk, he had a commanding countenance which did not appear to welcome any opposition, as I was to learn later.

One of his oldest friends was Esmond Baring, one of the London directors of the Anglo-American Corporation of South Africa; he was also the father of Peter's highly efficient secretary, Patricia, who became a great friend and ally of mine. In the middle of 1958 Esmond Baring told Peter that De Beers, the diamond mining section of

Anglo-American, had plans for the biggest diamond exhibition ever held. Could Christie's provide their rooms? Peter naturally seized on the idea, particularly as jewellery was one of his specialities; he saw that Christie's could make up some of the ground they had lost to Sotheby's through the tremendous publicity from the Goldschmidt sale. The exhibition could be held in the first two weeks of January when there was always a break in the sales programme. It was to be called the Ageless Diamond Exhibition and must still be the most valuable collection of diamonds ever to have been displayed under one roof. This was principally because there were four pieces of jewellery belonging to the Queen and one to Queen Elizabeth the Queen Mother, as well as some historic jewellery belonging to Christie's clients whom Peter had approached personally. The six most important jewellers in London also exhibited their best pieces. The proceeds of the exhibition went to the National Playing Fields Association and the Children's Country Holidays Fund at the Queen's special request.

The exhibition was a PR man's dream, not only because of the Queen's jewellery but also because of the free hand I was given by Sir Philip Oppenheimer, chairman of the De Beers Committee responsible for its design and mounting. I'm still amazed that he decided, after I had made a few suggestions at the first planning meeting, that the promotion of the exhibition should be left to PDA who were "on Christie's premises" – provided that they kept in close touch with De Beers's PR department. De Beers were spending £26,000 on mounting the exhibition and could well have insisted on running the show. However, Lionel Burke, the head of De Beers's PR department, was not put out in any way and a good working relationship developed immediately between us.

Jewellery and in particular diamonds were a new world for me, but Cecil Mann, of Garrard's, the Crown jewellers, was the perfect person to tell me everything I needed to know for the promotion of the exhibition. Cecil had looked after the royal family's jewellery for over thirty years, so he knew all the details of the pieces the Queen and Queen Mother were lending. Helped perhaps by a good bottle of claret, he expounded on the history of diamonds: how they are mined; "cleaved" when in "the rough" along a natural plane; how the gemstones are cut and "faceted", and finally polished.

One of the Queen's exhibits was a brooch made of two parts of the famed Cullinan diamond, the largest diamond ever found. Then there was Queen Alexandra's tiara, a present from some of her friends and similar to a Russian peasant's head-dress; and the twenty-one South African diamonds given to the Queen by the Union of South Africa on her twenty-first birthday, which she spent in Cape Town during the Royal Tour of King George VI. These were mounted as a necklace and a bracelet, and the Queen is said to refer to them as "my best diamonds". Lastly there was the Williamson "Pink", a 23-carat brilliant cut pink diamond – pink diamonds are very rare – which formed the centre of a flower brooch. It was given to the Queen as a wedding present by the late Dr J. Williamson, of Tanganyika, who owned the mine. Queen Elizabeth the Queen Mother lent the Garter Star which belonged to King George VI. The diamonds were a gift from the Union of South Africa in 1947. Garrard's mounted them as a Garter Star in 1948 and when the King wore it for the first time he was heard to comment, "Now I can compete with the ladies." Among the private pieces of jewellery there was the superb strawberry leaf tiara, belonging to the late Duchess of Northumberland; part of the historic Marie Antoinette necklace and a diadem which also belonged to her; and also the Eureka diamond, the first diamond ever to be discovered in South Africa.

Early in December we broke the story, which was sent out together with photographs of models wearing the most important pieces of private jewellery, and kept it running in newspapers, magazines, radio and TV up till Christmas. On the morning before the opening there was a special Press view which attracted a vast number of TV and radio networks, and British and foreign newspaper and magazine reporters. One of our most satisfying little hypes was through a boyfriend of Judy's who was responsible for the *Evening Standard* bill-posters. He was persuaded to do one with the heading "Queen's Jewellery for Christie's" and distribute copies throughout the New Bond Street–St James's area. Another was the franking of mail in the Mayfair–Piccadilly square mile announcing the charity exhibition at Christie's, so that many envelopes going into Sotheby's bore Christie's name.

Whether it was because of these efforts or not, the exhibition was a great success, the queue for admission extending round the corner in Bury Street in spite of freezing weather, and stretching into Christie's, up the stairs and twice round the gallery, duchesses rubbing shoulders with *Coronation Street* types. One of the most interesting sections of the exhibition was on diamond mining, which included a truck-load of "blue-ground" broken rock, illustrating the effort needed to get a gem diamond out of a mine. Even more fascinating was a diamond polisher at work, demonstrating the faceting of diamonds, which is done purely by the naked eye. Diamonds have a different number of facets according to their "cut" or shape, but a brilliant has fifty-eight facets and each one has to be at exactly the correct angle to the others, so that light is refracted and flashes in all the colours of the spectrum which is what gives diamonds their unique attraction. The Ageless Diamond Exhibition raised £8,500 for the charities and I hoped it had done Christie's some good as well.

Judy and I had now been at Christie's six months. We both quickly realised what an exciting place a fine art saleroom was to work in, compared with many office jobs. There were rarely moments of boredom, particularly for us because we had to keep in touch with every department, badgering them tactfully about whether they had any newsworthy works of art. However junior or senior, members of the staff could not but be affected by the general air of activity in the firm. It was not just the ebb and flow of the general public coming to the Front Counter with their paper bags filled with much-loved objects, or struggling in breathlessly with a picture under each arm to see if they were saleable. Everyone seemed to be on some pressing errand: secretaries with their notebooks scurrying to the warehouses, which ran a hundred yards back from the Front Hall and continued in the basement, for a cataloguing session; directors or technical staff bustling down the stairs on their way to the Front Counter to give an opinion on something which might be virtually worthless but on the other hand might be worth a great deal; others on their way out to see collections in different parts of London, the provinces or even abroad. When it came to a big sale it was the knowledge of all that had been done before and the importance of things selling well if the firm was to get more business which created the tension and excitement which is so much part of a fine art saleroom.

The staff of course was minute compared with Christie's 1,240 employees world-wide today. The number of sales was similarly small, 150 during the year compared with 1,400 now, world-wide. Two-thirds of the 30,000 lots we sold each year went for under £100. Efforts were made to get this point across so that people would not be put off by headlines of "fantastic prices". Peter took this so seriously that he wrote an article for the *Financial Times* spelling out the prices fetched in the late 1920s, and explaining how, allowing for the present value of the pound, 1958/9 prices were by no means extraordinary. This resulted in a telegram from Denys Sutton, then saleroom correspondent of the *Financial Times* but later for many years editor of *The Apollo* magazine, objecting to his having submitted such an article and accusing him of "disloyalty".

After the diamond exhibition 1959 started quietly. There is a natural cycle in the art auction world which results in three peaks of about a fortnight when the most important sales are held: at the end of March, June and November. Apart from the technical staff and directors, there was a small number of experienced retainers without whom the firm would come to a grinding halt. One such was Jim Taylor, the head porter, who had fifteen porters under his command (Jim had been a sergeant all through the Western Desert campaigns). Another was Roy Davidge, who was in charge of the Instructions Office where the auctioneers' catalogues are prepared, each lot having its confidential reserve price written in code and also any bids or "commissions" from people unable to be at the sale. Then there was Fred Nichols, the chief sales clerk; his was a job which required not only a head for figures – noting every price and keeping the running total – but the strength of mind not to become flustered. The auctioneer expected the sales clerk to have his eyes on the bidders as well, in case he himself missed something or someone, and also to know their names. Lastly, of course, there was the company secretary, Charlie Puddifoot.

To work with such people as Roy, Jim, Nick and "Puddie", to name only four, became a rewarding experience. I began to think that there was a paternalistic factor in fine art salerooms, particularly one as old as Christie's. Those on the staff in the 1950s and 1960s who did not have any great ambitions found being part of a family-type firm reassuring, irrespective of the appalling pay (it is very much better now) and its reactionary policies. There was great loyalty. Many did move on for perfectly understandable reasons, but many others remained and indeed are still there.

Our satisfaction with the results of the diamond exhibition was short-lived. Although we had some splendid Turner watercolours in the spring, followed by some important Old Master drawings from the Marquess of Northampton's famous collection and next a collection of Constables, there were far more important sales at Sotheby's, not only financially but from a prestige point of view. The highlight of their summer was the sale of Rubens's *The Adoration of the Magi* on behalf of the Trustees of the 2nd Duke of Westminster, who had died in 1953, leaving £17 million to be paid in death duties.

The Rubens had survived the war hanging on the staircase of Eaton Hall, the Westminsters' country seat near Chester, in spite of its having been requisitioned by the Army as a training centre for officers. Curiously the late Duke cannot have thought much of the picture or he would not have left it on the staircase of Eaton Hall or insured it for only £7,000. The Trustees did a good job and insisted on a reserve of £200,000, much more than any Old Master had ever fetched. Sotheby's need not have worried. There was considerable competition above that figure and the picture was eventually bought for £275,000 by Leonard Koetser, a Duke Street, St James's dealer with whom Judy and I often had our morning coffee. The National Gallery was asked by the Press for its comments on the price, and a spokesman was bold or stupid enough to say, "It certainly was not worth that sum. Even if we could have afforded it we would not have paid it."

It was some weeks after the sale that the "mystery buyer" became known. Michael Jaffé, the leading Rubens scholar in Britain and at that time Professor of Fine Arts at King's College, Cambridge (afterwards Director of the Fitzwilliam Museum), announced that the buyer was Major A. E. Allnatt, a property millionaire, whom he had persuaded to give it to King's. Allnatt had really wanted to donate it to the National Gallery. Twice he had arranged to see the Trustees and twice, amazingly, the meeting was cancelled. It would still be interesting to know why.

The day following the sale of the Rubens, Sotheby's fired another broadside by selling the Westminster Diamond tiara, which contained two enormous pear-shaped stones known as the Arcot diamonds, for £110,000. It was not surprising that, when the season ended, Sotheby's were able to announce sales totalling £5,750,000, virtually double those at Christie's.

However, long before these historic sales Pat Dolan had told me to write a report. Our first year of working for Christie's was up and I had to give recommendations for the future. In some ways what I wrote was highly critical, as it should have been, but it was otherwise pretty obvious stuff: "The picture department seems to PDA to be the crux of all Christie's problems . . . Collectors and dealers will not be convinced about Christie's authority on Impressionists until a completely new expert is brought in, someone who can be accepted without reservations . . ." Under "Christie's and the 'Dukes'", I see I said:

> Christie's fortunes were founded on close associations with the noblest families in the land. These were and still are very valuable contacts, but they must now be extended to the "new collector" who often comes from a very different stable, whether in this country or abroad . . .
>
> Christie's ability to survive on the type of contacts which James Christie built up seems also to have resulted in the last twenty-five years in a somewhat complacent attitude; a feeling that a normal commercial attitude towards getting and selling works of art is out of place in Christie's . . .
>
> Obituary lists from *The Times* should be circulated every morning to directors in case there was anyone with important works of art . . . Dossiers should be built up on families who might, for taxation reasons, have to sell art treasures in the future . . .

and so on. I was even so bold as to say that selling in guineas should be given up. Sotheby's didn't do it; silver, jewellery and books were sold in pounds sterling, so to the newcomer and even more to the foreigner the system was not only old-fashioned but inconsistent. This was too much, however, and Dolan told me to take it out as he knew it would infuriate Peter.

Patrick Dolan contributed the last page, telling the Board quite correctly that PDA was losing money from the account and asking for the fee to be raised from £3,000 to £6,500, a perfectly fair request. I don't know what Christie's reaction was. So far as PDA was concerned there was a deafening silence. However, towards the end of June I got a call from Lousada: "Would you like to have a drink on the way home? There's something I want to discuss with you. I'll call for you and we'll go to the Royal College of Art" (of which Lousada was a fellow and later chairman).

It may sound presumptuous but I guessed what he wanted to talk about; curiously it was the second approach I had had in a month. The first had been a summons to the headquarters of the Rank Organisation which needed someone to take charge of all their PR. Kenneth Winckles, the managing director, having heard of my experience in journalism and PR, said that my salary if I joined would be £15,000. In 1959 that was a lot of money, but could I work under

John Davis without getting a duodenal ulcer? I'd heard disagreeable accounts of him. On getting back to Bruton Street I took one of the secretaries out for a drink because her father was the director of Rank-Xerox, the most lucrative division then in the Rank empire. "Ask your dad what he thinks about this PR job which a friend of mine has been offered by his firm." The next day she told me, "Dad wouldn't wish it on his worst enemy." I wasn't surprised.

Lousada led me to a dark corner in the completely deserted bar of the Royal College. "Peter Chance has asked me to approach you to see if you would like to leave Dolan's and join Christie's and carry on running the Press Office there," he said. I thought that this might be the reaction of the Christie Board to Pat's increasing his fee, although obviously the offer would be much less than the £6,500 Pat was asking. My response was: "I would certainly like to join Christie's full-time, but it would have to be as a director. To do the job properly, or at least try to do it, I must have a voice on the Board."

Lousada reported back to Peter. I doubt if the Board originally thought of my joining them, but Peter had the bit between his teeth and asked me to see him the next morning. I told him I was very flattered at being asked to join Christie's. Had Lousada told him my feelings? "Yes, John, I'm delighted to say that my colleagues have agreed that after a probationary period you should join the Board." Charlie Puddifoot, the company secretary, was there making a few notes. I told Peter I would expect to be treated so far as remuneration and expenses were concerned like other directors, allowing of course for being very junior. What was the salary he was offering me? "The annual salary Floyd, Grimwade and Hannen receive is £2,500 and that is what I am offering you." The general public knew that secretaries were badly paid at Christie's but thought that the directors all drove Rolls-Royces. The truth was very different.

The salary Peter was offering me was the same as I was getting from Dolan, or thereabouts. I explained this and pointed out that, as I had no private income, there was not much financial incentive to move. I knew I would have to wait a full year before any possible increase in remuneration. I looked at Peter and said, "I believe the directors' bonus this year is going to be £750" – I don't know how I had learned this, but I realised that for once I was in a position to bargain – "would Christie's be willing to pay me the £750 as if I had been a director?" Today it sounds the most colossal cheek – akin to a footballer's transfer fee – and rather mercenary. Cheeky perhaps, but not the latter; we had two children now and every penny counted.

Peter took it very well and said he would have to consult his colleagues, which was only natural. I don't know what the reaction of the other directors was – I suspect it was not too friendly – but Peter had decided he wanted me to work for Christie's and brushed aside any opposition. The next day he told me the Board had accepted my request which he had supported and Puddifoot was there to record it officially. I was to join at the beginning of September, having given Dolan's a month's notice. "Oh, John, as a start, I think it would be a splendid idea if you produced an illustrated booklet with text of the past season's sales – have a look at the ones A. C. R. Carter of your old paper did for the years 1928 to 1931."

I walked back to Bruton Street knowing that I had to give notice but that I'd planned to go on holiday in mid-August to an hotel on the Helford River, Cornwall. Pat Dolan was in Geneva, Noel was on holiday, and Al Toombs, a nice American ex-journalist friend of Pat's, was in charge. I asked to see him and explained with some embarrassment that I had been offered a directorship by Christie's and thought it would be madness to pass it up. Al spoke to Dolan in Geneva while I was with him, and I heard his reaction from the earpiece of Al's telephone even though I was sitting the other side of the room; it was that of an infuriated bull. "Don't give him any holiday money, the double-crossing bastard!" He naturally thought that I'd pinched the account, which in advertising and PR is quite common. Years later he believed my explanation, took a great interest in Christie's gradual progress and we became close friends till his death in 1987.

I was under no delusions as to how lucky I was to be offered a seat on Christie's Board; it was quite a momentous step and the future sounded exciting although I knew it wasn't going to be easy. My mother couldn't believe it. Two of her uncles had had six-figure sales prior to the First World War, so she had been brought up with Memling triptychs, malachite tables and even Holman Hunt's controversial *The Scapegoat*, and she knew all about Christie's and quite a lot about the picture world; she couldn't understand how the firm could make her son, whose school reports and academic record had been disappointing, a director.

Feeling very cheerful I returned to King Street and remembering Peter's first instruction began collecting material from every department for the first of the twenty-five *Reviews of the Season* I produced for Christie's during my time there. The *Review* for 1959 was naturally very slender – all of forty pages – and very amateurish compared with the hardbacked 504-page books of the future. However, it had a colour plate on the front cover of Turner's lovely watercolour, *The Lake of Lucerne*, which had sold in March for the then world-record auction price of 11,000 gns ($32,450). I arranged with our catalogue printer for the galleys to be sent to Judy who would check them and send them on to me in Cornwall with pulls of the photographs selected. There in the hotel lounge I cut up the material Judy sent me each day and stuck it into a dummy, surrounded very often by elderly ladies incarcerated by the British summer and having to tolerate the smell of Gripfix; the dummy was then sent back to the printer so that he could produce a page proof which I could correct on my return to Christie's. It was a very ad hoc system but it seemed to work, and there weren't any bellows from Peter when the finished article appeared. The *Reviews*, which were sent out free to every catalogue subscriber as well as our free list, were produced like this until 1967/8 when we engaged a publisher to help me for the first time. The fact that they had to be produced while I was on my holidays was never commented upon, and I doubt if it occurred to anyone to consider the matter; as with so many things I found it was taken for granted.

In the middle of the summer Peter had decided it was high time that Christie's had a proper office in New York with a permanent representative. Sotheby's had had John "Jake" Carter ever since 1958. Christie's Board tended to scoff at any mention of his name because he had an accommodation address, operating from the suite of an old friend at 61 Broadway. They either didn't know or refused to recognise Jake's great talents. For ten years before the war and also after the war he'd built up the antiquarian side of Scribner's, the New York booksellers and publishers. During the war he worked for the British Information Service and afterwards was seconded from Scribner's to be personal assistant to Sir Roger Makins, British Ambassador in Washington. This if nothing else was recognition of his knowledge of America. Leaving that and his knowledge of books aside, his personality made him perfect for both his temporary diplomatic post and in 1958 his appointment as an associate director of Sotheby's.

It was perhaps significant that there was no one except Arthur on Christie's Board who had a comparable intellect. Peter had a good mind and was well read, but like many others of his class was in a social straitjacket because of the life he had been brought up to lead and his circle of friends. God knows he was not alone. The

Establishment in the City, banking and many other professions was renowned for its narrow-minded management and way of life. Most of Peter's friends would agree also that if he and Paddy had been able to have a family Peter's personality might have been very different.

Peter sought advice in New York about a possible representative for Christie's and Robert Leylan was recommended to him. Bob, as he was affectionately known to all of us very quickly, was a fine arts graduate of Harvard and for a number of years had been associated with the Paris and New York dealer Jacques Seligman. When he joined us in November he had just finished collaborating in the publication of a four-volume definitive work on Degas. Like Jake, Bob bought all his suits in Savile Row and his shoes at Trickers; he had much of his sophistication and as wide a range of friends in Britain and on the Continent as in America. All in all he sounded a good choice and has always remained a good friend not only of the firm but of those who worked closely with him. Bob took a chic little office on East 57th Street, New York's Bond Street, and went to work. However, he could not have been starting at a more difficult time, following the Goldschmidt and Weinberg sales.

Bob's appointment in November 1959 was the subject of my first Press release as a full member of Christie's. About the same time Peter was seeking Lousada's advice about a real expert for the picture department. Lousada suggested Walter Goetz and said he would arrange a dinner party so that Peter and Bill Martin could meet him. Walter, the son of a German father and French-born mother, was trilingual; he had also had an artistic education and knew the Paris art market where he represented Dudley Tooth, the well-known dealer. Before going there he had been a cartoonist for fifteen years on the *Daily Express*.

Anthony's dinner to introduce Walter to Peter and Bill came to nothing. Walter told me, "Naturally the state of the picture department came up. It was Bill Martin who said, 'Well, I don't know that things are all that bad. We sold that El Greco for 35,000 gns.'" Walter had made a point of keeping the conversation non-controversial and being ultra-polite but this gave him his cue: "I wasn't going to mention that sale," he said, "as I thought it might be a matter of some embarrassment as the picture was originally catalogued as Veronese School."

I doubt if it was this that resulted in Walter's not being offered a post at Christie's. I asked Walter for his impressions of the dinner. "Well, I think Anthony Lousada thought that with my knowledge of the Paris art market I might be of considerable help compared with, say, some Old Etonians and they were sounding me out as to whether I would be a suitable representative." I asked him why he thought nothing came of it. "I got on with Peter very well, but I know Anthony Lousada thought an anti-Semitic feeling was responsible, and I gradually came round to the same wavelength." It was water off Walter's back. He had told me, "I was sent to England in 1923, when I was twelve. I was probably one of the first Jewish boys to go to a British public school. There I had to get used to being called 'a dirty Hun' in place of 'a dirty Jew' which had been the case in Germany."

Whatever the reason for Walter's rejection, it was a lost opportunity for the strengthening of the picture department where he would have been as perfect in the job as Jake was for Sotheby's in America. Apart from the qualifications I have already mentioned, he was mature and experienced compared with the young recruits whom Peter was employing but who for one reason or another did not stay long. Eventually after four years the penny dropped, but by that time Sotheby's were even more established and we couldn't have bought Walter for £40,000 a year because by then he was buying pictures for American museums and important private collectors who trusted his judgment. To this day I don't know why Christie's did not realise that it was essential to engage a recognised art expert if they were to regain collectors' confidence in our picture department; they were just not thinking big enough. The young men Peter was taking on were excellent as a second eleven, but were no equal to Hans Gronau or even Carmen, because of their comparative youth.

Ian Lowe was the first recruit. He had taken a fine arts degree at Oxford and won the Laurence Binyon Prize in 1957. After spending the next summer looking at pictures and decorative arts in southern Germany he returned to England in search of a job. Peter saw Ian early in 1959 and he joined us in April on the princely salary of £500 a year. "Peter Chance said it was the most that a new employee had ever received at Christie's," Ian told me from the comfort of his office in the Ashmolean Museum where he went after being with us for two years and became Assistant Keeper until his retirement in 1988.

He was fortunate in one respect, he said, which was that he did not have to do his stint on the Front Counter. Shortly after he joined, Bill had a thrombosis while conducting a sale. "This left three of us in the picture department. Patrick was often away doing valuations and driving his Aston Martin; I was working 'on the hill'." ("The hill" was the nickname for that part of the passage to the back door which suddenly rose in line with Duke Street, St James's which runs parallel. It was here that every picture was stencilled and in the nearest warehouse the twice weekly "hill sessions" were held when pictures received their final attribution in the presence of the whole department.) "Brian was usually responsible for dealing with the public, at which he was not a master of the gentle word or encouraging gesture. I only stayed two years. My real reason for leaving was that I did not consider that there was enough thought given to training the junior members of the staff professionally. I did not think that with the tremendous pressure of work – sometimes I saw 300 pictures in a day – our cataloguing was sufficiently thorough. I thought that owing to the chaotic administration of the department I would not acquire sufficient serious knowledge at Christie's. Peter Chance was completely taken aback when I said I wanted to resign."

Ian's place was taken by David Barclay, who had just left the Courtauld Institute. Both Anthony Blunt – "I liked him very much" said David – and Professor Ellis Waterhouse knew that Ian Lowe was leaving Christie's and told David to apply for an interview with Patrick. David, who agreed completely with everything Ian had said about the department and also that Bill was "a most talented man but ruined by his father", lasted only six months because of a personality clash with Brian.

I do not think any of Brian's detractors would deny him his art historical knowledge. Equally I think Brian would agree that he could be a difficult colleague to work with and somewhat prickly at times. However, his occasional outbursts were not altogether surprising, especially in view of his sensitive nature. Ian and David were fortunate in having some private money to tide them over while looking for another job. Brian did not have such freedom; he had been at Christie's since 1958 and by 1961 must have felt considerable frustration over the difficulty of getting his views across either to Bill, whom he liked and respected, or to Patrick whom he regarded as "the reincarnation of Alec and opposed to any change".

Those who were to become Patrick's closest associates, who hadn't actually joined the firm as yet, will no doubt say that that is a monstrous libel. I regret to say that in my opinion there is no doubt that Patrick resisted for a long time any suggestions of changes in policy, whether they were to do with pictures or people. It was not long after I had been confirmed as a director that I crossed swords with Patrick myself and felt the full wrath of his intransigent attitude. I remember him stopping me at the bottom of the stairs one afternoon, I don't know why, and completely out of the blue saying, "I suppose you realise everyone on the Board thinks your ideas are insane and quite wrong for Christie's." I'm afraid I said, "Well, the Board could be wrong." If looks could kill I wouldn't be alive now!

Brian's view was: "I began to pressurise Bill as early as 1959 and onwards to have sales which were distinct in character but with little success. An obvious example were pictures which told a story, or 'Genre' sales. Patrick said, 'I don't know the meaning of the word,' but finally after months of haggling agreed to them being called 'Cardinal sales'." This was a reference to the numerous – appalling in my opinion – nineteenth-century continental pictures of cardinals, cavaliers et al. quaffing ale or in other scenes of jollification. These when grouped together fetched considerably higher prices than when lumped in with pictures ancient and modern as had been Alec's policy.

This was the first effort at specialisation and by the end of the 1960s it had spread to every type of picture – Old Masters, English, Modern British, Old Master drawings, watercolours, Old Master prints and Modern prints and of course Impressionist and Modern pictures and sculpture. However, it took all that time. Christopher Wood, who did not join till 1963, recalled how David Bathurst who joined the same year said he was called on to catalogue everything from Giotto to Jackson Pollock – "it was a bit of a crazy way to run an auction house". It is not altogether surprising, therefore, that Brian with his progressive ideas found his position so frustrating and that this provoked him into having disputes with his colleagues and not always treating Christie's customers with respect.

Brian will be remembered for a hilarious incident at the Front Counter – even if it was outrageous behaviour. One day while he was doing research for an Old Master sale, the Front Counter rang and asked him to come and see an old lady who insisted on speaking to an expert. It was the tenth interruption Brian had had that morning so he was not in the best of moods. When he got down to the Front Counter, the old lady said, "You look very young to be an expert." Brian told her in his plummiest voice that if it was any reassurance to her he had actually catalogued some of the Queen's pictures, which was true. "Well, what do you think of my picture then? What will it fetch at auction?" asked the lady. Brian looked at it with unconcealed horror and said, "I'm afraid, Modom, that we can't accept your picture for sale as it has not sufficient quality." There was a stunned silence. "Well, young man, what then do you suggest I do with my picture?" "If I was you, Modom," Brian replied, outraged at having his time wasted, "I should take it out into King Street and stamp on it." This was obviously quite inexcusable, but many other members of the technical staff, I'm sure, found it hard to control their patience with such petty interruptions.

Although no art expert, as early as 1960 I found Christie's failure to give the picture department any real credibility as depressing as Brian did. In two years nothing had been achieved in this direction. All the young men had left. After David Barclay came John Morrish and then Peter Cannon-Brooks, but neither stayed very long. What was obviously needed was someone with such an established name as an art expert that collectors would regain confidence in the firm and send us important pictures. The obvious man was David Carritt who in 1960 was only thirty-three, but whose genius as an art historian had been demonstrated years earlier by his astonishing discoveries and attributions which proved to be correct.

According to art experts his greatest discovery was of Dürer's *St Jerome in the Wilderness* at Raveningham Hall, the home of Sir Edmund Bacon, Bt, in 1957, when he'd only just become an art dealer. Many art scholars had seen this picture because Sir Edmund's collection was famous, but had not identified it as being by Dürer. It was unsigned, but the key to the discovery was the lion lying behind St Jerome. Colin Anson, a colleague first at Christie's who later joined Artemis, the international dealers where he has been for many years, told me, "It was totally characteristic of David's memory that he remembered the famous miniature drawing by Dürer, dated 1494, in the Hamburg Kunsthalle."

During the summer I had been on a river steamer party given by Professor "Teddy" Hall, who, as well as being a brilliant physicist, is renowned among hundreds of his friends for his splendid parties. I was introduced to Dr Christian Carritt, David's twin sister, and as we steamed up river she told me how unhappy her brother was as a dealer (he was also the very entertaining art critic of the *Evening Standard*). She felt that he was not cut out to be a dealer. Wasn't there a place for him at Christie's? I said I was quite certain there was; he was just the man we wanted.

A few days later I asked Peter if we could have lunch and told him towards the end of the meal that it seemed to me that the picture department needed strengthening. David Carritt seemed an obvious candidate. As far as I remember Peter hardly made any comment. Whether this was due to his being speechless at the effrontery of his PR man advising him about the picture department, I don't know. I doubt if he liked it, and just suggested that it was time to get the bill. Time would tell as to whether I'd made a useful suggestion, but I couldn't believe that he had not thought of David himself.

David recently had attracted a vast amount of publicity over his confirmation that eight large canvases of mythological subjects were by Guardi. These had belonged to Mrs Clodagh Shelswell-White and had decorated the ceiling of her home, Bantry House, overlooking Bantry Bay in southern Ireland. The panels were seen by the wily Dublin dealer Patrick O'Connor, who thought they might be valuable and persuaded the owner to sell them for about £12,000. Having taken them off the ceiling he rolled them up and took them back to his warehouse in Dublin. He then asked David Carritt to come over and give his opinion of them. David confirmed that they were undoubtedly by Francesco Guardi and even tried to buy them from O'Connor, but his father wouldn't lend him enough money. The panels were eventually sold – two of them to the National Gallery, Washington. David arranged the sale of four of the panels to Geoffrey Merton, an insurance broker, and was at least given credit for the correct attribution. They were later lent to the Royal Academy's winter exhibition, Italian Art and Britain. Peter must have been aware of the Guardis' being identified by David. He had himself seen them when they were still on the ceiling of Bantry House, but they were very dirty; there was no reason why he should have suspected them to be of importance.

Christie's negative reaction to employing Walter Goetz, as well as to considering David Carritt, was all the more serious for the strange treatment meted out much earlier to another promising recruit. Peter's apparent preference was for young graduates, but in the mid-1950s Peregrine Pollen had applied to join Christie's. Pollen was not a graduate but otherwise his background could not have been better from Christie's point of view. Educated at Eton and Christ Church, he was even a distant cousin of Patrick's. After doing his National Service, he worked his way round the world and then became ADC to Sir Evelyn Baring (later Lord Howick), Governor of Kenya.

The story of how he came to work at Sotheby's now takes a strange twist. Frank Herrmann relates in his book that Sir Evelyn had written to Lord Crawford, Patrick's father, to ask him for an introduction to Christie's for his ADC. Mr Herrmann tells me he was told this by Peter Wilson. However, Peregrine Pollen's version is completely different. He is quite unaware of any letter from Lord Crawford; but while he was still in Kenya he had written a letter to Patrick asking about a possible job. "I got from Patrick, I think you would agree, an exceptionally but charmingly pompous letter saying, 'I'm very busy. There are no vacancies at present, but when you come back from Kenya I'd be delighted to give you an interview.' I wrote to Christie's as opposed to Sotheby's because I knew nothing about anything and simply because the family tradition was at Christie's." Pollen's grandfather had formed a magnificent collection of Italian paintings which had been sold through Christie's to Duveen in 1927 for £620,000; and his grandmother was a sister of Sir George Holford whose pictures Christie's sold in 1928 for what in the late 1950s was still a world record sum. "Christie's was where my sympathies lay."

Not altogether surprisingly, when Peregrine returned from Kenya he joined Sotheby's. "I wasn't paid for the first three months. Apart from being surrounded by the remnants of two great collections I had had no formal artistic education. However, in November 1957 I joined Sotheby's picture department and in August of the next year, two months before the second Goldschmidt sale, I became Peter Wilson's assistant." It would be interesting to know who was really responsible for Pollen's not even being given an interview at Christie's – Alec or Patrick – and whether Peter knew about his interest in joining the firm. Patrick's letter was hardly welcoming to a cousin, however distant, whose forebears had had such important collections. What is certain is that Sotheby's employment of Pollen was a considerable gain for them and an unnecessary loss to Christie's. Pollen may not have had any artistic education but was quick to learn, to such an extent that he not only became Peter Wilson's assistant but in March 1960 was sent by him to run Sotheby's office in New York.

Early in 1960, Christie's were given a number of Old Masters from a Dutch collection formed before the war by the late Dr C. J. K. Van Aalst to sell. The Van Aalst pictures were the most important Christie's had been asked to auction since the new company had come into being. It was essential, therefore, that the sale went well. The highlight was Rembrandt's *Portrait of Juno*, a large baroque interpretation of the goddess venerated by Dutchmen of the artist's epoch. A brochure had been printed with the full history of the painting.

Patrick had authorised me to say that Christie's expected *Juno* to sell for £100,000. The Press release together with photographs attracted a lot of publicity. The day the news appeared in the papers Judy and I went over to the Bon-Bon for our morning coffee. It was full of dealers as usual and we sat down at a table with Leonard Koetser. "What's all this about *Juno* fetching £100,000?" he said loud enough for the whole café to hear. "I bet you £5 it doesn't," he said. "It's been completely flattened by relining – there's no impasto; you're mad to come out with a statement like that." There were rumblings of agreement. Judy and I left feeling very worried. Koetser may at times have been a bit naughty, but he knew his pictures. Judy and I learned quite a lot by talking to "the other side" during our coffee breaks. Personally I thought *Juno* an awful picture but that was of no relevance. I tentatively asked Bill Martin about the picture without appearing to criticise it. "Well, it should do well as he painted it in his late maturity. Mind you, it has been relined – because the original canvas was getting thin – and this tends to draw the paint back into the canvas, reducing what we call the 'impasto', so it's not in perfect condition." So Koetser was right.

The pictures were to be sold on April 1st. I remember the somewhat unfortunate date not only because of the sale, but because before it began Jo said to me in his nice Old-Etonian way, "Oh, it's today that you get your house colours," meaning that I'd survived my six months' probation and would now join the Board, "so let's hope for a good write-up of the sale." The Big Room was packed and I'd managed to get the TV there although I wondered then whether it was wise. There were some nice pictures in the sale: a splendid *Portrait of Rembrandt* by his pupil Carel Fabritius, a *Wooded River Scene* by Hobbema, a *Wooded Landscape* by Magnasco and *The Flooded Road*, a very attractive work by Jan Sieberechts, all of which sold well. When *Juno* came up there was a hush. Peter, who was taking the sale, started quite low and took it up slowly. There was dead silence in the room, a sickening and deeply depressing premonition of failure which I was to get to know well in the years to come. Peter bought the picture in at 50,000 gns, but I doubt if there was a bid of more than half that.

The result was another blow to the prestige of our picture department, and yet Patrick had been right not only about its attribution but about its provenance. He may have been unwise to come out with an expected price and never did again. It was a very good example of an auction house's difficulties and the waywardness of the art market.

A picture can arouse collective dislike one day whereas years later it may be a totally different story.

After the sale the Van Aalst Estate handed over the picture to the Hague dealer G. Cramer who sold it in 1966 to Bill Middendorf II, a former American investment banker and private collector. The asking price is believed to have been around $600,000. Ten years later, in 1976, Middendorf sold it to Dr Armand Hammer, President of Occidental Oil, for $3 million. Middendorf originally put it up for sale at Knoedler's for $5 million, but gave Hammer first refusal at $3 million.

There was no doubt in the minds of Mr Seymour Slive, former Director of the Harvard University Art Museums, and Dr Christopher White, Director of the Ashmolean Museum, Oxford, the acknowledged Rembrandt experts in America and Britain to whom I wrote, that *Juno* was by Rembrandt. Mr Slive said he tried to get *Juno* for the Fogg Museum in Harvard, but didn't have the funds. Dr White said, "I always found it extraordinary that there was no interest in *Juno* when it was auctioned." In *Hammer Witness to History*, Dr Armand Hammer relates that John Walker, an ex-Director of the National Gallery, Washington, considered it to be the finest Rembrandt in the world in private hands. But in April 1960 those favourable testimonies did not retrieve Christie's loss of face among the world's experts and collectors.

The 1959–60 sales season wound to its close. The most interesting sale in many ways had been the one we held on behalf of the appeal by the London Library, which after eighty years of being exempt from paying rates was suddenly faced with a £20,000 rate demand. Rupert Hart-Davis, the publisher and chairman of the library's appeal committee, asked Peter, an old friend of his, if Christie's would hold an auction of manuscripts donated by many of the library's members who had readily answered his appeal. It included E. M. Forster's *A Passage to India* (£6,500); *The Waste Land*, which T. S. Eliot had to write out again as the original manuscript had somehow got lost (£2,800); Lytton Strachey's *Queen Victoria* (£1,800) and a folio sheet and two notebooks of manuscript notes by T. E. Lawrence giving previously unpublished data regarding the subscription sale of *Seven Pillars of Wisdom* (£3,800).

The sale, which was held in the evening, totalled £27,000, and to show their appreciation the London Library made Christie's life members. More than half the total had been paid by Lew Feldman, a New York dealer and owner of the bookshop The House of El Dief.

I'd met him at home where he had been looking through my father's manuscripts as he bought for the University of Texas, which probably has the biggest collection of English manuscripts in the world. Just before lunch on the day of the sale I bumped into Lew in the Front Hall and he asked if I was doing anything for lunch. Knowing his importance I took him round to Overton's and we had a pleasant chat about the sale. Finally he said, "What do you think the sale is going to total, Mr Herbert?" "I haven't the slightest idea," I replied, "but I've heard £17,000 mentioned." He drew out his cheque book and said, "If I give you a cheque now for £17,000 could you arrange for me to buy the whole sale?" What a nerve! In the end he did actually pay £17,000, but he didn't get the whole sale. However, we got no commission, of course, although the sale may have done our prestige some good.

There had been many good sales of English and French furniture, silver naturally because Christie's had the edge over Sotheby's there, jewellery and even of Impressionists, but minor in Sotheby terms. When the end of season figures were released our knock-down total was £2.7 million compared with Sotheby's £6.8 million; the gap was widening.

We were just not getting enough good pictures, let alone collections of them. The reason should have been obvious. No one had any confidence in the department. It was a gloomy situation. The impetus of Peter's new broom did not seem to apply to the picture department even after the failure of the Van Aalst Rembrandt to sell. Nothing really constructive had been done except the appointment of Guy to improve its administration.

In 1961 the story was the same. Sales of furniture, jewellery, silver and other applied arts went well but there were no picture sales of real importance. There was the occasional extraordinary price such as the 9,500 gns ($27,930) paid by an American dealer for Holman Hunt's *The Lady of Shalott*, the highest price paid to date for a Pre-Raphaelite painting and indicating a revival of interest in the school. However, for the Old Masters we were getting the prices were sluggish, and there were no signs of any major Impressionist pictures.

Guy and his wife Biddy asked us to dinner, and after the meal I discreetly introduced the subject of David Carritt. Guy's reaction was non-committal and certainly not enthusiastic: "It's not quite as easy as that." What was it? Was it resistance from Patrick or could it possibly be that because the social mores of the time were not quite as broad-minded as they are today, David was not thought suitable? Whatever the reason, Guy was playing things very close to his chest, as he tended to do when asked questions he didn't wish to discuss.

What I couldn't understand was the apparent lack of concern. The sales total for 1960–61 was £3.1 million compared with Sotheby's £8.4 million, nearly £2 million more than their previous year. Pre-tax profits for the three years since Peter had taken over were, for the financial year ending March 31st: 1959, £35,000; 1960, £26,000; 1961, £32,000. Costs were inevitably going up, so without any improvement in picture sales I would have thought my colleagues on the Board would be worried. Perhaps they were; I certainly was and seriously wondered whether I had made a wise decision in joining Christie's after all.

Our Men in Havana

My admiration for Peter's energy on behalf of the firm was boundless, but when I learned of his Cuban adventure I was seriously concerned. I thought that the need for Christie's to get business had affected his judgment about what was an acceptable risk, and what might prove very damaging to our name, particularly in the United States.

It all started about the middle of 1962 when Patrick was approached by someone who said he was a spokesman for a syndicate, which even today must remain anonymous. They had thought up an idea to solve Castro's desperate shortage of foreign currency. Their suggestion was to make a cash offer for all the works of art confiscated when Castro seized power early in 1959. A large proportion of the works of art belonged to Americans. The idea was that Christie's should carry out an independent valuation. The syndicate hoped to auction the works of art at Christie's later for a profit, half of which would go to the Cubans. Patrick told Peter he thought he should see this spokesman and Peter did so. What is more, he happened to know the head of the syndicate well.

Peter decided, "after taking legal and financial advice", that he should at least go and see for himself the quality of the works of art and whether it was a viable proposition. Apart from Patrick, I doubt if many members of the Board knew where Peter had disappeared to – I certainly didn't; but Patricia Baring probably knew.

Peter was well aware of the risk he was running of antagonising American collectors, just at a time when we were trying to establish ourselves in New York. Secret discussions regarding travel arrangements took place outside Christie's. The syndicate were travelling independently via Curaçao, but Peter had been advised to fly to Jamaica, where he had to stay for two days incognito. He then caught a KLM flight on which a seat had been booked for him, but not in his name; he was told simply to present his ticket which was awaiting him in Kingston. It turned out to be the last aircraft into Cuba before the US–Russia missile crisis came to a head.

Havana was "an armed camp" Peter told me on his return. Young women as well as men were in camouflage uniform and everybody carried submachine-guns over their shoulders. I could not think of a more improbable person to find himself in such a situation than Peter – a pillar of the Establishment in his perfectly cut tropical suit, with little liking for or knowledge of the hoi polloi. In retrospect it tickled his sense of humour and adventure. What he couldn't have known was that the American fleet was about to encircle the island.

Peter was met by the syndicate's spokesman who had first approached Patrick, who took him to the Hilton Hotel where he was shown to a suite. (The hotel was otherwise filled with Cuban peasant families completely unused to twentieth-century amenities.) After freshening up Peter went downstairs where he was greeted by a high-ranking Cuban official and the head of the syndicate. They led him to the bar and offered a drink. "Rather foolishly," Peter told me, "I said, 'A whisky, please.' A glass of liquid was produced which might have been methylated spirits. I choked and my host, a minister of sorts, gave an order to his minions. A minute later two very tough security policemen came in and seized the unfortunate barman and marched him out. I cannot say I actually heard the shots ring out, but I imagined them."

The next day Peter was taken to the Villa Lobo where all the works of art belonging to former residents, apart from pictures and silver, had been stored together with the splendid Lobo collection. For five days, from morning to night, Peter was taken round by Castro's officials: "I shall never forget the curator of the Picture Museum where quite obviously there were many important works. She was very beautiful, dressed in jeans and a T-shirt with a submachine-gun over her shoulder and a pistol in her belt; she would certainly have liked to shoot me." Peter and the syndicate ate with the Cuban officials in private rooms and although there was no food in the shops they were well looked after.

Eventually the Cubans demanded a detailed inventory with prices. This was quite impossible for Peter or any one person to provide, so he suggested sending a team and quoted a substantial fee in the event of there being no sale. It was a tricky problem, for the syndicate would only buy if there was a chance of making a substantial profit after paying all expenses. There was no way of knowing whether someone in the Cuban hierarchy might have some idea of values on the international art market. To get round this problem it was decided to quote an inclusive figure for the different sections: pictures and drawings, silver and furniture, and jewellery and objets d'art.

At the end of five days Peter said he could be of no further use and should return to London to instruct a team to come out and conduct a valuation. However, leaving Havana was easier said than done. All regular boat and air services had ceased, so how was Peter to get back to London? Fortunately, to add yet another bizarre touch to his adventure, a Venezuelan basketball team had also become trapped in Havana and wanted to get home. Their Government graciously sent an old Britannia which flew the team and Peter to Mexico City. Peter had to be very careful on arrival as this was the first aircraft from Cuba since the crisis and he would have to show his passport. He realised that anyone with a British passport coming from Cuba was news, particularly since the Americans had announced that anyone landing from Cuba would be treated as a Communist. That in itself would have made all his many friends laugh, because few people were more "true-blue" than Peter. He prayed, therefore, that no journalists would be around. There was one man from the *Sunday Telegraph* but somehow Peter fobbed him off and ran across the airfield to an aircraft which was just leaving for New York. When he went to the BOAC desk in New York for a ticket to London, he realised he had for once no money because he had not been allowed to take any into Cuba. Plastic money in the form of credit cards didn't exist in those days, but British Airways on seeing his passport gave him a ticket on credit. On arrival in London he phoned Paddy who told him that rumours of American action against Cuba had been such that she had expected never to see him again.

Once back in King Street, Peter wasted no time in briefing Patrick and telling him to get a team together capable of valuing silver and jewellery as well as the pictures which were of course Patrick's responsibility. Michael Clayton, who had become Arthur's assistant in 1960, had some interesting things to say about what happened next: "In January 1963 Patrick asked me whether I would like to join him in a valuation behind the Iron Curtain. I jumped at the opportunity and then discovered that this in fact meant a visit to Cuba, the route being London–Prague–Gander–Havana." The third member of the team was Reggie Eyles, our jewellery expert.

"Prague, where we spent one night, was cold, bright and fascinating," Michael went on, "and we drank a great deal of slivovitz to keep warm. Next afternoon we took off for Gander, arriving in a blizzard about nine at night. We were ferried by bus to the terminal where we were to have dinner while the aircraft refuelled. Nobody told us, but unless one could produce one's passport, one wasn't allowed into the building. Patrick had left his on the aircraft and had to sit between the double-action automatic doors whilst Reggie and I carried his dinner to him, course by course; he was very cold by the time it came to coffee."

Havana, when they got there, was hot and humid. Their hotel was huge and modern and like everything else American, but after two years without spares very little worked, except the ice-cream machine which produced twenty-five different varieties. "We were obliged to live on daiquiris."

For Reggie it was not only their destination which came as a great shock. It became evident that he had never been abroad before and did not like foreign food. He ate Russian eggs for three days, until he discovered there was a shortage, and that anyone over the age of three caught eating eggs was liable to summary execution, whereupon he changed to salads. For security reasons he had not been told where they were bound, and he had only a thick serge suit to wear; with the temperature in the nineties, Patrick and Michael began to fear for his survival.

"We travelled everywhere with an armed escort," Michael continued. "Patrick and I went to various warehouses in which anything and everything had been jumbled together and one had to pick out the things worth valuing. I cannot speak for Patrick, but when faced with an aircraft hangar containing 800 different chests of assorted metalwork – pots, pans, pewter, silver and even coal scuttles – I gave up after the first fifteen or so and told my helpers to tip the contents of each chest on to the floor and stirred it with a broomstick to see if anything interesting showed up. As I recall, the total catch was a small dish by Paul de Lamerie." They also had to value the whole contents of a museum.

Meanwhile Reggie sat day after day in a small upper room of one of the banks looking at jewellery as it was brought to him, tray after tray, sweating profusely, only partly because of the heat, but mainly because two armed guards sat beside him with their submachine-guns digging him in the ribs. By this stage he had decided that coffee would be safe to drink and he would also occasionally eat some sliced fruit. The fact that he had lost his false teeth could have been an added reason for his slender diet. Patrick, of course, was in his element, relishing every aspect of the revolutionary environment – which barely touched the Christie team. One day they were even able to go shark fishing and just as Reggie was dozing off in his swivel chair, Patrick contrived to make his rod give the most fearsome tug so that Reggie nearly shot out of the boat.

"On one occasion we had to visit the Villa Lobo, a splendid cool white marble palace, filled with wonderful French furniture," said Michael. "We were met by the butler at nine in the morning bearing a tray with two glasses and a bottle of 1917 Hine. By eleven o'clock we had finished the brandy and French furniture prices had climbed to figures not dreamed of until the Getty Museum came on the scene twenty years later. We felt obliged to return the following day to revise our figures. This time there was no butler and no brandy – could he have been liquidated?

"All this time the syndicate were locked in discussions with the Cubans, who simply could not believe that they were prepared to buy at the figures put on by ourselves, sell on the open market in Europe and in the event of anything fetching more than a certain percentage share the bonus with the Cubans."

Because all the jewellery was in one place Reggie completed his task before Patrick and Michael and returned to London. The evening before he left, Patrick and Michael took him to a night club. By today's standards the performance was fairly staid but to Reggie it was an eye-opener and it was a shattered, not to say starving man, who was helped on to the aircraft the following day.

"In the event nothing came of the expedition, which may have been a good thing," added Michael. "The Canadian auctioneer who did get something for sale also had a bomb thrown into his saleroom. My one regret was that we never met Fidel Castro, who indicated that he would be pleased to see us after dinner one night. But we understood that he was going to make a speech, and as he did this the very day we arrived and it lasted four and a half hours, none of us felt we could face such concentrated brainwashing and in Spanish at that."

Meanwhile back in London Peter realised that he would have to brief me about the presence of the team in Cuba in case there was a Press leak. This was when he filled me in about his own trip as well. Although I was immediately horrified by the possibility of what the

Press could make of such news and what it would do to our efforts to get business from America, I couldn't resist a sneaking admiration for Peter's initiative. It was a pity he couldn't, it seemed, bring equal energy into revitalising the picture department.

Two days after Peter had told me about his travels and that the team were now on their way back I received an early call from the Londoner's Diary column of the *Evening Standard* who appeared to know not only of Patrick's presence in Cuba but virtually the full details of the syndicate's plan. For the one and only time in my life I decided to go down to Fleet Street and speak to the editor in the hope that I could persuade him not to run the story. I knew Charles Wintour, the *Standard*'s editor, well as we often met at parties, but I didn't think that this would have much effect. When I saw him he was very understanding but he said, "John, we have had these facts from a very good source and unless you categorically deny them you cannot expect us not to run a story; as an ex-reporter you know that perfectly well." The story was fairly mild, but it was the reaction of the foreign news agencies, and particularly of the London office of the *New York Times* and other American papers, that I was frightened about.

My wife and I were going out to dinner that evening, and I left our hostess's telephone number with our au pair girl in case she got any Press calls. It was standard procedure for reporters and the news desk to scan the evening papers as the afternoon wore on in case there were any stories which warranted a follow-up for the next day's paper. I was fully expecting a deluge of calls and warned my hostess. However, there was only one; true, it was from the Associated Press, the most powerful news agency in the world, but much to my amazement I managed to persuade the reporter there was nothing really in the *Standard* story without actually denying it. So we got away with it. But how had the *Standard* received such accurate information?

It wasn't until 1988 that I found out how the paper had got the story. Of all times it was during the "wake" at El Vino's, Fleet Street, that followed the funeral of Sam White, the *Evening Standard*'s Paris correspondent for forty years. I bumped into Gavin Young, an old friend of Sam's like everyone there. Patrick had told me on his return from Havana that he had run into him. I asked Gavin about their meeting. "I remember it well. It was just after the Bay of Pigs fiasco and before the missile crisis. I was on my way to one of the best black-bean soup restaurants where they also sold marvellous daiquiris. Suddenly I saw ahead of me, of all people, Patrick. I naturally asked him what he was doing there and he told me a few details, but said, 'Don't make too much of it.' Actually I didn't write a word and afterwards felt a bit foolish, but I was really there doing a political piece for the *Observer*."

However, on his return to New York, he said, he had a drink with John Richardson who asked him how his trip had gone. Gavin replied, "You'll never guess who I met – old Patrick." ". . . John suddenly stiffened like a pointer sniffing a grouse under a bush. I gave him a few details and then didn't see him for dust. In fact I was left paying the bill."

No harm was done, although poor Bob Leylan when he heard said to our New York lawyer, "That was a terrible thing for Peter Chance to have done. It might have jeopardised all our American business." The lawyer replied, "Well, I think it was a very bold thing to have done and anyway he wasn't caught." My sympathies, as I have already said, were mainly with Bob.

The Augustus John Studio Sale

James Christie's early success was due not only to his eloquence and personality, but also to friendship with the artists of the day. Four years after opening his rooms at the eastern end of Pall Mall, he moved to 125 Pall Mall where his neighbour was Thomas Gainsborough. They became firm friends and Gainsborough painted his portrait on condition he hung it in his "Great Rooms", as they were called in those days. James Christie offered other leading artists of the day, as well as Gainsborough, the use of his rooms to exhibit their portraits of the aristocracy. Such works were regarded as the height of fashion and apart from the Royal Academy show once a year there was no other public place where they could be seen. Not only did Christie in this way become great friends with the artists, but he also attracted the nobility to his auction rooms.

This practice also resulted in more than two centuries of studio sales, because when the artists died who had been helped by James Christie, their executors or friends asked him to auction the remaining pictures in the deceased artist's studio. It's not surprising that James Christie sold the pictures from Gainsborough's studio on his death in 1792, but his studio sales had in fact started in 1781 with the work of Nathaniel Hone. This set a precedent that was followed down the years by a whole string of similar sales – the studios of Reynolds, Landseer, Raeburn, Rossetti, Burne-Jones, Leighton, Sargent, and more than a hundred others right up to the present day.

The most interesting and indeed important studio sales since the war were the two following the death in 1961 of Augustus John. Augustus John was the last of an era and epitomised physically, intellectually and socially what the man in the street regarded as a Bohemian – a word that has long since gone out of vogue, as a result of more liberal social attitudes and the nature of contemporary art.

When John died at the age of eighty-three he left in his studio at Fordingbridge, near Salisbury, over a hundred oils and an even larger number of drawings dating from 1900 to 1956. Long before the first sale took place, the prospect of it aroused considerable interest in the international art world, not so much for the possible prices, but because it would reflect all the various stages of the artist's development.

Among the pictures in the first sale was his *Peasant Woman and Child*, painted in 1903, only a few years after leaving the Slade; this moving work was of particular interest as it was very similar in style to Picasso's contemporary blue period works. His *Portrait of a Gipsy Woman* reflected his enthusiasm for gipsy life, and his roamings in a caravan over England and Wales. In this context there were naturally many portraits of his wife Dorelia. There were others of his sons David, Pyramus and Robin, but none of his eldest son Caspar, who when his father died was Admiral Sir Caspar John, First Sea Lord. When Caspar decided to go into the Royal Navy, Augustus typically could not understand his eldest son subordinating his life "to one of discipline".

There was a fine portrait of Wyndham Lewis which recalls the storm which followed the rejection of Lewis's portrait of T. S. Eliot by the Royal Academy in 1938. Augustus John, one of Lewis's best friends, resigned in protest although he had been an Academician for ten years. (He was re-elected two years later.) Among portraits of the famous there were *Madame Suggia, T. E. Lawrence, Lord David Cecil, Cecil Beaton, Lady Ottoline Morrell* and *David Lloyd George*. There was also a very fine *Self-Portrait*.

Augustus John had died leaving £80,702 net after duty had been paid. All his assets were left in trust for life to his widow, Dorelia. Exemption was claimed by his Trustees for the works left in his studio but without success. This had brought about the sale. I became closely associated with the sale, which was certainly the highlight of our season, because apart from the obvious promotional possibilities, Peter had somewhat surprisingly suggested that I should write the usual "tactful letter" to the senior Trustee, even though Peter himself knew him well, offering our services if there had to be a sale.

The senior Trustee was Hugo Pitman, much beloved by all his many friends; he had been senior partner of Rowe and Pitman and a Trustee of the Tate. We had met just before the war and immediately hit it off. Although not even my godfather, he sent me a cheque for £100 as a twenty-first birthday present which by a remarkable coincidence I received exactly on the right day in 1945 while my destroyer was replenishing with the rest of the British Pacific Fleet. Perhaps Peter was right in thinking that for once the "tactful letter" might come better from a young friend of Hugo's than from the desk of the chairman. In any event Christie's were instructed to collect the pictures and drawings from Fordingbridge. This resulted in a strong protest from Dudley Tooth, Augustus's dealer, that he should be responsible for the sale and that Christie's would get only £26,000 for the studio.

There was no problem about interesting the Press in the sale; it was just a question of getting the maximum mileage. Apart from the immediate results of the Press release and a colour supplement story in one of the Sundays, I wanted to exploit the Photonews feature which the *Daily Express*, not a tabloid in those days and still edited by the great Arthur Christiansen, ran once a week. This was a half-page photograph with about 500 words of editorial underneath. John Rydon, the *Express*'s saleroom correspondent, whom I had known since my first days in Fleet Street, was keen on the idea, but there would have to be an exclusive photograph of Sir Caspar John in the picture warehouse looking at his father's pictures for the last time.

I recognised that it was fraught with danger to expose Sir Caspar to the possible whims of a sensational paper and spoke to Peter about it. "I think you're mad, but if Sir Caspar is willing, do it; go ahead, but God help you if it goes wrong." Sir Caspar readily agreed to see me and on arriving at Admiralty House I was ushered into his office, outside which stood two immaculate Royal Marine guards. Sir Caspar was a tall ascetic figure of a man with huge beetling eyebrows and the serious countenance of a Jesuit priest, although off-duty he could, I knew, let his hair down as much as his late father. Fortunately I had met him once on just such an occasion in Cornwall.

I explained to him the importance of stimulating public opinion and the necessity of getting the maximum publicity. I told him what the *Daily Express* wanted, and that there was a risk of an embarrassing headline. I would naturally try to prevent this, but there was no guaranteeing that I could. I didn't really expect him to say yes, but it took him only a few moments of consideration to do so, and arrange a time to come to King Street and be photographed in the warehouse with the pictures. We shook hands on it and he ushered me to the door. The Royal Marines snapped to attention and Sir Caspar said, "Show Sir Alan Herbert out"; even the greatest are prone to Freudian slips!

I admit to opening the *Daily Express* a few days later with a somewhat fluttering heart, but nobody could quarrel with the result: a half-page photograph, nice write-up and no maudlin headline. It may have been this and the sustained Press build-up which caused Dudley Tooth to drop me a personal note the afternoon after the first sale: "Congratulations. Very professional performance." It's encouraging to have one's slender talents occasionally recognised, but Dudley was a very nice man.

The results of the sale had indeed surprised everyone. The total for the first sale on July 20th, 1962 was just under £100,000 ($280,000), the *Self-Portrait* being bought by Freddie Mayor, a great personal friend and one of the most respected London picture dealers, for Lord Cowdray for 8,500 gns ($25,500), a very good price. An artist's works generally rise immediately after his death, but even so the prices for many of the drawings surprised everyone as Augustus had done some of them when his hand was not as steady as in his early days. Drawings with estimates of £25 went for ten times that amount, while superb early works such as his 1903 drawing of Dorelia and Euphemia Lamb went for 2,400 gns ($7,056).

By comparison the most important sale of Old Masters of the year was in November and totalled only £195,370 ($547,638). The one important picture, Claude Lorraine's *View of Carthage with Dido and Aeneas Leaving for the Hunt* did well, selling for 52,000 gns ($152,880), but otherwise prices were sluggish; we were just not getting sufficient important works.

It was in the same month that Peter added to our European representation by appointing Baron Martin Koblitz to be our representative in Austria. This received almost as much opposition as the appointment of Hans Backer – mainly due to his having been a dealer in London after the war. In those days members of the fine art trade, even though they were Christie's most important customers, were regarded as being definitely "below the salt", unless they'd been to public school. However, Martin had all the courtly charm of the *ancien régime* and soon won over everyone at King Street and began to send us valuable business. He also had the knack of finding out not only attractive but efficient girls to work for him, such as Elizabeth Lane, long since director in charge of valuations, and Charlotte Hohenlohe-

Langenburg, who was later to join Christie's team of representatives in Germany.

Even more important than Koblitz's appointment, Christie's announced in November that David Carritt would be joining them in the New Year, following Bill Martin's resignation because of ill-health. Bill had had a cerebral haemorrhage while taking a picture sale, after which he had returned to work for only a short time.

The penny had at last dropped. I think Guy had sounded out a prominent dealer friend of his about who was the best expert. Supported by Arthur, he finally suggested David to Peter. Peter Wilson's reaction was typical and not unfunny, even allowing for its bitchy note: "I've never seen a rat swimming out to join a sinking ship before." I naturally was overjoyed.

David Carritt as an art historian was a phenomenon. There are obviously many great art experts – museum directors, dealers and private collectors, some of whom are accepted as being the top authority about a particular artist – but David was in a class of his own. Walter Goetz told me: "I've never known anyone who had such a retentive visual as well as art historical memory." Hugh Leggatt, the well-known dealer, said, "He was a genius and had a better eye than anyone in the world." David Carritt certainly had a prodigious memory and an incredible eye for pictures, but what made him different from so many other experts was that he developed his visual skills at a very early age.

David was born on April 15th, 1927, of a Scottish mother and Scottish-English father who ran a small engineering business in Scotland. He had two sisters, Christian, the doctor I had met at the river party, and Heather, who was younger. The children were brought up in a strict puritanical way, none of them being allowed to read, even when they were teenagers, until 6 p.m. This was in spite of David's love of reading. Christian, perhaps because she was his twin, was particularly devoted to David and realised he needed a certain amount of protection. "At our first school, Norland Place, Holland Park, I told the staff that David was different from other people and had been from his birth. When we played hockey, I would be on the wing, and David would be full back, and I remember having as it were to play for two, as often I would have to rush across the field and say 'Come on, David' and give the ball a tremendous whack in defence of our team although it was really David who should have done it."

In spite of the rules at home, David started reading *Country Life* when he was still under eleven and before going away to school, and it was the pictures in great houses illustrated in *Country Life* which developed his interest in Old Masters. He confirmed that to me himself. "From the age of twelve," Christian continued, "it was perfectly obvious that he was destined to be an art historian. He had a photographic memory and never forgot a picture. It was when he went to Rugby that he started writing to the owners of the houses he had read about asking them if he could come and see their collections. One of the first to receive a letter from David was Colonel Hugh Brocklebank who had a house near Stratford on Avon and collected early Italian and English pictures."

Sir Brinsley Ford, the noted private collector who was a trustee of the National Gallery in the 1950s and chairman of the National Art Collections Fund for many years, was a great friend of Colonel Brocklebank's. He recalled the incident for me as some people may regard it as apocryphal. "Hugh had received a letter and presumed that it came from a master at Rugby, so was naturally very surprised when a schoolboy arrived on his bicycle and introduced himself. However, Hugh was always very kind to anyone who was interested in his pictures and he made no exception for schoolboys."

David went to Oxford, having got an open scholarship to Christ Church. Christian gave a laconic description of his career there: "He read English for his first term and hated it so switched to history. He was kept very short of money; did no work and got a First." When he came down he went to Italy for a long time – Florence, Siena and Rome – feasting his eyes on the pictures he loved. While in Florence he was encouraged by Bernard Berenson who said he had seldom encountered anyone with a finer eye for Old Masters.

He quickly became a friend of collectors and dealers all over the world, a friendship based not only on his staggering expertise – and this quickly came to the fore on his return from the Continent – but also on his tremendous personal charm. It may have been because of this quality that he was not suited to being an art dealer. Christian said, "David was very unworldly about money. He hated the financial side of pictures. Once he'd discovered a picture he lost interest. He wasn't any good at the business side. That's why he was taken for a ride by various dealers, and often never got his share. For instance for one of his first great coups, his identification of Caravaggio's missing *Music Party*, he only got a lunch and the thanks of the owner. Two years later it was sold to the Metropolitan Museum."

David also had tremendous moral integrity. Long before the

Guardis came to light he went to Ireland with a well-known dealer who introduced him to someone who wanted to sell his very important collection. Over lunch, perhaps because he had too much to drink, the collector started abusing Sir Alfred Beit, who lived nearby and whose collection is world-famous, in no uncertain terms. David said to the collector, "Sir Alfred is a great friend of mine. If you continue to be so rude about him I'm afraid I'll have to leave the table." The drunk collector thought he must be joking and continued in the same vein, and David got up and walked out. He was only twenty-six at the time and could have made a lot of money by buying the pictures from the rude collector. David's colleague who told me this story and wishes to remain anonymous regarded it as "astonishing moral courage".

David joined Christie's in January 1963. I'd never met him, although we must have been at Oxford about the same time, but had naturally read about his discoveries. We quickly became great friends, and indeed everyone at Christie's took to him. It was impossible not to like, let alone admire, David. Unlike many gifted people he never put himself on a plane above those who knew little or nothing about his subject. His undoubted genius did not make him frightening to the likes of me; indeed as he had been art critic on the *Evening Standard* for four years we were on common ground as regards the Press. This made him particularly valuable for me to have as a colleague because he would explain in terms I or visiting journalists could understand why a picture was important and what made it interesting; all without talking down to us or giving the impression that he was doing us a great favour. There was nothing pompous about him. He liked talking about his subject to people who were genuinely interested. What he refused to tolerate was pretentiousness.

The considerable strengthening of the picture department stemmed from David's arrival, but there were a number of other important additions during the year. After a few months David suggested that we should engage a specialist to look after Impressionist and Modern pictures, as there was none at present. He put forward the name of the Hon. David Bathurst, the son of the 2nd Viscount Bledisloe, who was working at the Marlborough Gallery at the time; before that he had studied under Gordon Washburn, Director of the Carnegie Institute, Pittsburgh. David joined us and was allocated a corner of the main Old Master picture warehouse.

The picture department was still under one huge umbrella; it was not until three years later that a separate Modern picture department was created. There was definite reluctance from Patrick to allow it to be autonomous. In spite of this David very sensibly split sales of Impressionist and Modern British pictures, which was a further advance towards specialist sales.

Another recruit to the Old Master picture side was Charlie Allsopp, the eldest son of Lord Hindlip and the present chairman of Christie's (King Street). He had joined the firm the year before and had no formal picture education, but soon picked up a great deal of knowledge in the way I have already described. There was also Christopher Wood, who joined the firm that year having won at Cambridge an art history degree under Michael Jaffé, who had just started his course. Christopher was taken on at £600 a year and after six months on the Front Counter was promoted to the picture department.

Guy Hannen was still acting as "picture führer", an assignment that, as was his wont and in spite of the annoyance it caused Patrick, he took very seriously. He spent hours at the hill sessions listening to Patrick, David, Brian and Christopher argue over what an attribution should be, the names of the artists mentioned very often meaning nothing to him. However, he did establish some discipline and made the team work to a schedule. This was essential if the printers were to get the manuscripts of each sale in time for the catalogue to be printed and posted all over the world one month in advance.

Christopher Wood, who has run his own gallery for over ten years, gives an interesting account of this period. In spite of his salary being only £600 a year Christopher was "absolutely delighted" when he was accepted by the firm in 1963. Having joined the picture department the following year, he sat in the office on the left at the top of the stairs leading up from the Front Hall with David, Brian, Noel Annesley – Brian's protégé who joined late in 1964 – John Hancock and, as from January 1965, Willie Mostyn-Owen.

Willie was older than the other new recruits, having travelled in France and Italy for two years after coming down from Cambridge in 1950. From 1952 till 1959 he worked with Berenson at I Tatti on a new edition of his famous "lists" of painters of the Italian Renaissance. In 1955, for Berenson's ninetieth birthday, he published a bibliography of all Berenson's writings. Willie was, therefore, a most important addition to the department as such work was invaluable training for cataloguing Old Masters. Being fluent in Italian and French and having worked at I Tatti he was a perfect colleague for David; they had a respect for each other, and Willie was able to add the very necessary element of orderliness to their work which was not David's strong point. Willie was also willing to spend hours in the Witt Library researching an important picture.

"As a junior," Christopher told me, "I count myself very lucky to have been involved in cataloguing with David, Brian and Willie. It was the most invaluable training one could have had. A tremendously good exercise for one's eye. The hill sessions were fairly daunting experiences, as Patrick insisted on seeing each manuscript, very often changing everything I had written and sometimes tearing the manuscript up. Patrick was quite a strict schoolmaster. I remember recalling this to him many years later and he said, 'Alec Martin was much worse.'" (Alec was indeed worse to the point of coarseness: "Come on, who's the f—— artist who painted this f—— picture?" One eminent dealer who was allowed to come in through the back door remembers hearing Alec talking in such terms to his junior staff.)

David of course was absolutely marvellous, not just because of his knowledge and eye, but pricking the bubble of pomposity with some outrageous *double entendre* when the discussion was beginning to get a bit tense. David also began the practice of inventing names of artists for pictures which were so bad that we couldn't think of an appropriate candidate. For instance, Christopher remembered a flower painting which was attributed to "Van Essa Bell", seemingly of Dutch origin, but really a corruption of Vanessa Bell. "Then one day I said, 'It's an absolute bastard.' 'That's it,' said David, 'Lawrence Bastard we'll call it.' And then there was a mythical Italian, Urini, and many others, but after a time we had to stop this somewhat frivolous approach, as the pictures not only sold but some of the names got into dealers' catalogues of their exhibitions."

On a more serious note I remember there was a hill session in progress and Patrick noticed that David, instead of concentrating on the picture being discussed, was looking at some pictures leaning against the wall. "David, please pay attention. What about this picture? Not those ones by the wall." David said he was sorry but Patrick must excuse him as he had to get some books from his office. Within a few moments he returned and studied the subjects of the pictures by the wall and the title of each work printed on the back. Each title was numbered and the label had been printed in a special way. Turning to a section in one of his books, David said, "Patrick, these pictures come from the Royal Collection. We'd better call the police." David's eagle eye for detail had seen the labels on the back, the numbers and the form of print and he realised they had come once from an important eighteenth-century collection. The reference books proved the rest. How many other art experts would have been so quick to see the truth? A hapless dealer in South London had innocently bought them from some "customer" and brought them to Christie's. Within twenty-four hours they were found to have come from St James's Palace, a hundred yards away.

Christopher said that when he first arrived everyone in the department, and this applied to Noel Annesley and John Lumley who joined us in late 1964, thought that the top direction was too stick-in-the-muddish and old-fashioned and needed to be given a shake. They felt Christie's had to be brought up to date. Peter was a remote figure and he gave the impression that he was an arch conservative, very reactionary and against any form of change. "However, when I became a director I got to know Peter well and found he was quite the reverse. Where Christie's was concerned he was not a reactionary at all. When I went to see him about the possibility of holding special sales of Victorian pictures he said, 'Splendid idea.' If I hadn't had his support I would never have been able to introduce them as Patrick, Jo, Guy and, I think, even Arthur were very lukewarm about the idea – 'Just Christopher wanting to do his own thing,' was their attitude. As you know, Victorian pictures have been great money-spinners over the last twenty years. No, I had a great respect for Peter in the end. Under his term of office Christie's became a great international art auction house and he must be given credit for it."

In the Board Room Peter reported that Parke-Bernet in New York was doing so badly that it would probably come up for sale. There was naturally discussion about whether Christie's could afford to buy it. Hambro's advised the Board in December that the maximum price they would recommend was $1 million compared with the asking price of $2 million. Borrowing this sum would have been impossible without accepting a Hambro representative on the Board, which we did not want. Financially, 1962 was Christie's worst year ever; the "sold total" for the year ending March 31st, 1963 not only fell compared with that of the previous year, but to such an extent that the firm actually made a loss of £6,000. Sotheby's knock-down total for the same period was £8.8 million, while Christie's was just over £3 million, an illustration of how difficult they were finding it to attract really good collections.

It was Christie's lowest point, so obviously they could not afford the interest payments which would have been necessary to buy PB;

anyway, as Guy wisely said – and it was on such occasions that Guy came into his own – we didn't have the staff to run it. Discussions with PB continued in order to make it as difficult as possible for Sotheby's to buy it, which they did the following year for $1.5 million. Even for them this meant raising finance on a massive scale and considerable risk, but taking risks was Peter Wilson's forte.

The results for 1963–4 were better, but only slightly, and Peter in the introduction to the *Review* mentioned "a noticeable shortage of Old Master pictures". Christie's did at least make a profit if only of £11,000. There were a few good pictures which, thanks to extra research by David, resulted in higher prices than might have been expected. One of these was Tintoretto's *Christ at the Pool of Bethesda* which in May achieved 45,000 gns ($122,735) compared with £3,360 in the 1927 Holford sale and £4,830 immediately after the war. David had provided new evidence for the catalogue which identified it with a *Raising of Lazarus* painted for a Venetian collector in 1573, thereby making it one of the few documented Tintorettos in private hands. It is substantiated facts such as these in a catalogue which are all-important to museums, dealers and serious collectors all over the world, and only a very able art historian can unearth them. The picture was one of thirteen Old Masters from the collection of Dr James Hasson, then aged eighty-two, who had been General de Gaulle's physician during the war.

Very different in every sense was the second part of the Augustus John studio sale which totalled a mere £33,405 ($89,050). Although most of the plums had gone in the first sale, there were some fine works such as a *Portrait of David*, one of his sons, which went for 3,200 gns ($8,957), while a lovely early drawing (1900–05) of a *Mother and Child* was bought by Her Majesty the Queen for only 400 gns ($1,176), an example of how the immediate interest after an artist's death quickly wears off; in the first sale drawings of that period fetched four-figure sums. The two sales totalled £133,500 ($368,056).

If there was a shortage of Old Masters there certainly wasn't of silver. The most important sale included twenty-five lots from the collection of Lord Brownlow, a lifelong friend of the Duke of Windsor's who, as "Mr Harris", during the last days of the Abdication crisis escorted Mrs Simpson on her journey from England to Cannes. Arthur pulled out all the stops for the Brownlow silver, and achieved a marketing plus by having it shipped to New York for exhibition prior to the sale. It was during this exhibition that Bob and Arthur learned of the Christie team's presence in Cuba which caused Bob so much worry. The Brownlow silver sold for £141,300 ($387,646), his famous James II chinoiserie tankards going for £17,000 ($47,600). These were sold again by us in 1969 – only six years later – for £56,000 ($134,000), having appreciated at a rate of 15s. or 75p an hour.

Anthony du Boulay, who had joined us in the Board Room at the beginning of the year, had some good sales including four Imperial spinach-green jade screens emblematic of the Four Seasons. These had come from a New York collector, which was encouraging, and sold for 40,000 gns ($117,600), a tremendous price. The uncarved jade for these screens, each of which measured 24 ins by 13 ins, was reputed to have been in the imperial vaults of the Russian Tzars and was given to the Emperor Ch'ien Lung towards the end of the eighteenth century. The panels were then carved by imperial command and placed in the Royal Palace. I was pleased that Anthony, who had joined Christie's in 1949 and had started a separate ceramics department as long ago as 1956, had at last been made a director. I had always felt guilty at becoming a director before him. Peter had warned Tony about my promotion and being the nice man he is (and a fellow-Wykehamist) he took it very well, although many wouldn't have done.

These and other good sales Christie's had, however, were nothing compared with Sotheby's 1963 season, which was exceptionally successful in all departments. It will be remembered particularly because of the success of the Fribourg Collection sale in New York. Not surprisingly, the gap between the two firms had stretched even further, Sotheby's knock-down total for the year ending March 31st, 1964 being close on £13 million compared with Christie's £4 million – a difference of £4 million more than the previous year.

However, 1964 saw the first signs of recovery at Christie's as a result of our having a stronger picture department. A number of private collectors had obviously regained confidence in the firm and it was also the year of David Bathurst's first two Impressionist sales. As specialised sales, these were a significant innovation although of minor importance compared to those today. David Bathurst may not have liked working with two of the toughest dealers in London while at the Marlborough Gallery, but it was probably invaluable training and the very opposite of the inertia which still to a certain extent pervaded Christie's. David set about the daunting task of wooing Impressionists out of American collectors with enthusiasm, energy and self-confidence, although the name of Sotheby's was on the lips of most collectors. As is often the case, the method he chose and which brought him success was simple in the extreme. He decided to make at least two trips to America each year and before each one he extracted from the books listing the major works of the most important artists the names of the owners – American collectors are far more willing to have their names published than those from other countries. From Christie's New York office he would then find out their addresses, ring them up and ask if he could come and see their collection. It was not only his cultured English accent, which is so popular with American women, that won him access, but, David told me, "Americans are far more willing than other nationalities to show complete strangers their collections – providing they have reasonable references."

Studying Sotheby's catalogues was also useful in order to approach collectors who appeared not to have swum into their net as yet. Following hours on the phone an itinerary would emerge and off David would go. I think Bob Leylan, although he brought us business, may have found it embarrassing to make these direct approaches to complete strangers. Sometimes, as on his first trip, David did not have to move outside New York. One of his first calls was to Mrs Norman B. Woolworth who gave him for sale in London the first picture Monet ever exhibited at the Paris Salon in 1865. This was *La Pointe de la Hève, Honfleur*, signed and dated 1864. By chance, at the Paris Salon the exhibits had been hung alphabetically according to the artists' names, so Monet's picture hung in the same room as Manet. The two artists' names were so similar that greatly to Manet's annoyance he found himself praised for a marine view by someone who was totally unknown to him. For a time he was convinced the stranger was playing a trick on him and he would not consent to meet Monet, then only twenty-five. Monet's picture, which was the highlight of David's first sale, sold for 20,000 gns ($58,800), the highest price by far that Christie's had ever obtained for an Impressionist work.

As an instance of the friendly reaction of American collectors, when David visited Mrs Woolworth she told him that her daughter, Mrs Pamela Woolworth Combemale, who lived in the same apartment block, had a number of Impressionists and that he should see her. By a stroke of luck Mrs Combemale was thinking of selling, so was delighted when her mother rang to introduce David. David told me that before he was shown the pictures a TV newsflash intervened in the form of John Kennedy's assassin, Lee Oswald, emerging from gaol and being shot by Jack Ruby. "We spent virtually the whole day in front of the box and it was not until the next day that I saw the pictures."

They were well worth waiting for. The pictures made an impressive group in November when they were sold in the best Impressionist sale we had held to date: Camille Pissarro's *La Route d'Osny, Pontoise*, 35,000 gns ($102,900), a superb Monet of Argenteuil in the sunset, 38,000 gns ($111,220) and two Sisleys, *Le Barrage de Saint-Mammes*, 24,000 gns ($70,560) and *Bouquet de Fleurs*, the only known flowerpiece by him which made 34,000 gns ($99,960). The sale also included one of Monet's splendid foggy views of London and the Thames which he painted from a suite in the Savoy Hotel – how he ever paid for it I don't know but Sir Hugh Wontner, chairman of the hotel for many years, assures me it is true – where he stayed in the autumn for three consecutive years. The series finally totalled forty-five paintings of which thirty-seven had been exhibited in 1904 by Durand-Ruel, the first dealer to back the Impressionists. The picture in our sale, *Charing Cross Bridge, Westminster*, which sold for 22,000 gns ($64,680) had not been in the exhibition, having been purchased two years earlier. David's efforts had been rewarded and the results of the November sale were encouraging not only to him but to the whole firm, which gained a lot of useful publicity all over the world.

The results of David's sales made it clear that Sotheby's were not the only people who sold Impressionists. An even more important highlight of 1964 was the announcement in July that Christie's were to sell the world-famous Northwick Park Collection belonging to Captain E. G. Spencer-Churchill, who had died on June 24th, aged eighty-eight. The sales would not be till the following year and many date the beginning of Christie's recovery from their success.

7

The Northwick Park Collection and the Ring

There had been a picture collection at Northwick Park, Moreton-in-Marsh, Gloucestershire, since early in the nineteenth century. At one time it totalled 1,500 pictures, owing to the passion of John, 2nd Lord Northwick, for collecting. When he died it was found that he had made no will or arrangements for his collection. His nephew George, who had inherited the title, was anxious to keep his uncle's collection intact, and offered the two other next of kin £80,000 for their combined share. They refused to agree, so there were sales lasting twenty-two days. The new Lord Northwick managed to buy back a number of important pictures and works of art. His widow bequeathed the collection to Captain Edward George Spencer-Churchill who gave it a new lease of life.

George Spencer-Churchill was sent to Egypt for his health at the age of thirteen. His stay there marked the beginning of his interest in the art of ancient Egypt. Spencer-Churchill's greatest delight was probably his antiquities, but he also loved Old Masters and added over 200 to those which the 3rd Lord Northwick had managed to buy back. These he catalogued as "The Northwick Rescues". Painted by major or minor artists, they had been lost to view for a hundred years owing to dirt, over-painting and over-varnishing; it was often merely an eye, an ear of corn, or a petal of a flower that excited Spencer-Churchill's curiosity and caused him to bid at Christie's and Sotheby's, which he visited nearly every week.

"The greatest thrill I get from collecting," Spencer-Churchill once said, "is when I am fortunate enough to rescue a damaged or almost entirely obscured picture which could not possibly have been giving pleasure to anyone, and finding it a thing of beauty when it has emerged from the hands of highly skilled restorers. One feels almost as if one had recalled the artist to life and got him to paint another picture."

I had read *Great Private Collections* (published by Weidenfeld and Nicolson in 1963), which included an appreciation by Patrick of the Northwick Park Collection, so I knew its importance. The historical details of the Northwick Park Collection have in the main been taken from this source. However, the excitement of preparing the Press announcement of what at that time was certainly the most important collection to be put up for auction since the war was somewhat marred for me. Peter rang down and asked me to go up to his room. There he introduced me to Lord Rockley, the senior Trustee, who appeared a somewhat forbidding character. Peter handed me a three-paragraph statement and said I was to give it to the Press. When I started to suggest that we would not be doing justice to the collection, Peter got very red in the face and firmly repeated his instructions. He told me afterwards that he had had a most difficult time – which was to continue until the collection was sold – with Lord Rockley, who had been responsible for the absurdly bald statement. The only thing to do was to send Judy up to Hatchard's to buy twenty copies of *Great Private Collections* and give one to each of the most important newspapers so that they could read Patrick's contribution. Expensive but effective, and there was no comeback either from Lord Rockley or Peter as to how the Press were so well-informed about the collection's most interesting items.

The work of organising the dispersal of this huge and varied collection had to begin immediately, because the Trustees had told Peter the house had to be empty by the end of September that year. A team of directors, technical staff and porters was sent immediately to Northwick Park to select the most important pictures and other works of art for a complete series of Northwick sales in May, June and October the following year. The remaining contents – ranging from quite good furniture and a mixture of porcelain, glass and silver which would attract the London fine art trade, as well as the locals, down to the servants' bedroom furniture and garden seats – were to be sold on the premises in a three-day sale in September. There was no time to be lost, therefore, with cataloguing the hundreds of items involved.

I needed to get to know the collection as Christie's had decided to hold an exhibition of the most important works in the first fortnight of the New Year. This had to receive the maximum promotion. Choosing a fine summer's day I drove up to Northwick Park for the first time. Architecturally the house came as a slight disappointment to anyone who had never seen it before. Denys Sutton, editor of *The Apollo* magazine for many years, wrote in an appreciation after Spencer-Churchill's death:

> Northwick Park . . . in its owner's day can hardly be called distinguished but the interior possessed that atmosphere which comes when a house has been lived in for several generations. Captain Spencer-Churchill was the right man for the house. He personified the great days when collectors bought what appealed to them, without their ear being tuned to the shouting in the market place.

By no stretch of the imagination could the house, which was built of sandstone, be called beautiful. There was a lake a little distance away, but no flower beds, and the weeds in the drive came right up to the front door. The roof leaked in places and there were rats. Brian, who was cataloguing the drawings, watercolours, prints and pictures, confirmed this in graphic detail later: "I was woken one night by a loud scuffling sound in the bathroom, and on investigating saw a large rat trying to jump into the basin where another rat was eating the soap. I nearly had hysterics." However, none of this had mattered to Spencer-Churchill. He had lived for the collection, and inside the house this indeed overwhelmed the senses.

When I arrived everyone was beavering away. Patrick took me round the main picture gallery where the pictures hung with only a few inches between them, in three rows right up to the ceiling. He said that Spencer-Churchill had told him on more than one occasion that he had given instructions in his will that Christie's should sell his collection when he died. Apart from Italian works, the collection was particularly rich in Netherlandish and early English works. At the far end of the gallery was a staggering array of Greek amphorae and vases, all of which had been bought by Spencer-Churchill, and which Richard Falkiner was busy cataloguing.

The collection of English portraits hung mainly in the "saloon", as Spencer-Churchill's cosy study was called. Here, as in the picture gallery, pictures hung side by side and one above another to form a solid phalanx of English history. There was Hogarth's *Portrait of Daniel Lock*, a Gainsborough *Self-Portrait* and a Romney of *Lady Hamilton*. Most important of all was Sir Joshua Reynolds's *Portrait of Warren Hastings*; this hung above the library table which had belonged to Hastings in his retirement in nearby Dalesford. On this were

200 Egyptian, Etruscan, Greek and Roman bronzes, all collected by Spencer-Churchill himself. There were cats, mice, ibises, goddesses and statuettes from Egypt, javelin-throwing warriors, athletes and mirrors from Etruria, reclining gods and deities and aes (late third-century BC bronze) coinage from Rome, weights from Babylon, early marble figures from the Aegean and early stone axe-heads from places as diverse as Southampton and Kenya.

In a case over the fireplace were three outstanding bronzes: the extremely rare *Chinese Wrestlers* from the Middle Chou period of about 600 BC; their right arms are locked and with their left they grasp each other's belts preparatory to attempting a throw. From Crete of 1600 BC was the Minoan bronze figurine of a *Bull with Dancer* – the only other figures of such importance are in the Heraklion Museum. Lastly there was a graceful stag of about 450 BC.

Richard Falkiner wandered in as I was looking at the antiquities. He had known the collection and in particular the antiquities, which were his special interest, since his teens as his family home was nearby. Spencer-Churchill, Richard said, was one of the kindest men and although the house was not open to the public, he had been delighted to show around anyone who was interested irrespective of their age.

In the drawing-room, the bedrooms and passages there were more pictures and works of art, and in the library I found Bill Spowers hard at work. Bill Spowers – "the Major", as the porters called him in view of what were undoubtedly some hectic years in the Grenadier Guards and Parachute Regiment – was Australian by birth, his forebears having arrived in Melbourne four years after the first white men. They became proprietors of the *Melbourne Argus* and *Australasian* but both these were sold after the war. Bill had joined the book department in 1960 and played a valuable role over the years, not only at King Street but later running our sales in Australia. I never saw him as a typical bibliophile, however. Immaculately dressed in his black suit, stiff collar and exciting striped shirts and with a diamond-mounted pin keeping his tie in place, he did not appear suited to the world of antiquarian books. Although somewhat small of stature he looked far more of a dashing blade. However, there was no doubt about his ability – colour-plate books were his speciality – and his capacity for hard work, epitomised many years later by the tremendous task of cataloguing and valuing some 65,000 books in the Chatsworth library. When I came upon him in the Northwick library he was cataloguing the superb illuminated miniatures in a fourteenth-century *Book of*

Hours which once belonged to Charles the Bold, Duke of Burgundy. As I was going out he said, "Oh, by the way, if you want a laugh at lunchtime, I'm going to do some water skiing on the lake." At twelve thirty everyone broke for lunch and made their way towards the 250-yard lake.

Bill had brought his hydroplane up on the roof of a Rolls. Having donned a wet suit and bravely putting on his mono-ski, he called, "OK," to Charlie Allsopp, who was going to drive the hydroplane. Charlie yanked the starter cord of the large outboard engine, slammed the engine into gear and the boat roared off. In spite of being jerked off the bank at such high speed, Bill managed to keep upright. Charlie timed his turn at the end of the lake far too late. Bill swung out with the centrifugal force and, realising that he was never going to make a complete turn, he let go the towline. He found himself heading at high speed for some rocks which had been dumped at the water's edge and a herd of cows who were peacefully drinking. However, when they saw this strange black-suited figure hurtling towards them they trotted off mooing loudly.

Bill had a rough landing and was lucky not to hurt himself, nor even break his ski. Patrick, his secretary, the Northwick Park agent, myself and others were roaring with laughter. Charlie then put the engine into reverse with the rudder hard over and capsized the boat, which added to our amusement. Although I found the incident as funny as everyone else, I remember feeling slightly uneasy, and wondering what Lord Rockley would have thought – I knew he made sudden unannounced appearances at Northwick Park.

Sure enough, Peter somehow heard about the incident and summoned Bill. "I nearly got the sack," Bill told me. "Peter said that if Lord Rockley had arrived while I was skiing or heard about it we would probably have lost the sale. I thought it was very unfair, as the agent was present and didn't raise any objections." Richard Falkiner said that it was "entirely in the Northwick tradition" because Spencer-Churchill had always allowed the locals to swim in the lake. However, I'm sure Peter was right, and Lord Rockley would not have been amused.

But Lord Rockley himself had been guilty of an extraordinary error of judgment. Brian told me that when he arrived at Northwick he found the house servants making a bonfire, in the courtyard outside the kitchen, of all the Northwick Park sale catalogues of 1859. Even if of little commercial value, these were of considerable importance as "provenance" for the catalogues Christie's were about to compile. Brian's pleadings to the men to stop were ignored and it needed Patrick's full wrath to rescue the catalogues.

By the beginning of September each department had made their lists and worked out the best composition of the sales. The National, British and Ashmolean Museums had, in accordance with Spencer-Churchill's will, selected those of the most important items which they wanted; not without some tense negotiations about values, which in the case of the antiquities were left to the still youthful Richard Falkiner although this was no easy task. Peter had told him the Trustees expected the highest possible prices, but it was very much a case of "how long is a piece of string?" because of the rarity of some of the pieces. I believe, for instance, that the Minoan bull went to the British Museum for £50,000 – a colossal sum for those days – having been bought from Spinks in 1921 for £100. Finally, before the house was emptied of the major items the Press were taken on a guided tour, and the BBC, after endless objections from Lord Rockley had been satisfied, were permitted to make a short TV film.

The 500 pictures in the house were then taken to Christie's depository in London, while the smaller works of art came to King Street. The porters were then able to empty the house of furniture, silver and the remaining contents which were sold in a marquee over the last three days in September. The house sale totalled £68,597 ($192,071) which now sounds ridiculously small, but the prices for the few remaining pieces of furniture of quality and other works of art in fact were high. A well-known dealer described it as the "craziest sale since the end of the war" – a bundle of walking sticks going for 76 gns. At house sales, medium quality or even very minor items often sell for prices which would never be paid in London, because such events can be a day out for the locals as well as for friends of the late owner. It is very easy for newcomers to auctions to find themselves overcome with a compulsion to bid, either because they do not wish to go away empty-handed or because they want to say that such-and-such came from the big house. This was particularly so in the Northwick Park sale because of Spencer-Churchill's popularity; the first five rows of seats were reserved for his friends.

The sale itself was well reported, but will really be remembered for the *Sunday Times*'s sensational exposé in November of art dealers' "rings" at auctions. As a newcomer to the art auction world I had not heard about the ring until I met Jack Baer, for many years now managing director of Hazlitt, Gooden and Fox, the well-known firm of picture dealers and a past chairman of the Society of London Art Dealers. Jack started dealing at the age of twenty-two and after a short apprenticeship was able with only £2,000 to take over the Hazlitt Gallery, opposite Christie's back door.

Jack and I became friends because we were members of the Ladder, a very cosy club just off nearby Duke of York Street which was run by a lovable elderly lady known as "Mossy"; in the 1920s and 1930s she had run the Gargoyle when most of its members were from the artistic, theatrical and writing professions, with a very different ambience from that of the strip club it has been for so many years. One day over lunch Jack said, "You know, you should get Peter Chance to do something about the ring." He then told me how he had been at one of our auctions and had been threatened by Julius Weitzner. Weitzner was a prominent picture dealer in New York and London with a base in Farm Street. Apparently he turned round to Jack and said, "Stop bidding, boy, or I'll break you." This was no idle threat because the ring could either force "recalcitrant" dealers to join them or prevent them from buying the pictures they needed to pursue their legitimate business by bidding them up beyond a price they could afford. Weitzner would try to soften his bullying tactics when he had received satisfaction by justifying them with such words as: "Just didn't want you to buy a lot of rubbish."

A ring – for those who don't know in spite of the vast amount of publicity they have aroused – is in being when a number of dealers agree not to bid on certain lots, thus destroying the element of unfettered competition essential for a proper auction. One dealer bids for those lots which have been selected by the ring and all the other members refrain from bidding; if he is successful the lots are secretly re-auctioned immediately afterwards – thus depriving the vendor of the proper market price. This nefarious practice is obviously illegal, and the 1927 Auctions (Bidding Agreements) Act was designed to prevent it, but it was certainly not effective in 1964. The basic reason was the difficulty of obtaining evidence of a ring; in addition the Act was not a sufficient deterrent to intimidate those wishing to organise a ring.

Works of art sold in the provinces are particularly vulnerable to being ringed, as country auctioneers do not specialise in them, and may be selling anything from "goods and chattels" to farm machinery most weeks. After a number of high quality works of art had been bought for suspiciously small prices in the early 1960s, the *Sunday Times* decided to carry out a thorough investigation. A particularly blatant example of the ring in action was at a Leamington Spa auction in 1962. A Chippendale bombé commode was knocked down for £450, but within eight hours was sold in the "knock-out" held in a private room at the Clarendon Hotel, Leamington, for £4,350. The new buyer was a Mr Roy Oliver, a wealthy Guildford dealer, who the next day phoned John Partridge, of Frank Partridge, the New Bond Street firm, and sold it to him for probably about twice as much. John Partridge said, "If I'd known that the commode was for auction, I'd have gone to Leamington Spa and bought it myself." The *Sunday Times* spoke to many of the dealers involved but decided to hold their fire until they had found further evidence.

The Northwick Park house sale provided it. Colin Simpson, the highly enterprising reporter assigned by the *Sunday Times* to the ring investigation, posing as a member of the ring, managed to get into the knock-out which was held in the snug of the Swann Inn, Moreton-in-Marsh, immediately after the sale. He had a microphone concealed up his sleeve, connected by a pocket transmitter to a receiver and a tape recorder in a van parked outside, which monitored the elaborate ritual that followed.

Some fifty dealers were present, three of whom were members of the council of the British Antique Dealers Association and one of whom was Major Michael Brett, the President, a Broadway dealer. I won't go into the complicated method by which members of the ring even if they weren't present received something, while the others received larger shares. Armed with the concealed recording equipment, Simpson questioned many of the dealers at the knock-out, including Brett who had been involved with the Chippendale commode sold at Leamington Spa two years earlier. The full-page article which appeared in the *Sunday Times* on November 8th, 1964 provoked a parliamentary and public storm and an embarrassing inquest in the BADA. Fourteen members of the council resigned as well as a number of other members.

The BADA tried to put its house in order. They made it a condition of membership that members signed a declaration that they would not take part in rings and put up a notice to that effect in their shop. In spite of the furore in Parliament, the Press, among the general public and also among dealers who detested the ring and were worried about the reputation of the fine art trade generally, many dealers took no notice of the BADA's directive and carried on as usual. Not surprisingly the *Sunday Times*, which managed to get a list of seventy-eight dealers who for various reasons had not signed the declaration, encountered considerable hostility when they enquired why they had not done so.

However, worse still was to come in 1968. In March of that year the contents of Aldwick Court, Somerset, were auctioned by the Gloucestershire firm of Bruton, Knowles. Aldwick Court was crammed with pictures, furniture and silver owned by Mr T. R. Bridson who had died the previous year after a somewhat solitary life. Incidentally, one of Bruton, Knowles's first people to start cataloguing was their furniture expert, Arthur Negus, who later became a household name as a result of the BBC TV programme *Going for a Song* – but he had no responsibility for the picture scandal that followed.

I remember David Carritt, who as usual had his ear to the ground, mentioning at a Board meeting that he believed a highly important Sienese picture was to be sold by Bruton, Knowles. This proved to be a *Madonna and Child* by the thirteenth-century Italian master Duccio. Duccio's works are so rare that there are few experts even in London who would be able to identify one. The picture was catalogued as "Sienese School – fifteenth century", although according to the *Sunday Times* it bore an inscription on the back that it was by Duccio. It was not altogether surprising, in view of the presence of Julius Weitzner, that there was little enthusiasm for the picture and it was bought by him for £2,700.

After the auction there was a knock-out at the Paradise Motel, Cowslip Green. I do not know what the knock-out price was, but Julius Weitzner bought the Duccio and let it be known that he would sell it for £150,000. The Director of the Cleveland Museum, Ohio, said he would pay that price, but it was refused an export licence for six months to allow time for the National Gallery, London, to find the money. This it succeeded in doing.

Under the provisions of Lord Waverley's report to R. A. Butler, Chancellor of the Exchequer, in 1952, criteria were laid down which represented the first attempt to protect Britain's heritage. The Chancellor of the Exchequer's Reviewing Committee on Works of Art was set up to decide whether an export licence should be granted. The basic criteria for assessing the importance of each work of art which museum directors were asked to consider were: 1. Is it so closely associated with Britain's heritage and national life that its departure would be a misfortune? 2. Is it of outstanding aesthetic importance? 3. Is it of outstanding significance for the study of some particular branch of art, learning or history? If a work of art was deemed to come within the Waverley criteria and was more than a hundred years old and had been in Britain for fifty years, an export licence would not be granted for up to six months to allow time for the national institutions most closely interested to find the sum, which had to be the market price.

As a result of the Duccio scandal and the uproar that followed, the law was toughened up slightly in 1969, but I doubt if it worried the ring much. The virtual impossibility of getting evidence of a ring was demonstrated when Anthony Lousada, at Peter's request following a letter from the Board of Trade, sent one of his most reliable managing clerks to a series of auctions at King Street. Not surprisingly, nothing came of his investigation.

Today, I am glad to say, the situation is very different from the 1960s. The days when fifty or sixty dealers would meet in a pub for the knock-out are gone. Nowadays it is also more difficult for the ring to operate in London because the market is much bigger, more international and far larger sums are involved. Most important of all, the expertise of London fine art auctioneers is of a very high order compared with what it was in the 1960s; there is far less likelihood of anything of quality slipping through without its appropriate reserve price – although no firm is infallible. There is also the very genuine desire of the majority of the members of the fine art trade to keep their house in order and thus maintain London's prestige as an honest market. Nevertheless it would be naive to pretend that there won't always be the possibility of a ring, and solicitors should recognise that it is unwise to give a country auctioneer the responsibility of dispersing a houseful of works of art, however unimportant they may look.

Leaving aside Julius Weitzner's activities in the saleroom, there was no doubt that he had a considerable eye for quality, but it was matched by his temerity; so much so that one almost had a sneaking admiration for the old rogue. One of the most flagrant examples of this was when S. Pearson and Sons, Ltd (Lord Cowdray's holding company for the *Financial Times* and many other interests, now Pearson plc), decided to sell a large picture which hung in the company's Board Room. The company sent it to Bonham's, rather than Christie's or Sotheby's. The subject of the picture was *Daniel in the Lion's Den* and Weitzner quite rightly decided that it was by Rubens. He approached Bonham's, bought the picture before the sale for £500 and managed to spirit it out of the country as it did not require an export licence, having been bought for under £2,000. Pearson's must have agreed to have the picture withdrawn from the sale but did not appreciate its importance in spite of the labels on the back which were evidence of its having been exhibited. Nor, apparently, did Bonham's. This was unfortunate as needless to say Weitzner sold it to the National Museum, Washington, for a six-figure sum.

8

How Rembrandt's *Titus* Was Sold

In 1965 Christie's went a long way towards recovering some of its lost prestige. It was not only the Northwick Park Collection, the most important items of which aroused a great deal of interest when they were exhibited in the New Year, but a number of other sales: Old Masters and other works of art from Harewood House, including the desk made by Thomas Chippendale; sixty-six Tiepolo drawings, all from an album which had been in Lord Beauchamp's library for many years and regarded as being of little value until seen by David Carritt; a good collection of Impressionist and Post-Impressionist pictures from Venezuela; Sir David Salomon's famous collection of Breguet watches; Oriental works of art and coins once in the collection of Alfred Morrison; and a great deal of silver from a number of grand houses. But the most memorable was the sale of five pictures from the famed Cook collection, because of the uproar and confusion which followed the auctioning of Rembrandt's *Portrait of Titus* for 760,000 gns ($2.2 million).

The Cook collection of Old Masters had once been one of the most important private collections in the country. It was begun in the nineteenth century by Sir Francis Cook, the first baronet, who was one of the shrewdest and most enlightened collectors of his day. The family's fortunes came originally from women's "foundation garments" as they were then called, made and sold by Cook, Son and Co. of St Paul's Churchyard. Sir Herbert Cook, the second baronet, enlarged the scope of the collection and for many years the pictures hung at Doughty House, Richmond. Following Sir Herbert's death in 1939 there had been gradual dispersals, either because of estate duty or because of the marital proclivities of the third baronet, another Sir Francis, who was now married to his seventh wife. Some pictures were on loan to museums, and the rest were in the house belonging to Sir Francis, who was a tax exile in Jersey.

How Rembrandt's Titus Was Sold

Sir Francis had invited Peter to Jersey to discuss the possible sale of five important pictures which he had still in his house. Peter took Patrick and David with him. The pictures they were shown were Rembrandt's *Portrait of his son Titus*, Velazquez's *Portrait of Don Juan de Calabazas*, a jester later in King Philip IV's service, Dürer's *Road to Calvary*, Turner's early landscape *Brentford Lock and Mill*, and Hogarth's *A Family Party*. Rembrandt's *Portrait of Titus*, which he had painted in 1650, was the most important picture of the group. Measuring 25 ins by 22 ins, it was not a great Rembrandt in academic terms – in fact it had an almost unfinished look about it – but it had great popular appeal. It portrayed all the tenderness one would expect from a father's portrait of a beloved son. The picture was once at Althorp, the seat of the Earls Spencer, and had been bought by Sir Herbert Cook, Sir Francis's father. It was, I gather, while Sir Francis was showing the pictures that David came into his own. His obvious love of great pictures and the enthusiastic way he talked about them, apart from the prices he suggested, undoubtedly helped to win Christie's the sale.

The initial announcement went without a hitch, but after that the sale of the Cook pictures, in particular that of *Titus*, took on a note of drama. It is no exaggeration to say that Sir Francis had a neurotic concern about the safety of his pictures and the difficulties of getting them to London, although today his views might well be understandable. Peter assured him that pictures and other works of art were flown to Heathrow every week from all parts of the world. However, Sir Francis was not convinced and refused to let his pictures be flown to Heathrow because of the stacking of international flights and air traffic control problems. Sir Francis also wanted to know what aircraft would be used for transporting the pictures and the number of flying hours in the pilot's logbook.

Peter asked Patrick, who had learned to fly at Oxford, what would be the safest aircraft. Patrick recommended a Dakota similar to those used for parachute drops, so a Dakota and pilot were hired from a company based at Gatwick. The day before the pictures were due to be collected, Peter began to enter into the spirit of the operation. He summoned Charlie – who with Jim Taylor, the head porter, was to accompany him – and sent him up to Swaine and Adeney in Piccadilly to buy a leather-bound cosh; he thought there might be an attempt to hijack the pictures on landing. Peter drove Charlie and Jim to Gatwick in his beautiful Bentley and they flew safely to Jersey in the Dakota.

On arriving at Sir Francis's house there was the usual traumatic discussion about details for the sale and confirmation of what prices we expected. A butler then announced that lunch was served. They had hardly begun when the phone rang. Sir Francis had given instructions that he was "incommunicado", so his lawyer answered it. He returned from Sir Francis's study looking somewhat abashed and said that Peter Wilson was on the line. Sir Francis said, "All right, I'll talk to him," and went next door. Peter and Charlie naturally feared that at the last moment Christie's were to be robbed of the sale. They could hear Sir Francis's raised voice saying, "What, only that? I expect much more," followed by the sound of the telephone being slammed down. Just at that moment Jim Taylor walked by outside carrying *Titus* in his right hand towards the van.

Sir Francis came back into the dining-room and said, "Bloody insult. PW said he would guarantee £500,000 for *Titus*; you can do better than that, can't you?" Peter naturally said, "Oh yes, of course," but inwardly thinking, "God, can we?" This assertion was, incidentally, an interesting example of Peter Wilson's self-confidence and willingness to guarantee a vast sum in order to get a really important piece of business or at least prevent his rivals winning it. True, the figure tied up exactly with what David had said, but Christie's had not guaranteed it. Nor did we ever quote it but somehow the figure began to be bandied about by dealers who were quite frank about us being over-optimistic.

As Peter, Charlie and Jim boarded the Dakota, a violent thunderstorm broke out which resulted in a bumpy flight. Peter said jokingly as he sat swathed in blankets against the cold – there was of course neither pressurisation nor heating in the Dakota – "This will cost Lloyd's a pretty penny if we go to the bottom with this lot."

A separate catalogue was printed for the Cook pictures, which were to be sold on March 19th after a hundred Old Masters from other collections. Great excitement spread through the firm, but in the picture department there was some concern about *Titus*; the reserve price, which of course was confidential at the time and I didn't learn it until the actual sale, was £550,000 with discretion. March was approaching and so far no one had expressed any interest. To make matters worse, Peter told Patrick that he had reason to believe that some time ago Agnew's, on behalf of Sir Francis Cook, had offered *Titus* for £650,000 to Norton Simon, the multi-millionaire founder of Hunts Food Corporation in California, but the deal had fallen through.

How Rembrandt's Titus Was Sold

Norton Simon had set up a foundation about ten years earlier for the acquisition of important works of art for the benefit of museums all over the USA; there were attractive tax concessions for such loans. Bob Leylan called Peter early in March to tell him that Norton Simon had rung him to say that he would probably be coming to the sale and had talked of special bidding arrangements. Bob had told him that he would have to speak to the auctioneer about these. On the Wednesday before the sale Simon called Peter and said he would be flying to London the next day, arriving at 9.35 p.m., and would like to see the Rembrandt, the Velazquez and some of the Northwick pictures that night. He also said he wanted a seat in the front of the main saleroom from which he could make a quick exit. I presumed this would be to escape the clutches of the Press who by now were as keyed up as all of us at Christie's – the three main American TV networks had said they wanted to attend the sale, as well as the BBC and ITN.

There had already been tremendous advance publicity. This was not only because of the fame of the Cook collection and the sentiment behind the portrait of Titus itself – "every father's son" – but in addition the amazing story of how *Titus* had first come to Britain. A fortnight before the sale Earl Spencer gave David the full details and he naturally passed them on to me to whet the appetite of the Press still further. It seems that in about 1815, George Barker, a picture restorer and dealer well known to the Spencers, missed his boat from Holland and had to spend the night at a farmhouse outside The Hague. In the morning he found hanging above his bed an enchanting picture of a young boy. When he expressed his admiration for the picture, the farmer offered to throw it in with the price of bed-and-breakfast: one shilling. It was Rembrandt's *Titus*. Once back in England, Barker presented it to his patron, Lord Spencer, whose wife Lavinia found it so beautiful that she said, "This picture must never leave the house."

Peter summoned Charlie on Thursday, the day before the sale, and said cryptically, "Do you read the *Financial Times*? No, probably not. Well, go out and buy a copy, also a white carnation and a pair of dark spectacles. I want you to meet Mr Norton Simon at Heathrow this evening and he will recognise you from these items. Hire a Rolls and bring Mr Simon to King Street. If his plane is late, ring me. As I'm taking the sale I want an early night, and Patrick can show him the pictures." Sure enough his plane was very late and Peter went home as arranged, and it was past midnight when Charlie and Norton Simon arrived at Christie's in the Rolls. During the drive into London

Charlie tried to establish some rapport with Simon, who didn't respond much.

Patrick greeted Simon and showed him the pictures. Simon gave them a cursory glance and then said he would like to discuss bidding arrangements. Patrick took him into Peter's room. After twenty minutes they both emerged, Patrick looking very worried. After he had arranged for the Rolls to take Mr Simon to his hotel, he came back and said to Charlie, "He's insisting on some impossible bidding instructions." Patrick had been forced to write these out twice on Christie's notepaper and both of them had signed each copy. The exact details of the "arrangements" can be seen opposite. In brief, if Mr Simon was sitting down he would be bidding for *Titus*; if he stood up he would have stopped bidding. If Mr Simon was successful in buying the picture it would be knocked down to Autolycus, a *nom de vente*.

Patrick had naturally told Mr Simon that his proposed method of bidding was far too complicated and that he would have to discuss it with Peter before the sale. Patrick drove Peter to Christie's the next morning and showed him the memorandum Simon had dictated to him. Norton Simon arrived at Christie's at 10.40 a.m., twenty minutes before the sale was due to begin, and was shown immediately into Peter's room. Peter told Simon that, as his proposals were so complicated, it would be much better to let his dealer, Dudley Tooth, who would be sitting next to him, bid for him. Simon would have none of that. However, he did agree so far as *Titus* was concerned that he should be regarded as bidding as long as he remained seated, that he would make no sign or call to indicate a bid and when he stood up it would mean that he had finished bidding. The major significance of this was that Simon said or implied that he would not bid openly. Just before he went into the rostrum Peter had time to tell Patrick, "It's all right, he's just going to be bidding when he's sitting down." The only problem was that Simon still had in his pocket his copy of the agreement which Patrick had countersigned and which implied that he might bid openly.

The tension among everyone involved with the sale was considerable because this was the most important group of pictures Christie's had had since Peter had become chairman, and probably since the Holford sale. It was essential for it to be a success. For the auctioneer, however experienced, nervous strain is quite natural though some never seem to be affected by it. Peter Wilson never seemed to show it. Peter Chance did. It is not only taking the sale that causes butterflies

AUTOLYCUS.

8. King Street. St. James's.
London. S.W.1
Telephone: Trafalgar 9060.

Friday March 19th

Rembrandt, Lot 105

Portrait of Titus

When Mr Simon is sitting down he is
bidding. If he bids openly when sitting
down he is also bidding. When he stands
up he has stopped bidding. If he then
sits down again he is not bidding until
he raises his finger. Having raised his
finger he is continuing to bid until
he stands up again.

Norton Simon Foundation
by Norton Simon

in the stomach; it is also the importance of generating competitive interest in the works of art being sold, particularly when they have high reserve prices. Allowances had to be made, therefore, for any crustiness on Peter's (and later Patrick's) part.

My responsibilities on big sale days were nothing to those of the auctioneer, but I confess to always having a slight feeling of stress. Relations with the Press were good, but trying to stop the hordes of reporters and photographers from blocking up the gangways tried my patience. In addition I was responsible for seeing that museum directors, dealers and private collectors were given the number of seats in whatever part of the Big Room they wanted. Trying to satisfy everyone was difficult as there was just not enough space; also it was obvious that a lot of people had no intention of bidding and were just coming for enjoyment. Closed circuit television was essential and had to be installed the night before and another auctioneer found to transmit the bids by telephone from the second or even third room. Many people implied they were so important that if they didn't get into the main room they wouldn't bid. As the years went by I got to know most of the dealers, foreign as well as British, and learned who was important and who was not. I rather liked this contact with the trade, who were very grateful if I managed to sit them where they wanted to be, although I often had to refuse £5 tips from dealers who hadn't been to our sales before. After a few years we developed a fairly sophisticated system of numbered and differently coloured seat tickets, having written to the dealers beforehand to find out their wishes.

Half an hour before the sale I would show the seating chart to whoever was taking it, so that he could see where the most important bids might come from. As the room filled up – people struggling down the narrow gangways to their seats, while others crowded round the walls – the sense of excitement mounted. The TV teams would be chatting on their rostrums having tested the lights immediately they had come in. Eventually we bought our own lights, but for many years a lighting company would come in the evening before the sale and take two hours to put up the huge 60 kilowatt lamps. I would get up in the rostrum to see whether the lights were angled right, then check with Peter (or Patrick) whether he would be happy with them. Satisfying both the TV lighting men and the auctioneer, who always complained about the glare of the lights, was an impossible task. Some of the cameramen seemed to think they were Zeffirelli – this, of course, was before the days of really fast film and halogen lights – and would exaggerate their need for light, while Peter, whose eyes were genuinely weaker than most, found the glare very difficult whichever way they were positioned. "I tell you, John, unless you get those lights right I'll stop the sale," he'd say with pre-sale bad temper. When they were switched on there was always a growl of, "Do we have to have those bloody lights?" but he eventually learned to live with them, even in Geneva where the ceiling of the auction room in the hotel was much lower.

Patrick's attitude was worse if anything, in fact just bloody-minded, partly due to pre-sale nervous tension, but also because he hated the whole idea of TV lights. "Nobody wants them and they make the room look like a bloody Hollywood film set," was his view. He may well have been right, but Peter Wilson had been under the glare and heat of the lights since 1956, and realised that the publicity resulting from TV, provided the sale went well, justified the discomfort.

On the day of the Cook picture sale there was no time for Peter to test the lights as he was with Norton Simon. He had asked me to look after Lady Cook, on whose behalf *Titus* was being sold (presumably for tax purposes), and bring her into the saleroom from the back and sit beside her in the third row, so I had to leave Judy to cope with the last-minute rush for seats. Sir Francis wasn't coming to the sale but had asked for a tape-recording to be made of his pictures being auctioned. Bill Spowers had a huge tape recorder and stationed himself between the rostrum and the front row. He was holding a microphone only a few feet from Norton Simon, who was in the second row beside his dealer Dudley Tooth. Douglas Ralphs, who had joined the accounts department about the time I became a director and was soon to become a most efficient and amiable company secretary and later a director, was in the Instructions Office on an open line to Sir Francis, so that he could relay the prices he heard through the public address system.

The TV lights came on a few lots before the Cook pictures so that the cameramen could make sure of their focusing, and a buzz of excitement went round the room. Lady Cook – a friendly and attractive woman – whom I had managed to get to her seat without drawing the attention of the photographers, smiled excitedly. Because of the competitive element between those in the audience and the auctioneer, particularly when a vendor has insisted on a very high reserve price, an auction of important pictures or works of art can be full of drama. In such cases the auctioneer has always to appear supremely self-confident and to have the room in his hand. Even if there is no enthusiasm for the lot in question, he has to try to generate it or seem to have done so by "taking bids off the wall". This is when the art of auctioneering comes into its own, for an auctioneer's first duty as the agent of the vendor is to sell his property for the highest price. In the case of the Cook pictures Peter had little to worry about except for the high reserve on *Titus*, but he did know he had at least one interested bidder, Norton Simon.

Peter always had a brisk and sometimes brusque manner in the box. Every auctioneer has a different style, but whatever it may be the first essential, as I have said, is that he keeps control of the room. Normally from the moment Peter said, "Lot 1," one knew there was no danger of anything untoward happening while he was in the box. The first Cook picture was William Hogarth's *A Family Party* which went to Colnaghi's for 38,000 gns ($111,720); next came Turner's early work, *Brentford Lock and Mill*, which was bought by Agnew's for 19,000 gns ($44,665); *The Road to Calvary* was bought in, not to anyone's surprise as there was a general feeling that it was by a follower and not by Dürer himself. Then it was the turn of Velazquez's *Portrait of Don Juan de Calabazas* which, after some spirited bidding, was knocked down to Agnew's, who we learned afterwards were acting for the Cleveland Museum, Ohio. The price was 170,000 gns ($524,790).

There was a staccato clicking of cameras as *Titus* was held up by the porter on the platform on the other side of the room from the rostrum, so that everyone could see it. "Lot 105 . . . Lot 105," intoned Peter. "One hundred thousand guineas offered." Now that I had nothing to do but keep a record of the prices I could relax and enjoy the sale. The undercurrent of excitement increased as the room became alive with bidding from many quarters – very different from the *Juno* sale. In four seconds Peter had taken *Titus* up to 200,000 gns in 20,000 gn. steps. In six seconds there was a verbal bid of 300,000 gns from Norton Simon, thereby breaking the agreement he had reached with Peter prior to the sale. Simon then made five further verbal bids which brought the price to 650,000 gns.

Simon then appeared to drop out and a bidding duel began between Geoffrey Agnew (he had not been knighted then) and David Somerset (the Duke of Beaufort now) of the Marlborough Gallery, which increased the excitement. Geoffrey Agnew raised Simon's bid to 680,000 gns; Somerset bid 700,000 gns, which Geoffrey increased to 720,000;

Somerset tried to increase it by just 10,000 gns, but Peter refused it as was his right, and said, "740,000 gns . . . 740,000 gns . . . one more, Geoff?" Agnew shook his head.

Peter then turned towards Norton Simon and said, "740,000 gns . . . 740,000 gns . . .740,000 gns, any more?" Still looking directly at Simon, "More? . . . bidding? . . . 740,000 gns, any more . . . more . . . 740,000 gns . . . bidding . . . 740,000 gns, for the last time . . . 740,000 gns . . . against you," said Peter who had been looking at Simon all the time. He then brought the gavel down and said, "Marlborough Fine Arts." This was greeted first by applause and then to everyone's amazement they heard, "Hold it, hold it." It was Norton Simon standing up. Peter said, "No. I said quite clearly: 'against you for the last time'." Norton Simon and Peter were looking daggers at each other and the room erupted in the face of what was obviously a serious difference of opinion.

Reporters and cameramen fought their way round towards the rostrum, some even climbing on the sales clerk's desk. There then ensued a most vulgar argument for two or three minutes with innocent *Titus* still "on the block", and Spowers looking highly embarrassed as he was right between Peter and Simon with the microphone recording the dispute. Everyone in the audience was asking loudly what on earth was happening. All this time the TV cameras were naturally rolling, the sale having gained an unexpected news angle with what the *Daily Telegraph* the next day described as "uproar". The hubbub from the seated crowd was so great that Peter had to rap his gavel several times to restore some semblance of order.

Finally Simon said, "All right, I will read what's in my pocket," and he dragged out the agreement. He asked Dudley Tooth to read it, which he did with reporters scribbling down the words and the audience leaning forward to hear: "'When Mr Simon is sitting down he is bidding. If he bids openly . . . he is bidding . . .'" Peter was not only angry, but not without cause somewhat flustered. "I am very sorry, I may . . . I have got this disputed bid, Mr Somerset . . . I am extremely sorry, I have got this disputed bid, I may have to reopen it . . ." Anthony Lousada had been asked to attend the sale and rushed up to the rostrum elbowing the reporters out of the way and told Peter he would have to start the bidding again. Not surprisingly David Somerset said, "I don't think this man should be able to open the bidding again." Peter replied, "I'm afraid my decision must be final. It's laid down clearly in the Conditions of Sale, if there is a dispute about a bid there is no alternative but to put the lot . . . continue with the bidding."

Peter reopened the sale: "Now, will you bid 760 . . . 760 . . . please, please, will you please be quiet, I am extremely sorry . . . this has never happened before, but I cannot refuse to accept this gentleman's bid for 760,000 gns." David Somerset remonstrated, "I think that after you had said four times that the bidding was closed – why didn't he bid?" Peter replied, "Through a misunderstanding which I can quite easily explain to you, not in public, but I'm afraid . . . I have my lawyer here and although I do not want to make a case of this, I must accept his bid for 760,000 gns. I am extremely sorry, Mr Somerset . . . so it is 760,000 gns . . . it is your bid . . . right?" said Peter, looking at Simon. "Right," said Simon. "It is 760,000 gns, 760,000 gns, any more? . . . 760,000 gns." With that Peter brought down his gavel and said, "Norton Simon Foundation." In pounds sterling that was £798,000 ($2.2 million), the highest price for any picture sold in Britain.

I was not present for the full dispute between Peter and Norton Simon as I thought Lady Cook would find the pandemonium not only distasteful but worrying, so I took her out when I heard Peter mention the words "disputed bid". (The verbatim account of the dispute between Peter and Simon is from the transcript of Spowers's tape recording.) I left Lady Cook in Peter's room and ran up to the kitchen to open a bottle of champagne which had been put in the fridge for what was meant to have been a celebratory drink after the sale. Now it seemed to be more appropriate as a nerve-calmer. I returned to the saleroom just in time to hear *Titus* being knocked down for 760,000 gns. Throughout the whole episode David Somerset behaved with great dignity, never – as many people might have done – losing his temper, even though from a business point of view he appeared to have suffered an unwarranted defeat. He must have been acting for an anonymous and very rich private collector who would probably be furious.

Once Norton Simon realised that the picture was his, he rushed behind the rostrum and out of the saleroom, down the back stairs and through an open door where the catalogues were delivered. He was followed not only by reporters and cameramen, but TV men with hand-held cameras and sound booms, and some even with tripods. When I got out into Duke Street, which is crowded at the best of times, I found Simon surrounded like a fox by a pack of hounds. The whole street was soon completely blocked and a traffic jam developed right up to Piccadilly.

The first question Simon was asked was, "Why did you bid in that way?" "I wanted to buy it anonymously," was Simon's reply, which in different circumstances might have been funny, but left even the Press speechless for a moment. At that point the law intervened, quite rightly telling Simon and the Press to move on as they were causing an obstruction. Simon set off surrounded by reporters towards King Street. I realised Christie's had to have their say, so I stopped the mob for a second to say that the chairman would hold a Press conference in one of the salerooms in fifteen minutes. Peter had gone to his room not unnaturally in a foul temper. Somewhat in fear and trembling I went in and told him quickly, before he could get a word in, that I had arranged a Press conference. He looked as grim as a bulldog about to attack and very red in the face, but when I explained that the Press could not be allowed just to have Simon's point of view he saw the logic, although it didn't alter his demeanour. When I asked Lady Cook if perhaps she would come along as well, as *Titus* was being sold under her name, she agreed immediately. Much to my surprise and relief all went well. The Press had drifted back and were already seated in the West Room, which had been used for closed circuit TV. Peter explained how the dispute had occurred; there were only a few questions and none of them barbed. Lady Cook was asked for her opinion and she backed Peter up perfectly, and said she thought the price tremendous.

Press reaction the next day was not too bad. The *Daily Telegraph*, in spite of the headline "Uproar as Rembrandt goes for £798,000", made it perfectly clear that Peter had offered it to Simon several times before knocking it down to Marlborough Fine Arts. *The Times* and other papers had stories in the same vein, while Osbert Lancaster immortalised the occasion in his inimitable way on the front page of the *Daily Express* with his pocket cartoon of Lady Littlehampton standing on her head. Immediately I saw it I rang the *Express* in order to get the original cartoon for Christie's, but someone had moved faster; however, Osbert Lancaster was able to arrange for us to have a photocopy of the original.

During the whole incident the one person who appeared to remain calm was the youngest in the room, Ray Perman, who had become chief sales clerk on Nick's retirement a few months before. For Ray, aged twenty-one, the experience of the *Titus* now stood him in good

"DON'T FORGET THAT BY PRIVATE ARRANGEMENT
LADY LITTLEHAMPTON IS STILL IN THE BILDING
AS LONG AS SHE IS STANDING ON HER HEAD!"
                                20.iii.65.

stead for future sales all over the world. (With five other boys from a school in Lambeth he had joined us five years before. He showed his organisational skills by creating order out of chaos in the catalogue department which had been made one of my extra responsibilities.)

The total for the whole sale on March 19th, allowing for the Dürer being bought in, was £1,170,529 ($3.2 million), the highest sum for any picture sale in Britain. However, as the Cook pictures had totalled £1,036,350 ($2.9 million), it didn't say much for the other hundred pictures and emphasised how lucky Christie's were to have got the Cook pictures and the Northwick Park ones which were to follow.

Irrespective of the unpleasant end to the sale, the price for *Titus* was remarkable and demonstrated in a different way from the Goldschmidt sale the lure of the art market. The previous highest price for a Rembrandt in Britain was £190,000 ($532,000) which was paid by Agnew's for his *St Bartholomew* in 1961, later acquired by Paul Getty. The highest price ever fetched anywhere in the world by a Rembrandt was the $2.3 million (£820,000) paid for *Aristotle Contemplating the Bust of Homer*, the property of the advertising millionaire Alfred W.

Erickson, when it was auctioned at Parke-Bernet in 1961. The buyer was James R. Rorimer, Director of the Metropolitan Museum, New York. This magnificent if sombre work was a very different type of Rembrandt and of far greater importance academically as an example of the artist's genius than *Titus*. *Titus*, on the other hand, was a highly attractive and saleable picture. The price it achieved showed that if two multi-millionaires decided they wanted a work of art there was no knowing how high they would be prepared to bid.

Peter, not unnaturally, was very upset by the furore caused by the sale of *Titus*. Many years later he described it to friends as "the worst moment of my life – the only comparable one being when on reconnaissance in 1944 in my scout car when I found myself surrounded by the German 10th SS Division". His concern for the firm was aggravated still further when on the Tuesday following the sale *The Times* printed a letter by Geoffrey Agnew, his cousin, which read in part:

> Christie's should never have accepted such an unpractical and ambiguous directive, especially on an occasion when large sums and a close finish were inevitable . . .
>
> During the subsequent altercation, Mr Chance, relying on the Conditions of Sale, Clause 1, "The highest bidder to be the buyer; and if any dispute arises between two or more bidders the lot, so in dispute, shall be immediately put up again and resold", put up the picture at 740,000 guineas and resold it to Mr Simon for 760,000 guineas. In doing this, he was, in my opinion, entirely wrong. The picture had been sold to the highest bidder. There was no dispute between bidders (as for example when two bidders bid simultaneously). The dispute was between the auctioneer and one bidder, because the auctioneer had failed to carry out the bidder's impossible instructions.
>
> I am afraid bidder and auctioneer, like everyone else, must accept responsibility for their mistakes . . .
>
> The point is of some importance. If the accepted practices of the auction room are to be disregarded, buying and selling there will become even more of a gamble than it is already. If the fall of the hammer means nothing, why have a hammer?

Although like everyone at Christie's I felt for Peter at this unexpected rebuke, which must have seemed like salt being rubbed into a wound,

Geoffrey Agnew had a point. The picture had been sold to the highest bidder and the dispute was between the auctioneer and one bidder (Simon) and not between two bidders as laid down in our Conditions of Sale.

Geoffrey Agnew could not have known, however, that Mr Simon had forgotten or chose not to remember the verbal agreement he had made with Peter before the sale. Peter could rightly argue that in not trying to come to an understanding with someone who had expressed great interest in *Titus* he would not be doing his client justice, which was to get the highest price. The trouble is that those new to the saleroom find themselves in a dramatic atmosphere which they have never experienced before; even hardened dealers admit that they hate bidding for really important lots, and when I have myself bid into six figures for private bidders I have experienced a considerable quickening of the heartbeat as the auctioneer forces the pace. It is not for nothing that "caveat emptor" has for years been the watchword for newcomers to auctions. Christie's were in fact lucky not to be sued by the millionaire for whom Somerset had been bidding. Anthony Lousada thought there was a definite possibility of a lawsuit, for millionaires don't like to be thwarted, and some might say Somerset's client was unjustly treated; he went as far as ordering his solicitors to impound Bill Spowers's tape but in the end he relented.

This was not the end of the drama over *Titus*. In spite of the huge price and all the effort that had gone into getting and selling it, Christie's did not do at all well financially from the sale. Dudley Tooth rang Peter during the afternoon and said he was speaking on behalf of Mr Simon who was taking the 3 p.m. plane back to New York. Dudley told Peter that Simon apologised for the misunderstanding and would like Christie's to apply for an export licence on his behalf. Peter had naturally considered this matter beforehand and everyone he discussed it with felt that there would be no difficulty in getting an export licence in a week or ten days. This was also the view of Terence Mullaly, the art critic and for many years saleroom correspondent of the *Daily Telegraph*, who the next day wrote, "In view of the large number of paintings in the National Gallery it is probable that it [an export licence] will be granted"; at the time of the sale there were about fifteen Rembrandts in the National Gallery. Unfortunately this forecast proved to be over-optimistic.

It was a full two months before the Committee for the Export of Works of Art granted a licence. They turned a deaf ear to Christie's entreaties that because of the number of Rembrandts in Britain the refusal of a licence was an unjustifiable use of the Waverley Committee's delaying powers.

For Christie's the delay was extremely serious, because Sir Francis Cook had stipulated before the sale that he wanted to be paid before the end of March, as he rightly suspected that the Chancellor of the Exchequer would introduce a Capital Gains Tax in his next Budget. Thus Christie's had to pay Sir Francis over £750,000 – allowing for the very small commission agreed beforehand and other expenses – without having had a penny from Norton Simon. This naturally resulted in hefty bank interest charges; efforts were made to get Norton Simon to pay these, but not altogether surprisingly he refused. Christie's received very little for selling *Titus* for such a huge price. In spite of this unhappy end to what we hoped would be a great sale, the pre-tax profits for the year ending March 31st, 1965, were up from £11,000 in the previous year to £98,000.

If the sale of *Titus* was something of a Pyrrhic victory, those of the Northwick Park Collection, which occupied two full weeks in May and June with further sales in the autumn and New Year, could not have gone better, though beside the six-figure sums fetched by Sir Francis's Rembrandt and Velazquez the prices may seem small – the highest being 78,000 gns ($229,320) for Pieter Brueghel the Elder's *Peasant Wedding*. I will only mention two other prices, both of them examples of Spencer-Churchill's "rescues": Dirk Bouts's enchanting *The Madonna and Child* sold for 15,000 gns ($44,100) and Nicholas van Verendael's *Vase of Flowers* – only an ear of wheat at the bottom of the picture being visible when Spencer-Churchill bought it – made 14,000 gns ($41,160). The total for the whole collection was £1.6 million ($4.5 million), which together with £700,000 worth of negotiated sales brought the grand total for the whole collection to £2.3 million ($6.4 million). The whole operation was therefore a great success, leaving even Lord Rockley happy and bringing valuable réclame to the firm.

It was undoubtedly the Northwick Park sales which were the springboard to recovery. They were followed in the autumn by the sale of forty-five Impressionist and Post-Impressionist pictures from Venezuela belonging to Mr and Mrs John Boulton, of Caracas. This was a coup for Bob Leylan and further proof that Christie's had a competent Impressionist department. It was an interesting collection because it had been formed by Mr Boulton's father, who, although living in Caracas, made frequent visits to Paris between 1922 and 1930, often accompanied by the painter Manuel Cabre.

The collection had remained unaltered since its formation and in the case of thirty-two of the paintings the original bills had been preserved. These thirty-two works, by Bonnard, Chagall, Dufy, Kisling, Laurencin, Monet, Pissarro, Soutine, Utrillo and others, cost Mr Boulton senior the equivalent of £3,789. When auctioned by Christie's they achieved a total of £136,143 ($1.06 million), a 3,500 per cent increase which even allowing for inflation was impressive. The pictures had not been bought for investment but for pleasure and were "fresh" – that is to say they had not been hawked around dealers beforehand – and of good quality. The prices reflected these all-important qualifications for any successful auction. One will suffice as an example of the reward a discerning eye in the 1920s could bring in 1965: Camille Pissarro's *Le Ruisseau à Osny*, which sold for 26,000 gns ($76,440), was originally bought for £560 in 1922.

The only worry David Bathurst had with this sale was that in Venezuela the stretchers of the pictures had become infested with weevils, and every day little piles of wood dust had to be swept up. The weevils were not interested in the canvas but would they eat through the stretchers before the sale? Fortunately they didn't.

When it came to the sale a nightmare which every auctioneer dreads seemed to befall David. It was nothing to do with the Boulton pictures. In the same sale there were two tiny panels by Seurat, *Champs en Eté*, painted in 1883, and *Maisons et Jardin*, from the year before. Although small, they were very fine works, so David was rather surprised when a bearded man in a macintosh, whom he'd never seen before, started bidding just when he thought it was all over and said, "36,000 gns [$105,840]." Somewhat reluctantly David knocked it down to him and said to Ray Perman through the corner of his mouth, "Who the hell's that?" However, before Ray could find out the second Seurat was held up. There was spirited bidding from all sides, but once again, the bearded man made what proved to be the final bid of 32,000 gns ($94,080). David thought the very worst had happened, that he had a crank on his hands. Then, as if reading his thoughts, the bearded man leant forward and handed up a card which read: "The bearer of this card is authorised to bid on my behalf. Paul Mellon." What had happened was that Paul Mellon's usual agent was unable to be present and had given the commission to one of his underlings. David told me that he came near to refusing the bearded man's bid on the second Seurat. Whatever the circumstances, to refuse a bid from one of America's greatest collectors – if not *the* greatest, and an Anglophile – would not have gone down well with him or with Peter.

This was not only a year of successful sales, which resulted in a pre-tax profit for the year ended March 31st, 1966, of £154,000 compared with £98,000 for the previous year, but also for administrative decisions: the purchase of our own printing works in order to improve production and distribution, a strengthening of our New York representation and the establishment in King Street of an "overseas office" to co-ordinate the efforts of our growing team of overseas representatives – Cesar Feldman had been taken on a year before following a visit by Jo Floyd to Buenos Aires.

I became involved with the purchase of our own printing works because I was responsible for delivery of catalogues to King Street and also their international distribution. Christie's had always used two printers, one a quite large firm based at Bletchley. The other was White Bros, started in the 1950s by Fred White in somewhat nondescript premises in Lambeth of which he had the freehold. To describe the firm as "small jobbing printers" would not be unkind, although Fred was perfectly capable of producing a handsome full colour illustrated catalogue.

Fred White's first wife had died and he was no doubt feeling a bit depressed. One day in 1965 he came into my office and asked if we could have a chat in private. His approach to me was because we spoke together almost daily about catalogue production figures or the collection of shipments to be taken to Heathrow. I took Fred across to the Golden Lion, our local, and over a beer he asked me whether I thought Christie's would be interested in buying him out. Lambeth Council had slapped a compulsory purchase order on him and he didn't feel like starting afresh. He was asking £38,000. I passed on the news to Guy, with the result that we acquired White Bros (Printers) during the summer.

This was one of the best deals that Christie's have ever done, because our catalogue demands were increasing and being self-sufficient would yield many advantages. Sotheby's used at least five printers, which was not half as efficient for such specialised work. Lambeth Council had had to offer Fred White alternative premises. The fact that they had been used previously as a pickle factory, and smelt like one the first time we visited the site, didn't matter. It was a post-war building, structurally sound, with a basement, ground and first floor. Being near to the Oval cricket ground, it was conveniently close. Fred White stayed on the Board which at first also consisted of Guy and me, to advise on the movement of machinery and future development.

One of the extra bonuses was that the whole catalogue dispatch department could be moved from the midden near the "hill" to the first floor of White's, where there was ample space for the latest labour-saving machines, such as the binder which automatically tied up bundles of catalogues with the tough string which had previously torn to pieces the hands of Doreen Edwards's staff. The integration of White's into Christie's enabled the whole process of the dispatch of catalogues to be simplified and accelerated; subscribers' catalogues could come up on the lift directly they had been bound instead of having to be loaded into lorries and unloaded again at King Street. Now the Post Office would come to the Offley works and collect bulk consignments of catalogues, instead of the boys having to take the sacks to the nearest Post Office.

From the moment that Bob Leylan had been appointed he received daily letters of complaint from American subscribers that they weren't getting their catalogues, and that no one replied to their letters to King Street. This indeed was why I had been lumbered with the task of reorganising the catalogue department, for which no director had ever before been made responsible. The backlash from American subscribers was so bad that it preyed on Bob's mind – he was, like many Americans, a stickler for efficient systems – so much so that it affected his personal life. A girlfriend of his on a visit to London told Patricia, Peter's secretary, that just when Bob was getting nicely amorous he would sit up and say, "Oh gee, I must make a note to write to John Herbert about the catalogue problem," completely destroying any hope of the long-awaited dénouement.

The need for stronger presentation in New York was obvious if we were to get more business there. Bob Leylan had tried his best under very different circumstances. Apart from the opposition of Sotheby Parke-Bernet, Bob found it difficult to tolerate the unbusiness-like attitudes which prevailed at King Street in his first years (not only in the catalogue department). His criticism was often justified, but led to bad blood with the departments concerned. Peter, therefore, had the unpleasant task of asking him to leave, unpleasant because he and indeed most of us liked Bob very much. Peter decided that it was essential for a senior director to take over the office, if only for a comparatively short period, so that Christie's presence would be more visible. Jo Floyd, therefore, went to New York for six months and was a great success because even if he didn't have Jake's intellect, he had his other qualities of charm and efficiency. First, though, Charlie Allsopp went out to hold the fort and in January was joined by John Richardson, the Impressionist expert who had been persuaded to join us. Apart from having written two much acclaimed books, one on Braque and another on Manet, John early in 1966 was mounting a ten-gallery exhibition in New York of Picasso's works. He was therefore a perfect reinforcement for the New York office where it was essential to have a recognised Impressionist expert.

A very different but equally valuable addition to our ranks at King Street was Dina Lieven. It was an inspired move of Peter's to ask her to join us even though she was sixty-three. Hans Backer, our invaluable European representative, had died the previous summer. Dina had been Hans's secretary in London for four years, and had thus been in and out of Christie's smoothing the none too easy path of the works of art Hans sent to us. During the next twelve years Christie's appointed representatives in every country this side of the Iron Curtain. The success of these European offices in first of all ferreting out works of art and then channelling them to London was very largely due to Dina. Her sympathy and understanding of the multi-national team who ran them, her perseverance and tact in getting King Street experts to co-operate and her indefatigable work at Geneva sales were invaluable. Initially, however, there was the inevitable suspicion of her because she was a foreigner but she was quickly accepted because she "could deal with foreigners". At long last Christie's was becoming organised so that the firm could face Sotheby's opposition on reasonably equal terms.

The Specious Orator

Christie's Bicentenary Year fell in 1966 and it was decided to celebrate this in the New Year of 1967 with an exhibition of magnificent pictures, all of which had been sold at least once by Christie's and which it was hoped would be loaned by museums and private collectors from all over the world.

The origins of James Christie, the firm's founder, remain remarkably vague for someone who became a household name, there being at least three conflicting accounts. The most favoured one is that he was born in Perth in 1730 of an English father and a Scottish mother related to Flora Macdonald. Christie had a brief career in the Royal Navy but resigned his commission as a midshipman before he was twenty and became apprenticed to Annesley, an auctioneer who carried on his business in the fashionable Covent Garden quarter of London. Within a few years James Christie decided to set up on his own in the same premises in Pall Mall as the Society of Artists of Great Britain, which in 1768 became the Royal Academy of Arts. The date, according to the first catalogue in the firm's archives, was December 5th, 1766, but there are one or two catalogues in the British Library from at least three years earlier, so young James had had a little experience by 1766. Nobody gave much for his chances, there being quite a number of established auctioneers in London at that time, but none, it seems, with the good looks, eloquence and personality of James Christie, then thirty-six.

It was a propitious moment to enter the art market. The wealth of the Industrial Revolution gave a considerable impetus to collecting and the Grand Tour of Europe had become fashionable, with the result that wagonloads of pictures, furniture, silver and works of art of all kinds entered Britain. This in turn brought about the establishment of more and more dealers in London anxious to satisfy the demands of individual collectors. Many dealers had already settled in London as a result of religious persecution in France. Until 1789 Paris was the most important art centre but the French Revolution destroyed it and gave a big fillip to the emerging London art market. Complementary to the large number of art dealers were the four firms of auctioneers, all of which were established in the eighteenth century. After Christie's and Sotheby's came Phillips, which was started in 1796 by Harry Phillips, James Christie's chief sales clerk, and is managed today by the highly enterprising Christopher Weston. Lastly there is Bonham's which was founded in 1793.

For some years James Christie's sales included chattels, as well as pictures and works of art, such as those in his first sale on December 5th, 1766: "2 Nankeen chamber pots. Sir Isaac Newton, Pope and Handel in bronze finely repaired by the late ingenious Mr Roubiliac; a 'Moonlight' by Cuyp [which fetched £3 11s.]; a pair of sheets and two 'pillow rigs'; four flat irons, a footman [what had he done to be there?], a grid iron trivet, etc. etc. etc." One morning Christie knocked down seventy-two loads of meadow hay "from a farm not two miles from St James's"; in another sale a barrel organ and a coffin, the latter, the catalogue explained, having been "made for a citizen who had made a remarkable recovery from a malady usually regarded by the medical profession as fatal".

Unlike today, before opening the bidding James Christie gave a considerable preamble: "Let me entreat you, Ladies and Gentlemen. Permit me to put this inestimable piece of elegance under your protection. Only observe, the inexhaustible munificence of your superlatively candid generosity must harmonise with the refulgent brilliancy of this little jewel. Will your Ladyship therefore do me the honour to say £50,000? A mere trifle, a brilliant of the first water, an unheard of price for such a lot, surely?" Christie's eloquence in the rostrum became the talk of London, and in due course cartoonists dubbed him "The Specious Orator". About 1770 he moved westwards to 125 Pall Mall, next to what became Schomberg House, in which Gainsborough lived and worked. The two men became firm friends.

In spite of his comparative youth and the competition from more experienced auctioneers, James Christie prospered. As early as 1769 he was selling Old Masters from abroad, some of which to judge from the prices must have had some quality. He also sold a surprising number of American School paintings, including works by Gilbert Stuart, Benjamin West, the Peale family and others. In spite of the

American War of Independence, American portraits, even of General George Washington, sold well.

One of the first one-owner sales of pictures from abroad was in 1797 for John Trumbull, an American who, on a diplomatic mission to Paris, realised it was a good time to buy paintings from families who had been ruined by the Revolution. Unfortunately the pictures arrived in the Pool of London on the Prince of Wales's birthday, which was a holiday for watermen. They had been celebrating and as a result the lighter loaded with Trumbull's crates of pictures went adrift and then sank, the crates floating down the river towards the sea. Fortunately some men had remained sober and recovered the pictures, which in spite of what had seemed to be a disaster for Mr Trumbull sold very well. There is no better example of the esteem those in high places held for James Christie than when at the turn of the century he was called in to value the magnificent pictures at Houghton which had been collected by Sir Robert Walpole, the first Earl of Orford. He valued them at £40,000; for this sum they were sold to Catherine the Great and most of them are in the Hermitage, Leningrad, to this day.

Lastly – for this book is about 1958–88 rather than the past – there was the sale in 1801 of Sir William Hamilton's collection, as a result of which James Christie crossed swords with Nelson. Sir William had been British Minister in Naples, but when the French were at the gates he decided it was time to go. Nelson was fortunately lying off the city in his flagship and took both Sir William and Emma on board. With them went Velazquez's *Portrait of Juan de Pareja*, the pride of Sir William's vast collection, and also a portrait of his wife, Emma, by Vigée-Lebrun. On entering the Channel the *Colossus*, which was carrying the rest of Hamilton's collection, was wrecked on the Scillies. Sir William arrived in England virtually penniless and put both the Velazquez and the portrait of Emma up for sale at Christie's. From his flagship Nelson wrote to Emma on March 10th, 1801: "But you are at auction my blood boils." In the next letter, having failed to have the picture withdrawn, he wrote: "How can any man sell your resemblance; to buy it many would fly. And for the original, no price is equal to her merits. Those of her mind and heart if possible exceed her beauty." He finally bought the portrait for 300 gns. "If it had cost me 300 drops of blood," he told Emma, "I would have given it with pleasure." These two letters today hang proudly in Christie's Board Room. As for the Velazquez, this was sold for 39 gns; but we will meet it again not only at the Bicentenary Exhibition but also in 1970 when it came up for auction.

It was these sales, and the association with the owners and such men as Charles James Fox, Burke, Sheridan, Garrick and Sir Joshua Reynolds and many other artists, that resulted in Christie's remaining in such an established position after the founder's death in 1803, when James Christie II took over the running of the firm. His two sons followed him and in 1831 were joined by William Manson. James H. B. Christie, the great-grandson of the founder, was the last member of the family to be associated with the firm and he retired in 1889.

Having done what he could to improve our presence in New York by sending Jo Floyd there and engaging John Richardson, Peter Chance, ever mindful of Sotheby's increasing sales total, decided it was time to expand eastwards. Peter had had many talks with Hans Backer about the problems of being based in Italy which had strict laws, as it still does, about the export of works of art. In March it was decided to explore the possibilities in Geneva. Anthony du Boulay, who spoke French well, was therefore sent out to reconnoitre. Almost a year later Christie, Manson and Woods (International) SA was formed.

Saleroom discoveries may sound as hackneyed a subject as record prices, but they cannot be altogether ignored as they are certainly important for the vendor, often of interest because of the circumstances in which the work of art was found, and demonstrate that the firm's staff is alert and expert. There are a number every year, which make good copy for the Press, as well as exciting the owner.

A discovery in 1966 which received world-wide publicity was the early Ming blue and white flask which Anthony spotted through the window of a house on an estate to which he had been taken to play tennis. The flask was sitting forlornly beneath the sideboard in the dining-room. Though it might well have been an eighteenth-century copy, Anthony asked his tennis partner if he could have a look at it. He was told by the maid that it got in the way of the vacuum cleaner! On close inspection, the flask fulfilled Anthony's most optimistic hopes, belonging to a rare group of early fifteenth-century porcelains decorated with a dragon design reversed in white on a blue ground. Only three such flasks were known, the others being in the Percival David Collection, London, and the Peking Museum. In all likelihood it came to Britain following the turmoil of the Boxer risings at the turn of the century. When put up for sale in November it achieved 24,000 gns ($70,560). In view of the flask's rarity it was an extraordinary coincidence when a second blue and white flask, similar to the one Christie's had sold, was brought to the Front Counter without the owner having read about the first. This one, like so many Chinese pieces, had been handed down in the family as having come from the Summer Palace, Peking, but had never been considered to be of any value. The decoration was almost a mirror copy of the first flask with a blue dragon on a white ground. Though of similar brilliant quality, it had not quite such startling composition which accounted for its making only 17,000 gns ($47,600).

Christie's were at last getting some splendid pictures. Among many that year were three superb works by Stubbs. The picture department took great pains to establish the pedigree of the horses – which showed that more trouble was being taken in making catalogue entries as interesting as possible. Two of them proved to be pure Arab stallions imported in Stuart times from North Africa. *Goldfinder* seen with mare and foal went for 72,000 gns ($211,680), the highest price to date for a Stubbs; the others also sold well.

More important still, though, was the Impressionist sale a fortnight later which included Van Gogh's *Portrait of Mademoiselle Ravoux* and a drawing, *Sorrow*, by the same artist. For Christie's this was a sale of historic importance not only because the Van Gogh portrait went for 150,000 gns ($441,000), more than any work by Van Gogh to date, but because both works came from the collection of the Reverend Theodore Pitcairn, of Bryn Athyn, Pennsylvania. The sale of the pictures was the result of two years' wooing of its owner by David Bathurst and the beginning of a series of sales from the Pitcairn Collection which received welcome publicity in the USA as well as Britain. Following the Woolworth, Combemale and Boulton pictures, it put our Impressionist department virtually on equal terms with that of Sotheby's. There was still some reluctance by American trustees to sell in London, so many of them chose Parke-Bernet. Thus David's success in getting the Pitcairn pictures was not only a major victory over the opposition, but also demonstrated to American collectors and trustees that Christie's could sell them as well as Sotheby's.

David, as I have already said, studied books on Impressionism such as those by F. Dault and John Rewald to find out the most important collectors before making his visits to America. The Reverend Theodore Pitcairn was one of those he rang up on his first trip. It seems amazing to me that Peregrine Pollen and Jake had not made any advances as yet to the Reverend Pitcairn. "The most famous picture in Pitcairn's collection was Monet's early work *La Terrasse à Sainte Adresse*, but when I first saw the collection in 1964," David told me, "I never mentioned the question of a possible sale. I was, however, rather astonished at such an important picture being hung in a pantry-cum-kitchen extension."

David obviously showed a keen interest in and appreciation of the collection, but never overplayed his hand and remained patient, believing correctly that an aggressive sales technique would be disastrous. With these shrewd tactics David grew so close to Pitcairn, a lean, white-haired, friendly man then about seventy-one, that he became a frequent weekend guest at his home in Bryn Athyn, about a hundred miles south of New York.

The Reverend Theodore Pitcairn was one of three sons of John Pitcairn, founder of the Pittsburgh Glass Co., PPG Industries. When he died he left an estate close to $20 million to Theodore and his brothers. In spite of his inheritance, Theodore Pitcairn chose the Church after university and was ordained in 1918 and served for several years as a missionary in Basutoland, before returning to the United States in 1926. He founded a separate church – the Lord's New Church – a splinter group of what is generally known as the New Church (Swedenborgian), itself based on the writings of the eighteenth-century Swedish scientist Emanuel Swedenborg.

Regardless of his chosen calling, Pitcairn became an art collector as early as 1921 and his first purchases were Van Gogh's *Portrait of Mademoiselle Ravoux*, Van Gogh's drawing of *Sorrow* and a third picture for the equivalent of $20,000 (£5,000). He was way ahead of his time in making such purchases, even if he could easily afford them. Mlle Ravoux was the daughter of the owner of the Café Ravoux, Place de la Mairie, Auvers-sur-Oise, where Van Gogh stayed from May 21st, 1890, and where he died on July 29th. Early in 1966 Pitcairn summoned David and told him that he would like Christie's to sell both the Van Gogh works, not only as his property but also on behalf of the Beneficia Foundation, Bryn Athyn, which Pitcairn founded in 1947 to support religious and musical charities. The foundation benefited from the full proceeds of the sale – £157,000 ($441,000) for *Mlle Ravoux* and £11,550 ($32,300) for *Sorrow*.

In December 1966 there was an important sale of Old Masters which will be remembered because of two pictures. One was a modello of the *Samson and Delilah* which Rubens painted on panel about 1609, probably for his friend Nickolaus Rockox, Burghermaster of Antwerp, which has been in the Cologne Collection for many years. As in the big picture, the modello showed Samson asleep with his head in Delilah's lap, while his locks were being cut by a male accomplice to rob him of his strength. Soldiers could be seen waiting outside the door to seize him. The circuitous way by which the modello came for sale is an object lesson for both auctioneers and museums. The modello had been bought sixty years earlier by a lady in a Yorkshire antique shop for a few shillings. Her step-granddaughter, who still wishes to remain anonymous, told me that it had been bought mainly for its gilt frame, the panel being badly cracked. She first of all took it to Sotheby's and asked for a written attribution and valuation. Some weeks later, having heard nothing, she called on Sotheby's. She was told the expert had been away on holiday and had not seen the picture yet, so producing the receipt form she insisted on taking the panel away – a good example of how business can be lost.

Next she decided to take it to the National Gallery. There she asked a junior member of staff, "Didn't Rubens paint a big picture of this subject?" and was told, "No, I'm sure not." However, he took the panel away and came back and said he could not find any reference to *Samson and Delilah* in the Rubens book. He then said, "Why not ask Christie's down the road?" The owner told me she wasn't impressed by him but took his advice, got a taxi to Christie's and went to the Front Counter, who rang up the picture department. By a stroke of luck, I was told, David Carritt had not gone to lunch and on seeing the panel immediately recognised it for what it was and the delighted vendor left it for sale.

The attribution by David was the basis of the Press release I sent out from details provided by Patrick. However, the facts I'd been given were not correct. It was only when researching this book that I discovered that the picture had actually been identified by Brian Sewell. Brian told me: "I don't wish to detract anything from David's brilliance, but this was one discovery for which I was responsible and not David. I remember the occasion vividly because Guy Hannen, who still in theory was in charge of the picture department, was doing his 'Führer bit', harassing me to get a catalogue off to the printers. Then suddenly a boy from the Front Counter arrived with a panel picture virtually 'two pieces of timber' [one of Brian's typical exaggerations]. I took one look at it and knew in my bones it was by Rubens. I said to the Front Counter boy, 'Don't let the lady leave and tell her that I'll be down as soon as possible.' 'What is it, Brian?' Guy said, 'What is it?' 'Guy, you've told me to finish this catalogue and finish it I will,' which I did after a quarter of an hour." Brian told Guy that he was sure it was a Rubens modello of a very important work. He then went down to the lady who had brought it in and told her it was a modello for Rubens's *Samson and Delilah*.

In January 1988, when Brian told me this, it came as a considerable shock. Fortunately I was able to obtain confirmation from the lady who had brought the panel in. I asked her, "Did the young man you saw at Christie's have a plummy voice?" "Yes, indeed he did. Just what I expected from someone at Christie's, but he was very nice and helpful and obviously knowledgeable," she told me. "Did he wear glasses?" I asked. "Yes, he did," she said. This was irrefutable proof that what Brian said was true, as David didn't wear glasses, and his voice certainly wasn't like Brian's. Finally Colin Anson, one of David's closest friends and colleagues in his final years, told me that David never claimed to have identified the modello.

However, that was not the end of the saga. Having completed his catalogue Brian went away to Spain on holiday. In his absence someone wrote an anonymous letter to the *Daily Telegraph* saying that everything they had printed about David discovering the modello was untrue and that it was another member of the staff. The *Telegraph* naturally didn't print the letter but told a reporter to ring up Patrick and ask him for an explanation. When Brian returned from holiday Patrick accused him of flagrant disloyalty and of having written the letter. Brian naturally denied this. All this may seem rather petty now and won't endear me or Brian to our ex-colleagues; but the incident does show that Patrick thought it in the firm's interests to enhance David's reputation whenever there was an opportunity to do so. The episode also throws an interesting light on the internal politics of the picture department and the pressure still felt from Bond Street. Finally, perhaps of more importance, when the Rubens panel came up for auction it achieved 24,000 gns ($70,560).

Unfortunately the réclame for the firm over the correct identifications of the Rubens panel was lost by a failure over another picture in the sale which taught many of us a lesson, not only regarding attribution but also the danger of over-promotion. The picture was another Rubens; probably his earliest treatment of *The Judgment of Paris*, the Orleans version of which has hung in the National Gallery for many years.

The background of the version Christie's had been sent is hardly credible. It had been bought in 1933 by a Mr Robert Savage, a Northampton picture framer who bought old frames from a dealer in York at an average price of 10 shillings; the dealer very often threw in the picture to clinch a deal. *The Judgment of Paris* was one of them and in 1966 Mrs Eva Savage, who had been widowed, sent it with thirty-nine other pictures to Christie's for sale. It was not a very distinguished provenance which may have accounted for the casual way it was catalogued first of all.

The picture had in fact been auctioned by Christie's on June 2nd, 1815, when it was Lot 27. The entry described it as: "The Judgment of Paris, Original by Rubens, a grand Chef d'oeuvre, differing in several points of Composition, from the Orleans Rubens of the same subject and size, to which this picture is a glorious rival . . ." In spite of this attribution the picture was bought in for 370 gns. This entry should have been rediscovered in 1966 from the original stencil on the stretcher; the whole point of having the stock number stencilled there is that pictures can be traced if they come up a second or even third time. Whoever had seen it first should have consulted the daybook which would have led to the attribution given above. Instead, in 1966 the picture department decided it was by Lankrink, a seventeenth-century copyist of Old Masters, and it was made Lot 183 in our last sale of the summer season.

Sir Oliver Millar, who was still then Keeper of the Queen's Pictures (but who had not as yet been knighted), had access to pictures in our warehouse and also on the hill. Even in the bad light there the picture had caught Millar's eye. He said later, "It smelt of Rubens." When the sale was on view Millar had a closer look at it and went in search of David Carritt, who had not seen the picture before, having been absent from the final hill session. When he heard Millar's view he rushed to the Big Room and was heard to exclaim, "Oh, my God." Michael Jaffé, the acknowledged Rubens expert, also confirmed Millar's opinion. Of even greater significance, Gregory Martin, who was still an assistant keeper at the National Gallery prior to joining Christie's, spotted it while walking round the rooms with his Director, Sir Philip Hendy. Unlike the El Greco in 1958 the picture was withdrawn, but not before a number of dealers had spotted it as being quite possibly a genuine Rubens and were looking forward to the sale. It was decided to keep the picture for the important autumn Old Master sale on November 25th.

The rumours about the picture being a long-lost Rubens reached the ears of the *Sunday Times*, probably through a dealer who felt thwarted. The paper once again put Colin Simpson on to an investigation in depth. I was on a beach in Tunisia when I opened the *Sunday Times* and read with horror Simpson's full-page story with quotes from Mrs Savage – whose address was meant to be secret – and others from Oliver Millar, Sir Philip Hendy and Michael Jaffé extolling it to the skies. Simpson as usual had done a thorough job, but it was the last form of publicity Christie's wanted at that time, months before the sale. I had left the office in the hands of Richard Walter, who had left both the *Evening Standard* and his next newspaper the *Daily Mail*, and I had taken him on as my assistant as the pressure of work had mounted considerably.

Good journalist though he was, I quickly learned that I had not made a good choice. Although a charming companion, he was incapable of fulfilling during the day his share of the many chores we had to handle; he was a compulsive talker on the telephone and in addition there was nothing businesslike about the way he worked, so that his desk was always littered with jottings about this and that. It was in this way that Colin Simpson, when he came to the Press Office to question Richard about the Rubens being withdrawn, found out Mrs Savage's address and got an exclusive interview with her. Evidently the picture presented hanging problems – it measured 52 ins down and 69 ins across – owing to the smallness of Mrs Savage's home; the only place where the picture could be seen properly was on a landing, but in order to admire it one had to retreat into the lavatory opposite.

The Press Office's job is to get the maximum publicity, but it has to be at the right time. A sensational write-up months before the sale can result in over-exposure and too much talk among dealers about condition or quality, so that the work is gradually "talked down"; moreover, "further research" can imply a huge reserve.

Mrs Savage's Rubens had so much human interest that the papers couldn't leave it alone. This just increased the speculation in the trade, whose noses had already been put out of joint by its being withdrawn, that the owner was expecting too much. The day before the sale the *Daily Express* picture desk rang up wanting to get in on the act and said they'd like to photograph the whole Board with the Rubens in the background, each director holding a work of art representing his department. The photographer was Michael McKeown, not only an old hand but an old friend; what he suggested may sound rather corny, but on the face of it was splendid publicity, for in spite of Simpson's article everyone at Christie's still expected the Rubens to sell well.

The photograph was taken in the anteroom: David Carritt was holding "his" Rubens modello of *Samson and Delilah*; David Bathurst a Matisse which Henry Ford II had sent us for sale the following week; Anthony du Boulay held the Ming vase he had spotted while going to play tennis; Arthur Grimwade a silver tankard and Albert Middlemiss, who had taken over from Reggie Eyles, held a diamond necklace as if he was saying his beads. I had naturally told Peter about the *Express*'s request and he had said, "Just come and get me when everything's ready." He stumped out of his room, obviously in a vile temper for some reason, sat down beside David Carritt and glowered at the camera. John Critchley, Roy Davidge, Ridley Leadbeater, from the Front Counter, and Jim Taylor, representing the staff, looked much happier.

The next day the photograph appeared across a page with an editorial about the Rubens below. It proved to be "hype" in its pejorative sense of exaggerated importance given to something which does not deserve it. When the picture came up for sale the room seemed to go dead and Peter bought it in for the pathetic sum of 24,000 gns: "No Bid". Yet almost immediately the National Gallery made an offer which, after consultation with Mrs Savage who not unnaturally had looked very sad as she left the saleroom, was accepted. The picture hangs today close to the Orleans Rubens.

Once again we had ended up with egg all over our faces. This was dispiriting and bad for the firm. Were we the victims of our own folly? Terence Mullaly may well have been right when he wrote in next day's *Daily Telegraph*: "The failure of this picture to sell and the price it reached occasioned no surprise to the art world. Its art historical interest had been swamped by the unrealistic estimates about the price it might fetch." Undoubtedly Simpson's article had been unfortunate because it allowed too much time for speculation, but I don't remember wild estimates being given out. The Press Office certainly hadn't issued any, although both Oliver Millar and Michael Jaffé had implied that it was of great value.

The real mistake was in attributing it to Lankrink and not spotting that it had been sold before. I asked a leading dealer why, even allowing for over-exposure of the picture and rumours of a high reserve, no one had tried to buy it. It was obviously a speculative picture but I would have thought it was worth a bid or two. The reply was, "I don't think the trade 'sat on their hands' out of pique, even though some people can be ill-disposed after a picture has been withdrawn. The fact is that it was an early Rubens and personally I didn't think it an attractive picture. Museum officials and art historians often get excited about a picture, but the question every dealer has to ask is whether it is saleable; and I didn't think it was. In fact I was rather surprised that the National Gallery snapped it up." It is of course standard policy for a museum to buy works which fill a gap in an artist's oeuvre. All in all it was a painful illustration of the psychology of the fine art trade and the correctness of Peter's favourite dictum which he never tired of shouting at all and sundry: "Get it right."

On a more positive note, in October Christie's had resumed wine sales which had been interrupted since the war. (James Christie's first sale had included wine.) Michael Broadbent, a Master of Wine, had joined us in July from Harvey's where he had been sales director. In September the new department was strengthened by Alan Taylor-Restell, whose hundred-year-old family firm of W. T. Restell in the City had been acquired in July. From the start the wine sales were a great success because of the expertise of these two men. They are completely different in character. Michael was quickly recognised throughout the world for his great knowledge of wine; he was also a man of boundless energy – writing many books in the course of time – and realised the value of publicity. Alan on the other hand was unassuming, but shrewd and respected by the wine trade for his knowledge just as much as Michael. He was also the fastest auctioneer of wine in London, almost of the same speed as Australian sheep auctioneers. Alan left Christie's in 1987; but the firm had been lucky to find two men of such calibre who could work well together, because their sales not only brought added revenue but considerable publicity. Sotheby's as yet did not hold wine sales.

Another innovation in October was a sale of models. This was purely Patrick's initiative, as apart from pictures he had a great love for well-made machines, whether they provided power for water-mills or traction engines, or were just models. For a couple of years I'd noticed a brass American horse-drawn fire engine and a railway engine complete with cowcatcher on top of Patrick's bookcase. Not only were the sales of models Patrick's idea but he found a steam fanatic with proper engineering qualifications to act as a consultant for the sales. This was Jonathan Minns, then still very young but who later was the inspiration behind the British Engineerium, outside Brighton, and since then of many other museums demonstrating Britain's industrial heritage. To get publicity before the first sale we persuaded Jonathan to drive a steam traction engine round the block very early one morning before there was any traffic. It was a splendid sight and great fun – Richard Walter's children sat on the carts the engine was pulling.

Frank Davis, that doyen of saleroom correspondents who was still working for *The Times* then, described the first sale in his inimitable style:

> The original James Christie who was game to sell anything from a chamber-pot to a tiara would have been enchanted yesterday. The occasion was nostalgic and nicely calculated to rouse the enthusiasm of man and boy, for the chief items were scale models of steam locomotives . . . The youngest person present was about six years old, and the oldest about 80 years young.

The American fire engine made 2,800 gns ($8,232).

Ever since the middle of the summer Peter and Patrick had been writing to private collectors and directors of museums all over the world asking them if they would lend certain pictures or drawings for our Bicentenary Exhibition. The response was tremendous and included Velazquez's *Portrait of Juan de Pareja*, the property of the Earl of Radnor but once, as we know, in Sir William Hamilton's collection; Albrecht Altdorfer's masterpiece *Christ Taking Leave of His Mother*; Canaletto's *View of Whitehall*; Constable's *The Young Waltonians*; Stubbs's *Gimcrack* and Degas's *L'Absinthe*. Altogether there were sixty paintings and drawings valued then at £5 million.

The design and mounting of the exhibition was the work of John Bruckland, a portly and genial architect/designer who had been responsible for mounting the Ageless Diamond Exhibition. Poster-size photostats of the title pages of historic sales of every kind formed an impressive introduction at the top of the stairs above the entrance to the anteroom. Immediately inside was Gainsborough's *Portrait of James Christie* which Mr Paul Getty had kindly loaned to us from his museum at Malibu, California. On each side of the portrait were shelves of bound catalogues demonstrating 200 years of fine art sales, something which no other firm of auctioneers in Britain could do. Round the walls of the anteroom were serried columns of captioned photographs in attractive dark green mounts. It was a staggering display and to a certain extent charted the changes of taste over two centuries, as each caption had the price which the picture had fetched, some of them on more than one occasion. There were sections of photographs of pictures by particularly famous artists that Christie's had sold – I think for instance there were at least twenty Rembrandts – which in many cases had formed the basis of museums' collections all over the world. The success of the exhibition was such that in slightly less than three weeks 15,439 people came to see it and £3,000 was raised for the National Art Collections Fund. I need hardly say that in the Press Office the maximum effort had gone into promoting not only the exhibition but the Bicentenary generally as from October, and it rightly received tremendous publicity in newspapers and magazines all over the world.

Before leaving the Bicentenary Exhibition, perhaps this is an appropriate moment to explain what had happened to Gainsborough's *Portrait of James Christie*. In the 1920s it was the property of James Archibald Christie, the founder's great-great-grandson, but he had nothing to do with the firm. In 1927 he decided to sell the portrait, and the trade very naturally made it known that if the firm was going to bid they would hold back. But the portrait had to be treated like any other property and a consortium of dealers, Agnew's, Colnaghi's and Knoedler's, bought it for 7,200 gns.

When the economic crash of 1929 came, the bottom fell out of the art market. Even such long-established dealers as Agnew's would have been in desperate straits if they had not owned the freehold of their premises. There can be no better illustration of the market conditions than that the dealers who had bought the Gainsborough portrait of James Christie found it impossible to sell it in spite of its being exhibited by each of them at various times. It was not in fact until 1938 that the picture was sold, Mr Paul Getty snapping it up for $26,500 (£5,419 at the dollar rate of $4.89 to the pound); this meant that the dealers took a substantial loss. There was no question of Christie's partners buying back the portrait after the auction because the price of 7,200 gns (£7,560) was equivalent to £177,419 according to the Retail Price Index in 1988; far beyond the partners' pockets. In 1938, even though it was a good year – the firm had been favoured with quite a number of good collections from America in the mid-1930s – the price that Getty paid, $26,500 or £5,419, was equivalent to £125,499 at the 1987 RPI value of the pound. Christie's partners therefore cannot be blamed for letting Getty buy the picture. (I am indebted to Mr Burton Fredericksen, Director, Provenance Index, and Senior Research Curator of The Getty Art History Information Program, and to Mr G. Cawley, Senior Manager (1987) of the St James's branch of Lloyds Bank, and his economic adviser for these statistics. Christie's have had an account with this branch of Lloyds Bank since 1835.)

A leading dealer told me that in 1988 that the price for the Gainsborough portrait would have to be reckoned as around £1 million. During the 1970s attempts were made to buy the portrait from Paul Getty but they were unsuccessful. Burton Fredericksen, who later had talks with Jo about Christie's getting the portrait back, says that Getty was never interested in selling it. He also makes the point that it was the first major painting bought by Getty, and has therefore a special importance for the Getty collection. There are no other English works of such quality in the collection, as far as I know, and I can't help wondering if the Getty Trustees, who are constantly being criticised in the Press, might not be prevailed upon to loan the picture to the National Portrait Gallery on a yearly basis. There have been reports of the possibility of other pictures being loaned, and if the Trustees agreed to the Gainsborough portrait being treated in this way they would win the gratitude of Britain, Christie's and the fine art trade. Early in 1989 I happened to meet Mr John Walsh, Director of the Getty Museum, and raised the matter. Without committing himself, he did not seem unsympathetic to the idea.

It was towards the end of the exhibition that Brian Sewell left. He had given Peter three months' notice in October and had worked it out with commendable diligence, considering the circumstances, doing a valuation of prints and drawings at Chatsworth. His decision did not altogether surprise me. He seldom appeared cheerful and I suspected he suffered stress and frustration working in the picture department, particularly in the early years.

He was a real loss to the firm, as Peter would be the first to admit if he was alive today. There are two versions of why Brian left. One is libellous and untrue and for the benefit of those ex-colleagues who still proclaim it privately I have checked that this is so. More important, Brian set Christie's picture department on a course which led to the much needed specialisation of sales, in spite of the obstacles which were put in his path. Nevertheless he admits that there was a great deal about working at Christie's which he enjoyed.

From the start there was animosity between Patrick and Bill Martin, for whom Brian had a deep respect. Then when Guy was put in charge of the administration of the picture department there was a new form of animosity to contend with – the battle between Guy and Patrick to be the acknowledged head of the department. "We could tell when there had been ructions in the Board Room or with Peter because the door would suddenly be flung open and in would come Guy saying: 'I think you realise that I am head of the picture department and what I say goes.' Yes Guy, we would say and he would take himself off. A few moments later in would come Patrick with his nose in the air saying, 'I hope you all realise that it is I who am head of the picture department.' For a time it was funny, but it eventually became an impossible situation."

That, however, was only half the story. Brian maintains, and I think he is right, that if the Board had earlier trusted those of their younger staff who obviously had talent and had given them at least some titular authority – as has been the case for many years now – recovery would have come much sooner. This is what Peter Wilson had done with his bright young men like Peregrine Pollen, Marcus Linell, Howard Ricketts and others. Brian went to the USA three times a year as from 1963. "I lost Old Master drawing after Old Master drawing because I didn't have the authority to clinch a deal. On one occasion I saw Robert Lehmann [Robert Lehmann was one of the great art authorities in New York and also a benefactor to the Metropolitan Museum] and he said, 'If Christie's can't be bothered to send me a director I'll go elsewhere.' I told Peter, and he was far more enlightened than anyone in the picture department, that I must be given some authority to take decisions."

I asked Brian what had made him finally decide to leave. He said that by 1966 Patrick had become an "incubus" (it is typical of him to use a word that made me reach for my dictionary) and that he could not contend with it any longer. The row over the identification of the Rubens modello can't have helped the relationship. Brian had been to Peter to explain the clash of temperaments. Even though he had his own department of prints and drawings it came under the general heading of the picture department; he had no autonomy – the Modern picture department had only that year been given theirs. "Patrick would come into my warehouse and suggest I reshaped a catalogue just in order to assert that he was technically head of the picture department." Brian eventually found this unacceptable so he went to Peter and said, "Every time I have been offered another job in the last eight years or so you have talked me out of accepting it on the grounds that I was destined to become a director. That it was inevitable. Now is the time I have to invoke your promise."

Peter told him to go away on holiday and to take as long as he liked. When Brian returned he went to Peter and said, "I'm back." Peter replied, "Give me three days to speak to the others." When the time was up Peter summoned Brian and said that he was afraid the answer was "No. It's Patrick." As a result Brian gave three months' notice. During that time Peter wined and dined him in an effort to persuade him to stay. "Even on my last day Peter came into my office and said, 'You can still change your mind; you don't have to go.'" However, Brian's mind was made up. An unhappy story and some may say one that need not be told, but it is very relevant to the slow development of Christie's picture department into the efficient one it is today with many sub-divisions, each one responsible for their own sales.

It suggests also that in spite of his Courtauld training Brian's face didn't fit which says a great deal about what the majority of Christie's Board thought most important. In some respects Brian did not have the Christie ethos. That is not a criticism but just a fact. He was yet another of a number of talented men and women who for various reasons found the King Street climate not to their liking. Their departure underlines the basic feature of any modern art saleroom. All such places contain a veritable fruit salad of personalities, each of which has varying degrees of sensitivity. These psychological facts have to be taken into consideration by top management.

10

Not "Just Gentlemen . . ."

By this time, if there were any justice in this world, Sotheby's would have ceased to imply to all and sundry that Christie's were just gentlemen trying to be auctioneers – a phrase that was part of the mythology of the art world as early as 1958 and still in use today. It was a period not only of successful sales at King Street, but also of foreign expansion. First, early in February 1967 Christie's Swiss company was formally incorporated under Anthony du Boulay, Michael Clayton and Dr Geza von Hapsburg. Geza had a doctorate in fine art, having studied at Freiburg University; more important, perhaps, he was the great-great-grandson of the Emperor Franz Joseph of Austria, a grandson of the last King of Saxony, Augustus III, and knew half the uncrowned kings and queens of Europe who were languishing in Portugal and elsewhere.

In New York Christie's found that they had outgrown the East 57th Street office originally set up by Bob Leylan, and moved nearer the action. The new location was 867 Madison Avenue, just down the road from Parke-Bernet and known to older New Yorkers as the Rhinelander Waldo mansion. Here John Richardson and Charlie Allsopp established themselves and were made directors of Christie, Manson and Woods (USA).

An even better example of willingness to break new ground was the firm's efforts to get business from the Soviet Union. These came to fruition in March with the sale of an Imperial Russian banqueting service made in St Petersburg about 1830 for Tzar Nicholas I. The sale was the direct result of discussions during the previous two years with Novoexport, the Soviet organisation responsible for the import and export of works of art, and a visit by Peter as a member of a London Chamber of Commerce trade delegation led by Lord Erroll.

The official discussions began, I think, in 1965 after Guy had heard from a friend of his, John Young, who was no stranger to doing business with the Russians, that they were short of foreign currency and were thinking of selling some of their huge surplus of works of art. John introduced Guy to Jimmy Scott who was then chairman of the Anglo-Soviet Trade Council. It was from him that Christie's learned that they should approach Novoexport, and he also agreed to help smooth the way.

Novoexport is based at 32 Highgate West Hill. Apart from trade in works of art, books, and every form of industrial machinery the address is well known to be a base for espionage but that was no business of Christie's. Letters were written, contacts were made and discussions held. The Russians naturally knew nothing about auctions, the advantages of which were explained to them and which they were invited to witness. The three most important officials were frequent guests at Board Room lunches and whether or not it was because of the whisky – they refused to touch the Stolichnaya vodka which had been specially put on ice – they always appeared friendly. Peter, Patrick and I could at least talk to them a little about their country as in 1963 we had been with our wives on Pauline Vogelpoel's first Contemporary Art Society trip to Russia. (Pauline is no longer Organising Secretary of the CAS having left in 1982 to live in Berne with her husband after twenty-eight years' tireless work, which was recognised by her being made an MBE.)

I can't help digressing a moment to illustrate the flashes of wit Patrick was capable of and which endeared him to his friends and colleagues and made one forget his bouts of ill-temper and unreasonableness. We had arrived at the famous mid-fourteenth-century monastery of Zagorsk, approximately sixty miles north-east of Moscow. It was a wonderful Indian summer day with a cloudless blue sky. It also happened to be an Orthodox Church feast day – Zagorsk being one of the few monasteries authorised to train priests even if in very small numbers. Peasants were climbing the steps leading to the open doors of the great church, its gold onion dome shining in the sun and the altar just inside bright with candles lighting up the icons. Each peasant kissed the altar, which was then wiped with a none too clean rag, and was given a tiny loaf of "holy bread" ("prosphera" as the Russians call it). Seating themselves on the steps of the church the peasants ate their loaves in the sun. Crumbs dropped on to the stone and pigeons began to circle. A gentle breeze scattered the crumbs which brought the pigeons down to peck at them. I told Patrick that he must take a photo but to wait till the pigeons got up and were circling round the golden onion dome. "Well, go on," Patrick said without a flicker of a smile, "you're the pigeon-raising officer (PRO)."

The only person who was unhappy about our courting the Russians was Count Alexis Bobrinskoy, a great-great-grandson of Catherine the Great. Alexis was commissioned by the last Tzar into the Irkutsk Hussars and fought all through the First World War against the Germans and then the Bolsheviks. After the Revolution he escaped to England. Alexis had been brought up surrounded by works of art, as his father had been President of the Imperial Archaeological Commission for thirty-two years. He inevitably found his way to Christie's and no doubt Sotheby's, and not only to sell some of the few things he had managed to bring with him when he fled from Russia. He had a fat cherubic face and was utterly charming, so it wasn't surprising that Peter added him to his band of émigré recruits in the late 1950s to help catalogue Russian works of art; needless to say it was on a most informal basis and he was paid an absolute pittance. To eke out a living he managed to get bit parts as an actor such as being an engine driver in an Ingrid Bergman film. He lived with his third wife, the Countess Olga, in a somewhat cramped flat, decorated with icons and portraits of Peter the Great and other Tzars, in the North End Road.

Alexis had not only been introduced to Russian works of art of every kind at an early age; he had actually discovered what for years has been one of the prize exhibits in the Gold Chamber of the Hermitage. In 1906 when he was only thirteen he accompanied his father to the vast plains of the Ukraine, where an archaeological team had discovered a barrow which was believed to have been built over the tomb of some Scythian chieftain. In those days it was a long and uncomfortable train journey, which ended in a horseback ride out to the barrow set in uninhabited country.

Work began next morning. The archaeological team led by his father worked all day and were rewarded for their efforts by unearthing the skeleton of the king himself with golden ornaments and swords beside him, while golden garment plaques were sewn to his cloak. Having emptied the tomb of all its treasures, Alexis's father and the team decided to call it a day and have a meal. Alexis, however, was so excited by the day's events that he stayed on the site and started probing the bottom of the grave with the trowel he had been given. Suddenly his trowel struck something solid; he gently scooped the earth away until he saw the glint of gold. Plunging his trowel deeper he uncovered a large golden comb. "Father, father," Alexis shouted, "I've found something, I've found something. A comb." His father shouted, "Don't touch it for God's sake, you'll break it." "I can't break it – it's heavy, it's solid gold," Alexis retorted. His father and the team came running over and to their amazement saw that Alexis had unearthed a ceremonial gold comb, eight inches long and six inches wide, with a cameo of fighting warriors across the top. It had been made for a Scythian chief by Greek craftsmen in the fifth–fourth century BC and was in perfect condition.

Alexis naturally was asked to meet the Novoexport officials at one of our Board Room lunches. Halfway through, the senior official said in Russian to Alexis, who had maintained a stony silence, "You should come back some time and pay us a visit." Alexis went white as a sheet and drew his hand across his throat. The official roared with laughter and said, "Oh, don't feel like that. Those days are over."

In spite of the hospitality and endless talk, none of the officials would commit themselves as to whether there was a chance of anything coming for auction. The Russian Ministry of Culture would probably oppose such a thing, we thought, even if the Ministry of Finance said it was essential. Then suddenly early in 1967 Christie's received a cable saying a consignment of porcelain would be arriving shortly by sea; no other details were given. It proved to be the Tzar Nicholas I service totalling 1,742 pieces.

Services such as the one we had been sent were originally used for imperial banquets held at coronations and ecclesiastical and diplomatic occasions; they were also brought out for the banquets held by the Tzars at the commissioning of officer cadets. The latter required huge quantities of porcelain because often as many as 200 officer cadets would sit down at one time. I am indebted to Alexis, who died in 1971, for the details which follow. Each of the "commissioning banquets" was attended by the Tzar who was the only person who could confer a commission. Not surprisingly because of the high spirits of the cadets and the vodka that flowed there were a large number of breakages, which resulted in the need for more services.

The banquets took place in either St Petersburg or Moscow and must have been glittering occasions. There were a variety of designs for the different types of plates in the service we had been sent. The majority, however, had gilt rims or gold grounds and were decorated in red, green and blue with the Imperial Arms of Russia – the double-headed eagle – in the centre or on the rim. The dessert plates had "Nicholas Tzar and Suzerain of all the Russias" inscribed in Cyrillic script round the centre. (Opinions naturally differ, but personally I thought they were appallingly vulgar.) To cater for modern-day requirements the whole service was split up into a number of different sized services and smaller mixed lots.

The Big Room was packed on March 21st not only with dealers and private collectors, such as Sir Isaac Wolfson, who paid 8,000 gns ($22,400) for a large dinner and dessert service, but also with restaurateurs such as Sir Charles Forte who in the end bought a number of lots for the decoration of the Café Royal. There was also an important official from the Ministry of Culture, Moscow, who looked very ill at ease compared with his London colleagues who by then were used to the pre-sale hubbub and TV cameras at the back of the room. The sale could not have gone better, the whole service being sold for £65,751 ($193,308). Virtually every lot had been sold. Typically Peter Wilson, immediately after we had announced the sale, summoned the world's Press and told them that Sotheby's had been invited out to Moscow to advise on a whole series of works of art sales, but as far as I know they never got any.

This was a good start to the year, for even if the Russian service had not made a vast sum of money it had won considerable publicity and showed that Christie's was looking for business from overseas and not just the shires. Many other, more remunerative sales followed of Old Masters, French furniture, silver, and clocks including an amazing Royal Tudor silver-gilt clock-salt which probably graced the table of Henry VIII. Early in July there was the seventh and final sale of the O'Byrne Collection of coins, bringing the total for the series to just over £118,000 ($330,400) – "today it would be over £2 million," Richard Falkiner, who was responsible for the success of the sales, told me.

In 1967 David Bathurst got his wish. The Reverend Theodore Pitcairn said he wanted to sell Monet's *La Terrasse à Sainte Adresse*. The succession of events leading up to David's being instructed demonstrates what it takes to get a great picture for sale. It started on a cold evening early in 1967 at Bryn Athyn where David was staying the weekend with the Pitcairns. David recalls Feodor, the Reverend Theodore's son, suggesting after supper in spite of the weather that they went for a spin on his snow-mobile, a kind of motor-bicycle on skis.

Mrs Pitcairn told her son not to be ridiculous: "David doesn't want to go out in this freezing weather on that machine." David certainly didn't want to, but ever conscious that nothing was beyond the call of duty when it came to getting business and pleasing clients or even those who might influence them, he said, "Yes, sounds a grand idea. Good to get some fresh air." That was the understatement of the year. Feodor and David mounted the snow-mobile and roared off into the forest. "Christ, it's cold. I must be mad," thought David. Unfortunately he didn't notice that Feodor had ducked his head, and consequently he hit an overhanging branch which knocked him off his pillion seat. The bridge of his nose had taken the full impact, and he found himself sitting dazed in the snow with his nose pouring blood. Feodor was naturally very apologetic and drove slowly home where his mother clucked over David and soundly scolded her son. "You might have killed him."

The next day David, his nose heavily bruised and with two black eyes, asked to use the telephone. It just so happened that Theodore Pitcairn's diary was open on his desk and he couldn't help seeing pencilled in "DW" for one day the following week and "PW" for another; obviously Daniel Wildenstein and Peter Wilson. It was evidently time to make a pitch for *La Terrasse*, the picture which initially prompted David to telephone Pitcairn. Long legal discussions followed, but eventually in the early summer there was a decision in Christie's favour.

La Terrasse à Sainte Adresse was painted by Claude Monet in the summer of 1867 when he was in desperate financial straits and had been forced to throw himself on the assistance of his father and aunt. The picture shows Monet's father seated in a cane chair in the garden of the family seaside villa at Sainte Adresse, outside Le Havre. It is a highly colourful picture, with hollyhocks, geraniums and other flowers in full bloom, while the tricolour and another flag fly from two flagpoles with the sea directly in front and the fishing fleet on the horizon.

La Terrasse arrived safely at King Street towards the end of the summer season, but was not to be sold until December 1st. Its prompt arrival was most fortunate; it meant that we could photograph it early and that full-colour advertising space could be booked in the most important art magazines round the world, which was generally impossible because of their six-week deadline. Even more important, our announcement late in September of the sale of the picture prompted CBS, one of the three main American TV networks, to send a team to make a film for *60 Minutes* about London being the "centre of the international art market" – this quickly became the most hackneyed catchphrase in journalism, even if it was a compliment. CBS intended quite rightly to go to both Sotheby's and Christie's, but the longest footage depended on who had the most important and newsworthy picture; for once Sotheby's could not offer anything in the same class as Monet's *La Terrasse*, particularly as it came from America and belonged to Pitcairn. So the team concentrated on Christie's, spending a week going through the vaults and filming the Front Counter service.

They were a tough bunch but very professional and friendly, provided that they received close co-operation. We nearly lost them one afternoon when they were doing a sequence on the silver vaults, with Arthur Grimwade expounding on silver like a river in spate. This was not quite what the chief cameraman had in mind and he said so. Arthur nearly walked out – he did once on BBC's *Going for a Song* – but by chance I had decided to check on how things were going and managed to calm both gentlemen down.

The CBS team said they would return for the actual sale, but wanted a platform at the back of the Big Room from which they could film the bidders in action and the expression on their faces. This meant putting up scaffolding each side and above the door through which all the pictures are brought for sale. It had never been done before and I thought Patrick would protest, but he didn't. The TV film went "coast to coast" and was invaluable publicity as *La Terrasse* sold for 560,000 gns (just over $1.4 million) which for many years was the highest auction price for an Impressionist sold in Europe. The picture was bought by Agnew's on behalf of the Metropolitan Museum, New York, where it is still one of the most popular pictures in that great museum.

Mr Pitcairn "had stopped by", as he told the Press afterwards, for the sale and was photographed with Peter who had taken it. Pitcairn explained how he had bought the picture in 1926: "My wife and I were walking down East 57th Street and saw it in a dealer's window. We bought it in ten minutes for $11,000 [then about £2,263]. I wasn't thinking of investment. We were both struck by its cheerful quality and thought this type of picture would give us a lift. At the time some people thought me rather odd. Monet wasn't too well known in New York." As for Mr Pitcairn, he gave all the proceeds to the Beneficia Foundation as usual.

It was about this time that *The Times* announced a new feature, the Times-Sotheby Index. This was a specious idea cooked up by my cunning opposite number at Sotheby's, Stanley Clark, over lunch with the late George Pulay, then City editor of *The Times*. When the idea was put to Peter Wilson he naturally welcomed it as preaching what was rapidly becoming his gospel – that art was a good form of investment – as well as having tremendous advertising potential for Sotheby's, all for free. Each of the Times-Sotheby Index series of articles would be researched and written by Geraldine Keen, as she was then before her marriage a few years later to the late Frank Norman, who wrote the musical *Fings Ain't Wot They Used t' be*.

The Press, whatever its many detractors may say, played a large part in helping to make London the centre of the international art market and later in promoting the foreign expansion of the two main auction houses. No one journalist had such an impact on the art market from 1967, whether on auction houses, museums or members of the fine art trade, as Geraldine.

When the idea of the Times-Sotheby Index was first mooted, Geraldine was twenty-seven and had just given up a job in the FAO in Rome, "because it was so appallingly corrupt". The offer from *The Times*, for whom she had worked for a short time before going to Rome, to compile an index of art prices – even though she then knew nothing about art – seemed too good to be true. Geraldine had got a Second in Maths at Oxford and then gone to Los Angeles University to do a post-graduate course in statistics.

To start with, Geraldine was on a three-month contract and provided with an office at Sotheby's where she quickly got to know all the experts and also Peter Wilson: "He was one of two geniuses I have met during my life." However, her contract soon changed because *The Times* realised that, although the index aroused considerable controversy if not unpopularity among collectors, dealers and certainly at Christie's, they had hit on a circulation winner. It was a time of rising prices and art auctions made news, so the feature immediately had a following. "The index was syndicated to the *New York Times*, *Connaissance des Arts* and elsewhere," Geraldine told me. "It was the only thing I've ever done which mainline newspapers wanted every month. Whether they should have done is quite a different matter."

The Times-Sotheby Index was a series of articles analysing the prices of works of art at auction, using a base date of 1951. Old Master pictures, Impressionists, twentieth-century contemporary paintings and works of art of every kind were to be subjected to Geraldine's research and calculator. The first index appeared on the front page of the review section of *The Times* one Saturday in November 1967 (not 1969 as has been stated in other books). However, it didn't really get going until 1968, when prices were buoyant and made good reading to financial pundits who saw no reason not to treat art like any other commodity.

As well as considerable controversy among dealers, the index aroused fury at Christie's not only because they disagreed with it in principle, but also because of the vast amount of publicity Sotheby's was getting by association with it. Collectors, dealers and auctioneers protested that works of art were in many ways unique, and that quality, condition and fashion had to be borne in mind; there were also the questions of insurance, what interest might have been gained if the money had been invested differently and the all-important point that works of art cannot be sold as quickly as equities. Generalisations about prices with graphs showing a definite upward trend could therefore be misleading. Thus many thought the index reduced works of art to something like the futures market. Inevitably it increased Peter's fury with *The Times* and gave him an immediate dislike for its author.

To be fair, most of these difficulties in comparing price levels were mentioned by Geraldine and she stressed that the index was compiled by scaling down or up the price paid for a picture (in the case of the first index which featured Impressionists) to an equivalent price for an average example of the artist's work. This involved a complicated mathematical formula and was questionable because the "grading" was handled by a Sotheby's expert and became a subjective opinion. However, as with all forms of qualifications, the reader probably tended to ignore them, I suspect, in favour of the seven graphs, which in the first article showed hard black lines rising steeply from the year 1951 to 1967 for the works of Renoir, Fantin-Latour, Monet, Sisley, Boudin and Pissarro. Another graph compared Impressionist prices with US and UK share prices; UK prices were just over 300 while Impressionists were nudging 900. Other indexes followed featuring Old Master prints, English silver, English glass, and so on. On October 12th, 1968, the index was headlined "The Art Market Booms On", and this was followed by articles on French furniture, twentieth-century contemporary paintings and other subjects into 1969.

When I interviewed her, I suggested to Geraldine that her index couldn't have helped but encourage the concept of art as an investment and that she had obviously changed her mind a few years later. On

Saturday, December 21st, 1974, she wrote a half-page feature for *The Times* which was headlined "Why British Rail may be on the wrong track with its investment in the art market". Geraldine's introduction read: "The time has come to dismember once and for all the idea that art is a safe investment medium." Her final words were: "There are and always will be marvellous opportunities for speculation in the art market . . . But the idea that art is a solid and safe investment medium is a fallacy."

Geraldine was remarkably frank in her reply to my question. "To be honest about it, I came back from Rome to set the index up and had just broken off with a man I thought I might marry, and so I was very much alone and miserable in London when I started work on this." She'd never been near the art market before and was working away on these records, trying to see how possible it was to set them into some statistical order. She used to stay awake through the night worrying about it and trying new ideas. There was one stage when she was beginning to understand the market and its problems and in her heart of hearts she decided that an index was impossible. "Then I thought if I tell *The Times* and Sotheby's that an index is impossible, that will destroy my job, which is the only thing I've got left about me at the moment. And so I decided, and I've always felt slightly guilty about this, that I would bash on and produce something although I was aware that it was not going to be rigorously significant. And it's always seemed very odd that that little cheat that I did opened out a career that has been enormous fun for twenty years. Usually when one cheats, one gets bitten back – retribution comes."

So she didn't ever seriously believe the charts. She felt that to the extent that averaging was possible and in following a trend she had done it as well as it could be done. Since *The Times* weren't trying to do it daily or monthly – it was just a trend over a number of years – they were reasonably significant charts. "On the other hand of course it didn't take into account the loss of interest, insurance and so on and there's no doubt that seeing these charts made everyone think that art was an investment medium."

Peregrine Pollen, who was still in New York, thought it a brilliant PR coup, but quite nonsensical – "meaningless statistics, but every week or fortnight we appeared to be top of the league. It was a major policy mistake to stop it." Other members of Sotheby's disagreed. They regarded the index with suspicion and even contempt for reasons already mentioned. The index folded in 1969 because of its increasing unpopularity among the dealers, and also because the Inland Revenue started using the prices against Sotheby's valuations for probate when clients did not necessarily want the highest figure.

However, worse was to come, or that's the way Christie's quickly saw it, for in April 1969 Geraldine was appointed saleroom correspondent of *The Times*. Few journalists can claim, as she can, to have forced two world famous firms to change their hallowed practices by sheer persistence and strength of mind. I remember our first meeting. I saw this small girl get out of a battered German bubble car, dressed – I hope she will not think me ungallant – rather like one of Augustus John's gipsies, with wisps of hair flying in all directions.

What quickly caused great concern at Sotheby's and even more so at Christie's was Geraldine's statistical approach to sale results. The time-honoured custom, which Fleet Street, to their eternal shame, had accepted for years, was to give knock-down totals of sales, which meant including lots which had been bought in. As an ex-journalist I had been struck by this economy with the truth at the first sale I attended. Guy Hannen was behind me and at the end of the sale he said, "The sale clerk will give you the total for the sale. Get that and the ten top prices and give that to the Press." I queried this by saying, "Surely the clerk's total includes lots which haven't been sold?" A steely look came over Guy's face and he began to pale, which I learned was a bad sign, and he said, "Don't worry about that, Herbert. Just do as I say. That's the way it's always done, here and at Sotheby's."

It's not surprising that Christie's and Sotheby's went into a state of shock when Geraldine challenged this long-established practice and immediately brought a statistical slant to her stories. This aroused the wrath of the two main auction houses and led to attempts by both of them to bend both Geraldine and *The Times* to their view on how sales totals should be reported. Their failure to do so resulted in more heated words in Christie's Board Room than on any other subject during my twenty-six years as a director, and considerable unpleasantness for me personally.

11

Tokyo Here We Come

The year 1967 was one of reconnaisance overseas, first to Australia where regular sales were to be held in Sydney and Melbourne from 1968. Bill Spowers was made responsible for these, which grew in importance. Even more far-sighted – worthy of the sixteenth-century Merchant Adventurers even if somewhat more speculative – was the decision to hold a sale in Japan. It all started with a conversation between Anthony du Boulay and John Harding about what social and cultural changes in Japan's traditional life would result from their huge post-war wealth.

The background to this first British auction in Tokyo might have come straight from an Evelyn Waugh novel. An objective observer could be forgiven if he felt on reading John's curriculum vitae – not that he has ever written one – that he was not quite "Christie material", let alone suitable to represent the firm in what could prove a costly experiment. John's schooling had been far from orthodox in the Christie sense. The son of an Army officer, he had left preparatory school before he was fourteen and joined the Southern Railway (as it still was in 1944), hoping that he could wangle his way on board one of the cross-Channel steamers as he had set his heart on joining the Merchant Navy. His wish was granted sooner than he expected as he was drafted aboard the 12,000-ton converted cattle ship, SS *Biarritz*, which he found was on her way to the Normandy beaches loaded with cardboard coffins. After the war he continued happily in the Merchant Navy for ten years and was studying for his Second Mate's ticket when in 1954 his ship the SS *Lake Michigan* was stranded in Tokyo harbour with engine trouble.

The ship was laid up for several months and John, then acting Second Mate, was often on duty on the gangway preventing the crew smuggling the ship's property ashore, while on the dockside there was an elderly Japanese preventing the unauthorised getting on board. In spite of this somewhat menial task the elderly man was a junior director of a shipping company and told John many things about his country's culture which aroused John's interest. He also introduced him to his family including his daughter, with whom the inevitable liaison developed which later proved of considerable importance to Christie's. One of the first forms of Japanese life to which John was introduced was judo, and in six months he had attained the rank of 1st Dan, a remarkable achievement for a Westerner.

From this he progressed to kendo, or sword-fencing, and this was the beginning of his interest in Japanese swords which in Japan are venerated as much as Old Masters or Impressionists are in the Western world. Those of us who worked with John later were surprised to learn that when given shore leave he would head straight for the museums rather than the bright lights of the Ginza. John's interest in swords led him naturally to Tsuba – sword guards, which are intricately hand-forged and often decorated with silver, gold and other soft metals – as well as to lacquer, sculpture, screens, Buddhist works of art and Japanese porcelain.

He returned to Britain in 1956 and started a business restoring antiques as members of his family had been doing for four generations. He also assiduously visited museums all over the world, making an intensive study of Japanese art. In this way, although something of a rough diamond – especially to many at Christie's when he eventually joined them – John Harding developed an eye and an appreciation of Japanese culture. Indeed, without his almost psychic understanding of the Japanese mentality, Christie's would not have been the first foreign auction house to hold a sale in Tokyo.

In 1966 Anthony du Boulay and Anthony Derham, his assistant, had taken on an ex-Army officer who was supposed to be a Japanese expert. Although he may not have been responsible, a Japanese dagger disappeared from the warehouse. The insurance company was called in and discovered that the ex-Army officer had a prison record for theft, so he had to go. However, before he did so he suggested that Christie's should employ someone called John Harding to whom he had always turned when he was stuck for how a Japanese artefact should be catalogued. Not perhaps the best referee, but in those days there were very few people in England who made any pretence of knowing about Japanese art.

It was in this rather strange way that John was taken on as a consultant in 1966. "I was paid £300 the first year, told to come in every Thursday, and given one shelf in the Chinese warehouse," he recalls. However, before long he was producing sales particularly of Japanese swords which were very successful. One of these included a magnificent thirteenth-century Tachi (blade) made by a famous swordsmith whose name is so revered that a Japanese dealer stood up and bowed when it came up for auction.

Another of John's sales was not so successful; in fact it holds the record for the most unsuccessful sale Christie's have ever held. Nevertheless it had great repercussions. John had persuaded Anthony du Boulay that modern or nineteenth-century Japanese prints would sell well, and he had a collection from South Africa totalling over 200 of them. Today they would sell well, but John was twenty years too early with his idea. The knock-down total was £2,000, of which only £200 was sold. Anthony came to him in near-hysteria, saying Guy wanted an explanation and if John didn't come up with one which would restore some faith in his judgment he'd probably be fired. It was as a result of the disastrous sale that Anthony and John had their talk about Japan the next day. John said that the only way to find out what the Japanese wanted was for him to go to Tokyo. Anthony spoke to Guy, who backed John's proposal and sent him off to reconnoitre Tokyo. His mission was to make sure that the most important dealers in Tokyo knew about Christie's, and that the Western art which it was thought many Japanese would now like as well as their own was available at Christie's. To help him John had taken on Tajima Misuru, whom he had met in London, as permanent representative because of his knowledge of the local market.

John found that Christie's name was virtually unknown in Tokyo and, to make matters worse, that Sotheby's had been asked to hold a sale during British Week in June 1969. When he approached the British Embassy to ask if Christie's could hold one as well, he was told "No" by the Cultural Attaché, Sir John Figgess, who ironically later became director of Christie's Oriental department. It must have been a very trying time for John. Tokyo is a confusing city, the buildings being numbered by the date when they were built rather than in numerical order, so it is difficult to find one's way about; in addition John's Japanese was virtually non-existent.

In desperation he decided to seek out the girlfriend of his seafaring days, and also, if he could find him, the only important dealer he knew, Mr Gintiro Fugishiro of the Osahi Art Company. It was obviously essential for Christie's to hold a sale before Sotheby's if the latter were not to gain a great advantage. The possibility seemed remote because of Tokyo's auction laws. In order to stop stolen property from coming on to the market, the only people the police allowed to hold auctions were dealers registered with them. The dealers are members of clubs, the most important being the Bijutsu Club.

After a long search John found his girlfriend, who offered to act as interpreter. She told him that if Christie's wanted to hold a sale the only way was to combine with the Japanese dealers and the best place to hold it would be the Bijutsu Club. Apart from dealers being the only people allowed to take part in an auction, their role is very different from that in Britain. Big collectors needed a dealer as a front for tax purposes, so that purchases were not made in their name and did not reveal their wealth. If Christie's produced the right works of art, it would be the Bijutsu Club dealers who would be bidding, not so much for themselves but for the big collectors. The logic of her suggestion was indisputable, but to the Board of Christie's it was virtual heresy. Fortunately they didn't know about it until it was a *fait accompli*. I doubt if anyone who had gone through the normal Front Counter training would have dared to take John's initiative.

Not being governed by public-school orthodoxy, John began the most extraordinary series of meetings – each one taking hours and involving innumerable cups of tea – which in the end were not only responsible for the sale taking place but also for its success. Fugishiro confirmed that the only chance of the auction being a success was for Christie's to "join the team", and introduced him to the Bijutsu Club. The club agreed to an auction, provided that Christie's had the approval of the Ministry of International Trade and Industry and the police. A stumbling block arose because the police said the ministry had told them Christie's would have to have the support of the British Embassy. This meant going back to Sir John Figgess.

This was where John pulled a fast one on Sir John, if the truth be told, as he promised him that Christie's would not hold an auction in British Week provided that the Embassy helped the firm when they did hold one. "I let Sir John take it for granted I meant the following year, as he did not think there was time for us to organise a sale before British Week," John told me. "By the time he found out the truth it was too late for him to do anything about it." Having reassured the police about the British Embassy's views, John thought he would have to bribe them to get a licence. His girlfriend disarmed him by saying,

"No, not at all. Just take the Inspector two enormous jars of mixed boiled sweets." Feeling very foolish, John walked into the Bijutsu area police station and plonked the jars of sweets down on the desk. The Inspector did not look in the least surprised and, when he heard what John wanted, said that provided he gave him guarantees that nothing imported had been stolen he could have a licence.

Finally the Bijutsu Club asked for a cable from Peter and Guy confirming that they wanted John to make these arrangements. John had been writing regularly to Guy explaining his plans and progress. I remember Guy showing me one of his letters which described his meetings with little comic drawings. John agrees he had a somewhat warped sense of humour. When his negotiations were going badly, he would sign his letters with a woebegone face, tears pouring down his cheeks; other letters were signed with an upturned mouth and smiling face. Curiously, it did work as a form of communication between Guy and John. Following the Bijutsu Club's letter the Board heard the awful truth that Christie's were for once going to do business through dealers. After much huffing and puffing from Arthur and others, confirmation was sent. Even so, the Japanese dealers could not believe that John was capable of producing a Modigliani and other such works, so Guy had to go out before Christmas 1968 to reassure them of Christie's capabilities.

On his return technical departments – and of course the world in general – were told that it had been decided to hold a sale in Tokyo in conjunction with the Bijutsu Club in May 1969, as if it was the simplest thing in the world, instead of having taken nearly two years to arrange. Every department was whipped into action by Guy to find works of art for sale, an order which was not greeted with enthusiasm by those who could ill afford to dilute their King Street sales. Many dealers were approached who might have had works of art on their hands for some time. Even so, every lot had to be hand-picked for the Japanese market and there were only four months in which to find them. Collectors and dealers had to be convinced about the prices Christie's could get for them in Tokyo, although until they'd been there no one could possibly know. At the same time Christie's promised to pay for the return of all those lots which failed to sell. If they misjudged the interest in Japan the shipping bill for unsold lots could prove expensive.

While John Harding was wheedling his way round the Japanese and British alike there were other important foreign developments during 1968. A Paris office was opened (Sotheby's had opened one the year before) and the Princesse Jeanne-Marie de Broglie appointed as our representative. On the other side of the Atlantic a base was established in Montreal to sell pictures and books of Canadian interest, once again to a certain extent following Sotheby's lead. (They had held their first sale in Toronto the year before.) In New York Jerry Patterson, a well-known bibliophile who had previously been head of Parke-Bernet's book department, joined John Richardson and Charlie as a director of Christie's New York. In Geneva the first sale was held at the luxurious Hôtel Richemond where all Christie's sales have been held since. It was of continental porcelain, mainly Meissen, which had come by descent from Augustus the Strong of Saxony. The announcement of the sale aroused a considerable amount of opposition from the Geneva dealers and they even threatened to boycott the sale. However, Dr Andreina Torre, probably the most important porcelain dealer in Switzerland, operating from Zürich, told them in so many words, "Don't be so childish," and the sale was a great success. At the end of July as usual Christie's announced their sales figures for the season – "world-wide" for the first time – which were just over £10 million net ($24 million), an increase of 45 per cent; but Sotheby's were still a long way ahead. The knock-down totals were £11.7 million compared with £30 million for Sotheby Parke-Bernet, which naturally included a large contribution by Parke-Bernet. It was vitally important for Christie's, therefore, that the sales in Geneva and elsewhere were not only successful but increased in number.

The year 1969 was dubbed "Christie's International Year". That was Guy's idea and a good one, because in addition to the Tokyo sale which was to be held late in May, there was Christie's first sale in Montreal, further sales in Sydney and Melbourne and, most important of all, Christie's first jewellery sale in Geneva. Preparations were also made to hold sales in Rome.

The first few months of the year were spent cataloguing for the Tokyo sale. The response from both dealers and collectors had been much better than expected. Altogether over two tons of works of art ranging from Impressionist and Victorian paintings, Greek and Persian pottery to Oriental porcelain and English arms and armour were packed in a container, insured for £600,000 ($1.4 million) and flown across Canada to Los Angeles where they were shipped to Tokyo.

The "manuscripts" (descriptions of each lot written by the respective expert) for the sale had been sent weeks before to Nagoya, a provincial town a hundred miles south of Tokyo, where the catalogue was to be printed under the guidance of John Harding and Taji. Neither of them had ever edited, let alone designed, a hardbacked 256-page catalogue with colour illustrations or been involved with the catalogue manuscripts of paintings. Guy had given them strict instructions: "The catalogue has got to be in Christie's usual style – not a Japanese version." Then by coincidence I had the opportunity to contribute in a small way to the correct look of the catalogue. Just before John and Taji were due to start work on it, Michael Green, our shipping manager, came to me with a free ticket from Sabena Airlines which had just been granted routing facilities. It had to be given to a director, and as I had to liaise with the shipping manager over flight arrangements for catalogues he brought it to me. On my arrival in Tokyo, jet-lagged and generally exhausted after the long flight over the Pole, John Harding whisked me off on the 100 m.p.h. Silver Bullet train to Nagoya. I had hoped after a good sleep to go to Kyoto and generally see the sights but there was no time.

John said that perhaps I could give him and Taji a hand correcting the proofs. "We're OK on the Oriental side, but you probably know more about pictures." For the next week John, Taji and I sat opposite the Japanese printing team, who bowed every time I pointed out a printing mistake. John would then give me a kick which meant, "For God's sake don't lose your temper even if it is the third time they've done it, because of Japanese susceptibilities to loss of face." For instance, the word "inkeeper" kept appearing, because the Japanese couldn't understand that "innkeeper" had two "n"s. We ate – only chopsticks were provided – in the next room where the Japanese slept each night on the floor on "tatamis", or rush mats.

After six days John and I signed the corrected proofs and they were sent off to the printer. I returned to London without going to Kyoto. Some weeks afterwards Peter, Guy and others flew out for the sale. The catalogue had been printed on time in both Japanese and English, with a red hardbacked cover bearing the title of the sale and Christie's medallion in gold leaf, and the same in Japanese on the back. Considering there are 2,200 characters to the Japanese alphabet, the catalogue was quite an achievement as there weren't any complaints of mistakes from the Japanese as far as I know. Guy was, I gather, well satisfied.

Mr Keizo Mitani, chairman of the Tokyo Art Dealers Association, took the first session of Oriental works of art and arms and armour, each lot being announced in Japanese and English. Peter took the evening session of paintings, the first auction he had ever taken in his socks – it is the custom in Japan to take off your shoes on entering a building. Both sessions were an unqualified success from the vendors' point of view. The prices for many nineteenth-century narrative and landscape paintings by comparatively modest artists were higher than those which could be expected in London. This brought smiles to the faces of those dealers who had consigned them and had come to listen to the telephone link-up with Tokyo in Guy's room in King Street. The interest in Impressionists was considerable, Modigliani's *Portrait of a Young Farmer*, which had been sent for sale from America, making Yen 51 million (£59,574), compared with the equivalent of £22,320 when sold at Parke-Bernet five years before. Even more surprising was the Yen 29 million (£33,875) paid for Renoir's portrait of *Madame Henriot*, a rather large middle-aged lady, which had fetched only £5,500 in 1962. The sale totalled Yen 695 million (£812,652), all in all a very satisfactory operation which, even if it did not yield a great profit because of all the costs involved, brought Christie's to the attention of the Japanese and showed the world that the firm had considerable enterprise. The *Guardian* put it succinctly in the headline of its story on the sale: "Christie's Takes Japanese Market by Storm".

Earlier in the month there had been the all-important first jewellery sale in Geneva. This included forty-six lots belonging to the late Nina Dyer, an ex-model who had been married first to Baron Hans Heinrich Thyssen-Bornemisza and more recently to Prince Sadruddin Khan. Guy had had a big hand in getting the sale. It was a sad but not unusual story. In spite of the wealth of her husbands neither marriage proved happy nor lasted very long and she was only thirty-five when she committed suicide. Her husbands had, however, lavished superb jewellery upon her. It was just the type of sale Christie's needed to get the Geneva base off the ground because it attracted not only dealers from all over Europe, the Far East and America but also *le beau monde* who enjoyed the fact that it had been made a black-tie occasion.

It was by far the most important jewellery sale for which Albert Middlemiss, previously of Cartier's and before that Garrard's, had ever been responsible. He produced a hardback catalogue in three languages and with many colour illustrations. The Nina Dyer jewellery had to be collected by Guy and Albert from a Paris bank and then taken to Geneva. Helping Albert was François Curiel, the son of a Parisian jeweller, who had just joined him as an assistant.

When everyone was seated satisfactorily, Peter mounted the rostrum, very debonair with his white hair flowing back in a natural wave. He took the sale in French (a practice which after a few years was stopped as it could lead to "franglais" problems), enjoying the glamour of the occasion and the prices which were way above expectations, totalling in all Sfr. 12.7 million (£1.2 million) of which Nina Dyer's jewellery accounted for nearly half. The previous record for a jewellery sale had been £596,000 in 1966. The top price was Sfr. 1.1 million (£111,947) for a 32.07 carat emerald cut diamond ring by Harry Winston, the New York dealer, which was bought back by him. It had been given to Nina by Prince Sadruddin Khan. The 16.38 carat emerald given to Nina by Baron Thyssen as an engagement ring went to Van Cleef once again for Sfr. 280,000 (£23,369). Then there were her famous sapphire and diamond panther jewels, a parure by Cartier, the five pieces going for Sfr. 203,000 (£19,749).

The success of this first jewellery sale in Geneva was almost as important for Christie's as the Goldschmidt sale was for Sotheby's. The significance of the sale was not purely its financial success, but proof that Christie's strategy in establishing themselves in Geneva had been correct so far as Europe was concerned. None of the pieces could have been sold in London because they would have incurred duty and purchase tax on being imported into the country – only unmounted stones and jewellery over a hundred years old can be imported into Britain free of tax. The success of the Dyer sale was not lost on many people in the highest tax bracket in London. Jewellery could be transported easily and the Swiss banking system was the most confidential in the world. For once Sotheby's were unable to compete, as they had opened an office in Zürich only that year.

Many contributed towards the success of Christie's Geneva but it was undoubtedly Hans Nadelhoffer, the firm's jewellery expert, who was responsible for attracting not only more sales of the quality of Nina Dyer's property, but works of art of all kinds. Christie's had been very lucky to get Hans. From 1966 to 1968 he had been working for Edouard Gubelin, the most respected jeweller in Switzerland, who had a private laboratory with all the latest machines for telling the quality of gemstones. Hans's resulting knowledge of jewellery and his professional approach soon impressed collectors and dealers all over the world. His cataloguing could not be faulted and prior to each sale the jewellery was beautifully presented on blue velvet "plateaux" and mounts. After a few years dealers from all over the world came to trust him regarding the quality of a stone, and would know that if they phoned him he would not exaggerate its fineness for the sake of Christie's. Geza von Hapsburg obtained vast amounts of works of art from "members of royal houses" including many by Fabergé, while others in the Geneva office or at King Street were responsible for getting silver, porcelain, gold boxes, art nouveau and art deco and also wine; but there is no doubt that it was Hans's jewellery sales which gave Christie's Geneva its prestige. It was a great sadness to his friends when he died in 1988.

During its first ten years Christie's Geneva sold Sfr. 430 million (over £130 million) worth of jewellery. This is a measure of the financial importance of those sales to the main firm and one of the reasons why Christie's was able to go public in 1973, long before Sotheby's, for all the latter's apparent success. Selling some of the lots demanded strong nerves and really skilled auctioneering because the reserve prices in many cases were enormous. The sales did not always go smoothly. Seeing the bids at the back of the long ballroom was difficult, so, to start with, "tennis umpire ladders" were used. Anthony du Boulay used to perch himself on one halfway down the room to indicate bids at the back, sometimes I'm afraid creating confusion rather than helping to stop it because he got so excited. There were some real slanging matches with Peter getting very red in the face.

The trouble was often sparked off by Roger Varenne, the most powerful dealer in Geneva. To begin with, he insisted on sitting towards the back surrounded by his cronies. This proved disastrous as he would often bid looking down at his catalogue and just lifting a hand, which made it impossible for the auctioneer to see him. Varenne is no longer with us; apart from being very conscious of his importance as a dealer, he suffered from diabetes which may have been responsible for his aggressive attitude and apparent desire to make trouble. I remember one sale when Guy physically had to hold him down, because he kept getting up and arguing with Peter. In the end Christie's made him and his friends sit in the second row and he was told to bid through François Curiel. There were many undignified scenes which were extremely unpleasant to witness, but they must have been even worse for Peter. Fortunately the TV cameras were never present during these ugly moments.

When we first began to hold sales in Geneva it was all very relaxed because there were only two or three a week; so much so that Peter, who enjoyed getting away from the frustrations and back-biting of

King Street, often accompanied by Paddy, his wife, would suggest going to the Griffin, one of the local nightclubs, for an hour or two's dancing and drinking. The whole Christie's team was invited, not just directors. However, within a few years there were so many sales and the expenses of mounting them were so great that such frivolity ceased. It was hard work, but there was the satisfaction of achieving success by working together. Most of the team were young, but were still exhausted at the end of the week. The exception was Dina Lieven, who although nearly seventy somehow managed to stand behind the jewellery display cases all day, discussing the lots in four languages if necessary and being utterly charming to everyone. She was marvellous.

Everyone from directors to porters snatched their meals in the hotel's canteen, a practice which added to the general feeling of a united effort and enabled everyone to keep in touch with the latest problem. To get to the canteen Christie's staff had to go through the kitchens and occasionally their electrically operated sliding doors would produce Marx-Brothers-type situations. Colleagues deep in conversation would step on the rubber patch in the floor outside the kitchens which activated the doors and walk in, only to come face to face with a waiter carrying a huge tray of boeuf en croûte or lobster Thermidor.

Just inside the doors also were the switches for the TV lights which were particularly unpopular with Peter in Geneva because the ceiling was low. Geneva sales were often of international interest which meant that Swiss, French and Italian TV and in particular Juliane Stephan, the Robin Day of West German TV, were only too delighted to cover our sales as a change from the dreary routine at the Palais des Nations; so, in spite of the growls from Peter and entreaties from my colleagues on his behalf, the lights had to be on for the top lots. (Varenne and his gang were by then sitting in the second row and caused no trouble.)

Back in London, one of Geraldine's first reports as *The Times*'s saleroom correspondent brought nothing but pleasure. It referred to a Rembrandt *Self-Portrait* and a long-lost Tiepolo ceiling painting, "the most important old paintings to reach a London auction room for several years". This made the Old Master sale of June 27th of particular interest. Christie's had already sold the self-portrait twice, once in 1879 when it fetched 1,250 gns and again in 1884 when it made 1,800 gns. In June 1969, Mr Norton Simon bought it through a dealer and without "uproar" for 460,000 gns ($1.1 million). The price was in line with the picture department's expectations, although art experts would probably say that the *Self-Portrait* was a greater work than *Titus*. The latter, however, had such appeal that it attracted more than one millionaire, as well as museums, to bid much more for it.

It was very nice to have a Rembrandt *Self-Portrait* to sell, but undoubtedly the picture which captured the public's interest was the ceiling painting by Giovanni Battista Tiepolo. The subject was a magnificent *Allegory of Venus Entrusting Eros to Chronos*. The tracking down of this picture was an example of David Carritt's genius, not only in art-historical knowledge, but in ferreting out long-lost works with detective-like research. The existence of the picture and four small grisailles must have been well known at the turn of the century when they decorated the drawing-room of Bute House, the residence of Henri Louis Bischoffsheim, at 75 South Audley Street, Mayfair. Their importance must have been overlooked when, on the death of Mr Bischoffsheim's widow in 1922, the mansion was acquired by the Egyptian Government as their embassy.

Between 1922 and 1964 the Tiepolos must have been seen frequently by visitors to the United Arab Republic embassy (as it had become after the fall of Farouk), and one would have thought that their presence would have been remarked upon in art circles; but no. Professor Antonio Morassi had published in 1962 a complete catalogue of Tiepolo's paintings which listed the UAR's ones as "London, formerly Bischoffsheim Collection" and referred to an article of 1876 in which they were described as forming part of a ceiling of "one of the grandest houses in Mayfair, London, present whereabouts unknown". David was browsing through this book one day and read this small entry. His sister Christian told me that he kept on referring to it when she was driving him home to his Mount Street flat after parties. It's surprising really that no one guessed their whereabouts before David did, because there are not that many houses capable of accommodating a ceiling painting which measured 115 ins by 75 ins. It just showed that David read unceasingly and remembered everything. I can imagine the gleam in his eye when, on turning to the Post Office directory, he saw "United Arab Republic Embassy" at the previous Bischoffsheim address. His request to the Cultural Attaché asking if he could have a look at the works of art in the embassy was immediately granted, and there the great Tiepolo was found together with the four smaller ones. That was in 1964.

Late in March 1969, after consultation with Cairo, the Ambassador decided that the pictures not only represented a great fire risk, as they could not be moved quickly, but they were also irrelevant to UAR art collections. Accordingly Christie's were instructed to sell the pictures; the proceeds would be used to help finance the conservation of the temples in Egypt. The first I knew about the sale was when Peter rang me one weekend at our Chichester harbourside cottage – I was in the bath at the time – and told me he was off to America and he wanted me to take charge of the removal of the paintings from the embassy to Christie's. "And don't delay – the picture's got to be photographed in colour and the printer's screaming for the catalogue" were his last words.

It was easier said than done. The main painting was in a huge gilt frame which was screwed into the ceiling. We got a scaffolding up quickly and a team stood by to take it down. They stood by for two days because of the delay getting it insured from the ceiling to the floor; the underwriters we'd been told to go to were friends of Peter's – the usual hopeless "old pals" act. In desperation I went to Doug Ralphs, who had taken over as company secretary on the death of Roy Davidge, and he got cover from the firm Christie's now use all the time.

We held a full-scale Press conference to announce the sale with the Ambassador present, and David spoke with the ease of both an art historian and an ex-journalist. When it came up for sale the Tiepolo was bought by the National Gallery, who till then had no important work by Gian Battista, for 390,000 gns ($982,000), the highest price to date ever paid for an eighteenth-century master. And what about the glaring emptiness in the UAR's main reception room ceiling? The Ambassador discovered, I do not know how, Mr John Lewis, an artist of Loughton, Essex. Prior to the sale he asked him to paint a copy for £350. Having seen the original Tiepolo and taken its dimensions, he painted a copy with the huge canvas in a stretcher standing vertically in between the banisters of his small house, which was a remarkable achievement.

The season ended with a world-wide sold total of £11.1 million – £1 million up on the previous year – but Sotheby's was still far ahead if their knock-down total was anything to go by, £40.3 million compared with our £15.2 million. In spite of this, the autumn of 1969 showed in no uncertain terms that Christie's picture department had won back the confidence of collectors, the Old Master sale held before Christmas having yet another Rembrandt; this time a *Portrait of an Old Man* which was bought by Edward Speelman for 300,000 gns

($756,000). It had been sold on behalf of Sir Brian Mountain whose father, Sir Edward, had bought it in 1937 for 7,000 gns – "a sum considered so remarkable that his final bid was greeted with a spontaneous outburst of applause". However, a far more significant price in the same sale was the 260,000 gns ($655,200) paid by Norton Simon for *The Flight into Egypt* by Jacopo da Bassano. Hitherto the highest prices had been commanded only by the biggest names, and Bassano, though a respected figure in late Renaissance painting in Venice, had never before excited much interest in the saleroom. The huge price paid by Norton Simon underlined a growing trend that works of impeccable beauty, preservation and authenticity did not have to be by the biggest names such as Rubens, Rembrandt and Titian to fetch high prices.

12

"Two Million Two Hundred Thousand Guineas. Any More?"

The year 1970 was even more "international" than 1969, and the Press coined the phrase "Have Gavel Will Travel". It wasn't an exaggeration, for in the first few months of the year there were nine sales in Montreal, one in Ottawa, four in Melbourne, one in Tokyo and four in Geneva. During the whole 1969–70 season there were over 400 flights by directors and technical staff to produce these sales which totalled over £4.6 million ($11.1 million), compared with £2 million ($5.2 million) in 1968–9. The total for the whole season for the first time showed an improvement compared with Sotheby's, so morale at King Street was high. Christie's world-wide knock-down total till the end of July was £20 million, a 31 per cent increase, while Sotheby's London total was £25.4 million, an increase of only £200,000. Sotheby's New York sales amounted in theory to another £20 million, but during 1969 Wall Street suffered a major setback which naturally affected art prices and in particular Impressionists. For ten years the prices for these works had increased the most because they were the natural buy for the American nouveau riche, apart from the real collectors; the failure also of twentieth-century contemporary art at SPB was particularly damaging to those dealers specialising in such works, as no auction house so far had held such sales.

SPB may have had its problems as a result of the Wall Street collapse in prices, but Sotheby's London was in financial difficulties also. As in New York there were signs that a period of inflation was round the corner; this was aggravated by the "special arrangements" which Peter Wilson had been providing in order to get collections of Impressionists. Many Sotheby directors were shocked by Wilson's deviousness, not just because a large number of the pictures were now being bought in but because they didn't agree with his methods of doing business.

Christie's occasionally discussed the question of guaranteeing. I remember in particular David Bathurst arguing that it was impossible to get business from American collectors or their trustees – the Edward G. Robinson collection was his target at the time – without making provision for special terms and I think he was quite right; but the Board never agreed to it so far as I can remember, and would certainly never even have considered the wheeler-dealing Wilson loved so much. This difference between the styles of the two firms may well have been responsible for Christie's not going through the agonies which befell Sotheby's years later. However, Christie's did feel, like Sotheby's, that the sale totals given to the Press should be the knock-down totals – that is, they should include those lots bought in – and that it was in the vendors' interests that the printed price lists should not reveal what was bought in, because it made resale afterwards more difficult and could devalue the work of art.

Geraldine's interest, some might say fixation, about the subject arose because when she was doing the Times-Sotheby Index she became conscious that there were two definite types of price. For instance, the Sotheby expert would say, "Oh, that's a crazy price, that was unsold, you can't use that." "So that my first controversial thing," she told me in 1988, "was hitting at the administration and structure of the market." Her feature, headlined "Secrecy in the London Auction Houses", was of course highly controversial.

A few weeks earlier the late Chancellor Adenauer's collection had come up for sale, and this naturally aroused a lot of interest. There were thirty-nine pictures in all – most of them by German artists – which used to hang in Adenauer's country house at Rhondorff, near Bonn. They were now being sold on behalf of Mr Heinz Kisters from Switzerland. I remember showing them to Terence Mullaly, the *Daily Telegraph*'s art critic and saleroom correspondent – he knew far more about pictures than any of his colleagues – and he enthused about them. However, when it came to the sale no one was interested and only four pictures were sold.

I think David Carritt had seen them beforehand and had said they were all right. However, unknown to him they may have been hawked around the trade, which is fatal to any auction, or perhaps the trade felt the circumstances in which the collection had been formed might have been suspect. In view of Adenauer's name there was a large international Press turnout which poured into my office and also pursued the owner. The result was so disastrous that there was no disguising the truth, so I came straight out with it and told the Press that only four pictures had been sold. Geraldine immediately piped up, "You aren't being serious, John?" It seemed she did not think I could announce such an appalling result so nonchalantly, but what else was I to do? It was not our standard practice; but the results had been so bad that it was ridiculous not to give them. Moreover her article was illustrated and the caption read, "A portrait attributed to El Greco bought in at Christie's at 40,000 gns in their Adenauer sale; on this occasion Christie's publicly announced that only four out of 36 pictures had been sold." Mr Kisters amazingly was all smiles and when he was interviewed didn't seem all that disappointed.

The failure of the Adenauer sale gave the market an attack of the jitters; but, again, the whole episode underlines the danger of analysing art auction results by pure statistics. The failure of the Adenauer pictures had nothing to do with inflation or even art and was fortunately followed a week later by a sensationally successful Impressionist sale which restored confidence. Two pictures dominated this sale, Seurat's *Les Poseuses (petite version)* and Picasso's *Self-Portrait* which he painted in 1901 when he was only nineteen.

Seurat's *Les Poseuses* was from the collection of Henry P. McIlhenny, the Philadelphia collector. John Richardson had been responsible for getting it for sale. Seurat was working on it from the autumn of 1886 till the spring of 1888. John Russell, for many years now the *New York Times*'s art critic, wrote in our annual *Review* that he thought the picture was one of the three or four most beautiful works of art to come on to the international art market since the war. When it came up for sale the "petite version" was bought by the American dealer Richard Feigen on behalf of Artemis for 410,000 gns ($1,033,000), but I think that Henry McIlhenny had expected more. Artemis was a comparatively new art investment company which had been formed by the late Baron Léon Lambert, of the Banque Lambert, Brussels, and Baron Elie de Rothschild, of Paris. Their original idea was to buy works of art of high quality and lend them to museums and then after sufficient time had elapsed sell them for a profit. For many years, of course, they have been perfectly normal dealers. Sadly at the end of 1970 we lost David Carritt to them. I understand that when Patrick said goodbye to him he said, "I don't know how we're going to get on without you!"

The Picasso *Self-Portrait* was a wonderful picture, and personally I preferred it to the Seurat. Although penniless at the time, Picasso had painted it with all the bravura of a successful painter, his handsome assured head set off by a vermilion lavallière and snowy smock. To make the picture even more convincing, Picasso added the word "Yo" (Spanish for "I") as if to persuade himself and the world that far from eking out a living in a Montparnasse garret, he had actually taken Paris by storm. Despite a show at Vollard's gallery in 1901 and the picture's being No. 1 in the catalogue, Picasso did not prosper. By the winter he was virtually starving – a fact that is reflected in the pathos and self-pity of his next great self-portrait, the picture that ushers in the blue period. Soon fortune smiled on him. Who could be more appropriate than Hugo von Hofmannsthal, the Austrian librettist, to be the buyer of this painting with his first royalties from *Der Rosenkavalier*? On June 30th it was sold on behalf of Mr Michael Zimmer of New York – which demonstrated that the New York team were getting through to private collectors there in spite of SPB – for 140,000 gns ($353,000). The buyer was the New York dealer Spencer Samuels – an example of the London art market bringing in invisible earnings in the form of his commission.

I must mention one other painting in this very good sale, Monet's *Les Bords de la Seine, Argenteuil*, one of his most superb early works. Painted in 1872, it was sold in Paris in 1912 for the equivalent of £1,070 – just about the time when Sir Hugh Lane was regarded as a madman for paying £1,000 for Renoir's *Les Parapluies* (which pathetically the National Gallery refused to hang and which we now share every five years with Dublin). The Monet was bought for the then staggering price of 240,000 gns ($605,000) by Mr Ronald Lyon, a rags-to-riches property tycoon.

All in all it was a good summer for Christie's and not only for picture sales. Arthur Grimwade in the silver department had had as good a season as David Bathurst and sold a number of gold pieces apart from silver. The highlight of his year, though, was a Charles I silver inkstand made in the style of Christian van Vianen. This belonged to an old friend of Peter's, the late Major-General Sir George Burns. After staying with Sir George at his big house near Hatfield one weekend, Peter told Arthur that his host had shown him a silver inkstand of 1639 which he would like to sell. "1639," said Arthur, "I didn't know any were made so early. I must consult my card index." Arthur's card index must be unique. I asked him about it. "My dear boy, in the 1930s there wasn't much to do, so I itemised every piece of important silver we sold back to 1830." Sure enough, in a catalogue of 1893 there was a reference to the inkstand's sale for £446 8s. or 48s. an oz, a large sum in those days. Even in 1893 the inkstand had been described as in the style of van Vianen. It was a remarkable work, almost sculpture-like, being 16 ins wide with two candlesticks and stands in the form of lions' feet. The sides were chased with scenes representing the Muses associated with the pen and elaborate scrollwork. When it came up for sale in July it was bought by Cyril Humphris, the well-known dealer, for £78,000 ($187,000), a tribute to Arthur's enterprise and industry in working out the past history for the catalogue. Indeed, Arthur was universally admired for his scholarship and untiring research work.

The autumn was memorable because of our first sale in Rome which took place only after typical Mafia-like opposition. Harry Ward-Bailey, who had taken over the Italian office after Hans Backer's death, had hired the Villa Miani on Monte Mario, one of the nine hills overlooking Rome. It was to be a two-day sale of Old Masters and nineteenth-century pictures, prints and drawings. From the first announcement there was strenuous opposition from the local auctioneers. Four of them challenged Christie's right to hold an auction in Italy and filed suits with the police to stop them doing so. Harry and Christie's Italian lawyer eventually had to seek the help of the British Embassy in order to get the necessary licence, without which the police would not even allow Christie's inside the villa's grounds. Up till the morning before the view was meant to begin, the licence still had not been granted, even though the lorries with the pictures were outside the gates. It was only in the evening that authorisation was given and the lorries trundled in. Jim Taylor was faced with getting the pictures hung during the night if they were to be ready for the view the next morning. He had brought with him Albert Watts, who is still loyally working for the firm, but otherwise a dozen Italians had been hired for the job. The last time Jim had seen an Italian had been in the Western Desert, so he took great delight in cracking his verbal whip over them; none of them understood English, but they got his message and the pictures were up by early morning.

Besides Harry the Christie team consisted of Patrick who was to take the sale, Willie Mostyn-Owen as linguist, Ray Perman and Richard Walter, my assistant, who took full advantage of his opportunity to erect a Press bar. Just about breakfast time flames and smoke were seen coming from the garden. Who started the fire was never discovered, but it took some time to put it out because the fire brigade's hoses leaked so badly that they resembled a garden sprinkler. After that Christie's were given Carabinieri guards, who took up positions all round the villa armed with submachine-guns, while a helicopter chattered overhead. The sale was a qualified success and those that followed were accepted by Italian auctioneers and dealers without demur. They have since gone from strength to strength, particularly after Christie's moved their office to the Palazzo Lancellotti in the Piazza Navona, although because of the legislation regarding the export of works of art they will never match those held in Geneva. The fact that the first one took place at all said quite a lot for Christie's team – whom the general public might think unable to cope with the obstacles and threats which come their way.

A fortnight later Christie's Geneva had the best series of sales to date – gold boxes, objects of art, a superb collection of Fabergé and some magnificent jewels which were sold in the evening. The next day there were two sessions of continental porcelain, maiolica and faience. The results were not only the best yet, but better than those for years to come because of the quality. However, the view began with an unfortunate incident, in some ways more dramatic than those in Rome. I had sent Richard Walter ahead to handle the Press conference before the view began. He was to work with Monica, Geza's German-born wife. In the early days of the Geneva office Geza had asked me out to lunch with Monica. In those days he was not quite so self-assured as today; he was also very poor for someone who expected to be able to wear a clean shirt every day. Eventually he had plucked up courage and asked if I thought Monica could help with the PR and be paid for doing so. Monica not only spoke English and French well, apart from her own language, but was a bright girl, so I had said it was an excellent idea.

I arrived at the Hôtel Richemond early in the evening and went straight to Room 107 which was always assigned to us as Press Office. I walked into an atmosphere that was charged with drama; there were Geza, Anthony du Boulay, Monica and Richard, the latter two for some reason drying their eyes. Apparently Richard had allowed his egotistical nature and Napoleonic complex to get out of control and when Monica questioned certain Press arrangements, a furious row developed, which ended with Richard reaching up – Monica was several inches taller than him – and shaking her by the throat. Not surprisingly she screamed; Anthony rushed in from the next room – which was en suite – and Geza happened to be passing and recognised his wife's screams. Monica and Richard were separated and apparently both burst into tears. Not knowing what had happened, but realising every eye was on Richard, I suggested to him that we went out and had dinner, over which he told me what had occurred. It seemed that anything could happen at Christie's sales and probably would – which in the coming years proved only too true. However, it did not take long for Geza to be able to afford to change his shirt every day, so Monica ceased her PR activities.

The high peak of 1970, let alone the autumn season, was the sale of Velazquez's *Portrait of Juan de Pareja*, the property of the 8th Earl of Radnor. The picture had been included in the Bicentenary Exhibition but few of us thought it would ever come up for auction. Its importance as a picture was indisputable and it was very unlikely that any other work by Velazquez of equal quality would ever come up for sale. "I happen to know," Hugh Leggatt told me, "that it was at the top of the National Gallery's 'paramount list'" (the secret list of pictures in great houses in Britain which the National Gallery would like to have on its walls).

As mentioned earlier, the Velazquez had been in the collection of Sir William Hamilton until after his return from Italy, when he was forced to sell it at Christie's in 1801. The portrait then went for 39 gns but the buyer's name was not recorded. Ten years later it was acquired by the 2nd Earl of Radnor for £151 14s. 5d. and remained at Longford Castle, the Radnor seat near Salisbury, until 1970.

"Jake" Folkestone, as the 8th Earl is known to his friends, and his Trustees were faced with massive tax bills on gifts the 7th Earl had made in his lifetime, as he had died in 1968 before the lapse of the seven years necessary to obtain exemption from death duties. Christie's advice was sought and Jo Floyd, an old friend, took charge of the discussions, naturally aided by Patrick and also by Christopher Ponter, who had joined the firm in October after twenty years in the Estate Duty Office of the Inland Revenue. For the last five years he had specialised in Estate Duty and Capital Gains Tax so far as they related to works of art – gamekeeper turned poacher, one might say.

Martin Davies, Director of the National Gallery, had not surprisingly made an offer for the picture, but the funds available to the gallery then were not what they are today; however, the offer would of course have been tax-free. And the top rate of tax would heavily reduce the proceeds of any auction. Jo had to convince Lord Radnor and his Trustees that Christie's considered *Juan de Pareja* to be of such quality and art-historical importance that at auction it could exceed all expectations, even allowing for the tax factor. The talk must eventually have got down to what sum Christie's thought it could make. I don't know what price Jo suggested, but the sale of *Titus* may well have been mentioned as an illustration of what Old Masters of great importance could fetch, even though it was a very different kind of picture.

Jo stressed, I suspect, that the importance and desirability of the Velazquez to museums all over the world meant that it could fetch an unheard-of figure; no picture so far had fetched £1 million, but I wouldn't be surprised if that figure was mentioned. Today undoubtedly the interest of museums is world-wide, but in 1970 it basically meant American museums. What the National Gallery had offered was not mentioned, but Christopher was asked to get his calculator out and determine what price allowing for tax the picture would have to sell for to make a certain net sum. Finally it was the case made by Jo, who could be most persuasive and convincing, which won the day and Jake opted for a sale by auction.

Apart from the Velazquez, which was the last lot, it was not a great sale but everyone was there; museum directors from all over America and Britain, dealers from America and Europe as well as Britain and millionaire private collectors who with their wives or friends had come to see the fun. As picture followed picture the suspense among Christie's staff was painful, in spite of the "stiff upper lip" look of Jo standing behind the rostrum. I'd given instructions for the TV lights to come on a few lots earlier, and there was a buzz of excitement and a clicking of cameras as *Pareja* was held up by the porter on the dais on Patrick's left.

Patrick, whatever his innermost thoughts, appeared as cool as a cucumber and started the bidding with a quiet "250,000 gns, 250,000 gns, thank you." He took it up quite slowly – there appeared to be no shortage of bidders including Willie Mostyn-Owen bidding on the telephone for a private collector – till it reached and quickly passed the magical million gns; I remember digging my fingers into Richard Walter's right shoulder with excitement. Hugh Leggatt came in at this moment but did not last long, and the bidding developed into a duel between Geoffrey Agnew and a youngish man in the second row, almost directly below Patrick. Up and up went the bidding till it passed 2 million gns. The man in the second row nodded gently. "2,200,000 gns, 2,200,000 gns – any more?" said Patrick looking at Geoffrey Agnew. "One more, Geoff?" He shook his head. "No? Any more? To you, sir," Patrick said looking down at the man in the second row as if he had been knocking down a 200 gn. picture. Ray Perman sent his assistant round to get his name. I didn't know the man and I don't know whether it was Patrick's one-upmanship to pretend that he didn't know the son of the most powerful picture dealer in the world, Daniel Wildenstein, of Paris; it was his thirty-year-old son Alec, who was vice-president of the New York end of the business, who had bought the Velazquez.

Across the road in Pruniers, which has long since become a Japanese restaurant, was Daniel Wildenstein, Alec's father, waiting for news. I doubt, however, if he was really worried, as he had instructed Alec to buy the picture whatever the price, and being the wealthiest of all dealers he could do so. The Velazquez had fetched £2,310,000 ($5.5 million) and for many years was the most expensive picture sold at auction. For Christie's it was a great day and in particular for Jo because he had been proved right, and he had a happy vendor, who would no doubt spread the gospel regarding the good advice he had been given.

The impact of the sale was so great that the Post Office used an agency photograph showing the painting being sold on huge hoardings on the Underground as part of their promotion of Premium Bonds. Eventually of course the picture moved to the Metropolitan Museum, New York, where Douglas Dillon, the president, described it at its official unveiling the following year as one of the half-dozen most important acquisitions by the museum.

13

The Gap Closes

It had been a successful autumn, but unknown to most of us while we were occupied with the run-up to the Velazquez sale, Jo was already involved in discussions with the Trustees of the late Mrs Anna Thomson Dodge, the car-maker's widow. Mrs Dodge had died aged 103 the previous June, leaving a huge art collection assembled for her by the legendary Lord Duveen and an estate exceeding $100 million (£41.6 million). The Old Masters, French furniture and tapestries, porcelain and silver decorated her mock French château, Rose Terrace, in Grosse Pointe, the suburb which makes life bearable for the Detroit rich. Christie's had been asked for an appraisal – and so obviously had Sotheby Parke-Bernet.

However, before the development of what proved to be an even greater sale than Northwick Park – particularly as it was American – there was the negotiated sale of Rogier van der Weyden's long-lost masterpiece the *Portrait of St Ivo of Chartres* to the National Gallery. This was the last picture which David Carritt discovered as a director of Christie's.

Most of David's discoveries were under strange circumstances, and this was no exception. Lord Dunnally, who had been made Christie's first representative in Ireland, had asked David back in 1968 to see a picture belonging to the late Joan, Lady Baird, an old friend of his, which was in her cottage at Bray beside the Thames. On entering the sitting-room David saw over the mantelpiece the portrait: "I realised it was one of the most beautiful, important and rare Flemish pictures in the world." (It was not, however, the picture that Lord Dunnally had thought worthy of David's attention.)

For two years David researched the picture to establish the authenticity of the portrait of St Ivo of Chartres, sometimes known as "the lawyer of the poor"; the picture had hung for many years unrecognised at Mauldslie Castle, Lanarkshire, and had passed by descent to Lady Baird's husband who had predeceased her. The discovery was important as Rogier van der Weyden (1399–1464) ranks, after Jan van Eyck, as one of the rarest and most important fifteenth-century masters.

The negotiations regarding the picture's value went on for months and proved extremely complex as *St Ivo* was the first major painting to be sold to the nation, as was Lady Baird's wish, where the liability for Estate Duty was governed by the revised provisions of the Finance Act, 1969. Although Jo and Patrick were nominally responsible for the sale it proved to be a first challenge for Christopher Ponter. A gross price of £800,000 was finally agreed upon, but when allowance had been made for Estate Duty and Capital Gains Tax the net cost to the National Gallery was substantially less than £500,000. After months of restoration the National Gallery announced the purchase on March 1st and gave credit to both David and Christie's. However, there was no mention of Christie's in the Press; in those days newspapers seldom bothered about reporting who had been responsible for negotiating the sale. In any case they could argue that the story was stale news as it had been in the *Observer* in February, but with no mention of Christie's, which was very disappointing. Richard Walter had been responsible.

After the sale of the Velazquez I had had to fire Richard, having learned that the Geneva office had refused to have him out there again after the incident with Monica. It was unfortunate as I and many others in Christie's liked him. It was not therefore a pleasant ten minutes in the Board Room for either of us. The next day I rang up Sue Rose and invited her to lunch. For many years Sue had been saleroom correspondent of the *Yorkshire Post* but was then working on the Londoner's Diary column of the *Evening Standard*. When I offered her the job as my assistant she jumped at it, and we worked well together for many years. She naturally had to work out her notice so couldn't join us immediately.

About a month after he was fired, Richard's story regarding David's discovery of *St Ivo*, which was still meant to be confidential, appeared in the *Observer*. I suppose there was a natural temptation to take a swipe at me and Christie's. However, considering he was out of a job when I took him on, as both the *Evening Standard* and the *Daily Mail*, in spite of his journalistic ability, had asked him to leave, he might have thought twice about taking advantage of his position, and at least have mentioned Christie's.

The Gap Closes

For Christopher Ponter, I'm sure it was the beginning of an exhausting but satisfying period of his life, and a lot more interesting than working for the Inland Revenue. It was essential for collectors with works of art of national importance to have some financial strategy for the future, so that their descendants wouldn't be landed with tremendous tax problems. However, many solicitors found themselves out of their depth when it came to the pros and cons of a negotiated sale or one by auction. Christopher, having had a legal education and keeping up to date with the ever-changing tax system, soon won the respect of solicitors. Equally, as the national heritage became more and more a matter of public concern, museum directors found in him someone they could talk to, even though his duty was to the private collector. His quiet but shrewd manner of negotiation, rather than the aggressive way other colleagues tended to talk, won the regard of collector and museum director alike.

Negotiated sales began after the war as a result of the 1956 Finance Act, whereby works of art of a pre-eminent nature could be accepted by the Treasury in lieu of Estate Duty, and allocated to the appropriate national institution, the notional cost being met from the Land Fund. (Hugh Dalton, when Chancellor of the Exchequer, had set up the Land Fund from the sale of surplus war material.) It was recognised that taxation was the major reason for such sales and a quarter of the tax payable was remitted; this came to be known as "the sweetener". Thus, in some cases negotiated sales can be as advantageous to the vendor as to the national museums, which can receive acquisitions without having to dip into their slender purchase funds. There have been many changes in the legislation since 1956 and as a result of these and the huge rise in prices which can be expected for highly important works of art, the number of negotiated sales has mounted. There is no doubt that Christie's have been entrusted with far more than Sotheby's.

The first thing I knew about the forthcoming Dodge sale was when Arthur bounced into my office one evening with the look of excitement of a boy telling his father he has scored three goals in an important match. Arthur suggested a drink in the Golden Lion across the road and he had a willing listener. After his time in New York, Jo had been the obvious ambassador to send to see the Dodge Trustees, who wanted an appraisal. So, accompanied by Arthur, Anthony du Boulay and Anthony Coleridge, Jo flew off to Detroit and over two weeks his team completed a valuation of the huge collection.

Jo must have emphasised to the Trustees Christie's long connection with Old Masters and also the forthcoming Velazquez sale. Old Masters have an affinity with French furniture and there had been many good sales of the latter at Christie's recently. Jo could also point to the Old Masters Charlie Allsopp had managed to get from a famous Newport, Rhode Island collection – solid evidence of the confidence of another American estate in selling works of art at Christie's in London.

For once Sotheby's reaction was surprisingly muted. Peregrine Pollen admitted that Sotheby Parke-Bernet were not quick enough and lost the Dodge Collection due to treating it as a routine matter. "We did not take it seriously enough and only sent one director. You sent a team, and you'd had those wonderful pictures from Newport, which must have helped." The Trustees gave Christie's the sale towards the end of February. According to the *Daily Telegraph* the American auction world was "stunned to learn that a London house had won the right to sell one of the country's greatest private collections". To impress American collectors further with Christie's expertise it was essential to exploit the Dodge Collection's PR potential to the maximum.

The story of Anna Thomson Dodge has a Cinderella quality. She left her native Dundee when very young and set sail like hundreds of others for the New World. All she had was her ability to teach the piano. She settled in the small Michigan town of Niles where she fell in love with a mechanic named Horace Dodge, who also had an interest in music. When they were married in 1896 Horace had 75 cents in his pocket, 45 of which went on their honeymoon suite for the night and 20 cents for breakfast. So they started life with 10 cents and lived with Horace's parents.

Horace opened a bicycle factory with his brother John, but quickly branched out into making parts for Henry Ford. By 1910 they were making most of the components for the Model "T" Ford and owned 10 per cent of the Ford Motor Company. However, Horace had a flair for bigger things – and for what we now call the mass production line – and in 1914 the Dodge brothers began building their own cars with the proceeds of the sale of their Ford shares, which brought in $50 million; gradually their car stable grew to include Chrysler, De Soto and Plymouth as well as Dodges. Horace did not live long enough to enjoy the fruits of his success, as he died in 1920.

Perhaps because she came from Scotland, Anna invested the $59 million Horace had left her wisely in tax-free bonds issued by municipalities. These earned her in interest, it is believed, an average of $1.5 million a year for the next fifty years, so she emerged almost unscathed from the Wall Street crash of 1929. Anna had married again in 1926. Her husband, Hugh Dillman, was an unsuccessful actor and they were divorced in 1947. However, their first fourteen years together were happy ones, with Dillman teaching Anna to enjoy the good things of life including the best champagne and Beluga caviare. It was during this period that Anna developed her passion for eighteenth-century France and devoured every book on the subject. She became so knowledgeable that Hollywood film moguls turned to her for advice, and she gradually came to see herself as Madame de Pompadour the second, to the extent of commissioning Sir Gerald Kelly to paint a huge portrait of her in spite of her age. For this she had a dress made exactly similar to the one worn by Madame de Pompadour in the famous portrait by Boucher – with a deep décolletage and a frothing mass of bows.

In the early 1930s, Anna Dodge decided to embark on her dream and build herself an "eighteenth-century French château" which was to be called Rose Terrace, on the banks of Lake St Clair and in Grosse Pointe Farms. This is or was the motor car "millionaire's row", where the Fords, Firestones, Packards and others have all had their homes at one time or another. Naturally the best experts were engaged to build and design the interior of the château: the architect was the Philadelphian Horace Trumbauer and the well-known firm of Alavoine carried out the interior decoration. It was this firm which brought in Joseph Duveen, the art world's super-salesman, who is rumoured to have paid Alavoine $400,000 for introducing him to Anna. His instructions were to fill Rose Terrace with pictures, French furniture, tapestries, silver, Oriental porcelain and other works of art fit for a Queen; an assignment tailor-made for Duveen. The 75-room château took four years to complete. After the third year Anna sailed away on the 257-ft steam yacht *Delphine*, named after her daughter, which Horace had given her. She would return in a year, during which time, she said, her Versailles was to be brought to opulent completion.

While the house was being built Duveen combed Europe and as far afield as Russia for works of art and wrote frequently to Mr and Mrs Dillman, as they still were, on what he had found. His letters are gems of salesmanship angled towards those who are as yet new to spending large sums on works of art, but are determined to win the

175

admiration of their neighbours. Each of his letters was calculated to overcome any sales resistance from Anna or her husband.

Duveen was naturally astute enough to drop a name or two: ". . . You may be interested to know that my uncle and former senior partner sold this set to the late Mr Pierpont Morgan some 25 years ago for the famous Fragonard room at Prince's gate, London." Then there was Duveen's "nothing but the best" ploy: ". . . I assure you that you will not see such a set in either France or Germany; its like does not exist in any private collection, nor has any dealer anything comparable to it. Indeed I do not hesitate to say that no individual in America has such a set of this period." Finally there is an ecstatic description followed by "to hell with expense" advice:

> I wish I had thought when Mr Dillman was here, to have had
> the chairs placed in front of the Boucher tapestry. I had this
> done today, and really the whole ensemble hums in one
> delightful tone – it is a perfect symphony of glorious
> colouring . . . There is no great house in Detroit, so may I
> suggest that you have here a wonderful opportunity, by indulging
> yourselves, to show Detroit what such a house would really
> mean. After all, suppose you do spend a little more than you
> intended; does it really matter? . . . I fully appreciate the
> reference to Mrs Dillman's thought that the house may cost
> more than she anticipated, but is this not always true? I have
> rarely known of anyone building a fine house – and I have been
> concerned with very many – where the expense was not greater
> than was anticipated. But in this connection, may I say that we
> can always arrange payment to suit your convenience . . .

An instalment system for Mrs Dodge?

It took more than one pint for Arthur to recount the glories of the Dodge Collection even in the somewhat dowdy atmosphere of the Golden Lion. Not surprisingly he had been entranced by being able to read Duveen's letters, to such an extent that he had memorised certain passages and the pub resounded with Arthur's recitation.

Duveen had asked whether it really mattered if the collection turned out to have cost more than anticipated, which was $2.5 million. Evidently not, although when in 1936 Anna returned in the *Delphine* her first reaction might well have shaken salesmen weaker than Duveen. Everyone who had had a hand in creating Rose Terrace was there to greet her, with Duveen in his customary morning coat at the head of the line. He escorted Anna off the pier into the house where she scarcely gave a glance to Boucher's two huge pictures, *The Bird-catchers* and *The Fountain of Love* – traditionally thought to have been painted to the order of Madame de Pompadour for Louis XV – and began to climb the grand winding staircase. As she reached the top she turned and spoke for the first time: "Duveen, this simply won't do."

Presumably Anna relented. She certainly should have done, as Duveen had indeed brought together a collection a Queen could be proud of, so much so that her friends, members of her own family and the servants referred to her as "the Queen". The French furniture was remarkable for the number of pieces with a royal provenance. Somehow this huge collection, totalling in all many hundreds of pieces, not only of pictures, but furniture, tapestries, porcelain, silver, sculpture and works of art, was packed up and transported in a BOAC 707 cargo jet to London Airport – Sir Francis Cook would have been surprised – which landed safely. The collection was unpacked under police guard, with Jim Taylor very much in charge. The only exception were the two Bouchers, 116 ins by 133 ins, which where too big to get into the aircraft and had to travel by sea.

The only thing to go wrong regarding the sale of the Dodge Collection was the initial announcement to the Press. I normally gave an important story exclusively to *The Times*, because Geraldine had shown that she and her editor were really interested and prepared to give good saleroom stories the most space; the story would also of course go to the agencies, and to the provincial and foreign Press. However, in the case of the Dodge Collection, as it had everything a newspaper dreams about, I decided to give it to my old paper the *Daily Telegraph*. To give every important story to *The Times* might tend to make them feel they had an automatic right to such stories, and anyhow it was a little unfair, I thought, on other quality papers.

The *Telegraph* saleroom correspondent at the time was Robert Adam and I knew he'd do his best, particularly as I had been partly responsible for his getting the job. I told Bob about the Dodge Collection and that he could have it to himself, but asked him to be sure that his news editor and the chief sub-editor realised the significance of the story: that it was the biggest collection as yet to come to London from America, and that it had been owned previously by a once penniless music teacher from Dundee. Bob did full justice to the story, but the subs cut it to about five inches, with no double-column top and photograph as it deserved. It would never happen today, but the *Telegraph* sub-editors at that time failed to see the human as well as the art interest in it.

Not unnaturally my colleagues couldn't understand why the Dodge Collection had received such meagre treatment; you had to have worked on the *Telegraph* to do that. And why had I given it to the *Telegraph* in the first place? All in all, the Press Office had boobed and I was bitterly annoyed about letting the firm down, apart from appearing incompetent. Bob was equally furious with his colleagues. The only thing to do was to let the dust settle and resurrect the story with a new "top" – if we could find one.

The arrival of the huge pair of Bouchers provided the perfect answer. Christie's couldn't get them in through the back door without taking the doors off, or making some temporary structural alterations. Knowing the *Telegraph* sub-editors' delight in the prosaic, I was willing to bet this would seem worthy to them of a double-column top with photograph; the rest of the Dodge story could follow. I was right: the sub-editors swallowed the bait and gave Christie's all the space the story originally deserved. After that the PR campaign went well; particularly important was a feature in the *Telegraph* colour supplement by Ian Ball, who'd been in the *Telegraph* news room with me and was then one of the paper's New York bureau, of which he has since for many years been the head. I gave him all the facts and he contacted the Trustees who let him see the Duveen letters.

The announcement that Christie's were going to sell the Dodge Collection resulted in a number of other really important Old Masters and pieces of French furniture being sent for sale. Collectors are always pleased to see their property sold in good company. Among the Old Masters was a pair of copper panels by the sixteenth/seventeenth-century German master Adam Elsheimer, which turned out to have come from his famous Frankfurt tabernacle; the panels had been brought to the Front Counter, having been found in the owner's outhouse with a lot of other pictures.

Then there was Caravaggio's long-lost masterpiece *Martha Reproving Mary for Her Vanity* which belonged to a South American collector. David had been tipped off by an artist friend of his that it might be by Caravaggio, and flew out to see it, although he was very sceptical about its being "right". Caravaggio died when he was thirty-nine, so works are exceedingly rare; in 1971 the National Gallery had only one fully accepted work by him. However, David returned convinced that it was "right". He explained that the picture had remained undiscovered because it belonged to a family who, apart from this one picture, had no works of art. This meant that the house was not visited by people interested in pictures. "The picture was not completely unfamiliar to me, because what is probably the best copy hangs in the library at Christ Church, Oxford, and I saw it almost daily while I was there," David told me. It had taken eighteen months to get the picture out of South America so its inclusion was a lucky coincidence. To mention only a few of the other stars, there was Lord Derby's Van Dyck, *Four Negro Heads*, Bellotto's *View of the Castle Sonnerstein on the Elbe at Pirna* and Veronese's *The Martyrdom and Last Communion of St Lucy*, the finest work by him to appear on the market for many years.

However, by far the most important picture was Titian's *The Death of Actaeon*, the property of the Trustees of the Earl of Harewood. This huge picture depicted Actaeon, the hunter, fleeing from Diana, the Goddess of Hunting, whom he had disturbed while she was bathing with her attendants. Diana has discharged an arrow at Actaeon, which turns him into a stag, so that he is attacked and devoured by her hounds. For the last ten years the picture had been lent by the Harewood Trustees to the National Gallery.

Jo was responsible for pre-sale negotiations with the Trustees' solicitors about this prize picture and called me up one day to discuss when we should announce its forthcoming sale. It was then the middle of February, and in view of the picture's having been removed from the National Gallery for cataloguing I suggested it should be as soon as possible, provided he could give me a few days to write a release and get organised with black and white photographs – our Press list was very large and every photograph had to be captioned on the back. I told Jo it would be a general release, unlike that of the Dodge Collection. Nobody apart from Jo, Patrick and my staff knew when it was going to be released, but Jo had to get the agreement of the Trustees and the solicitors; they concurred and said they looked forward to good coverage.

At 5 p.m. on the day before the release was due to be distributed by hand throughout Fleet Street, I got a call from Peter Hopkirk, a reporter on *The Times*. "Are you going to sell Lord Harewood's Titian, *The Death of Actaeon*?" he asked. "Sotheby's aren't and Lord Harewood's solicitors told me that there would be an announcement in due course." My heart sank. The filing cabinets were full of releases all in addressed envelopes, and the solicitors and Trustees had been told it would be given to the Press the following day. This may seem a trivial matter, but some Trustees and solicitors tend to think the Press are public servants whom firms such as Christie's can virtually instruct. The grander their client, the more filled with self-importance they can become; they get very upset if what they have been told does not work out and they are not slow to make their feelings known. "I don't know, Peter," I lied, "I'll have to ring you back."

I got Jo on the phone and explained that Lord Harewood's solicitors had virtually admitted the picture was going to be sold, but hadn't thought of warning us that *The Times* was on to the story. I asked Jo to get the solicitors to authorise us to release the story immediately; otherwise it would be only in *The Times* and it was too big a story for that. Needless to say the solicitor was in a meeting. The minutes ticked by. I knew the saleroom correspondents would be going home soon or to the nearest pub. My best-laid plans seemed to be going awry again.

Eventually the solicitor rang Jo and having heard what had happened gave us the go-ahead. That was the good thing about Jo; if you explained the wherefores and the whys he'd back you up, having in any case briefed you properly in the first place. I rang Peter Hopkirk and said, "Oh yes, Peter, we are going to sell the Harewood Titian. I'll have a press release down to you in ten minutes." "You'll do what?" screamed Hopkirk, not unnaturally outraged at seeing his scoop disappearing before his eyes. "I'm sorry, Peter. I know how you must feel, but I've got a job to do as well and that is to get the maximum coverage here and overseas. It's not enough for the papers and agencies to pick it up from your first edition." That is what would have happened, but at that time of night the story would never have got the space it deserved.

There then occurred one of the most hilarious episodes in dealing with the Press in all my time at Christie's – as I realised once it was over. While I was waiting for Jo to ring down with the solicitor's decision, I told what staff I had – Sue Rose was not to join us until the following week – my plan. There was Patricia Stirling, generally known as "P" (for many years now Mrs Ranald Noel-Paton), and a rather frivolous youth, Johnny van Haeften; he had only been taken on because his father and godfather, who had a huge collection and used to invite Peter down to shoot, asked him to give Johnny a job. There was Carolyn Scott, known as "Chop", my advertising girl, who like Patricia was to be with me for about eight years. Chop would have to look after the office while the rest of us went down to Fleet Street with the Press releases, using Johnny's MG Sprite.

Having spoken to Jo, we just managed to pile into Johnny's small car – Patricia although a very attractive girl was not exactly sylphlike – and hurtled round St James's Square. In spite of the urgency I suggested to Johnny that he wasn't Steve McQueen and that it would be a good idea to arrive alive at Fleet Street. Our first stop was outside the centuries-old pub the Cheshire Cheese, because by then it was after six and I thought some of the saleroom reporters would be there. Patricia came with me and I told Johnny to deliver the release to Hopkirk at *The Times* and to Anthony Thorncroft at the *Financial Times* and then come back and wait for us here. Sure enough, propping up the bar of the Cheshire Cheese was the late John Rydon of the *Daily Express* and Bob Adam of the *Daily Telegraph*. "Put your glasses down, lads, there's work to be done," I said and showed them the release. John said with mock severity: "This really is intolerable. We're off duty relaxing from our labours and you barge in with a story. It's not only a rather unusual way to distribute your releases, but I've never known it to be done before." I then told them what had happened and they bustled back to their offices to tell their night news editors that there was a big story he knew nothing about. This would need space so he would have to tell the chief sub-editor to reserve some.

Johnny meanwhile was not having a happy time. He told us later that Hopkirk was not only incensed at being given the release but threatened to debag him. Johnny sensibly thought that for once it was no time for his usual banter and left. After leaving the Cheshire Cheese, Patricia crossed the road to the Press Association and Reuters building and left a bundle of releases for both agencies and other papers with offices in the building, and then ran down Fleet Street, round the corner to the Associated Press; I went to the *Daily Mail* and United Press International, the all-important American news agency. Giggling like a schoolgirl Patricia came puffing back up Fleet Street, and went into hysterics as Johnny told us what an awful time he had had, while driving us to the *Guardian* where we handed in our last release for Donald Wintersgill.

All somewhat unorthodox, but it worked: the Titian story received tremendous coverage – which no doubt the Trustees and solicitors took for granted. But how on earth had *The Times* got wind of the sale? During the next week we found out how and why Hopkirk was so particularly furious, so much so that he was going the rounds of all the saleroom reporters trying to get me and Christie's "blacked". Fortunately they were all good friends and he was told not to be silly and that in my position he would have done exactly the same. One of them told us that an old lady from Budleigh Salterton had been inadvertently responsible for tipping off *The Times*.

Some weeks earlier Peter Hopkirk had managed to get hold of a copy of the National Gallery's paramount list of pictures and written a feature about it. The old lady from Budleigh Salterton read it and decided to make a special trip to London to see some of these wonderful pictures which were on loan to the National Gallery. By chance she chose the day after *The Death of Actaeon* had been removed to Christie's. When she got home, she wrote an indignant letter to *The Times* about the Titian not being there; the letters editor smelt a story and passed it down to the news editor who passed it on to Peter Hopkirk to investigate.

Before the week was out I got a call from William Rees-Mogg, editor of *The Times* (he had not as yet been knighted let alone raised to the peerage). In quiet, punctilious tones he upbraided me for "unprofessional conduct". The last thing I wanted to do was to have a row with someone for whom I had a great respect. I reminded him of the large number of exclusive stories I had given his paper and said that Christie's were very grateful for its obvious interest. There were times, however, when it was my duty to get the maximum coverage and I'd been employed to do this because of my journalistic experience. If, as on this occasion, my responsibilities clashed with the desires of *The Times* it was unfortunate. After all, the Press reserved the right to print news – and I'm not referring to gossip – regardless of the feelings of or inconvenience to the people or businesses it concerned. Sometimes that could be justified as being "in the public interest", but in my opinion and that of our clients the sale of the Titian was not such an occasion. Rees-Mogg probably did not agree, but he has never held it against me and has been friendly whenever we have met.

Christie's was packed with sightseers from the middle of June 1971 when the Dodge Collection, together with all the other magnificent works of art which were to be sold the following week, went on view. The spacious rooms – so different from those of Sotheby's – have never looked better. It was like coming into a palace. Even allowing for the "mega-pound" Old Masters and Impressionists sold since, Willie

Mostyn-Owen, who was responsible for the catalogue, agrees there has never been another sale with so many Old Masters of such great quality.

The Dodge Trustees were not disappointed, the whole collection selling for just under £2 million ($4.8 million), of which £382,000 ($916,800) had been for Anna's jewellery which had been sold in Geneva. The pair of Bouchers were bought for 400,000 gns ($1.1 million) by the Getty Museum at Malibu, California, as were the *Four Negro Heads* for the same sum. Four rustic scenes by Fragonard went to the Detroit Institute of Art for 110,000 gns ($264,000). The finest piece of Anna's French furniture was Martin Carlin's writing table which the Grand Duchess Marie-Feodorovna, later Tzarina of Paul I, had bought in Paris, for her bedroom in the Palace of Pavlovsk. This was bought by Mr H. Sabet, an Iranian living in Paris, after a spirited duel with the Detroit Institute of Art, for 165,000 gns ($415,800). A magnificent pair of Louis XV ormolu and marquetry commodes, which traditionally decorated one of the hunting lodges of the Kings of Saxony – the ormolu and marquetry fronts showing a deer fleeing through a forest – were also bought by the Getty Museum for 80,000 gns ($201,600).

The highest price in the Old Master sale was naturally for the Titian. This was bought by Julius Weitzner for 1,600,000 gns. When Peter, who was taking the sale, knocked it down to him, Weitzner for once appeared rather disconcerted, as if he had not really meant to buy it. Whether he was playfully bidding up the Getty, no one will ever know, but it came as no surprise when it was announced a few days later that the Titian had been bought from Weitzner by the Getty Museum for £50,000 more than the auction price. This was a quick profit without the worry of having paid a vast sum and the inevitable wait, after finding a buyer, for an export licence. The National Gallery in any case was determined to put up a fight for the Titian. With the help of the NACF and the Pilgrim Trust, and their willingness to devote the whole of their £400,000 purchase grant, they were successful in persuading the Government that the Titian must be saved. Lord Eccles, Paymaster-General with special responsibility for the Arts, announced that the Government would advance £600,000 against the National Gallery's future grants, if the final £231,500 could be found. The Government undertook to match every pound raised by a public appeal. In this way the full £1,763,000 was paid to the Getty Museum.

There was only one disappointment about the sale – Sir Denis

Mahon, the acknowledged expert on Caravaggio, did not feel he could lend his name to the attribution of the picture in the catalogue; and there was no real provenance. This and the rarity of the artist's works put doubts into dealers' and museum directors' minds, particularly as the picture needed considerable cleaning and restoration. The result was that it was bought in at 130,000 gns. Nevertheless this did not stop Hugh Leggatt and Mahon approaching the owners and, after having it cleaned by the National Gallery, negotiating a sale on their behalf with the Detroit Institute of Art. David's opinion of the picture was fully vindicated. It's not always clear to the Press, let alone acknowledged by them, the difficulties that auction houses face with certain works of art. There is also the very natural competition of dealers to get their hands on really important pictures.

This great Old Master sale was followed by one of Impressionists early in July which almost equalled it for quality. The emphasis was on works by Renoir, and in particular those collected by Georges Charpentier, France's leading publisher in the 1870s. The highlight was Renoir's *Le Pêcheur à la Ligne* which was the very essence of Impressionism, evoking a languorous summer's day and showing a man fishing on a river bank, while his prettily dressed companion reads the paper. David had first seen its glowing warmth and the Renoir family portraits in the clinical atmosphere of a Swiss bank vault. The owners of pictures can sometimes show no appreciation of what they have inherited; or perhaps they just prefer to have the proceeds from their sale. The Tournon-Charpentier heirs had chosen to settle in Costa Rica. *Le Pêcheur* was bought by Sir Nigel Broakes, chairman of Trafalgar House.

As a result of the Dodge Collection, the Titian, the Renoirs and many successful applied art sales the 1970–71 season's world-wide total was just under £25.3 million (knock-down), an increase of 25 per cent compared with the previous year's. The gap between it and Sotheby's total sales, a gap which some years had been as much as £20 million, had been greatly reduced; in London Christie's sales had exceeded Sotheby's by £4 million. The improvement in the relative positions could not be put down purely to the Velazquez, Dodge and other sales. The year before, when Christie's announced the 1969–70 season's figures, *The Times* had headlined Geraldine's article: "Hard Year for Art but not for Christie's." Christie's couldn't expect a better headline than that, but no one commented on it, least of all Peter. The fact was that for Sotheby's the chickens were beginning to come home to roost, as a result of the economic climate, complete lack of credit control and Peter Wilson's overweening self-confidence in his methods of getting business.

In 1969 there had been the crisis on Wall Street which resulted in Sotheby's bought-in figure rising from the normal 10 per cent of the value of sales to 25 per cent. The lack of confidence on Wall Street brought falls on the London Stock Exchange and in turn in the London art market, particularly silver. From 1966 to early 1969 English silver prices had risen at an unhealthy rate, as a result of investment buying. Christie's were approached by many rich people asking for advice and they had been passed on to the best dealers. In the face of the huge demand, the dealers had to buy more stock and sale prices rocketed. The Stock Exchange crisis put an end to the silver boom and prices plummeted; worse still, some dealers found their clients were unable to pay. It's a matter of fascination now, though not then, that the date when the silver crisis shook the whole art market can be placed exactly.

Early in 1969, Norman C. Hurst, a discerning silver collector, asked Arthur to sell what remained of his collection but stipulated that it had to be before April 1st. Arthur sold Mr Hurst's 131 lots on March 26th for £118,964 ($285,513), giving him a 245 per cent profit on what he had originally paid – he had given Arthur many of the original bills. Mr Hurst had hit the peak of the market, because on April 2nd prices fell drastically. Apart from the effect of the Stock Exchange collapse, the silver crisis coincided with the 1969 Budget which made works of art even of museum quality liable for duty if sold within three years. Roy Jenkins, the Chancellor of the Exchequer, in his Budget speech said the "pursuit of art for loophole's sake will become less worthwhile".

Christie's silver sales fell from £1.3 million in the 1968–9 season to £881,000 in 1969–70, the year *The Times* described as a "Hard Year for Art . . ." In spite of that, Christie's sales rose from £15 million to £20 million, while Sotheby's sales improved by only £300,000. "In the face of these difficulties," wrote Geraldine, "it is quite remarkable that Christie's have succeeded in increasing the volume of their trade by one third. It is in fact a reversal of the story of the past decade which has seen Sotheby's move from one sensational success to another, while Christie's battled to hold their own." When therefore Christie's in 1970–71 improved their position with a further 25 per cent increase on the previous year, it was an even greater demonstration that

Christie's were catching up their rivals. For Peter it must have been a particularly satisfactory season for it was announced that he had been made a CBE.

Sotheby's on the other hand were in real financial trouble because, apart from the silver crisis, they had a vast amount of book and jewellery payments outstanding. A former Sotheby's director told me that well-known book dealers had been offered three months' interest-free credit. Some of these had overdrafts far exceeding the credit limit. The bought-in figure on books rose from 3 per cent to 25–30 per cent and even 40 per cent. At Christie's there was nothing like such a financial problem. Under the eagle eye of Guy Hannen, who chaired the Management Committee meetings, the chief cashier had to produce a list of dealers who had exceeded their agreed limit, and if necessary Guy would write a stiff letter threatening to withdraw interest-free credit. Debts on books in any case were minimal compared with those at Sotheby's, where books were the traditional backbone of the firm. Also in 1971 there were the additional costs of Sotheby's Belgravia. In 1969 Howard Ricketts, the firm's brilliant arms and armour expert, had thought up an idea for a completely separate saleroom for Victorian works of art and art nouveau. He had written about this to his friend Marcus Linell, who had become the firm's youngest director at the age of twenty-three and had been sent to New York to run the works of art department. Linell was more than enthusiastic about Ricketts's idea and began planning the organisation while still in New York.

In January 1971 he returned to run Sotheby's Belgravia which was established in the old "Pantechnicon" building in Motcomb Street and quickly proved itself. However, there were inevitably extra costs – in particular it meant finding a new depository which cost a lot more money. This made Sotheby's financial situation even more disastrous. The overdraft soared to over £1 million and Tony Holloway, the financial controller, gratefully accepted the life savings of one director. "It was a dire moment and it was in the trough of 1971 when the cigarette offer came along."

The offer was £100,000 from W. D. and H. O. Wills, the Imperial Tobacco Company, for the use of Sotheby's name for a new cigarette to be called Sotheby's Reserve. Marcus Linell told me that there was also to have been a valuable royalty payment if the cigarette was a success. When Peter Wilson put forward the idea he met instant opposition and "catalysed a level of discord among the directors that had been dormant for some years". In spite of the threats of resignation from Marcus Linell, whose father had died of lung cancer when he was in his teens, Tim Clarke and Howard Ricketts, Peter Wilson was determined to get Board approval for the cigarette offer. To people like Howard Ricketts, "It had nothing to do with auctioneering. Most important of all, it didn't enhance the reputation of the company." Wilson sent Pollen over to New York to persuade the Parke-Bernet Board to agree; they did, and Peter Wilson got his majority.

It was the beginning of the crack-up of the family aspect of Sotheby's. As a result Tim Clarke, Howard Ricketts and Marcus Linell all threatened to resign with the proviso that if the cigarette failed they would stay. After four years it was withdrawn from the market, but by then the failure clause did not operate. Marcus Linell was so taken up with Belgravia that he stayed, but Howard Ricketts, who had felt himself at loggerheads over a number of policy decisions, left and has become a most successful arms and armour dealer. Tim Clarke stayed as a consultant, while Michael Webb, who had run the furniture department with such success, retired to Yorkshire. It was from this moment that Peter Wilson's star ceased to be in the ascendant and the firm – in spite of some famous sales such as Mentmore and Von Hirsch – was unknowingly, it seemed, heading for disaster.

Christie's were in a sounder state. At long last the firm was much better organised thanks to the specialisation of sales and by 1971 departments had been strengthened with new experts. Gregory Martin, Sir Alec's grandson, had joined the Old Master department, having been an assistant keeper in the National Gallery; Francis Russell and Anthony Browne were valuable new recruits for Noel Annesley. The smaller departments such as porcelain had been split into English and continental porcelain, glass, and art nouveau and art deco with specialists in each subject working under Hugo Morley-Fletcher. Likewise the Oriental department under Anthony du Boulay had specialists in all types of Chinese and Japanese art. Coins and medals – Richard Falkiner had finally been dubbed "socially unreliable" by Peter and asked to leave – had been taken over by Raymond Sancroft-Baker, who like Richard was a coin enthusiast from an early age. Then there were new departments such as modern sporting guns for which there was a great second-hand market, owing to the time it takes to make a really good shotgun; Christopher Brunker, who had previously been responsible for these sales at Knight, Frank and Rutley, started a department which has gone from strength to strength.

The growth continued through the 1970s to take in musical instruments, medieval jewellery and by the 1980s twentieth-century decorative art.

On the Continent, Christie's appointed their first representative in Scandinavia, Lillemore Malmstrom, who had worked in a modern picture gallery, while another new office was set up in Düsseldorf where it was planned to hold sales. There had been two more sales in Italy and a number in Australia, all of which, if not producing a huge profit, were in their way successful and promoted Christie's name abroad.

Thus the firm was in much better shape to face the 1971–2 season which began with the house sale in Detroit of what was left of Anna Thomson Dodge's collection. The team, led by Jo, consisted of Anthony Coleridge, myself and Patricia, and Ray Perman and his assistant Brian Coulter. Jim Taylor, protesting loudly as he had never flown the Atlantic before, had preceded us in order to get the house ready for viewing and to train the fifteen black porters who had been engaged by a local firm of auctioneers, with whom we were to be in association as they were going to sell the house.

Detroit, the biggest motor car manufacturing centre in the world, is not an attractive city. The "uptown" or business and financial sector is remarkably small considering the wealth generated there. From the airport we drove through the skyscraper district and were quickly out into "downtown" Detroit, which is a depressed area. After half an hour's drive we came to Grosse Pointe Farms, a green suburb with magnificent trees. There couldn't have been a greater contrast to the slums we had driven through, and considering the nearby poverty it's surprising that it wasn't a more frequent target for racial protest.

Rose Terrace lies back from a broad boulevard with a long drive and huge garden in the front; the garden at the back slopes down to Lake St Clair. Anna's "château" had a French look, but was not a particularly beautiful building. I set up a Press Office in the bar – nothing unusual in that in America – which was just to the left of the front door. Sufficient eighteenth-century pieces of French furniture and works of art had been left behind for the house sale to attract dealers from Europe as well as America. Not only dealers and collectors would be interested; the house was bound to attract a lot of attention from both the Press and the public, because nobody except the very rich had ever been inside Rose Terrace. The desire of some members for a memento of their visit, even if only a door-handle, had already

been considered. David Stalker, the senior partner of the local auctioneers, had engaged twenty-six security men, half of whom were in plain
clothes, while the other half were in uniform with a revolver at the
hip.

Mrs Dodge had not been renowned for her generosity to Detroit,
even after the slump. The only money she left to the city after her
death was, I think, for the erection of a fountain in her memory. Anna
had outlived some members of her family; those that remained,
one gathered, were behaving like characters straight out of *Dynasty*.
However, "below stairs" Anna did look after the large number of
ladies on her staff, most of whom seemed to have a different coloured
hair rinse every day. They gave us a great welcome even though they
were soon to be unemployed. More important, there was Gus, who
had the key to the cellar, where there was very good wine and many
bottles of Dimple Haig whisky, which Anna's second husband had
bought at a quarter of its proper price when Prohibition came in. We
all ate together at a huge deal table in the basement kitchen in a very
democratic way, with Jo tucking into a breakfast of waffles and maple
syrup and everything else which is part of the American start to the
day. A few yards inside the basement Gus showed us the secret door
which led to the Dodge speakeasy where during prohibition days there
must have been some heavy drinking.

Armed with a camera, Patricia, Ray and I went on a tour of the
house, which, even without most of the art collection, was fascinating.
Sir Gerald Kelly's vast portrait of Anna still dominated the drawing-
room, while upstairs her bathroom had gold-plated taps and brass
shower jets on both sides all the way up the walls, which provided
almost a jacuzzi effect. We slept in the staff bedrooms on the top floor
– squirrels running round the roof outside – with very simple furniture
compared to what had been in the rooms below.

When the view opened, the queue to see the house stretched 200
yards down the drive and half a mile down the boulevard outside. By
the end of the first day 2,500 people had been through the house. In
one of the garages I found one of the original Dodge cars and pushed
it out. Rather unkindly, without even allowing her time to do her hair,
I summoned Patricia, so that she could be photographed getting out
of it by the hordes of photographers who had arrived. Thanks to the
Associated Press this photograph went round the world, somewhat to
Patricia's embarrassment. Michael Leapman, from *The Times*'s New
York bureau, arrived with other reporters and TV networks, so Jo

and Anthony were kept busy giving interviews several times a day. When the day's view was over and the crowds had gone, we relaxed in the kitchen over a glass or two of 1929 Dimple Haig, which had to be strained through a sieve because the cork had softened since Prohibition days.

Once the sale started everyone had to lend a hand late into the night getting the results out. It all went well although the total at the end of the three days was only $596,000 (£261,435). The weather was kind to us and when the last lot had been sold, Jo stood in the sun outside the marquee autographing catalogues for the locals.

When the Press had been given the results and we'd phoned London, I started packing up for our return. In doing so I came upon a Christmas card with a huge Father Christmas on the front. Inside I read: "To Momma. I don't want a million dollars. I just want $999,999 and 99 cents." It was signed by one of Anna's sons and must have been overlooked by one of the blue-rinsed maids when they were clearing up after Anna's death. Horace was the only real person in the Dodge family.

14

The Hot Seat

"The market expanded in America as a result of PR. Let's face it, none of the successes of Sotheby's and Christie's looked at as auction business would have been possible without what you and Stanley Clark were doing. That had created an enormous market which we both took advantage of." This is Peregrine Pollen's view of the significance of PR following Christie's opening of their Park Avenue office in 1977. It may appear to some people an overstatement. Nevertheless PR, publicity – call it what you like – was of considerable significance to the growth of the New York art market, and in the London art market from 1958.

However, one of the reasons, apart from their long history, why Christie's and Sotheby's are household names is that even before either firm employed professional public relations staff the quality newspapers covered their daily sales regardless of their importance or even news interest. There are no two other organisations in Britain apart from the Houses of Parliament and the Stock Exchange – and they are collective institutions – which are favoured in such a way. This is a phenomenal sociological fact. Logically one would assume it reflects the public interest in art auctions. Today that is true not only because of sensational prices, but also because of a developed interest in pictures and works of art. However, in the late 1950s and 1960s this certainly wasn't the case. Only collectors, dealers, museum officials and perhaps the gentry were interested in regular saleroom reports, until of course something like the Goldschmidt sale took place. The effect of this long-standing policy was not healthy. Christie's certainly – and I suspect Sotheby's partners reacted in the same way – took the daily coverage for granted; they didn't realise how lucky they were, compared with other commercial companies.

After the second Goldschmidt sale the news editors woke up to allotting space according to the importance of a sale, and sometimes there wasn't any space available for Christie's. Peter hated the Press – many people do – and reacted in a highly volatile way as the gap between the two firms' turnovers increased. He ignored the fair treatment Christie's received when they did have a good sale. It was really a reflection of his personal feelings towards Peter Wilson and Sotheby's generally. He refused to accept that Sotheby's, for the moment at least, was the leading firm of fine art auctioneers. I was often tempted to quote to him and the Board in general: "The fault . . . is not in our stars, But in ourselves, that we are underlings." But this would not have been constructive.

It was not only the newspapers. Frank Davis's weekly saleroom feature in *Country Life* was read and scanned for the number of photographs featuring Christie's. One of my secretaries, Victoria Gilmore – "Vicki" – had the unenviable task of taking my copy of the magazine to Peter. More often than not he would start protesting to her about Frank Davis's treatment of Christie's, and then in stronger language phone me and instruct me to pass on his views to Frank. I did once mention to him Peter's protests and he said, "Tell Peter Chance not to be so silly." Frank, whom Peter sometimes referred to as "that ex-trade union leader" – he had actually many years ago been industrial relations officer at the United Steel works at Scunthorpe – told me how some wag of a dealer at the BADA dinner one year had seen Peter Wilson striding off to his seat in one direction and Peter Chance stalking off in the opposite: "Interesting placement; Peter the Great and Ivan the Terrible." (Peter Chance, you will remember, had been christened Ivan.)

It was all fairly absurd because I can remember in my early days at Christie's being with Peter when a deputation representing the British Antique Dealers Association came to protest about the use of Christie's photographs and prices in Frank's articles. They said this made it very difficult for them to sell their stock. Needless to say they did not get anywhere, and eventually found that the more organised world-wide publicity Christie's and Sotheby's managed to generate, the more the whole London art market benefited, as Peregrine said about New York.

It was not surprising, therefore, that after an amicable period to begin with, relations between Peter and me deteriorated to such a degree that my secretaries put their hands to their ears when he came on the phone to complain, which was most mornings. Every outburst

Albrecht Altdorfer: *Christ Taking Leave of his Mother* (circa 1513). This German masterpiece hung at Luton Hoo from 1904 till its sale to the National Gallery, London, was negotiated in 1980 on behalf of the Trustees of the Wernher Estate. For many years the net price obtained by the Trustees represented an open market value considerably in excess of any record price in the world for any painting. In 1885 it had been bought at Christie's for 23 gns (£24 3s).

Diego Velazquez: *Portrait of Juan de Pareja*. Sold in 1970 for 2.2 million gns ($5.5 million) on behalf of the Earl of Radnor. This was the first picture ever to be sold for over £1 million and the auctioneer was Patrick Lindsay. Bought by Wildenstein's, the picture was acquired the following year by the Metropolitan Museum, New York. In 1801 Christie's auctioned this picture on behalf of Sir William Hamilton. It fetched 39 gns (£40 19s).

Giovanni Battista Tiepolo: *Allegory of Venus Entrusting Eros to Chronos*. Discovered by David Carritt on the ceiling in the main drawing-room of the United Arab Republic's embassy in London. Bought by the National Gallery, London, 1969 for 390,000 gns ($982,000).

Duccio di Buoninsegna: *The Crucifixion* (circa 1300). This radiant panel, measuring only 59.7 cm by 38 cm, once hung in Patrick Lindsay's nursery at Balcarres, the family seat. It was auctioned by him on behalf of his mother, Mary, Countess of Crawford and Balcarres, in 1976 for £1 million ($1.7 million). The buyer was Ray Perman, the chief sales clerk, on behalf of a private collector.

Gilt-bronze figure of St John the Evangelist, circa 1200, 9.5 cm high. Sold to the Victoria and Albert Museum in 1972 for £36,759 ($88,200).

The Star of South Africa, the pear-shaped pendant diamond of 47.69 carats. Sold in Geneva in 1974 for S fr. 1.6 million (£225,300).

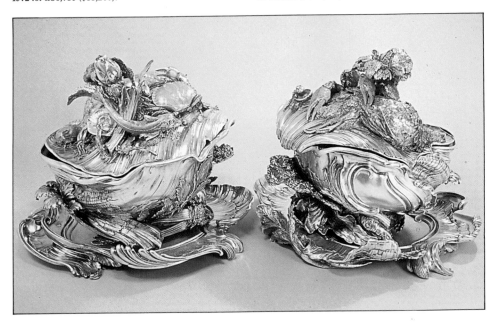

Pair of Louis XV silver tureens and stands made for the Duke of Kingston by Juste-Aurèle Meissonier, Paris 1734-6. Sold in Geneva in 1977 for S fr. 2.4 million (£612,500). The tureens are masterpieces of the rococo style.

Charlie Allsopp, chairman of Christie's, London, selling Van Gogh's *Sunflowers* for £24.7 million ($39.9 million) in 1987.

£ 22500000
$ 36292500
SF 54675000
FF 228150000
YN 540000

CHRISTIE'S

CHRISTIE'S
LONDON

Russian banqueting service totalling 1,742 pieces made in St Petersburg (Leningrad) about 1830 for Tzar Nicholas I. Sold in 1967 on behalf of Novoexport, Moscow, for a total of £65,751 ($193,308).

A portion of the Nanking Cargo on the seabed before being raised from the South China Sea by "Captain" Michael Hatcher and his crew. The 160,000 pieces of mid-eighteenth-century Chinese porcelain and 126 bars of gold were auctioned in Amsterdam in 1986 for £10 million ($14.2 million).

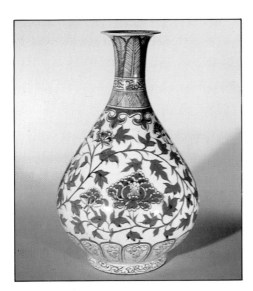

Chinese underglaze copper-red pear-shaped vase, second half of the fourteenth century. Sold in 1984 for £421,000 ($606,528).

Mother-of-pearl and polychrome Boulle marquetry bureau, circa 1720. Sold in 1987 on behalf of the Trustees of the Knole Estate for £1.2 million ($1.9 million). This exceptional piece of furniture had been in an attic at Knole for many years. In spite of its jewel-like appearance there is no documentation about its place of origin or who made it.

Pablo Picasso: *Jeune Arlequine*, 1905. Sold in 1988 for
£20.9 million ($38.4 million). © DACS 1989.

A brilliant auctioneer and an intrepid racing motorist and pilot. The late Patrick Lindsay with his beloved Spitfire.

Jo Floyd, chairman of Christie's, London, from 1974 to 1984 and of Christies International from 1976 until 1988, taking the sale of French furniture in 1983 which consisted of only fifty-four lots but totalled just over £2 million ($2.9 million). The sale included the celebrated Louis XVI porcelain-mounted writing desk by Martin Carlin. Originally the property of the Tzarina Maria Feodorovna, it was bought by the J. Paul Getty Museum for £918,000 ($1.3 million). The desk was sold as part of the Dodge Collection in 1971 when it fetched 165,000 gns ($415,800); it can just be seen in the left-hand corner, while Geraldine Norman stands to the left of the auctioneer.

ended with what was his favourite instruction to everyone: "For Christ's sake get it right." I thought at one time it was going to be my epitaph. The fact that I had got him into the *Sunday Times*'s prestige Portrait Gallery feature, with a photograph by Douglas Glass and write-up by John Russell, even before I had been made a director and in spite of Sotheby's having taken the lead (which made Peter Wilson demand similar treatment), was of nothing. Jake Carter in the Garrick told Arthur, "You know what we call Peterborough? Herbert's Column." Having written many paragraphs for Peterborough when I had been on the *Telegraph*, I knew to the nearest line not only the subject matter but the style that they liked. It didn't make any difference because Peter took *The Times*, although he saw the cuttings book each morning.

Stanley Clark had a far easier task. Not only had Sotheby's as a result of the Goldschmidt sale wrested the position of No. 1 saleroom from Christie's, but his chairman had an astonishing charisma which made him attractive to the media – and he recognised what skilful PR could do to help Sotheby's further. He would often call Stanley at 7.30 a.m. to ask his advice, which was encouraging for Stanley. There was never, for instance, any argument about TV lights. Stanley also, being an outside consultant with his own firm, wasn't burdened with all the other responsibilities I had: the catalogue department, advertising, the monthly forthcoming sales notice, charity sales and the *Review of the Season*.

John Lumley and certain other directors were kind enough to commiserate with me sometimes. John had said, "I think you've got the worst job in the firm." Things must have been bad, because when I looked through my records I realised it was towards the end of the 1960s that I began to scan the advertisements in the Sunday papers for another job. I even went as far as going to see Bill Deedes, or rather the Rt Hon. William Deedes, when he was Minister without Portfolio in one of Macmillan's governments. I'd always been interested in politics and wondered if there was an opening for an ex-journalist. I'd first met Bill when I was on the *Telegraph*, for whom he wrote parliamentary pieces for Peterborough. He was sympathetic, but not hopeful. He didn't think I'd find the Central Office any less frustrating than my present job, and even if I managed to get attached to a minister, there was always the question of what to do if he lost his office. It was only due to my wife's wise counsel that I stayed: "It's no use expecting to be appreciated in your job, but you're lucky to have it however awful it may be at times. You not only like having the connection with Fleet Street and being able to use your journalistic experience, but the actual art side is obviously interesting. So stop feeling sorry for yourself." She was right and so I stayed and have never regretted it, although the pressures not only continued but increased.

It was when the Times-Sotheby Index appeared, followed two years later by Geraldine's becoming saleroom correspondent of *The Times*, that life really became difficult for the Press Office and in particular for me. And then Geraldine's campaign for information on bought-in lots brought about not only a real row but a running battle for many years.

Before embarking on this painful subject I hasten to reassure readers that any journalist asking me or one of my staff if a lot had been sold was told the truth. There was never any pressure from above to do otherwise. It's true we didn't volunteer information on bought-in lots, if we weren't asked about them, and the standard procedure was that the total given would be the knock-down and include bought-in lots. Geraldine, once she was confident of her position, decided this was not good enough; she wanted, certainly when it came to important sales, every price in the catalogue and whether the work was sold and if so who the buyer was. With this information she could work out the percentage sold and bought in. It was strange that no other journalist had ever asked for such basic information before.

The trouble with Geraldine's demand for a complete statistical report of a sale was that it could result in an unbalanced account. As with the Times-Sotheby Index, statistics were only half the story; the quality, condition and importance in the artist's oeuvre of a lot and whether it had been bought comparatively recently could all influence the result. However, the sub-editors naturally seized on the "BI" percentage after a particularly unsuccessful sale because it made an easy headline. For Christie's or Sotheby's, the daily harping on about the percentage sold and unsold could do serious damage not only to both firms by deterring foreign vendors, but by depressing the market generally. I was regarded as being putty in Geraldine's hands. Guy would say, "You've got to talk to her in a more positive way." I asked him what he expected me to do if she demanded to know the buyer of each lot; he surely did not want me to lie to her. I wasn't willing to do so in any case, as it would have been the nadir of PR.

After fifteen months of being saleroom correspondent, Geraldine decided to launch an "investigative" attack on saleroom practices. I can't remember her telling me or even hearing that she was going to do this. However, the top brass of both Christie's and Sotheby's knew about it and for once they were united; normally when Christie's name was mentioned, "Peter Wilson's lips would curl with distaste," according to an ex-director of Sotheby's. Both chairmen decided that every effort should be made to get Geraldine's article suppressed. My colleagues never mentioned this to me or what they planned to do, which showed what they thought of me. It also, I think, showed a lack of courtesy.

So Peter Wilson, accompanied by his cousin Lord Westmorland and Peter Chance and Jo Floyd, went to see William Rees-Mogg, editor of *The Times*. Rees-Mogg listened politely to what they had to say and then said *The Times* would be going ahead with the article as he thought it in the public interest. The auctioneers retired abashed and furious. I learned this only when interviewing Geraldine for this book. Geraldine's view was, "It was a sledge-hammer to crack a nut, wasn't it?" But was it?

Years later Geraldine wrote: "The art market as a whole is an extraordinary business. Art values are the product of a weird mix of cultural, aesthetic, psychological and financial pressures – always in a flux, always dependent on human nature." That was a far more accurate assessment of Christie's and Sotheby's problems, as well as those of art dealers who were equally worried by her reporting. Not surprisingly it took her years to come to that conclusion.

Investigative journalism has been all the rage for many years and often does noble work on behalf of the public interest, although those under investigation may not welcome such attention. However, it can prove heady wine for the journalist concerned; as he or she "scratches away for the facts" – to use Geraldine's apt phrase – the adrenaline count rises and on occasions the balanced viewpoint is in danger.

Geraldine's article was headlined "Secrecy in the London Auction Houses" with a sub-head, "Geraldine Keen examines the traditional art sales practice of buying in". The article basically emphasised the anxiety in the art market that summer (1970) about how far falling stock markets – most particularly Wall Street – were going to affect prices. It was difficult for the public to interpret auction results because auctioneers were unwilling to publish price lists showing what lots had been bought in. My reply to that would have been that *The Times*'s headline "Christie's Impressionist Sale: 50 per cent Unsold", which appeared before the Chance/Wilson delegation to Rees-Mogg, could well be far more harmful to the interests of those for whom she was writing because it was damaging for the London art market, if she did not qualify such statistics with the many factors affecting prices I mentioned earlier. Price lists were hardly relevant as the number of subscribers was minute, and dealers always sensed or found out through the grapevine when an important lot had been bought in, as Geraldine went on to say. Salerooms act as agents for the vendor and if it is known that a work of art was unsold, its potential future value at least for a time may be seriously reduced. This was the salerooms' basic defence for not revealing unsold lots in price lists and Geraldine in her article accepted this point. Such was Peter Wilson's concern when he read *The Times*'s headline about Christie's 50 per cent BI sale that he rang me up, although he had only just arrived from New York, and said, "What are we going to do about this woman?"

The attempt to suppress Geraldine's feature having failed, the hostility to her sales results articles continued, except of course when we had had a good sale and got a good report. Nothing was said then. Nothing also was said when she wrote lengthy articles about particularly important works of art which were due to be sold by Christie's. Pre-sale publicity was if anything more important than post-sale, as that depended on results and I couldn't do anything about them.

For many years now I and indeed other Christie's directors have been good friends with Geraldine. However, when she became saleroom correspondent this happy relationship did not exist. I knew we were stuck with her and had to make the best of it. I therefore decided to give her these important pre-sale stories on an exclusive basis, not because I thought she might be more reasonable, but because she was interested and intelligent and as Rees-Mogg was keen on art auctions he would give her proper space. It was a policy of permeation and education also. The more she talked with Christie's experts, the more she would learn about the whole business. Thus Geraldine would come in and see Willie, Gregory, Hugo, Arthur or whoever was in charge of the sale. This worked well from all points of view. The articles were well written in a paper most of Christie's potential clients read and were virtually guaranteed a lot of space; no other paper could be trusted to be interested enough. Equally, every journalist likes to get an exclusive story. My policy appeared to be completely lost on Peter, Jo and Guy. Curiously, Sotheby's or Stanley Clark didn't seem to make any effort to pursue the same policy, so that Geraldine was just as much accused by Sotheby's of being pro-Christie's, as she was condemned by Peter for being in Sotheby's pocket.

There were times when I fought back at him and even won. In the autumn of 1969 we had the only Impressionist sale Christie's have ever held in Geneva. The most important picture was Gauguin's *Bonjour Monsieur Gauguin* (in emulation of Courbet's famous *Bonjour Monsieur Courbet* in the Louvre). All in all the sale went well, the Gauguin going for Sfr. 1.3 million (£131,707 – $329,000), believe it or not the highest auction price at the time for the artist. It was bought by Dr Armand Hammer, President of Occidental Oil, who had flown into Geneva in his private jet and landed in a snowstorm – his was the last plane to be allowed to land. Hammer tells in his autobiography how immediately after the sale he was offered "a huge profit" by a Greek millionaire whose plane had been forbidden to land in Geneva. Hammer told him the picture wasn't for sale.

On Monday morning of the following week there was a Board meeting and towards the end Peter began a tirade about the Geneva Press results. Naturally all his venom was directed at Geraldine. He said the whole Board was disgusted. Fortunately I had thought something like this might happen and had the press cuttings book by my feet. Very quietly, and naturally "with due respect, Mr Chairman", I told Peter that I couldn't understand his complaint as the sales, particularly the Impressionist and jewellery sales – the latter had included the historic Mancini pearl earrings given by Louis XIV to Maria Mancini, Cardinal Mazarin's niece – had got good coverage. I also said that I hadn't had any complaints from other directors, and as regards Geraldine I knew that she had gone to great lengths to be present at the Impressionist sale even though it meant taking a night train from Italy where she had been covering a Sotheby sale.

I then lifted up the cuttings book and showed him and other directors the results, which included a large photograph of the Gauguin in the *Financial Times*. Peter, like all those who think the object of their wrath is unlikely to stand up for him- (or her-) self, looked a little put out. "Well, has anyone else got anything to say?" Absolute silence and the meeting ended. I gathered up my papers and the press cuttings book. On the way downstairs Guy caught me up and said, "One up for you. That was well done." That was nice of him. Perhaps the rest of the Board felt deep down that Peter's attitude was often unjustified.

Nevertheless, the nagging and inquests at Board meetings continued. "I tell you, John, there's nothing, in my opinion, which is not beyond the line of duty when it comes to controlling that woman." I wonder what Geraldine would have done if I'd taken him at his word. The absurd thing was that by now it was 1972; the sales of the Velazquez, the Dodge Collection and the Titian, apart from immensely important applied arts, had all brought lustre to Christie's name. There wasn't any need for such concern about Sotheby's, because even if they were still ahead in terms of sales totals, Christie's had reestablished itself as an auction house very different from that of 1958.

Peter's attitude towards the Press and in particular Geraldine was verging on paranoia. More time was spent on discussing what to do about Geraldine at Board meetings than on any other one subject. Paranoia may seem an exaggeration, but it is not. The *OED*'s definition refers to "mental derangement", "spec . . . characterized by . . . delusions of grandeur". In spite of his many great qualities this aptly described one side of Peter's character.

The situation was not improved by a report that late at night in New York Geraldine had let rip at the whole commercial art world, and among other things said, "I hate the guts of both you and Sotheby's." The occasion followed a reception for Harry Ward-Bailey who had taken over the Rome office after Hans's death, and was now about to take over the New York office, John Richardson having been persuaded by Knoedler's, which had been bought by Dr Armand Hammer, to join them. It so happened that Geraldine was in New York with her husband Frank Norman and both had been invited to the party.

When it had finished Christie's directors, Arthur Grimwade and David Bathurst, who were there from London, took them both up the road to a restaurant where the drinking continued. Geraldine must have been "in her cups". Apart from her remark about both firms of auctioneers she implied that everyone involved in the art market was living off the backs of artists of the past. The incident would not be worth mentioning if it hadn't added fuel to the fire; and it was also felt that she was no doubt egged on by her husband who was branded as a Communist. The whole evening had an element of farce as Harry Ward-Bailey without telling anyone left the party before it had ended, as he had decided at the last moment not to take up the appointment.

Long before this incident I had often wondered, although Geraldine and I had built up a good working relationship, whether she bore any animosity towards Christie's, which with all its Old-Etonian and Establishment attitudes even I found exasperating. Had this lighted a fuse of left-wing contempt which could possibly influence her reports, if only subconsciously? When I interviewed her for this book at the home of her charming mother in Oxford I asked a point-blank question about the incident and her feelings towards auctioneers. Because of the Times-Sotheby index, she said, she got to know Sotheby's people first and found them charming, intelligent and full of humour. She was so much in Peter Wilson's good books that he told her he hoped she'd join the firm when the index had run its course. When she became saleroom correspondent she found that Christie's experts were just the same.

Commenting on the incident in New York, she said she didn't think there was any time when she hated Christie's. There were two points: first, Christie's were very sensitive about her previous connection with Sotheby's; secondly, Christie's "top brass" had behaved "very very rudely" towards her. On one occasion Patrick had rung her up and insulted her for half an hour – I was standing outside his office wincing at the noise while Ray Perman was deafened, having been summoned to produce the auctioneer's catalogue.

There was also another occasion which I knew nothing about. Geraldine remembers being asked by Jo if she would come to see him and Guy. She thought it was going to be a cooling-down meeting. Instead Jo and Guy both went at her hammer and tongs, insulting her knowledge, her honesty, her abilities as a journalist; it was a fantastic bit of real rudeness. She couldn't remember exactly what it was about, probably some article attacking the way Christie's had behaved; there might have been a couple of questionable factual pieces which they disliked but which depended on how people read the facts. "It was a real bashing. I was staggered when I came out, not because I was so hurt, but that two grown men, well brought up, could have behaved in that way to a young girl. It simply wasn't the way to behave. If they were very angry, they should have done it politely, point by point, not just shouted at me. So it's perfectly possible that I could when pissed have said, 'I hate Christie's,' in New York straight after this kind of thing. But I certainly have never had any ill-feeling towards Christie's." She got on well with Arthur Grimwade, who was always most helpful, David Bathurst, David Carritt, Noel Annesley and John Lumley, and Hugo Morley-Fletcher was a special chum. So apart from the three "top dogs", relationships were good.

There was also the theory that Geraldine was a Communist – the result of her diatribe in New York. Frank, her husband, was said to be a card-carrying party member. Geraldine continued, "It was so extraordinary getting this back from the trade; nothing could have been more untrue. Frank having come from nowhere adored the good things of life. If you are born without certain things, you value money, eating and drinking and being posh, far more than if you're born to it. Because you've got there by your own effort. As for me I've never been a political creature. I think people were trying desperately to explain why someone should criticise the art market and upset its fine old customs, and I think the reason was that there had never been a journalist operating in the art market before. Saleroom correspondents had just been 'Misters'."

As a result of the New York incident there were further Board Room discussions about Geraldine, and I was asked for my views. I said that there was nothing to be gained by shouting at her, considering writs, visiting Rees-Mogg (much to my embarrassment I had been on one such visit with Peter after the Chance/Wilson one), or complaining about her reports, unless there were real factual errors. The only way to improve the situation was to try to educate her about the genuine difficulties of art auctions. I suggested that the auctioneer should speak to her after she had been given the results by the Press Office to explain the background of the sale, which could defuse the BI factor. I think this was regarded as rather feeble and not dynamic enough; I certainly don't think it became established practice until Jo became chairman, but it worked then.

Peter was still determined to prove that Geraldine was biased against Christie's, and in 1973 he asked Arthur to do an analysis of her news stories regarding both firms over a year or so in column inches. I couldn't think of anything more pathetic, particularly for one of the directors most respected inside and outside Christie's to have to do. In any case it wouldn't prove anything, any more than some of Geraldine's statistics. The power of publicity is not measured purely in column inches, but by where the article appears and its style. Eventually the analysis was done and Arthur reported that Geraldine gave approximately 24 per cent more publicity to Christie's than to Sotheby's; this was because of my policy of giving her exclusive information for pre-sale articles, apart from the fact that over the last few years our sales had improved tremendously.

This didn't satisfy Peter and a few months later he demanded that there should be an analysis done over a year of every national daily and London evening paper's publicity on the two firms. This seemed not to be directed this time so much against Geraldine, but appeared to be an investigation into my stewardship of the Press Office. I gave Johnny van Haeften and Carolyn Scott this chore which took them several days. Once again because of pieces in Peterborough, the *Times* Diary and Londoner's Diary – Sue Rose, my assistant, was responsible for many of them – Christie's once again came way ahead in column inches. Having been in the job well over ten years I regarded the analysis as a personal insult, and a further example of Peter's paranoia. However, although angry about the insinuations of the exercise I was determined to keep cool, as everything from the sales point of view was going well, and there was even exciting talk that we might go "public".

I also thought of the many good points about the job. During my twenty-six years with the firm I was lucky to have some splendid girls working for me, with the exception of one raven-haired beauty who thought she could twist me round her little finger just when the *Review* was going into production. I chose most of them myself – in a somewhat unorthodox way sometimes, I admit. At wedding receptions or parties I may have appeared unfit to make a sound judgment, but talking to them when they were relaxed worked. After Judy, who had come with me from Dolan's but left when she got married, came Angela Pinney, Vicki Gilmore, Debbie Drooglever, "P" Stirling, Carolyn Scott, Annie Breitmeyer, Mandy O'Flynn, Georgina Hirst and Marianne Law. Then there was of course Sue Rose, my able assistant, and Johnny van Haeften, who always wanted to be in the picture department and now can show them how wrong they were not to give him a chance, because he's a most successful dealer. In December 1978 Sue Rose left for the Arts Council where she has been doing a splendid job ever since. She was a great loss not only professionally but as a friend. In her place I took on Peter Rose, no relation, who had been an associate editor of the *Montreal Star*. There were others who for various reasons didn't stay long, but the above were the hard core. It was a happy office because we worked as a team and I am very grateful to them not only for their hard work and loyalty but for their friendship, even if the general atmosphere at times appeared to be more like St Trinian's.

Nor was it all depressing. Apart from the big sales, there were always many opportunities for getting publicity whether it was in national, provincial or foreign papers. Sometimes they arose as a result of discoveries by technical staff on overseas trips, such as the fourteenth-century Chinese wine jar which Tony Derham while on a valuation on the Continent in 1972 recognised as being one of only three in existence. The jar was being used as an umbrella stand at the time, but was sent for sale and fetched £220,500 ($573,300).

Another remarkable Chinese work of art was the copper-red pear-shaped vase which a Scottish couple took to our Glasgow saleroom which we had opened in 1979. They'd been to the world-famous Burrell Collection in Glasgow and were surprised to see on display a vase resembling the one which formed the base of a lamp in their home. Christie's Glasgow examined the vase, which fortunately had not had a hole bored in its base for a flex, and confirmed their hope that it was of a very rare type dating probably from the second half of the fourteenth century. The couple had inherited it in a family division carried out literally in the form of a lucky dip – a description of each object had been written on slips of paper and put in a hat. At the time the two beneficiaries were rather disappointed, but when the vase sold for £421,000 ($606,528) in 1984 they changed their minds.

One of the prettiest little objects, in the discovery category, was a gilt-bronze statuette which was found by Arthur Davey, a Suffolk farm worker, while he was hoeing weeds. The four-inch figure was not surprisingly covered in mud and Arthur's wife took a wire scrubbing brush to it in complete ignorance of its value. Once cleaned it rattled about on top of the dashboard of Mr Davey's van; he even offered it to his son, who tried to swap it with a friend for a Dinky toy, but he had only a tractor and Mr Davey's son knew all about tractors. Eventually a local farmer with an interest in antiques heard about it and brought it to Christie's. With the help of the Victoria and Albert Museum the figure was identified as St John the Evangelist, probably part of a twelfth-century crucifixion group which had been vandalised years ago. It was thought that the figure, when found to be gilt-bronze, was thrown away as being too dangerous to sell, and came to the surface only after a mechanical digger had gone through the ditches alongside the field Arthur Davey was hoeing. When it came up for the sale the V and A paid £36,759 ($88,200) for it.

But for real hype there is nothing to beat something which has wildlife – whether bird or beast – as the subject of the story. Early in 1984 Harold Catchpole's Dickin Medal was brought in to Raymond Sancroft-Baker who gave it a provisional valuation of £250. The People's Dispensary for Sick Animals was founded by Maria Elizabeth

Dickin, and the Dickin Medal came to be regarded as the "Animal VC". In 1946 it was awarded to Mercury, a Blue-Hen, for the "most outstanding single performance" by any one pigeon on special service . . . one of 16,554 missions flown by British pigeons throughout the last war, of which only 1,842 were successful. Mercury's heroic mission took place on July 30th, 1942, and consisted of a 480-mile non-stop flight across the North Sea.

Mr Catchpole, son of Mercury's owner, told us that the Army took two birds from each of fifty fanciers all down the East Coast. The birds were given special rations of grain to strengthen them. When the time came for them to go into action they were put into baskets and parachuted out. On this mission Mercury was the only one to come home to her nest in Cemetery Road, Ipswich, with a special message in a tube on her leg.

Peter Rose was principally responsible for promoting this story. The results were amazing and world-wide. We received a telephone call from a former US airman in Texas who had spent the war years parachuting pigeons as opposed to people into Europe and couldn't resist putting in a bid. However he was beaten by Mr Louis Massarella – known to fanciers for his world-famous pigeon stud near Loughborough – who paid £5,000 ($7,750) for Mercury's medal.

Simple, sentimental and even corny stuff though it may be, it's what a Press Office exists for when there's no big sale in the offing. When projected by people who know what they are doing such stories can, as Peregrine Pollen suggested at the beginning of this chapter, have a considerable effect on the commercial success of an auction house. I must admit it was also very satisfying to arouse the interest of the Press with such material.

15

Christie's Goes Public

On November 12th, 1973, Christie's went public and Christies International plc was born. The question about whether to go public and when had occupied hours of talks between Peter and other members of the Policy Committee and Hambro's for months. If anyone in 1963, the year that Christie's made a loss of £6,000, had said that ten years later the firm would have had a sufficient number of profitable years to justify a public issue of shares, I think they would have been told they were mad. Nevertheless, as a result of Peter's leadership and hard work by everyone, Hambro's thought Christie's profits since 1968 would be acceptable to the City. They were as follows:

Profits *1968 – June 30, 1973*	*Adjusted profits before Tax*
18 months ended 30 Sept. 1968	£139,000
12 months ended 30 Sept. 1969	£90,000
15 months ended 31 Dec. 1970	£514,000
12 months ended 31 Dec. 1971	£562,000
12 months ended 31 Dec. 1972	£1,113,000
6 months ended 30 June 1973	£1,167,000

It was a remarkable turn-around in the company's financial record, considering its public image compared with Sotheby's, and the latter's gimmicks such as the Times-Sotheby Index, cigarettes and Peter Wilson's "special arrangements" for certain sales. Only 37 per cent

(7.5 million) of the 10p shares were offered to the public at 70p each, the rest being "A" shares which were retained by the directors as a defence against any predator. "C." Berens masterminded the whole flotation on behalf of Hambro's, smoking sixty cigarettes a day in spite of having only one lung and being responsible for two other public share-issues at the same time as Christie's. Throughout the operation he remained completely unruffled, compared with the Christie contingent, except when it came to the full-scale Press conference at King Street. Then he was worried that Richard, his son, by now head of the *Daily Express*'s William Hickey column, might cause a disturbance or ask embarrassing questions. Meanwhile Peter, Jo and Guy were worried about how the offer would be received by the City, and in particular whether the price per share – 70p – would be considered reasonable. When the application for shares opened on October 15th, the offer was eleven times over-subscribed.

Christie's could not have gone public if Guy had not kept a tight control on costs from very early on. In 1973 Jonathan Price, an accountant who had joined the firm the previous year, became finance director with instructions to do the same. Better financial husbandry, together with the gradual improvement in the firm's sales from 1965, resulted in a strong balance sheet. A few details of the more interesting sales and expansion are necessary to show how and why the profits increased so much, at a time when Sotheby's finances were, as can be seen later, in a very different state.

The year 1972 marked a turning point in the revaluation of English paintings. A June sale totalled £972,000 ($2.5 million) and contained a number of works which fetched prices which up till then one would only have expected of high quality Old Masters. The highest was 140,000 gns ($482,000) for Romney's *The Gower Family* – the previous highest price for the artist being £60,900 for *Mrs Bromley Davenport*, which Duveen had paid as long ago as 1926. (This had been one of the prices mentioned in the article Peter wrote for the *Financial Times* way back in 1958, making the point that allowing for the fall in the value of the pound prices were not so "fantastic".)

A very different work was Samuel Palmer's *Harvest Moon*, which was so small that it had to be kept in a showcase. It was one of the most exciting discoveries of the sale, the owner having brought it to the Front Counter quite oblivious of its value, or that his family had bought it at Christie's in 1909 for 5 gns, the vendor being the artist's son. When it came up for sale it fetched 44,000 gns ($120,120).

However, the most memorable sale of 1972 for those of us at Christie's was that of Impressionists from the Leo Rogers collection which John Richardson had managed to get. The sale, a week after the Samuel Palmer had been sold, had to be postponed a day as the world's currency markets were closed prior to a major readjustment of the rates of exchange. There had been an important sale in the morning so the Leo Rogers pictures were billed for the afternoon, which in those days was very unusual. Whether or not Peter, who took the sale, had had some particularly good claret (to which he was very partial) at lunch, I don't know but he took the sale at a gallop. It was a tour de force of auctioneering as it was not by any means the easiest of sales, many of the pictures being sold at just over the reserve price. The total was £856,320 ($2.2 million), the highlight being *Portrait du peintre Moise Kisling* by Modigliani, which went for 100,000 gns ($273,000). Peter looked quite surprised at the congratulations he received from many of his colleagues; to him it was just another sale.

In the autumn there was another milestone, the first complete week of Victorian works of art. This was organised by Christopher Wood, whose *Dictionary of Victorian Artists* had been published the previous year. Christopher had been responsible, thanks to Peter's backing, for the first Victorian picture sale in 1968, and the huge sums which have been paid since for such works show how important this initiative was. However, every department seemed to be doing well: Noel's drawings, watercolours and prints (32,000 gns – $80,604 – for a print of Rembrandt's *Ecce Homo* and 90,000 gns – $226,800 – for Picasso's *Vollard Suite*); some splendid French furniture and Oriental porcelain – Tony Derham's 210,000 gn. ($573,300) "umbrella stand" has been mentioned already; and a magnificent group of gold snuff-boxes from the New Jersey home of the late Charles Engelhard, an American platinum millionaire but famous also as a racehorse owner and winner of the Derby, the St Leger and the 2,000 Guineas. It was undoubtedly the finest sale of gold boxes since 1904 – Sotheby's couldn't boast such history. There was the final portion of the great coin collection formed by the late Sir Charles Oman, the eminent historian, and his son, C. C. Oman, late Keeper of Metalwork at the V and A. This was sold after Richard Falkiner had left, but the whole collection was brought to him originally because of his early specialisation in coins.

Then there was the first sale of veteran and vintage cars which also inaugurated Lord Montagu's National Motor Museum at Beaulieu.

This was naturally Patrick's initiative because of his personal love and enthusiasm for such cars, on and off such circuits as Silverstone, Goodwood and Thruxton, where he was much respected as a racing driver. Nevertheless, he had some terrifying crashes – not because he made mistakes but because, as can happen in all sports, things beyond his control went wrong. I doubt if any other member of Christie's has been driven at 146 m.p.h. down the A1 – not the M1 – after a publicity outing, ironically to promote the future sale of a very much slower means of transport, to wit a Blériot monoplane. "Out of interest, John, how fast have you ever been in a car?" – as if it was likely that I had been faster. It wasn't lack of confidence in his driving that had made the blood leave my hands and feet so they were icy cold, but just the fear that some old dear might come crawling out of a side turning.

The car sale at Beaulieu was the first of many, not only there but in Geneva regularly, and later Los Angeles, Texas and Oklahoma and more recently Monaco, not forgetting the annual sale during the Earls Court motor show. Some sales were obviously more successful than others, but thanks to Patrick's knowing the late Michael Sedgewick, one of England's natural eccentrics but a man who knew everything about the innards of ancient cars, these sales became a world-wide example of yet another side to Christie's expertise, which as with Michael Broadbent's wine sales Sotheby's was never able to equal. Abroad the Düsseldorf office held its first sale, the Rome office its third sale and Geneva as usual two five-day sessions during the year, all of which did well.

The next year, 1973, was equally successful and gave the profits a significant heave, the June Old Master sale totalling £3.2 million ($8 million), Cuyp's *Woody River Landscape* from an American collection being knocked down by Patrick for 580,000 gns ($1.5 million). Another picture of particular interest was Gérard David's *Christ on the Cross between St John the Baptist and St Francis*. Although one of the most important Flemish primitives to come up for sale since the war, ranking in significance with Rogier van der Weyden's *Portrait of St Ivo*, this picture had been found with a lot of bric-à-brac in the vestry of All Hallows Berkyngechurch by the Tower. It had originally been given to the Rev. "Tubby" Clayton, the founder of Toc H and Vicar of All Hallows from 1922 to 1963. When it came up for sale it made 160,000 gns ($420,000).

Applied arts were doing just as well. Among many silver sales

Arthur had a field day in June when he sold a rare pair of Queen Anne chandeliers, followed by the first of three sales of the famous Ortiz-Patino collection of gold snuff-boxes which made a grand total of £823,410 (just over $2 million); Chinese porcelain included the Ming Wu Ts'ai jar which Sir Ilay Campbell, who had been our Scottish representative for some years, had discovered in a seedy Glasgow tenement but sold for 70,000 gns ($183,750).

It was a year also of enthusiasm and imagination. David Bathurst was responsible for Cyril Connolly's being taken on as a consultant on modern books, thus giving the department a shot in the arm as well as producing a sale. A most unusual and academic sale was that of Egyptian sculpture discovered between 1895 and 1897 by two English ladies – I can't help feeling they must have looked rather like Margaret Rutherford – in the Temple of Mut in Asher, near Luxor, for which the ever-popular "Lizzie-Anne" (now Lady Elizabeth Hastings) was responsible, since she had taken an extramural degree in Egyptology. Another new form of specialisation was the watch and clock department under Simon Bull.

Overseas sales results were certainly helpful to the profit figure for the first six months, Guy taking the May jewellery sale in Geneva which achieved the highest total to date of Sfr. 20.9 million (£2.6 million), many of the lots coming from American owners. A new departure for Geneva was the sale of top quality French furniture, mainly belonging to the owners of lakeside houses. In Düsseldorf the second sale included Russian icons collected by Jean Herbette, when he was French Ambassador in Moscow after the First World War; the prices achieved emphasised the importance of selling where the interest is greatest. Still in Europe, offices were opened in Amsterdam and Madrid, while on the other side of the world the picture sales in both Sydney and Melbourne, in their much smaller way than those at King Street, were a success. All these sales and developments in 1972 and 1973 not only enhanced Christie's image but pushed the profit curve up at a steeper angle, which made going public easier.

When all the excitement of the successful share issue was over, I couldn't help wondering why Sotheby's, whose net sales in 1972–3 were £71.7 million compared with Christie's net total of £33.8 million, hadn't yet gone public; perhaps behind all the hype their balance sheet was not so good? When in 1988 I questioned Marcus Linell, who was then director in charge of Sotheby's financial services, he took a very laid-back view. "The only point in going public is if a firm needs extra capital or its directors want to get their money out," he said, turning the question to imply that Sotheby's didn't wish to go public and Christie's had only done so because Peter wanted to be in a position to get his money out. Peter certainly didn't wish a repeat of the 1958 drama over Sir Alec Martin's shares, but it was a somewhat ingenuous attitude for Linell to take, although perhaps inevitable in view of Sotheby's position.

Sotheby's overdraft problems following the silver crisis in 1969 were alleviated to a certain extent in July the following year when Jacob Rothschild's Investment Trust bought 20 per cent of Sotheby's equity for just under £3 million. Linell was quite correct about the reasons why firms go public, but the fact was that Sotheby's couldn't possibly have done so at that time, even though some directors were keen to get their money out, because the profits record simply wasn't good enough.

Following the announcement of the Rothschild Investment Trust's deal, the *Financial Times* and other financial journalists pointed out that in 1969 Sotheby's pre-tax profits had dropped from a peak the previous year of £934,000 to £859,000 "because rising costs have been eating into profits"; some of the extra costs were due to Belgravia. In the current year (1970) profits were expected to be lower. Compare this situation with Christie's profits record as set out at the beginning of this chapter and how it climbed in 1971, 1972 and 1973, and it is difficult to believe the two firms were in the same type of business.

The Rothschild Investment Trust had had a financial relationship with Sotheby's since 1966, but fundamentally the 1970 deal provided Sotheby's with only a breathing space. It proved in any case a mariage de convenance because quite soon afterwards Jacob Rothschild bought control of Colnaghi's, one of the oldest and most prestigious Old Master picture and drawings galleries in London. Peter Wilson was furious, regarding it as desertion. However, Rothschild was first and foremost a banker, and his stake in Sotheby's was merely like any other investment he might make.

Curiously his purchase of Colnaghi's nearly had calamitous results for Christie's because Rothschild immediately looked around for new expertise. He approached both Noel Annesley, who was mainly responsible for the reputation Christie's drawings, watercolours and prints department was then acquiring, and also Gregory Martin, as today in charge of Christie's Old Master sales. I don't know what they were being paid, but all our salaries were ridiculously low. Jacob Rothschild must have made them a very attractive offer because in principle both said "Yes," much to the sadness of all of us.

I remember talking to Noel over lunch at what was then our favourite local Italian haunt, Casa Mario in Duke of York Street. I told him I didn't think he would like being a dealer with the fundamental moral position of not always offering a collector a true price, but rather one that the market would bear. In the end, mainly due to the length of time the solicitors took to draw up the contracts, both had second thoughts. Christie's in a way had the last laugh as Jacob had already printed a huge quantity of new writing paper bearing the names of both Noel and Gregory, which of course had to be pulped, but to a Rothschild that was not much of a loss.

In 1971 Peter Wilson found himself in a completely new financial dilemma because the perennial problem had been aggravated by the extra costs of opening Belgravia. "Sotheby's suddenly found itself strapped for cash . . . in a general economic climate that veered from the merely depressing to the disastrous." When Wills cigarettes made their £100,000 offer, Peter Wilson was therefore determined to take advantage of it, in spite of all the internal misery and damage to morale it caused.

Then in 1972 Peregrine Pollen came to the rescue. Peregrine had returned from New York as Peter Wilson's heir-apparent – or that's what the public as well as Peregrine thought. In fact he joined Lord Westmorland, Peter Wilson's cousin, as joint deputy chairman. Peregrine had no specific department, but was asked to try to get some order into the financial situation, particularly the question of advances and guarantees. In New York the giving of guarantees had been common practice, in order to improve Sotheby's bargaining power when negotiating for important collections, although Christie's had never, to my knowledge, been so bold. In November Sotheby's made public what was hitherto a private practice, by announcing what Geraldine described as a "revolutionary new scheme of guaranteed auction prices in New York" on the occasion of Parke-Bernet's annual meeting with the Art Dealers Association of America. This basically meant an extra 7.5 per cent vendor's premium up to the guaranteed price; if the bidding went further, the normal 10 per cent commission would apply. The success and rights and wrongs of this will be discussed in a later chapter.

It must have been in 1973 that even Peter Wilson, not one to lose his nerve, began to see the writing on the wall and the need for professional financial reorganisation. The following year one of his non-executive directors, Lord Jellicoe, introduced him to Peter Spira, then a vice-chairman of Warburg's of which Jellicoe was a non-executive director. Wilson offered Spira the post of group finance director and after much deliberation he accepted and joined Sotheby's in October 1974.

I asked Spira why he had left the security of a merchant bank for such a "hot potato" as Sotheby's. He admitted that there might have been an element of naivety in his decision to join, "because I didn't realise Sotheby's *was* such a hot potato". However, after twenty years in the City he thought it was time for a change and that Peter Wilson's offer was a very attractive and unique opportunity, very different from industry, in which he wouldn't have wanted to work. "So I took the plunge." Little did he know how deep and cold the water was to be.

"I can tell you, I got quite a shock on my first day," he told me, "because I'd been shown a paper in June which showed that the estimated profits for 1974 were £5 million before tax. By the time I got there in October that figure was down to £2.5 million. When we started looking at how the year would work out – this was just about the beginning of the 1974/75 oil crisis – it looked as if we would be very lucky to make £1 million. The graph instead of going up was going sharply down." The profits before tax for 1973 were £3.5 million on a net sales total of £71.7 million, compared with Christie's half-year profits of £1.1 million for net sales of £33.8 million. "A number of things were clear: the figures were unreliable, the cost control was weak and the credit control was equally poor."

The first thing Spira did in order to bring the finances under control was to ask clients to whom Sotheby's were giving as much as £250,000 credit to provide a modest bank reference. "I felt that if one was going to behave like a banker and give credit, one should behave like a prudent banker." So for several months Spira went round the top dealers explaining that he wasn't impugning their credit or honesty, but that it was a rough, tough world. The Shah could be assassinated at any moment while owing £1 million to a dealer who, through no fault of his own, would be unable to pay Sotheby's; prudence dictated that some modest steps be taken to get bank references and a business-like relationship. After he had talked to them most were perfectly reasonable, but it took a lot of time. The real trouble was that Peter

Wilson tended to support the complainants. There was no doubt that my assumptions had been correct concerning why Sotheby's had not gone public before Christie's.

16

The Buyer's Premium

Christie's 1973 autumn season was the most successful to date in the firm's history, which must have pleased the 4,000 people who had bought shares. The increased sale trend had continued. During the three months there had been 150 sales in London and twenty-six sales overseas, compared with 115 sales in London and twelve overseas in the autumn of 1972. The overseas sales had totalled £4.2 million compared with £2.3 million a year earlier, contributing significantly to the year's profits.

The highlight of the 1973 autumn sales was the collection of Sidney J. Lamon, an American financier and diamond merchant whose New York apartment housed superb French furniture, continental silver, Renaissance jewels, French and German porcelain and Italian maiolica. Everything in the collection was of high quality because Lamon had been advised by the well-known dealer Sammy Rosenberg, who was also a friend from boyhood days – they had been in the same scout troop in Holland before emigrating to America. The collection sold for £1.6 million ($3.8 million).

In spite of the buoyancy of the art market during the autumn and the first six months of 1974, the general economic situation could not have been worse. In 1973 the OPEC countries had quadrupled oil prices which affected the economies of nearly every Western country, resulting in declining purchasing power and a domestic inflation rate approaching 27 per cent per annum. Manufacturing companies and businesses generally had been hit by reduced orders. Prices on the Stock Exchange had naturally tumbled and to add to the domino effect there was a secondary banking crash which caused many businesses, particularly in property, to go bankrupt. Christie's were to learn that it generally takes about a year for such catastrophes to filter through to the art market. So for the first half of the year sales results continued to be good.

Most important of all was Frederick M. Mayer's collection of Chinese porcelain, acknowledged as being one of the finest in the world, which was sold in June. Frederick M. Mayer arrived in New York in the late 1930s when there were still signs of the depression. Undeterred he succeeded in building up both a real estate and a stockbroking firm, and for the second time in his life began making an art collection. In 1945 he bought his first piece of Chinese porcelain and from that moment he became preoccupied with the development of the art of China.

Anthony Derham by deft diplomacy was responsible for winning Mr Mayer over to Christie's when he decided to sell. Collecting had been a pleasure for him for many years, but Mr Mayer eventually realised that his feelings for his collection had subtly changed. A stream of scholarly visitors to his apartment emphasised the extraordinary values of objects for which he had paid nominal sums; his friends had burglaries; insurance premiums reached figures for which he had not long ago been able to buy good pieces. He no longer enjoyed his things and though he realised that he would miss the pleasure and interest of showing them to students of Chinese art he decided to auction the entire group. The eye with which the collection was assembled was more than vindicated by the sold total of £2.2 million ($5.3 million). Sadly, Mr Mayer died shortly after the sale and was unable to enjoy its success.

Peter had informed the Board in March that he was going to retire from being chairman at the end of the season, in July, although he would remain chairman of Christies International. It would be almost forty-five years since he had joined the firm and sixteen years since he had become chairman. When Peter took over the company in 1958 it was old-fashioned and out of touch with reality; the sales total was £1.6 million ($4.4 million) and the profit £35,000. Thanks to his energetic and imaginative leadership Christie's had become a public company and he was able to inform the first annual general meeting of Christies International on May 21st that the pre-tax profit was £2.17 million compared with £1.1 million in 1972. The City columnists were impressed. "Art: A market that bucked the trend. Come rain or shine, economic crisis or boom, the fine art market appears to move inexorably upwards," said the *Sunday Telegraph*; "Confidence in Christies International," said the *Financial Times*.

However, it was no time for Christie's to rest on its laurels because £696,000 of that pre-tax profit was from sales overseas. This said something about UK margins and costs and brought about a review of the development of the whole firm at home and overseas. Most important of all was an analysis of the cost of selling lots at King Street, particularly those of comparatively small value and large size (thus taking up valuable storage space) and of little international interest. It was pointless including such lots in catalogues which were mailed all over the world. This matter was becoming acute but by the autumn a solution had been found.

In May Peter took a particularly successful jewellery sale in Geneva which must have been a satisfying occasion on which to bow out. This totalled Sfr. 24 million (£3.3 million), and included the beautiful pendant stone the Star of South Africa. The main pear-shaped stone of 47.69 carats had a historic glamour because its discovery started the South African diamond rush in March 1869. There was no shortage of bidders and it was eventually knocked down for Sfr. 1.6 million (£225,300).

It was a coincidence of course, but Peter had chosen the right time to retire; in the autumn of 1974 the recession really began to bite. The interim statement issued on October 9th spelt it out: the profit before tax had dropped to £843,000 for the six months ended June 30th compared with £1.1 million for the same period in 1973. For Jo Floyd it could not have been a worse time to take over the responsibilities of chairman. In an interview with the *Daily Telegraph* he said: "It's a time of horrible uncertainty . . . we are not insulated against an international depression. So one must be cautious . . . The first six months have been very successful from the point of view of trading. But obviously we are fighting the same desperate battle against inflation and expenses as everyone else."

Costs had to be cut and decisions were taken which would save £600,000 a year: these involved the closure of the Los Angeles, Madrid and Tokyo offices and ultimately staff redundancies. The year 1974 ended on a sober note. At a Board meeting on December 11th Guy said grimly that action must be taken to produce a "slimmer and more efficient group". Jo undoubtedly hated wielding the axe, but in January 1975, twenty-six of the 250 staff were retired or made redundant – all those retired had far exceeded normal retirement age. Directors took a voluntary 10 per cent cut in salary. (It was lucky for Mark Wrey that I had wanted an extra assistant the previous autumn; otherwise, being on the Front Counter, he might well have been one of those made redundant. Instead he joined me and is now doing my job, having been made public relations director in December 1987.) Those who were made redundant soon found other jobs.

In order to solve the problem of small value lots, the long-established South Kensington auctioneers Debenham and Coe were acquired in the autumn. The new company, Christie's South Kensington, would start operating as from February. In this way the sale of small lots would be rationalised in a profitable manner and release valuable storage space for important works of art. For vendors the advantages would be twofold. First Christie's would be able to offer for sale works of art in the lower price range far more quickly than at King Street, so that secondly it would be possible to pay them much sooner.

Paul Whitfield, who had been made a director in 1970, and Bill Brooks, who had been managing director of Debenham and Coe for many years, would be joint managing directors. Bill Brooks was an ebullient character, as the whole London art market knows, and at times had quite a touch of James Christie's method of encouraging bids. He welcomed the amalgamation as being a logical conclusion to Debenham and Coe's progress during the past four years. In 1973 Debenham and Coe's turnover was approximately £1 million. Little did Christie's or Bill realise that this very necessary step was going to prove so profitable, outstripping in time the undoubted success of Sotheby's Belgravia. Spira told me that it had been extremely difficult to persuade Peter Wilson that it was essential to change the method of selling the vast number of lots of small value, as the old system just didn't make commercial sense. "In that way he just didn't have a feel for modern business."

In 1974 the British economy was in a parlous state. The Stock Exchange had reached an all-time low; the Financial Times Index was at its lowest ever figure of 60, interest rates were up to 13 per cent and a three-day week was imposed on industry. It was quite obvious that in the prevailing financial climate further steps towards profitability had to be taken. The pre-tax profits announced in April were £1.55 million compared with £2.17 million for 1973. Sales had remained virtually static. The decline in profitability was mainly due to King Street sales; overseas profits had increased from £696,000 in 1973 to £754,000 the previous year. The economies, redundancies and rationalisation at the lower end of the business through Christie's

South Kensington, which had been operating well since February, had been swallowed up by inflation. Action had to be taken to pay for the huge increase in operating costs such as printing and postage, two of any auctioneer's greatest expenses, and telephone charges, which had tripled.

Sotheby's were obviously suffering from similar cost problems and had made thirty-one of their staff redundant. Spira's warning to his colleagues and dealers, that if credit was going to be given bank references should be provided, proved only too prescient. Prices for Chinese ceramics had begun to rise startlingly in 1970 and reached boom proportions in 1974. The highest prices were paid by two dealers, Hugh Moss and Mrs Helen Glatz – an elderly lady of German origin who had come to London after her release from a concentration camp. But in April 1974 there was a revolution in Portugal, the home of Mrs Glatz's client, Manoel Ricardo Spiritu Santo. The nephew of Ricardo Spiritu Santo, a leading banker and collector, he was unable to send any money out of the country. Sotheby's had to take many of his purchases back, but by July prices had plummeted. This was just the kind of situation that Spira had argued could happen. Mrs Glatz was nowhere to be seen at Sotheby's July sale.

By now inflation was more than 20 per cent and for Christie's the financial outlook for the year was decidedly bleak – at best a profit of £250,000 on sales of £25 million. It was about this time that Christies International shares reached their all-time low of 23p. (I wonder if anyone had the sense to buy shares then. I doubt if many people anticipated in 1975 that they would be worth over £7 in 1987.) It was essential for Christie's to increase its revenue, but it could not be done by increasing the vendor's commission; that would only blunt its (and indeed London's) competitive edge compared with continental auctioneers. The alternative was to adopt the continental practice of levying a charge on the buyer, although this has always gone into the coffers of the country (or canton in the case of Switzerland). Christie's did not think this would place them at a disadvantage with Sotheby's who were believed, correctly, to be in the same boat. Sotheby's Board had endless meetings and eventually it decided to go ahead with a buyer's charge, but to wait for Peter Wilson's return from a foreign trip before announcing it. Christie's Board beat them to it, announcing on May 31st that a 10 per cent buyer's premium would be introduced as from the autumn season and the vendor's commission reduced to a flat 10 per cent with no charges for illustrations, advertising or UK insurance; the premium would not, however, apply to Christie's South Kensington where the commission was 15 per cent. Before publicly announcing the premium, Jo as a matter of courtesy sent a letter round to Peter Wilson explaining Christie's decision. That was on Friday, May 30th. On Tuesday, June 3rd, Sotheby's announced that they would follow suit. Jo had also written to the dealers' associations stressing that it was essential to give the premium "a fair trial". He also told them that the normal introductory commission given to dealers would be doubled to 4 per cent. These letters had no effect and there was an immediate furore in the fine art trade and charges of "collusion".

Reams have been written about the rights and wrongs of the buyer's premium and the wicked auctioneers, so I don't intend to repeat all the arguments, particularly as today the fine art trade throughout Britain is in good health, although virtually every auctioneer has introduced a buyer's premium. British dealers had always had to pay the sales tax at Paris auctions and had done so quite happily at Sotheby's first sale in Monaco which happened shortly before Christie's decision. However, they were outraged at the idea of also having to pay on purchases in London.

Christie's, Sotheby's, Phillips (who decided first to make capital out of not imposing the premium, although within a year they had been forced to do so) and Bonham's are all businesses which have to be run at a profit. Certainly up to the late 1970s Christie's and Sotheby's were high-cost, small-profit operations. Both were highly competitive and dependent on getting works of art from abroad, which British fine art dealers were also only too keen to buy.

The fact that the terms of sale were better in London for vendors was the reason it had become the centre of the international art market. Fine art auctioneers may be a service industry but they are affected by costs and market conditions in the same way as any other business. If there was any need for justification of the premium it was provided by the financial figures for the first six months of 1975. When Peter came to give the year's results just before Christmas, estimated it is true, he emphasised even more the need for the premium. The London group's pre-tax profit for 1975 was £485,000, which was approximately the amount raised by the premium less the reduction of the vendor's commission. This was in spite of some sensational prices.

The next six years – it was not until 1981 that the fine art trade finally agreed to withdraw their attempts at litigation against Christie's and Sotheby's – were an unhappy time. Dealers and auctioneers may be on different sides of the fine art fence, but they are interdependent. Fine art auctioneers depend primarily on the fine art trade, British and international; neither could do without each other. In the course of business many genuine friendships had been built up over the years and the premium dispute put these under strain. Some dealers took a common sense view that they would take the 10 per cent premium into consideration when bidding. But the majority did not. The first form of protest was a boycott at the first Sotheby sale in the autumn and an attempted one at Christie's, but this kind of demonstration fizzled out quickly, as the fine art trade still had to carry on. There was never in any case a united front for this type of action; some dealers who walked out asked friends to bid for them.

When the Department of Prices and Consumer Protection questioned Christie's in September 1975, they accepted in the end Christie's assurances that the premium decision had been made independently. However, this did not satisfy the fine art trade, whose anger saw no bounds, eventually three years later reaching the stage of trying to take legal action against both firms of auctioneers. The matter was discussed in chambers in the Chancery Division, but the dealers, having taken note of the acceptance by the Department of Prices and Consumer Protection of Christie's explanation, decided not to pursue their claim for an injunction pending trial – perhaps for fear of legal costs, but also because some realised that the wrangling over the premium wasn't doing the market any good. For the moment that was the end of public protest, but the bitterness of the dealers continued and was to be voiced some years later.

Sotheby's were if anything in even worse odour with the dealers and general public than Christie's because just before Christmas 1974 it was learned that the British Railways Pension Fund had decided to invest 3 per cent of their vast resources in works of art, relying on the advice of Sotheby's. This was the brainchild of Christopher Lewin, a collector of antiquarian books but by profession an actuary and one of those responsible for the annual investment of British railwaymen's superannuation funds. The decision was criticised on several grounds in a lengthy feature by Geraldine on December 21st. The question was not only whether it was appropriate for a pension fund to invest in works of art, but whether there was not a conflict of interest in Sotheby's acting as advisers to the fund; how, as agents for the vendors, could their advice to the fund be unbiased?

The person at the centre of the storm was Annamaria Edelstein, originally assistant to Philip Wilson, Peter Wilson's son, who was responsible for the production of *Art at Auction*, the counterpart to Christie's *Review of the Season*. In that capacity Annamaria naturally got to know the heads of every department. Although she was employed by British Rail from 1974, it was too much for the general public, let alone journalists and dealers, to believe that she wouldn't either overtly or covertly be influenced into discussing the affairs of the fund. Annamaria not surprisingly gave only one interview to the Press, so it was not seen that her character was in itself a safeguard.

Annamaria had worked with Philip Wilson on *Art at Auction* for six years. During this time she came to know his father very well, went on holiday with him and like many people admired him and learned a great deal from him. At the same time, as she told me in 1989, Peter Wilson thought she would be a good person to help British Rail because she had worked on *Art at Auction*. As with Christie's *Review* this inevitably gives the editor, as Annamaria said, "a smattering of knowledge of every subject and also an idea about prices". "Peter Wilson also knew that I was bloody-minded and thought that was a good characteristic for somebody who had to put a collection together without being influenced by anyone, including him." I asked her if Peter Wilson tried to make use of her. "Of course he did," she said with a laugh. "Of course he did. I just used to laugh at him, because he was so transparent." Annamaria told me that no one ever knew when she was bidding as she always did so through a dealer she knew well. Her relations with the fund were not always easy. "I used to have the most terrible fights because they didn't like my suggestions, and I threatened to resign three times. I was given the job because I was not a complete idiot, and can tell a liar as well as any person. I got to know a number of directors at Christie's, in Geneva and New York, whom I came to trust and who gave me good advice." In the final analysis Annamaria was not only "bloody-minded", but she also had integrity. It was this that people found difficult to believe.

Peregrine Pollen, who initially had a considerable amount to do with the fund project, said very much what came to be my view after talking to Annamaria. "No auctioneer is ever going to be considered to be honest. It's a dirty business and always has been. An actress from the eighteenth century was automatically considered to be a whore and auctioneers are automatically even now considered to be corrupt. However honest they are, and Christie's and Sotheby's try to be honest in major ways, they will never be trusted because it's a chancy game. There was never a conflict of interest, and the defences against a possible conflict of interest were carefully thought out and carefully built and solidly built. But it was a splendid stick to beat us with, and it was helped by the unions in British Rail; Geraldine added her weight, and even Bernard Levin who equated it with putting money on the third race at Uttoxeter. I can see no difference between having British Rail as a heavy buyer and Norton Simon. They were equally unpredictable."

Nevertheless I agree with Geraldine, senior members of the trade and even ex-Sotheby directors who thought Sotheby's should never have become involved. Whatever well-meaning safeguards were built into the system, there was no way it could avoid being interpreted as a conflict of interest – not that Peter Wilson worried about that. He wanted new buyers in the market.

However, there was another side to the controversy. Were works of art a justifiable form of investment from an actuarial point of view? Peter Spira is quite clear on this aspect: "My view was that interest rates were about 6 per cent and at that time it was not unreasonable for a pension fund to put a very small percentage of its assets in works of art provided it was long-term. A year or two later when interest rates were 10 or 12 per cent Sotheby's attitude, or Peter Wilson's attitude particularly, was that it was still a sensible thing to do. In my opinion in these changed circumstances it was no longer sensible." Sir Peter Parker, who took over British Rail from Lord Marsh, probably agreed, because in 1980 the fund stopped buying, having spent £40 million on 2,000 objects.

In spite of the controversies sales went on. Just before the news broke of Sotheby's connection with the British Railways Pension Fund, King Street passed another milestone in December 1974 with their first contemporary art sale. This was organised by Jorg-Michael Bertz, Christie's talented Düsseldorf representative. Jorg had already mounted a sale of contemporary pictures in Düsseldorf which had aroused considerable interest. From now, until the appointment of Babs Thomson in 1984, Jorg was responsible not only for collecting contemporary art for sale, but for creating a completely new department at King Street and getting support for it. The importance of catering for the interests of a new group of collectors on this side of the Atlantic quickly became apparent.

The huge canvases Jorg brought us from the Continent were not to the taste of many of us, but curiously did not clash with the highly important eighteenth-century French furniture which happened to be on display at the same time. The sale in the grim autumn of 1974 attracted a huge audience of all ages, even if many of them didn't have any money. Considering the economic climate it went well. It was the beginning of a most important development in the picture department. In America the sums paid for such works were tremendous and continued to rise. Jorg taught all of us in the Press Office the importance of knowing the different forms of contemporary art – Minimal Art, Conceptual Art, Constructivism and so on. When we opened in 1977 in New York such sales were of even greater importance, not only financially, but from a PR point of view.

To add to the financial worries, at the beginning of 1975 Christie's was the target of a gang of thieves who by clever faking of receipt notes stole jewellery worth £240,000. In addition the year started with the biggest non-event of my time at Christie's, which perhaps understandably I have never forgotten. One morning early in January, David Bathurst burst into the Press Office, in itself an unusual event. I and my staff obviously had to keep contact with every department so we would do the rounds of the various offices. However, many colleagues, regardless of whether they were directors or technical staff, made a habit of popping in either because they had something they thought would be interesting to the Press, or just to chat up my secretaries. These visits were welcome as they helped to establish a rapport which was important, apart from keeping at least me (if it was confidential) in touch with the latest developments.

The only director who hardly ever came in was David Bathurst, so his arrival obviously meant something special was in the wind. He asked me to produce an advertising campaign for an important Impressionist picture, taking in newspapers and magazines, from Los Angeles to Hong Kong together with the cost as soon as possible. It was not all that difficult and I went up to his office with it. The picture was to be sold on April 15th, so we should book space immediately if we were going to get into certain magazines. David authorised this and I asked for suitable copy for the advertisement. He handed me the manuscript for the catalogue and I copied down the details. The picture was Van Gogh's *Portrait of Patience Escalier*, a local gardener wearing a big hat, which the artist had painted in Arles in 1888; it was to be sold anonymously. In the middle of February I thought that if we were advertising this picture all round the world, we should get some free publicity by giving it to the Press, and went upstairs to discuss it with David. He agreed and handed me a photograph of the picture and told me there were no other details I could use other than what was on the manuscript which would go in the catalogue.

Just after I'd got back to my office Geraldine walked in. "Want a story, just for yourself?" I said, offering her the details I had had typed out together with the photograph. Before giving it her I looked at it carefully and thought it was familiar. I suddenly realised I had seen a pastiche of it in Guy's office, which had been painted by a convict in Wormwood Scrubs who has since sent him many more artistic efforts.

Next morning at seven thirty I went downstairs, collected the papers, made myself a cup of tea and got back into bed. I had just had time to unfold *The Times* and see the Van Gogh in the bottom left hand corner when the telephone rang. "For Christ's sake what's happening?" Needless to say it was David Bathurst. I asked what was wrong. "Exclusive on *The Times* front page was just what we wanted, considering the lack of information." "Yes, but I told the owner [whose name I still did not know] that it wasn't going to appear till Wednesday." I told David that he'd never mentioned Wednesday to me and as far as I was concerned had given me a free hand. "But you don't understand, the owner hasn't even told his wife he's selling the picture." "I'm sorry, David, but I'm not psychic. You should have told me in detail when you wanted the news to appear and if there were any other problems to be borne in mind." Geraldine had in fact done some homework and quoted what Van Gogh had written in his letters about the portrait: "I imagine the man I have to paint, terrible in the furnace of the height of harvest time." But no owner's name.

Soon after I'd got into the office John Rydon of the *Daily Express* rang wanting to know who owned the picture and also a photograph. I told him I couldn't oblige. The picture was due to appear in colour on the front page of our monthly forthcoming sales magazine. I sensed disaster. If the picture was as important as the advertising programme implied it must be in the Van Gogh books, which normally gave the owner's name. If so, any reporter worth his salt would be able not only to find it out but also get a photograph. Sure enough, next morning the story led the *Daily Express*'s William Hickey column, with a detail of a photograph of the picture. It was the property of 68-year-old Chester Beatty, son of the late copper millionaire, who till now had always favoured Sotheby's. I gather Jo had been working on Beatty's solicitor since November. When he agreed to sell it through

Christie's, Jo had told him the ownership of such an important painting couldn't be kept anonymous. However, Beatty, like many rich and powerful men, refused to see the logic of what Jo had said. I don't know what went on between David and Beatty because events moved so fast. Directly it appeared in *The Times*, Martin Summers, the smooth good-looking director of the LeFevre Gallery, had rung David Somerset, head of the Marlborough Gallery, and suggested a joint approach to Beatty to buy the picture for "around $2 million", he told me in 1987.

Beatty accepted the dealers' offer immediately, no doubt outraged at not having had his way and presumably having had to pacify his wife. There was also of course no commission to pay. Chester Beatty was probably also infuriated by William Hickey's question: "The real poser is not who is selling but why? Two years ago it would have certainly fetched more . . . Today the market is down. Hardly the time to sell . . . So sensitive is our anonymous owner that Christie's absurdly refused to supply me with a photograph of the painting. It was quite easy to get one from an art gallery." I suspect Rydon had been to the Courtauld Institute which would have been able to give him chapter and verse.

I don't blame David for being mortified as he thought, probably quite rightly, that he had on his hands the first £1 million Impressionist. Instead he was instructed to hand the picture over to dealers, whom he naturally knew well. The picture still appeared on the front page of our monthly magazine, so rubbing salt into the wound. No rockets descended on the Press office; nor should they have done, but it left a scar to this day. The incident underlined the importance of briefing the Press Office properly, as Jo, Patrick, Arthur and others always did. It also made me wonder about David's casualness.

In 1975 there were definite signs of gradual recovery from the recession: Albert had a jewellery sale which included a superb sapphire and diamond brooch which made £160,000 ($384,000). Jo sold a Louis XVI black lacquer and ebony writing-desk and cartonnier by Martin Carlin for £157,750 ($362,825) – sales of French furniture during the 1974–5 season totalled £3.8 million ($8.7 million). Then there were the prestigious Stefano della Bella drawings; even some notable Old Masters – Pieter de Hooch's *The Soap Bubbles* achieving a new record for the artist at £147,000 ($338,100), while Canaletto's view of *The Old Horse Guards and Banqueting Hall from St James's Park* was bought by Roy Miles, a comparatively new dealer who had previously run a ladies' hairdressing salon, for £105,000 ($241,000). It was the most expensive picture Miles had bought to date and he was no doubt pleased when the Mellon Center for British Art at Yale said they would like it.

There was also a historic wine sale, when Château Lafite and Château Mouton-Rothschild sank their differences in order to shake the sluggish fine wine market into activity and to correct the severe over-reaction to excessive prices caused by inflationary demand and speculation during the 1971–3 period. The managing director of Château Mouton-Rothschild was asked by the French Press why he was selling through Christie's and his reply was: "Nous avons choisi Londres et non pas la Salle Drouot [then the main Paris auction house] pour cette vente aux enchères, pour profiter de la clientèle internationale de Christie's." Sotheby's never got anywhere near threatening the dominant position Michael Broadbent and Alan Taylor-Restell had achieved for Christie's wine auctions. Château Mouton-Rothschild were aware of this, not through hearsay, but because many thousands of cases belonging to Bass Charrington had been lying in the château's cellars at the time of the Bass sale the previous summer, and the results had been noted. The Château Lafite/ Mouton-Rothschild sale in June consisted of some 6,000 cases of twenty of the best vintages from 1945 to 1971. The wine sold for £438,222 ($1,008,000), and inspired Jak of the *Standard* to draw another splendid cartoon of a Hell's Angels type "caff" with the wine on the slate menu. It was as a result of sales like this that in 1979 the French Government made Michael a Chevalier dans l'Ordre National du Mérite, second to the Légion d'Honneur.

Finally in his December Impressionist sale, David had a large number of works which belonged to the late Fletcher Jones, a Los Angeles computer tycoon who had killed himself while piloting his own plane. The collection included Picasso's wonderful *Self-Portrait* which made £283,500 ($567,000) compared with the £147,000 ($353,000) Christie's had sold it for in 1970. (The reader may notice that there is no longer any mention of guineas. This last vestige of the eighteenth century had been abandoned at the beginning of the year and prompted Patrick to get the cartoonist Michael ffolkes to produce an amusing Bateman-like cartoon which has hung in the Board Room ever since.)

Full economic recovery came in 1976. It was also the year Peter resigned as Chairman of Christies International, but not before the financial results had been announced for 1975. These bore out the warning Peter had given at Christmas. In spite of the sales mentioned above and many others, the profit before tax was £1.9 million compared with £1.5 million for 1974; sales in 1975 totalled £39.2 million compared with £40 million the previous year. There just hadn't been sufficient good business at King Street to make an impression on costs. However, there was no doubt that Peter had saved Christie's. He didn't leave without one last crack at Geraldine who before Christmas had suggested that the art market might be shifting from London because of the buyer's premium.

Geraldine's thesis was, in my opinion, ill-reasoned and it did not tally with the results of our picture sales in the autumn. I drafted a letter to *The Times*, but was told by them that they didn't publish letters from public relations officers even if they were directors; so I went to Jo who agreed completely, but found it quite amusing to see me getting all steamed up about one of Geraldine's articles, when generally I was defending her. Jo signed the letter, and Peter quoted part of it in the annual report: "It is surely proof of the confidence of foreign collectors in the London art market that over a quarter of the lots in our important Old Master sale on 28 November came from abroad, while in the Impressionist sale on 2 December no fewer than 79 out of 94 works in the morning sale belonged to foreign vendors from 10 different countries, while buyers as usual came from all over the world."

An encouraging sign of a full recovery in the market was Patrick's July Old Master sale which thanks to a number of great works achieved a total of £2.9 million ($5.1 million). One of these was Duccio's *The Crucifixion*, which will be remembered not only for its price but also its radiance. Patrick sold it on behalf of his mother, Mary, Countess of Crawford and Balcarres, for £1 million ($1.7 million), but who the buyer was still remains unknown, except to Ray Perman, who as sales clerk had been given instructions to bid for it. When Patrick was a boy, the Duccio had hung in his nursery.

The applied arts departments were equally busy, particularly Hermione Waterfield and Bill Fagg, late of the British Museum, who were producing their first catalogue of the Hooper Collection of Tribal Art, which covered virtually every tribal corner of the globe. The amazing thing is that James Hooper, who had died in 1971, had formed his collection almost entirely of purchases from missionaries, explorers, servicemen, colonial officers and traders, and left Britain only three times in his life, none of which was in the search for tribal art. By profession he worked for the Thames Conservancy which gave him time to devote to tribal art. In 1912 his father had given him a native spear which he hung in his bedroom. Having cleaned it, he wondered who had made it: what did he look like and where had he lived? "Thus my curiosity was aroused and I spent my time searching curio shops for tribal objects and weapons to form a small collection." When the fifth sale was held in 1980, the total had reached £2.8 million ($6.6 million).

So far I have not mentioned many sales of books. The book department was minute compared with that of Sotheby's and always seemed to be riven by staff dramas. However, in spite of these, under the flamboyantly dressed and good-humoured direction of Bill Spowers the department achieved a startling increase in turnover: major sales included illuminated manuscripts from the famed Chatsworth library; books, manuscripts and letters from Siegfried Sassoon's library; seven sumptuous folios from the Houghton *Shahnameh* (*Book of Kings*, Iran's national epic) which fetched £785,000 ($1.3 million); in the following year the Evelyn Library and of even greater importance the splendid library of Arthur Houghton Jnr, of New York, which was sold in two parts a few years later.

There was one outstanding book in 1976. This was Lieutenant William Bligh's weather-stained pocketbook account of the 3,500-mile voyage in the *Bounty*'s whaler after the mutiny. Cast adrift almost in the middle of the Pacific, Bligh successfully sailed the open whaler to Timor, in the East Indies, an amazing feat of seamanship and navigation. Bligh's "account . . . kept in my bosom as a common memorandum of our time" consisted of 107 pages of autograph text, not surprisingly untidily written, with ink-blots and weather stains, twenty-two pages of navigational recordings and nine sketch charts. The document records his moods of doubt, exasperation and despair. It is almost certainly the first draft of the version later sent to the Admiralty. One can picture Bligh sitting in the sternsheets recording in intimate detail the physical characteristics of Fletcher Christian and the other mutineers. The existence of the pocketbook outside Bligh's family was completely unknown until brought to Christie's. It found a fitting home in the National Library in Sydney, Australia, after being sold for £55,000 ($93,500).

That summer Christie's could take pride in the publication of Arthur Grimwade's *London Goldsmiths 1697–1837: Their Lives and*

Marks which was the result of twenty years' research, much of it being done by getting up at 6 a.m. To quote Frank Davis of *Country Life*: "It is one of those monumental reference works which inevitably defy the passage of time."

Some important decisions had recently been taken. Early in the year Christie's bought the freehold of Langley Works, near Vauxhall Station, which was to be the new home of White's, the printers, as they were outgrowing the original Lambeth works. More important still, the first initiatives were taken to acquire a New York saleroom. Guy did the legwork and negotiating, the Board finally agreeing in June to lease part of the old Delmonico Hotel, 502 Park Avenue. Once a firm decision had been taken, there was no time to lose if the saleroom was to be in action next summer.

In September, therefore, Guy went to New York to take charge of the final problems over the lease and the refurbishment of what had been the hotel's ballroom, restaurant and lounges. If you're going to start a saleroom, you need some art experts and administrators. Early in the autumn Anthony du Boulay, Ian Kennedy, who had been in the Old Master department for some years, Anthony Phillips, who had been Arthur Grimwade's assistant, Stephen Massey, who would run the book department, and Ray Perman, who would train the "attendants", as porters are called in America, joined the resident New York staff of Christopher Burge, François Curiel and of course Guy. It was an exciting time, for directly they arrived everyone had to set to work to get a series of sales together for next May, although the conversion of the building had hardly begun. The team left in a confident mood because by then the interim figures were available and showed that the pre-tax profit for the first six months of 1976 was £1.7 million, compared with £664,000 for 1975, nearly three times greater.

During the autumn there was another good Impressionist sale with more than three-quarters of the works from abroad, and sixteen sessions in Geneva totalling Sfr. 19.9 million (£4.9 million). These sales helped push the pre-tax profit for 1976 up to £3.6 million compared with £1.9 million the year before; nearly twice as much. The gap between Sotheby's and Christie's sales was not only narrowing, but Christie's at last were going to be able to compete on the same footing as Sotheby's with their own saleroom in New York.

17

Peter the Great and Ivan the Terrible

By early in 1977 the art market had recovered and Peter Spira's financial strictures on Sotheby's, although highly unpopular with the technical departments, had brought the firm's accounts into some semblance of order. In February, four years after Christie's had gone public, Spira advised the Board that Sotheby's were in a position to do the same. Considering that their annual world-wide sales had often been three times those of Christie's, it speaks volumes for the state of their balance sheet that they were in no position to do so before – but this point was lost on the Press.

On June 1st the flotation of Sotheby Parke-Bernet, to give the group its new title, was over-subscribed twenty-six times, the initial share price being 150p. The issue was completely different from that of Christie's. There were no "A" shares owned by the directors for reasons of security. This was obviously to enable Sotheby's directors to get their money out if and when they wanted; some had wanted to do so since 1971. Eighteen months later the shares had risen to 380p. The offer document had forecast a profit for the year 1977 of £4.6 million. This was comfortably exceeded. In the following year sales increased by 30 per cent to just over £161 million, with a pre-tax profit of just over £7 million.

These figures sound very impressive until compared with Christie's, whose sales in 1978 totalled £98.9 million with pre-tax profits of £5.6 million: although Christie's had had approximately only two-thirds of Sotheby's sales they had achieved 80 per cent of Sotheby's pre-tax profits. The significance of this was picked up by some City editors.

The three largest shareholders were Peter Wilson, Peregrine Pollen and the Rothschild Investment Trust; it will be remembered that Jacob Rothschild had bought 20 per cent of the equity in 1971 which it had been hoped would help bring about a public flotation much earlier. Peter Wilson could boast that his firm sold more works of art than any other firm of fine art auctioneers. Peter Chance could reply, "Maybe, but Christie's is more profitable." How did Peter Wilson raise Sotheby's sales totals so dramatically and, more important still, how did his business methods compare with those of Christie's?

There is no doubt that Peter Wilson was a phenomenon who changed the whole character of the London art market. Even his critics agree that he had a most remarkable eye for works of art of all kinds, was a brilliant auctioneer, and had an unusually imaginative entrepreneurial mind. His golden years were from 1957, when he became chairman, until 1969. Unlike Peter Chance, he had more experienced colleagues on the Board and of his own age to help him: Anthony Hobson (books), Carmen Gronau (pictures, mainly Old Masters – Peter Wilson himself looked after Impressionists), Richard Timewell (furniture), Jim Kiddell (ceramics); Tim Clarke (works of art and glass); Graham Llewellyn, whose first job had been behind the jewellery counter of Harrods (jewellery); and Fred Rose (silver). The fine art trade's general impression of the two firms was given succinctly by Jack Abbey, President of the British Antique Dealers Association in 1958, at the association's annual dinner, when he referred to "the young hussy of Bond Street and the old lady of King Street".

Peter Wilson and his colleagues were far more imaginative and keen to get intelligent recruits and train them in the best possible way than Christie's were. Three at least applied to Christie's as well as Sotheby's – Peregrine Pollen, Richard Day and Howard Ricketts – but for various reasons all three ended up at Sotheby's, and all of them became directors when in their twenties. Christie's had taken on young men with arts degrees, such as Christopher Wood, Hugo Morley-Fletcher, Noel Annesley and John Lumley, who had all studied at Cambridge under Professor Michael Jaffé, but there wasn't the same stimulus and imaginative training that there was at Sotheby's.

Among those who joined Sotheby's in the late 1950s and early 1960s were Marcus Linell, Howard Ricketts, Richard Day, Richard Came, Michael Webb, the late Bruce Chatwin, and Michel Strauss. Unlike at Christie's, those wishing to join technical departments became porters. Jim Kiddell, the great ceramics expert, believed that people's eyesight began to deteriorate when they were fourteen. This partly accounts for the fact that Marcus Linell, who was to run Sotheby's Belgravia and later become managing director, was offered a job when he was sixteen. "I think I better get my O levels first," he told Kiddell, but to me he said, "It was tremendously exciting to be offered such an opportunity so young even if it was for £6 a week."

According to Linell the "porter system" was a fairly random method of training and there were a lot of casualties who didn't measure up to what was required. The philosophy was to get people working in a department where they would see a great deal and handle the objects, rather than get a fleeting glimpse of them as they crossed the Front Counter. The ex-public school boy porters were frowned on at Christie's for some reason. They did exist, but as far as I know Philip Hook, who resigned in 1987 to join David Bathurst and Henry Wyndham in the St James's Art Group, was the only one to be made a director. David Messum is an even more outstanding example of what rewards the art market can bring to those with perseverance, however humble their beginnings. David, having come straight from school to be one of Jim Taylor's porters – "a wonderful way of learning the business" – spent a short time in the drawings and watercolours warehouse working for Brian and Noel and then graduated to Bonham's where he catalogued pictures. He has been a dealer for many years, with such success that in 1988 he bought a five-floor gallery opposite Sotheby's St George's Street entrance and specialises in British Impressionist pictures.

The Sotheby's trainees were quickly struck by Peter Wilson's energy, determination and ambition for the firm and not surprisingly they admired him, although they recognised that the success of the company lay also in the abilities of Anthony Hobson and Tim Clarke, and "they were a remarkably bright trio". Marcus Linell expressed very clearly the charismatic effect Peter Wilson had on his trainees. "His determination always ran ahead of whatever was achieved, which was wonderful, so that he always wanted to and did step from one achievement to the next, always upwards, dragging – he was leading from the front – others along in no uncertain way.

"It was terribly exciting. It was like being in some sort of troika with him whipping the horses on, and you were panting along behind, thinking, 'My God, what a wonderful life this is,' and it was extremely exhilarating going from peak to peak and certainly at the time of the Goldschmidt sale one thought that that sort of thing could never happen again. It was an extraordinary phenomenon because the value of the sale was quite a large proportion of the annual turnover so that how on earth next year could you do what had been done last year?"

Richard Day, who joined Sotheby's in 1958 at the age of twenty-two, became director in 1964 of the drawings and prints department. He had been the first boy at Stowe to take Art and Art History as an A level. After doing his National Service he put on a bicentenary exhibition of James Gilroy's prints in a gallery in Kensington. An old lady came in mainly to get out of the rain. She asked him what he wanted to do and he said join Sotheby's or Christie's. Having seen the exhibition she asked him to come and have a drink; and there he met Carmen Gronau, who told him to apply to Peter Wilson for an interview. "I saw him twice. He was extremely nice and asked interesting questions and finally offered me a job. Initially I was in the book department but I was very lucky because they allowed me to go every afternoon to study prints in the British Museum." Carmen eventually asked him to catalogue Old Master drawings, of course under her final approval. In 1964 Carmen combined the prints and drawings departments and Richard Day was made a partner and told to run it.

Richard Day stressed like Marcus the enthusiastic atmosphere which made Sotheby's hum like a dynamo in his early days. "Eight of us all had tea together each day. It was made for us by Mrs Janner, the cleaning lady, and we had it in her broom cupboard. It was a wonderful time for exchanging information, and discussing what was turning up in one's department. You'd learn as you talked over tea, just as undergraduates learn from their contemporaries." There were no cultural broom cupboards at Christie's.

Howard Ricketts started collecting arms and armour when he was seven, having been given the part of King Arthur in his pre-prep school play for which he needed a sword. This aroused his interest and he began buying arms and armour at auctions when he was fifteen. He joined Sotheby's in 1959 at £5 10s. a week. There wasn't much demand for arms and armour in those days. There were very few known collections or reference books and what there were were very expensive, so Ricketts had to teach himself. He researched collections abroad which gave him valuable experience. "I was twenty-four when I became a partner in Sotheby's, but it was only because Peter Wilson happened to hear that I'd been offered a job by the Metropolitan Museum. The great thing about Peter Wilson was that if he recognised that anyone had a particular passion for a particular subject he would put them into it, and if they swam they swam and were put on the Board eventually. I was a special case."

Peter the Great and Ivan the Terrible

Peter Wilson's restless energy was stimulated still further by the sales which resulted from the success of the second Goldschmidt sale; he encouraged his young men to go out and get business. Howard Ricketts agreed when I raised the question of ruthlessness with particular regard to those who hitherto might have been regarded as dealers' clients. Before the Goldschmidt sale it was normal for many collectors not only to buy through a dealer but to approach a dealer if they wished to sell, even if the work of art ended in an auction house. Peter Wilson changed all that. "Yes I think we were ruthless, and if you went round with Peter Wilson, you learned how to get collections and it was a very exciting time. One felt one was in direct competition with the trade." Marcus Linell was of the same opinion: "The antagonism from the dealers was inevitable."

However, Peter Wilson's eyes were really on America which he regarded as the golden land of opportunity. After the success of the Fribourg sale, which had been won only after offering what were very tough terms for Sotheby's, Peter and Peregrine Pollen set their sights on Parke-Bernet who were making only about 1 per cent on their capital. The death in September 1963 of Leslie Hyam, Parke-Bernet's president, gave them their chance, but it meant an enormous financial risk. But risks were nothing to Peter Wilson; he thrived on them and this was only one of many. As Peregrine Pollen said, "Peter was an imaginative gambler. The Fribourg sale was a risk. Every sale was treated as a risk until we went public. All Sotheby's coups were basically risks. If we lost money it didn't matter so long as we got the sale and did it imaginatively and that's what we were trying to build on."

Buying Parke-Bernet could only be done with extra finance on a huge scale and Wilson was attacked by many of his partners, particularly Anthony Hobson, Richard Timewell and Fred Rose. Peregrine made a passionate appeal to go ahead and standing up at the Board meeting said, "And if we can't find anyone else to run PB I'll run it myself." In order to solve the financial problem Wilson sought the help of Hermann Robinow, an investment banker who after leaving Warburg's founded with Clifford Barclay Barro Equities – not surprisingly they were dubbed "the barrow boys".

Robinow was extremely influential in providing financial advice. He realised that banks wouldn't understand sales of works of art or trust them, but they would value real estate. He believed, therefore, that it was crucial for a service industry to have a collateral of real estate with which if necessary it could find funds to purchase works of art. Wilson took his advice and within the next fifteen years or so acquired a large amount of property in the New Bond Street, Conduit Street, St George's Street and Maddox Street quadrant, all of which is now of course worth a vast amount more than was originally paid for it. However, one of Robinow's earliest and most valuable contributions was an imaginative refinancing scheme whereby partners were able to extract capital without selling their shares. It also enabled the partners to avoid a tremendous lot of tax. In this way the bright young men like Marcus were able to get shares because the profits had been mortgaged and they were "terribly cheap". "It was wonderful because you had a bunch of very contented people."

There were no incentives at Christie's in the 1960s for young but valuable staff or even directors. In those years the firm was probably not in a financial position to act on such advice even if they had been given it. I doubt, however, if Hambro's Bank would have been able to stitch together such a clever scheme. Peter Chance would never have left his friends in an Establishment bank like Hambro's and taken advice from someone like Robinow. Once again it was imagination and business flair which enabled Sotheby's to advance in so many directions. It was only towards the end of the 1970s, by which time the shares had recovered from the recession, that a share-option scheme was offered to certain directors at Christie's.

Finding money to buy Parke-Bernet was no problem for Robinow; he quickly arranged a $1.5 million eighteen-month loan through the Morgan Guaranty Trust. However, having bought Parke-Bernet, Wilson and Pollen were faced with a problem. In 1964 in America auctions weren't fashionable; they were associated with "chattels" and the dispersal of a family's effects. What was needed were some major sales to get Parke-Bernet off the ground.

That was Peregrine Pollen's first objective once Parke-Bernet was part of Sotheby's and he was more than equal to it. It had to be an Impressionist and Modern picture sale because after the Goldschmidt sale that was what was smart, valuable and attractive. A sale was scheduled for April 14th, 1965. Considerable thought and imagination went into its planning, because it was as much a public relations affair as a commercial exercise. It was to be an evening – black tie – occasion to give it snob appeal and there were to be two auctions. In between there was a benefit dinner at 980 Madison Avenue which was transformed to resemble the interior of the Café de la Nouvelle Athènes in the Place Pigalle where Degas and Manet drank together, and where Degas in 1876 painted one of his most famous pictures, *L'Absinthe*. The menu was printed in the style of the day and there were six-foot-high photographs of all the artists hanging round the room. Pollen told me: "It was a very dramatic evening. A marvellous Degas of dancers which had literally been brought to us over the Front Counter, sold for $410,000 (then a very high price), and the two sales totalled $2.3 million. That was our PR debut in New York. It was great fun and a great success." This was the kind of marketing on a grand scale which Christie's did not learn until comparatively recently.

Peter Wilson also revelled in the policy of offering special terms regardless of the risks. Sometimes he didn't have to. Occasionally when he was chasing a picture Robinow "would give him a bid" so that he could be sure of selling it for what the owner wanted. "Robinow was a wealthy man and could do it." Offering advances was regarded as "normal business". It was towards the end of the 1960s that the "purchasing of collections" began although it created a lot of Board Room battles and was kept secret for as long as possible, because it raised the question of a conflict of interest. Sotheby's could always raise money because they had the collateral in real estate. Christie's couldn't have done so, even if they had been so inclined, as they had sold their freehold.

Peter Wilson also encouraged people such as Pollen, now that he was in charge in New York, to work out special terms if he had the nerve. "It was entirely due to Peter that any of us did anything imaginative." A prize example for which Pollen was responsible was the sale of eight Impressionists belonging to a Long Island collector called Clifford Klent; these included Renoir's superb *Pont des Arts*. Pollen told the owner that unless the Renoir fetched over $1 million Parke-Bernet would not take any commission on any of the pictures. "The world record for a Renoir at that time was $225,000. It was a colossal gamble. The picture fetched $1.5 million and we got full commission on the whole sale. But that's the kind of gamble which is difficult to take once you're a public company, particularly if the sale is going to be a major percentage of the annual turnover. That attitude developed a sea change once we became a public company."

It was a foreign world to Christie's who in Peter Chance's day very rarely even suggested either an advance or a guarantee, or special terms of any sort. The Board almost to a man, with the exception of David Bathurst who had the difficult job of prising pictures out of Americans, was psychologically as well as financially opposed to such ways of doing business. In the final analysis they may well have been correct, but it might have been sensible to have given them a little more consideration before Christie's went public.

Apart from the difficulty and risks of raising money for Christie's at that time, Peter Chance and indeed most of his younger colleagues believed in the orthodox style of fine art auctioneering in which they'd been trained. In any case I don't think that Peter Chance had Peter Wilson's self-confidence to back his own or his colleagues' judgment about the value of an Impressionist, or other works of art, with an advance. I remember well the matter coming up with regard to the Edward G. Robinson collection of Impressionists. David pleaded for a little assistance so that he could bargain with the Trustees. I supported him and Peter said, "Do you realise you are risking your money as well as the firm's?" For David Bathurst in his search for pictures in America this attitude posed great difficulties.

Wilson's policy was diametrically opposite, as Peregrine Pollen and Peter Spira confirm. It can be described as sales at any price. Sotheby's had to be seen to be selling more and more even if they were virtually buying or providing large advances for what they were selling. The risks inherent in such a policy came to a head over the "Higgons affair". Madame Higgons, the French wife of an English-born dealer (né Higgins), proved a good source for Impressionists in which Peter Wilson, still head of that department as well as being chairman, was naturally particularly interested. In return for a number of such pictures the Higgonses received advances.

Peter Wilson's intermediary was Michel Strauss, the French-born and much respected present director of Sotheby's Impressionist department. Strauss, whose grandparents had a superb collection of Impressionists which he never saw as they had to be sold in the 1930s depression, told me he had wanted a career in the art world from the age of seven. After taking an art degree at Harvard, followed by a post-graduate degree at the Courtauld, he was recommended to Peter Wilson by Douglas Cooper as a possible assistant. He joined Sotheby's in 1961 at the age of twenty-five and started cataloguing Impressionists straight away.

Strauss was perfectly frank about the Higgons affair. "They found pictures in France and in order to help them purchase them we made advances in a normal business way." This worked perfectly until the market took a downturn, as it did following the Wall Street and Stock

Exchange collapse in 1969/70. A number of Higgons's pictures failed to sell and the Higgonses ended up owing Sotheby's money on advances. It was then that the Board learned the full details of what had been going on. Strauss said, "The Board didn't know the day-to-day details. There was no requirement for them to do so. The Higgonses soon sorted the matter out by providing some more pictures. There was nothing underhand or secretive about it. It was a storm in a teacup. You know what PW was like; he did what he wanted. That was the foundation of the success of the business. You invest to make money." However, that was not how Robinow, the finance director, saw it. He "made a great fuss about it, saying he hadn't been told about it and some others on the Board got worked up".

Marcus Linell, a past managing director, put it another way: "The basic problem was that Peter in his capacity as chairman, together with Michel Strauss, who was very young and inexperienced, got carried away by the success of what they had been doing. At a certain point the Board realised what had been going on. Initially we were very worried and then the worry receded. It was just over-enthusiasm." Over-enthusiasm or not, the Higgons affair like many other special arrangements of Peter Wilson's added to a growing feeling of disharmony among junior and senior directors.

Talking to Strauss in April 1989, twenty years later, I agreed that in retrospect it was a storm in a teacup. "Christie's may not have made special terms then but they do now," Michel said. Nevertheless, just as Peter Chance didn't agree with making advances, so there were certainly Sotheby directors then who were worried by such a policy. "It's extraordinary when you think about it, but until the late 1970s the competition for Impressionists wasn't really there, because David Bathurst didn't have the ammunition to compete." That was quite true and obtained until David took over Christie's New York.

The Higgons affair in a way was the end of Peter Wilson's "golden period". There was increasing criticism of his methods. The Times-Sotheby Index had already aroused the wrath of the dealers and criticism of genuine collectors; and even many members of Sotheby's didn't like its commercial hype.

Following the Higgons affair Robinow became finance director and arranged for Jacob Rothschild, who had worked under him at Warburg's, to buy a fifth of the equity. According to Richard Day, Rothschild was brought in to engineer an eventual flotation. "This was done to try to capitalise all the work we had done as partners and

I was worried about what my shares were worth." But it was not then to be, as we have already seen. Robinow decided he'd had enough and left, as did Richard Day; Robinow wrote to him, "Great minds think alike."

The furore over the Higgons affair was overshadowed by the 1969 collapse of prices and the overdraft position which had soared to over £1 million. This was where the real estate helped to prop up the balance sheet. In spite of Peter Wilson's anger over Geraldine's article about bought-in lots, she still says that she considers him a genius. "I loved Peter Wilson. His mind went so much faster than mine that it took me a fortnight to catch up."

During this time also there was a classic case of the lengths to which Sotheby's would go to get a whole collection. This was the sale of the largest and best collection of antique firearms in the world, totalling in all some 1,500 pieces, some of which had been in the Hermitage until the 1920s. It was the property of William Goodwin Renwick, a Boston lawyer, who had retired to Tucson, Arizona, where he installed it in the gunroom – at the wrong temperature, so that some of the decoration of a number of pieces came apart. There it remained unseen by anyone until Mr Renwick's death.

For once Christie's had the ball at their feet. Their arms and armour expert, Peter Hawkins, was way ahead of Sotheby's. He had done his homework on the collection and knew the attorney who was handling Renwick's estate following his death. When he arrived in London he took him to see Peter Chance. For some reason they did not hit it off and the attorney went off to Sotheby's. Undeterred by this reverse Hawkins prevailed on Peter to let him fly to Tucson to catalogue the collection which, in his opinion, was perfect auction material. Peter backed him and told the Board that he should be sent out.

Peter alerted the attorney that Hawkins was coming and the attorney was rather tickled by the Englishman's enterprise, in view of the fact that John Hayward of Sotheby's, who had been Keeper of Metalwork at the V and A, had valued the collection by then. Peter Hawkins catalogued the collection in three days and valued it at just under £1 million, considerably more than Hayward's figure. Wilson phoned the attorney and was told by him that Christie's were going to auction it.

A fortnight before he was due to leave Sotheby's (having resigned over the Wills cigarette affair), Ricketts heard about the Renwick situation. He went to Peter Wilson and told him he thought he could get the collection for Sotheby's. Wilson phoned the attorney and was told that the contract with Christie's was about to be signed. Peter Wilson persuaded him to allow Sotheby's to carry out another valuation. Ricketts and his successor David Jeffcoat flew off to Tucson where they had to catalogue the collection in three days. Ricketts's figure was bigger than Hayward's but still less than Hawkins's. Before leaving London Ricketts had suggested to Peter Wilson that if Sotheby's could not get the collection for auction, he had a client who could have been interested in acquiring it. A short while later Peter Wilson phoned the attorney again and told him he had a buyer for the whole collection; was he interested? The attorney said yes and through Peter Wilson's client the collection was bought for $1.6 million which was equivalent then to £623,000, considerably less than Hawkins's valuation.

I remember talking to Peter Hawkins when he returned almost in tears, utterly exhausted physically and emotionally. The collection was bought from Peter Wilson's client shortly afterwards and sold in twelve sales between 1972 and 1976 for £3 million, providing Sotheby's with a handsome profit which they needed owing to the oil crisis. Peter Wilson kept the fact that he'd bought the collection from his colleagues and the dealers until it leaked out, so that the last sale was sold as Sotheby's property. This is where the "genius", as Geraldine called him, showed a Jekyll and Hyde quality. Incidentally, it was reasonable that there had been such variance in the valuations, because a number of the pieces had no predictable value. A gun estimated by Sotheby's at £20,000 was bought by John Partridge on behalf of the Metropolitan Museum for £125,000.

About the same time as Ricketts and Hawkins were fighting over getting the Renwick sale, the London art market formed for once a united front – auctioneers and dealers – regarding the damage Value Added Tax would do. Her Majesty's Customs and Excise were proposing to introduce this tax across the board, without any exceptions. This would have been disastrous. But the final decision of Anthony Barber, then Chancellor of the Exchequer, was that works of art from abroad would not be liable to VAT.

Even on this matter Peter Wilson is portrayed in Nicholas Faith's book *Sold* as the hero of the hour. Such was his charisma that an admiring outsider said, "He buried it with four phone calls!" The apparent success of Sotheby's had created in people's minds the idea that Peter Wilson could do anything. In fact, however, he played a very small part in the discussions of the joint committee representing Christie's and Sotheby's and the Society of London Art Dealers and the British Antique Dealers Association. The auctioneers and the fine art dealers agreed that Sir Anthony Lousada should act as an independent chairman, and he was basically responsible for the outcome of the talks. "Looking back on my whole career in the law it was undoubtedly the most time-consuming job I had ever done." Discussions continued throughout 1973 and Lousada addressed committees in both Houses of Parliament, and finally took both Peters – "this was the only time Peter Wilson came into the discussions" – and Geoffrey Agnew to see the Chancellor of the Exchequer. Finally Lousada was telephoned by Customs and told that they would make "certain arrangements with the art market". These have been entirely satisfactory to both sides for the past fifteen years, and it is hoped that there will be no change in the future.

In 1972 Peregrine Pollen returned from New York. Everyone took it for granted that he would be Peter's successor and I'm sure Pollen had been given that impression. However, it was quite difficult to fit him into a job because Lord Westmorland, Peter's cousin, had been deputy chairman for some years. It must have been a difficult time for Pollen because for over seven years he had run Parke-Bernet and had had complete autonomy. Sotheby's like Christie's was departmentalised; where was Pollen to go? To begin with, he was asked to sort out the financial chaos. He brought in the guarantee system which had operated in New York, whereby the vendor would pay an extra 7.5 per cent on top of the normal 10 per cent for whatever result was guaranteed, and 10 per cent above that figure. Initially this was a private matter in particular cases. When the fine art trade learned of it there were more rumbles of discontent.

There then occurred one of those tiny incidents which can betray people's innermost character. Geraldine wrote two fairly innocent paragraphs for the *Times* Diary about the return of the heir apparent and that clearly this was Peter Wilson's successor. "I don't think Peter Wilson shouted at me at the time." However, a year or eighteen months later when Geraldine went to see Peter Wilson on some matter he produced these paragraphs and said, "It's an absolute lie, how could you have written this, I'm never going to retire at sixty-five, I'm staying at Sotheby's."

"It seemed to me quite extraordinary that he'd hung on to this tiny cutting and had all this venom eighteen months later. I think in essence he couldn't bear handing Sotheby's over. He was married to Sotheby's, working from 7 a.m. till midnight; he used to lie in bed ringing people up all over the world. Anything that suggested that he was going to be separated from his 'bride' would really cut into him – anything that suggested that Sotheby's was other than him, and that there was such a thing as Sotheby's without him. I think that a lot of his bad behaviour at the end was part of his agony of separation."

Peter Wilson's psychological reaction to Geraldine's Diary story showed him in terms which became more and more his true self as the years went on. He was no longer talking as much to Carmen Gronau, who had always been such a steadying influence on him, according to Richard Day. Nor was it surprising that Pollen not only had no real department or job, and that Peter Wilson gradually withdrew from him.

During 1973 and 1974 there were a number of other examples of Sotheby's sophisticated commercial approach which worried the London fine art trade. There was the sale of the sporting pictures collected by Jack Dick, a New England businessman, indicted for forgery and grand larceny by the American Internal Revenue Service. The IRS wanted to get their hands on the pictures. Not even this deterred Peter Wilson, but it led to questions in the House of Commons. The Dick furore was followed by yet another, over the collection of Señor Antonio Santamarina, an Argentine citizen. The Argentine Government claimed that it had been exported illegally. When the Press asked how the collection was sent for sale, Sotheby's replied, "No comment."

Finally towards the end of 1974 there was the controversial decision by the British Railways Pension Fund to invest in art through Sotheby's. For the trade it was the final straw. (If they'd known that Peter Wilson had typically persuaded British Rail that when the time came to sell – which they started doing in 1988 – only Sotheby's would be used, they and perhaps many railwaymen would have been outraged. By then British Rail might have got better terms from Christie's.) The dealers now regarded Sotheby's as encroaching on their legitimate function, even more than they had done in earlier years.

In April 1974 Geraldine wrote a reflective piece on Sotheby's style of doing business. She concluded: "It is perhaps also worth noting that Christie's has not in general followed Sotheby's innovations. It continues to act as an agent for the vendor only; it is less secretive, being perfectly open with the Press for instance about what sells and what doesn't sell. Its operations are also highly successful indicating, perhaps, that some people prefer tradition."

It is interesting that all Sotheby's major coups, with the exception of the sale of the great Rothschild/Rosebery collection at Mentmore later in 1977, were foreign sales. The firm had been very successful in America but there was no doubt that by now a lot of people in Britain were not prepared to do business with Peter Wilson. As an ex-Sotheby director put it, "We didn't have the class of business in this country which Christie's had, and to a certain extent that applies to this day."

I asked Peter Spira how he found Peter Wilson as a chairman when he joined Sotheby's in 1974. He said that like most people there was good and bad in him. He was a brilliant auctioneer. Tremendously persuasive, he had great charm and was really very successful at wheedling business out of all sorts of people. He had immense energy – he would fly round the world at a drop of the hat; he was tireless in his lust for business. He was motivated by something that somewhat surprised Spira, with his experience of the very competitive world of merchant banking, where merchant bankers can cut each other's throats during the day but are happy to sit down to dinner together in the evening. "Having come from that atmosphere, I was amazed by the depth of his antagonism towards Christie's."

Peter Wilson was mesmerised by sales figures. There was great jubilation when Peter or some other colleague landed a £1 million or £5 million sale. "I would be the spoilsport and ask what the commission was going to be; any special terms or costs? To begin with they more or less told me to shut up. All that mattered was more sales because Sotheby's would be outdoing Christie's, and even if we didn't make any money out of it, that sale would bring in more sales. That was an attitude I certainly tried to change when we went public in 1977. I said people should become more conscious of the profit element. I think basically Peter didn't think in terms of running the business in a business manner."

I think it must be obvious by now that Sotheby's, even though they did go public, was doomed because of Peter Wilson's character and failing health. However, Wilson had such a strong personality that his staff were overawed by him. Spira had got the financial situation under control, but obviously was fighting unending battles to bring about a more businesslike attitude throughout the firm.

There is no doubt that Peter Wilson was a genius in many ways, but in his latter years his talent became destructive, so far as his firm was concerned; his unorthodox methods, although brilliantly successful for a time, eventually brought about Sotheby's downfall. However, from 1956 to the end of the 1960s there is no doubt that Sotheby's *was* Peter Wilson. His leadership was far more dynamic and imaginative than at Christie's. With the exception of Peter and Arthur Grimwade, the rest of Christie's Board were no match for Peter Wilson's colleagues whatever their ages.

Although both Peter Chance and Peter Wilson had been to Eton, the difference between the two men could not have been greater. Wilson was not interested in clubs and shooting, only in Sotheby's, and above all wanted to forget his early years as an advertising representative. Peter Chance was well-read, clubbable by nature, and enjoyed giving parties to his many friends. I can remember many enjoyable evenings at his house in my very early days when often everyone ended up dancing; there was Peter tieless and with his coat off beaming away beneath the perspiration. There was no pomposity on those occasions, nor on many others such as his birthday parties on the river which I used to organise for him.

However, there was another side to Peter Chance which was of real significance and less known. His interest in pictures and works of art was not purely commercial and because he was chairman of Christie's. He was a very sincere and active patron of the arts. He loved beautiful buildings and helping in their restoration and was for many years chairman of the Georgian Group; he also helped the National Trust and the Victorian Society.

Apart from saving Christie's, one of the things which I think gave him the greatest pleasure was the restoration of St Paul's Church, Deptford. Built by Thomas Archer, St Paul's was in ruins when Lord Rosse, who had been chairman of the Georgian Group before Peter, first showed it to him. Father Diamond, the present incumbent, had then a congregation of six. Peter promised to match the grants given by the Government from time to time for its restoration. As a result of that help, the church has long since been "the pearl in the heart of Deptford" as John Betjeman described it, and has a congregation to match it.

I don't think Peter Wilson had much time for genuine patronage of the arts; he certainly wouldn't have given any large sums for such work, as one of the strange sides of his nature was his financial meanness. Many of his colleagues agree about this; not only did he never have any money in his pockets, but he even went to the trouble of taking side roads when driving to his Riviera château, Clavary, in order to avoid having to pay the tolls on the Routes Nationales.

Undoubtedly more modern and imaginative policies would have helped Christie's in 1958. There was none of Sotheby's dynamic approach to business-getting, their showmanship or their enlightened attitude towards recruitment and training. Valuable time was lost in getting the picture department on a modern footing. Nevertheless, Peter Chance's achievement in restoring the fortunes of Christie's was remarkable. He certainly had as much determination as Peter Wilson, but he had no wish to stray from the orthodox role of the fine art auctioneer. Not for him the commercialised hype of Sotheby's.

Christie's innovations weren't gimmicks. The re-establishment of wine sales before Sotheby's with two real experts; the acquisition of printing works first in London and later in Holland, and so achieving important economies; the rationalisation of the sale of less important works of art by developing Christie's South Kensington; regular vintage car sales and model sales; the introduction of an Estate Duty advisory service and the acquisition of Robson Lowe, the most prestigious firm of stamp auctioneers: these were all solid achievements. Expansion overseas was done in a circumspect way, only when there was sufficient cash to do it. It took time to make up all the lost ground, so to the general public Sotheby's until the mid-1960s appeared to be the dynamo. However, once Christie's had gone public, City editors respected the strength of the firm's balance sheet for which these policies had been responsible.

18

A Bad First Night in New York

The first few months of 1977 were overshadowed by the opening of Christie's saleroom in New York which was to be in the middle of May. However, for the Press Office and me in particular what became an unforgettable nightmare began one sunny morning early the previous autumn. Suddenly a large lady in a bright floral dress bounced into the office and said, "I'm going to be your PR officer in New York." Jo Floyd just then rang down to say Letitia Baldridge would be coming to see me and could I tell her something about Christie's.

Letitia Baldridge was a larger-than-life figure with a voice that could shatter glass, but for all that she was a jolly person. After a few moments' chat I wondered what her qualifications were for what was going to be a highly important job. I learned much later that Stephen Lash, a "Brooks Brothers" American but also an ex-Warburg's man who was to be in charge of the trusts and estates department in New York, had selected her. He had been over to London earlier on an indoctrination course into Christie's ways, and had been told to find someone who could help with the overall launch of Christie's New York. For this she was perfect, as she had assisted President Kennedy during the 1961 inauguration and had been Jackie Kennedy's "Chief of Staff" from 1961 to 1963. In 1987 she brought out a 500-page *Complete Guide to Executive Manners*. Stephen Pile in his criticism of the book for the *Sunday Times* said that her qualification for writing it was that she had spent years telling people how to behave in assorted US embassies. He described her as "a splendid ungainly woman who seems to do everything wrong herself . . . and looked so much like Mrs Thatcher that people get confused". Following President Kennedy's assassination Letitia had left the White House and set up her public relations firm; but as I was to find in May her knowledge of dealing with the Press was on the whole limited to getting the names of the "beautiful people" into the glossy magazines which feature American social occasions, rather than hard news stories.

After an hour's briefing and loading Letitia up with background material, details of record sales and photographs, it was time for lunch. Jo had asked me to join him with Letitia and some others at Overton's where the whole subject of PR in New York could be discussed further, as well as the timing of the actual announcement of Park Avenue's opening series of sales. The lunch got off to a bad start with Jo having to tell Letitia to keep her voice down as "a lot of the trade come here". "Gee, this is just like being in the CIA," she replied. Letitia was good enough to say that she'd had a lot of help from me, but wanted some more human-interest photographs of Jo: "Of you shaving or something like that." Jo replied, "I'm afraid I shave in the bath; it may seem unhygienic to you, but there it is and I'm not going to have the Press in my bathroom."

After lunch while I was dictating a letter to Anne Breitmeyer, my new PA (Patricia having left to get married), Jo popped his head in and said, "I don't think I can stand her." "She's not my choice," I replied, but needless to say she flew off that night with a signed contract. By chance I got into the office early next day, and when the phone rang it was Letitia. "What on earth are you ringing for at this time of day, you must have only just arrived?" "Oh Gawd, John, it's awful. I've lost all that material including the announcement, which Jo said was secret. I'll probably get the sack. I don't know where it could be; could you look in the john?" I promised to do my best. It wasn't in the "john", but I found it quite quickly; the large pile of papers had been sitting on the reception desk of Dukes Hotel, the other side of St James's, where she'd stayed one night. I rang her back and said she could go to sleep with an easy mind and that Jo wouldn't know. I didn't see her again until I arrived in New York with Anne, whose help I knew I would need.

Christie's had been lucky to get such a prestigious site for their saleroom as the Delmonico Hotel building on Park Avenue; it was described by Brendan Gill, the well-known *New Yorker* critic, as a "romantic skyscraper confection of the 1920s". The Delmonico had been bought by a consortium which wanted to find a long-term tenant for that part of the hotel which could not be used for their apartment venture. Guy was in his element, and after some fairly hard but reasonably amicable bargaining was able to negotiate a 25-year lease for approximately $265,000 a year. "It worked out at $10 a square foot, which was fairly good, as it must now be worth well over $50 a square foot in that part of New York." To transform the ballroom into the main saleroom and other space into galleries for exhibiting works of art and also offices was a huge undertaking.

In March, while the work was in hand, I flew out to New York to collect material for the special monthly forthcoming sales notice and other advertisements which were to feature the new saleroom. Christie's New York were still operating from their Madison Avenue offices. There was great activity there and in Park Avenue and it was a useful opportunity to see the work in hand and to meet the new staff who had had to be engaged.

Christie's were feeling fairly bullish when I got back. The Board had just been told that the pre-tax profits for 1976 were £3.6 million compared with £1.9 million for the previous year; nearly twice as much. And 1977 already promised to be good. In late March there had been a near £1 million ($1.7 million) continental porcelain sale, which included the only complete set in private hands of sixteen Italian Comedy Nymphenburg figures made in 1760 by the great Franz Anton Bustelli. A week later an Old Master drawing, whose owner had no knowledge of its importance when he brought it to the Front Counter the previous autumn, had sold for £104,000 ($176,800). This was due to much detective work by Noel Annesley who had proved it to be by the sixteenth-century master Sebastiano del Piombo; while in Geneva at the end of April Christie's in two days sold £4.6 million (Sfr. 20.4 million) worth of jewellery. By the end of the season the sales were going to total £66.4 million ($114.2 million) compared with £1.3 million ($3.6 million) twenty-five years before.

During these spring sales the work of converting the ballroom part of Delmonico's went on apace and was completed just in time. When Jo, Patrick, David, Charlie, Jeanne-Marie, Geza von Hapsburg, Hans and other visiting firemen like myself and Anne Breitmeyer arrived everything looked very smart. Above the entrance was a huge gilded medallion of James Christie's profile. This was very eye-catching, and a great contrast to the anonymity, in those days, of King Street. Inside there was a broad carpeted staircase over which hung a huge Murano glass chandelier leading up to the Front Counter, for those who didn't want to take the elevator. It was all very impressive. "It cost us about $1.4 million to get into New York – that is rent, renovation, legal fees and so on," Guy told me some years later, "but by the end of the second six months we were operating at a profit."

Guy had done a splendid job master-minding the whole operation, for to find suitable premises, convert them and then train local staff required tremendous organisation. Supporting him were Christopher Burge (Impressionist paintings and sculpture), Ian Kennedy (Old Masters), Anthony du Boulay (porcelain), François Curiel (jewellery), Anthony Phillips (silver), Stephen Massey (books), and Stephen Lash (trusts and estates). Together they had managed to get just over eight days of respectable sales. Ray Perman was at work at seven thirty every morning training a team of attendants in how an auction is run – how to transform a gallery where works of art have been on view into a saleroom, how to handle works of art – and sorting out endless snarl-ups for Guy.

All in all it was a considerable feat which Sotheby's, although they may have had problems initially with Parke-Bernet, never had to face. Press reaction to Christie's forthcoming debut was considerable and highly favourable, as American dealers and collectors were delighted that Sotheby's monopolistic position was at last going to be broken. Apart from carrying out all the negotiations and overseeing the plans, Guy had found an advertising agency which interpreted brilliantly the significance of the moment. Particularly effective were the advertisements in the *New Yorker*, drawn by one of their cartoonists: one was of a typical high-society cocktail party, with in different ways Christie's arrival on everybody's lips; another was of a traffic jam of Cadillacs in Park Avenue all trying to get to No. 502, our new address.

The attitude at Sotheby Parke-Bernet, in spite of their great lead, was one of "extreme jitters". This was aggravated by Christie's decision to import the 10 per cent buyer's premium for which they had had to get the approval of the New York Consumer Affairs Department. None was so angry as John Marion, who had succeeded Peregrine Pollen as president. Very unwisely, as it turned out, he let his feelings run away with him and in an interview with the *New York Times* he declared the buyer's premium "as welcome to 1970s America as the Stamp Act was to 1770s America", and said that Parke-Bernet would not follow suit.

Peter Spira rightly saw the danger to the SPB group of this outburst. "John Marion entrenched himself even before Christie's opened in New York." Many at Sotheby's thought that Christie's would get Sotheby's business. They would go to every client and say they would sell their property for no vendor's commission because they would be able to afford it. Sotheby's allowed this to go on for eighteen months, during which time Christie's took business away from them which Sotheby's had tied up. That single decision cost Sotheby's a tremendous lot of business. It was not quite that easy for Christie's to start with, however.

Christie's Park Avenue was buzzing with excitement and activity on our arrival. Ray Perman showed Anne and myself into the "Press Office", which was about the size of four telephone boxes and had no air conditioning. We were introduced to Julie Michele – a very nice and efficient girl she proved – who had been told to help us with any problems. The first thing to do was to find Letitia Baldridge, or "Tish" as she liked to be called. She duly appeared and I could tell that she was quite glad to see me, as she had never before been on the crest of a wave of such potential publicity.

I asked Tish what TV networks were coming and what were the arrangements regarding lighting. I had had a quick look at the main saleroom and seen that none had been installed permanently in the ceiling, as I had suggested to Guy, and that the gangways down each wall were very narrow. Tish said she really didn't know as she hadn't contacted them, thus confirming my fears about how experienced she was at dealing with the media. I knew that the BBC were coming and quickly contacted the three main American networks – CBS, NBC and ABC – and suggested they came over so we could discuss the lighting situation; I didn't want all of them turning up with lights when one set would do.

Christopher Burge popped his head in and asked me if I'd like a look at the Impressionists, the first sale of which was to be a black tie affair on the evening of May 16th. Poor Christopher had had the worst job. We had to open with a sale of Impressionist pictures. Getting a collection of quality when there was a deadline to meet was no easy task. However, Christopher had on his list of collectors a Mr Sydney R. Barlow, a banker from Beverly Hills, who had some nice pictures. By chance Mr Barlow did want to sell some of his collection and chose eighteen pictures, one of which was Cézanne's *Study* for his world-famous *The Card Player*. The evening sale would consist of fifty-one pictures, the first eighteen being from the Barlow Collection, which would have a catalogue to itself.

As I walked round the main saleroom they looked an attractive bunch, until I read the full caption stuck alongside each picture. Unlike in London, "estimates" were the order of the day. Some years earlier the Art Dealers Association of America had made representations to the powerful Consumer Affairs Department which finally decreed that if estimates were to be published the reserve price could not exceed the top estimate and "normally did not exceed the low estimate". Consequently you did not have to be a mathematical genius to gauge what the so-called secret reserve price might be; "reserve prices" at Parke-Bernet had always been anathema to American dealers.

In 1977 the Impressionist market could not be said to be as buoyant as Christie's would like and the estimates looked very high. Although he was outwardly displaying confidence I sensed Christopher's anxiety, because the success of Christie's opening virtually depended on the results of his two sales, there being a less important one on the day after the evening debut. We passed a huge and appalling Van Gogh of harvesters at work. I commented on it and Christopher said that they had actually got a selling bid on it.

During the week before the sale Anne and I were kept hard at it answering Press enquiries as well as getting to know all the people who covered art auctions, in particular the formidable Rita Rieff of the *New York Times* whose demands for information I quickly found were almost impossible to satisfy. She had been on to Guy asking for Christie's record prices, so I went to see her in her office hoping that it would show that Christie's wanted to establish a smooth working relationship; I suspect, however, that this just increased her egotism. She was preparing a big feature comparing the success of the two firms, for which she wanted record prices in every department. I had most of these, but she kept on asking for more together with the dates, so at one point in her office I was speaking to King Street and Park Avenue at the same time. When her article appeared two days later it did not make good reading for Christie's. The only prices that Rita decided were better than those of Sotheby's were those achieved for the Velazquez and a silver corkscrew. However, Rita was an exception to the rest of the art reporters.

The pre-debut fever and pressure from the Press mounted as the days went by, but it was satisfying working with American journalists; in the main they are very professional. The only trouble was the heat. Even when Anne and I came out of the front door at about 7 p.m. or later, the temperature seemed to hit us like a furnace.

During the week before the opening there were two receptions, each for a thousand people. Jo and Guy were photographed in front of Gainsborough's *Portrait of James Christie* which the J. Paul Getty

Museum at Malibu had kindly loaned to Christie's for the occasion. The receptions went well. There was unlimited champagne and smoked salmon and in spite of the numbers there didn't seem to be a crush. One of the first to arrive was New York's tiny Mayor Abe Beam, seemingly indestructible in the face of the city's financial crisis; ambassadors, important collectors, museum directors, dealers from all parts of the world, socialites and a sprinkling of Press. Everyone was most complimentary, reflecting the wave of favourable publicity so far. However, some dealers remarked about the estimates. Barlow had bought his pictures in the early 1960s so it shouldn't be too soon for him to sell. It all depended on the state of the market.

The sale on May 16th was due to start at 8 p.m. Every seat – roughly a thousand – had been taken in the main room, and also in Regine's, the neighbouring night club, where transparencies were to be flashed on to a screen as each picture came up for sale, as well as in what was normally exhibition space. Closed circuit TV had been installed to cater for these areas. There was the usual hubbub while everyone took their seats with that deliberate slowness of the very rich or self-important who wanted to be seen and certainly would not demean themselves by hurrying just because the sale was due to start or other people wanted to reach their seats; many waved or shouted to friends just as if it was a cocktail party, and in some ways it was a social occasion – but not for those working for Christie's. I doubt if there was anyone who did not feel tense and was not praying that the sale would go well after all the effort that Guy and his team had put into getting everything organised. To add to the delay there was the problem of accommodating TV camera tripods without blocking up the gangways each side; the only way was to open up the fire doors which gave sufficient space but must have been strictly illegal.

Jo, who was going to take the sale, climbed into the rostrum, not a hair out of place, and smiling that smile we all knew so well; every inch what Americans think of as the typical debonair upper-crust Englishman. In contrast I was already in a muck sweat as some TV networks had not taken any pre-sale film, so while the crowd poured in I had to hold up Renoir's *Baigneuse Couchée*, a large and quite heavy picture of a nude, in the very cramped space behind the screen where all the pictures were stacked before the sale. Christopher Burge and others stood at strategically placed telephones to take overseas bids, and Ray Perman sat down with that philosophical smile of his at the sale clerk's desk. Having tested the closed circuit TV telephone links,

Jo rapped for silence with his hammer and read out the announcement about the buyer's premium which the Consumer Affairs Department had ordered to be read every hundred lots and began the sale.

You don't have to be an art expert to know whether a sale is going well or not. Anyone who works in an auction house and is present at sales can soon tell. It's not a question of the number of visible bidders, but of the atmosphere in the room and whether the auctioneer slows his pace and delays longer before knocking down a lot. The first few Barlow lots went reasonably well, but then came Cézanne's *Study* for *The Card Player*, the most important picture in the sale and the subject of the wrap-around cover of the Barlow catalogue. Cézanne had done a series of pictures of card players at Aix, culminating in two great works both of which are now in museums. There did not appear to be any great enthusiasm even for this marvellous little picture. However, there was at least some bidding: Hans Bergruen, the Zürich dealer, went up to $450,000 (£264,705), but it was not enough and Jo bought it in at $480,000. Presumably the reserve was about $500,000. The next lot was Degas's *Danseuses Russes* which sold well for $264,000 (£155,294), while one of Camille Pissarro's views of the *Boulevard Montmartre* (they were painted in 1897 under different weather conditions) made $275,000 (£161,764). That in effect was the Barlow sale. Out of eighteen pictures, only ten had been sold for a total inclusive of buyer's premium of $1,059,300 (£623,117).

These results did not bode well for the second half of the sale. This consisted of thirty-three pictures. The most important of these was Renoir's nude *Baigneuse Couchée*, the picture I had been holding up for CBS TV. This sold for $660,000 (£388,235) so I hoped my efforts wouldn't be wasted, while Picasso's *Buste de Femme* made $330,000 (£194,117). The total for the second part was $3,770,866 (£2,218,235), bringing the sold total with premium for the evening to $4,830,166 (£2,841,273), 54.8 per cent in money terms. Out of the thirty-three pictures in the second half only thirteen had sold, or 39 per cent. Altogether, therefore, only twenty-three pictures out of fifty-one had sold, which in Geraldine terms meant a 55 per cent BI total; not good, in fact disastrous.

As the crowd started slowly to make their way out, I went to Ray to check the results. He looked at me sympathetically: "God knows what you're going to say to the Press." Tish had been taking a back seat in the preliminaries for the evening, but I had asked her to organise drinks in large quantities because there would have to be a Press conference after the sale. The speed at which the crowd was moving out of the main saleroom was snail-like. I was impatient to get out but couldn't barge my way through. I was thinking of what I was going to say, and inadvertently I let the felt-tip pen I was still holding with my catalogue at chest level touch the silver lamé dress of the woman in front of me. She turned round, saw the pen and with venom in her voice spat out, "You've ruined my Paris gown." I apologised profusely, gave her my card and told her to ring tomorrow morning. "God, what a night," I thought. Even before the sale began I gathered from Ian Ball, my old colleague from the *Daily Telegraph*, that there'd been the most appalling accident on top of the Pan Am building further up Park Avenue. One of the helicopters making the regular breathtaking flight from Kennedy Airport had crashed on landing; two rotor blades had been smashed off and there'd been a number of dead and injured amongst those waiting to board.

After my clumsiness with my pen, but having put the top on it, I squeezed past the irate silver lamé lady, who was already telling her companion that she was going to sue Christie's. I thought I'd already caused so much indignation that I might just as well hurry along. Apologising to everyone I passed, I reached after fifteen minutes the room near the Front Counter where the Press conference was going to be held. There were at least five TV network teams and sixty other journalists waiting impatiently for me. To my amazement, all the drink had gone, so Tish couldn't get even that right.

I made my presence known and there was silence, save for the whirring of the TV cameras three feet away from me. I was even more conscious of the reflection in a mirror on the wall of the faces of Jo and Guy, their eyes boring into my back and obviously worried about what I was going to say. Jo had called me in during the morning to discuss this particular point. I'd said that it all depended how the sale went. Provided we had half a dozen good prices, buyers' names and foreign interest, that should protect Christie's from a bad BI headline. "But what if it goes badly?" Fortunately Christopher Burge was present and had chipped in with the fact that the New York Press always asked for the BI figure and that Sotheby Parke-Bernet always gave it. There was no question of Christie's not giving it. Jo and Guy had not suggested that, but that I should be able to devise a "positive way" of getting the results of the sale across without mentioning the disappointments. That was easier said than done. Guy saw to it that he never had to speak to the Press, while Jo as chairman either made special announcements or gave interviews with such a bland manner that few journalists ever asked any tough questions. Giving the sale results was a very different matter and I suspected that the New York Press would be very much like Geraldine.

I began my spiel with the knock-down total for the evening of $7.2 million and then ran through the highest prices which being so few told the whole story. Standing to my left was a large tall elderly man scribbling furiously whom I gathered was the Associated Press representative – and thus immensely important. "What do you mean by the 'knock-down' total?" he asked. I explained what it was. This prompted a girl reporter in front of me to ask, "Mr Herbert, there didn't seem to be much bidding" – quite right, there wasn't. "The results reflect the present market conditions for Impressionists and were in line with expectations. There was bidding on the telephone from European and Japanese private collectors and dealers as well as from many American private collectors, which shows the interest in the sale." If they wanted a statement that should do them, I thought, and they could quote it, together with the price and a photograph of Renoir's *Baigneuse Couchée* which would have made page 3 of the *Sun* any day. As this had been bought within the top estimate, it couldn't really be said to be a good price, but as estimates were not in those days printed in the catalogue they probably didn't know that. I couldn't believe I was going to get away with such waffle and prevarication.

Sure enough, the young girl reporter said, "Please, Mr Herbert, could you just tell us how many pictures sold?" So out it all came: twenty-three pictures had sold out of fifty-one, for a total of $4.1 million (£2.4 million). The Press left satisfied at last; what's more, it was a better story than they'd expected as Christie's, after all the razzamatazz, had egg all over their faces. Jo and Guy had disappeared, their worst fears realised, no doubt, about the way I would handle the situation, and Anne and I dejectedly had to carry on telexing the bad news to foreign journalists, King Street and our European representatives.

The next day the publicity was horrendous, and there were the inevitable recriminations, but there was nothing I or anyone else could have done. It was just bad luck that market conditions in 1977 were really not favourable. The next year there was a turn-around in the New York Impressionist market. A year after that Sotheby's sold Barlow's bought-in pictures in London. Cézanne's *Study* of *The Card Player* was bought by Hans Bergruen for approximately twice as much in pounds sterling as he had bid at Christie's debut. Christopher asked him, "Why didn't you buy it with us in 1977?" "I just couldn't," Hans replied, "the market was not favourable." Endorsing this opinion were the number of private bidders in America, a total of fifty-six. The New York trade had just sat on their hands. Equally significant as I had mentioned at the Press conference were the number of European and Japanese bidders, contradicting suggestions, no doubt made by Sotheby Parke-Bernet, that the buyer's premium would frighten dealers and private collectors away.

On the morning of May 17th not many people were talking to me. John Whittles, another old colleague from the *Daily Telegraph* who'd left the paper, about the same time as I'd done, for the top PR job in Lockheed Aircraft in Los Angeles, came on the phone: "For Christ's sake, John, I've never seen such bad publicity, what the hell's gone wrong?" Ian Ball, still at the time of writing (1988) New York bureau chief of the *Daily Telegraph*, was the next friend to phone: "I guess you could do with a drink. Come up to the office first, and I'll introduce you to the boys." He also gave me the teleprinter tape of the Associated Press correspondent's story which went not only right across America, but round the world. The intro read: "Christie's went to the floor last night in a vain attempt to wrest the monopoly position from their arch rivals Sotheby Parke-Bernet . . ." I stuffed it in my wallet as a memento.

When I got back to the office I rang the AP man, as I knew we had to try to get some favourable publicity and he was the best man to set the wires buzzing if we could only give him a good story. I suggested we met, and he said he'd be delighted and that he was sorry things had gone so badly. To help establish some relationship before we met, I took a chance and asked him if he had ever known Eddy Gilmore, Vicki's father, and a Pulitzer Prizewinner who had had a lifetime's career with Associated Press. He had of course; in fact he'd taken over from him in Moscow during the war. I told him he was a great friend of mine; I knew Eddy wouldn't mind me exploiting what was absolutely true. "Gee, that's great. Any friend of Eddy's is a friend of mine. Come on up and have a drink directly you've finished work."

His name was Stanley Johnson and his apartment was only fifteen minutes' walk away, just off Park Avenue. It was a relief for once to get away from my colleagues in Christie's and the atmosphere there and to talk to someone with whom I was immediately on the same wavelength. He introduced me to his wife who consoled me about the results of the previous night, and hoped I understood her husband's position. I told her that there was no question of any ill-will over her husband's story, he was only doing his job. "Come on into my cuddy where the air conditioning is on, my wife likes the heat." We talked and drank whisky for a long time. He was pleased to have someone to reminisce with, particularly as I'd known Eddy Gilmore. "You know, we AP correspondents were more important during the war than some of our ambassadors," was one of his more amazing remarks. However, he was a nice chap and could obviously be useful.

Before going I said that in the following week there was a natural history book sale in which he might be interested. I had brought the catalogue along. None of the sales in between – the second Impressionist sale (as depressing as the first), the jewellery, silver, tribal art and nineteenth-century pictures – had any news interest. However, among the natural history books there was "a double elephant folio" edition, because of its great size, of John James Audubon's *The Birds of America*, the largest and most sumptuous colour-plate book ever produced. Audubon, with his long hair and woodsman's attire, was the quintessential American Frontiersman. The 436 hand-coloured plates of birds were the result of his early life in the American wilderness and were printed in London, 1827–38. Each bird not only looked incredibly lifelike and was shown in its own habitat, but the colour printing, considering the date, was superb. "The sale's in the evening, I'll ring you here." "Do that," my new friend said, "if it sells well it will certainly make a story. Before then I'll study the catalogue." I tottered back to my apartment in the Delmonico building fairly drunk but feeling happier. Even if the Audubon did go for a big sum, the publicity would never make up for the first night, but I'd done what a PR man should do.

During the intervening days there were two developments, one good and one bad. Our accountant challenged the silver lamé dress lady, when she rang up, to produce the receipt from the Paris fashion house she said she had bought it from, or at least the dress so that he could see the label. Christie's never heard any more from her. The second matter concerned Van Gogh's terrible picture of harvesters which Christopher Burge had said would be sold. For some days before our arrival a personable youngish man, quite well dressed, had come in on several occasions and expressed interest in the picture and finally left a bid which he carried out at the sale, to the photographers'

Sir Alec Martin, Christie's managing director from 1940 to 1958. His autocratic regime particularly in the post-war years did the firm great harm.

The author showing Rembrandt's *Portrait of Titus* to the Press prior to its auction in 1965 for 760,000 gns ($2.2 million).

Mr Norton Simon, of Los Angeles, scowling at Peter Chance during the dispute which arose as a result of his special bidding arrangements and produced uproar over the sale of Rembrandt's *Titus*.

Christie's Board and senior staff in 1966 with Rubens's *Judgment of Paris* hanging at the back of the anteroom. Most of the directors are holding an example of their specialist subject.

1 William Mostyn-Owen, Old Masters
2 Peter Chance, chairman
3 Jo Floyd, deputy-chairman, later chairman
4 John Critchley, furniture expert
5 The author
6 Richard Falkiner, coins and gold boxes
7 Anthony du Boulay, Chinese porcelain
8 David Carritt, Old Masters
9 Michael Broadbent, wine
10 Guy Hannen, managing director
11 David Bathurst, Impressionists
12 Arthur Grimwade, silver
13 Ray Perman, chief sales clerk
14 Roy Davidge, company secretary
15 Patrick Lindsay, Old Masters
16 Albert Middlemiss, jewellery
17 Frank Ayres, porter
18 Ridley Leadbeater, Front Counter manager
19 Jim Taylor, foreman porter

Peter Chance, chairman from 1958 to 1974, auctioning Monet's *La Terrasse à Sainte Adresse* for 560,000 gns ($1.4 million) on behalf of the Reverend Theodore Pitcairn. The picture was bought by the Metropolitan Museum, New York. A platform on scaffolding was put up over the back entrance to the saleroom for a CBS TV crew.

The historic Louis XVI writing-table made by Martin Carlin being taken away for safe storage on its arrival with the rest of the Dodge Collection at London Airport in 1971. It is being carried by Jim Taylor, wearing the trilby hat, and another porter.

Anthony Derham, Oriental ceramics director in 1972, with the mid-fourteenth century underglazed red and blue wine jar which he discovered in a collection on the Continent. Such was its rarity that when sold it fetched £220,500 ($573,000), a world record price at the time for any work of art other than a picture. When Derham found the vase it was being used as an umbrella stand.

Patrick Lindsay in action in the rostrum, auctioning
Turner's *Dutch Boats in a Gale: Fishermen endeavouring
to put their fish on board,* known generally as the
Bridgewater Seapiece. Turner painted it as a companion
to the Duke of Bridgewater's *A Rising Gale,* by Willem
van de Velde the Younger, and it set the seal on his early
success. When sold in 1976 it fetched £340,000
($604,860).

The Press in action at the Chanel wardrobe view. Hordes
of reporters and photographers from newspapers,
magazines, radio and television networks all over the
world featured the sale in advance as well as afterwards.

Sheena Cousins (left) and Elizabeth Flach (right), two of
the models engaged for the Chanel wardrobe sale in
1978, with Madame Lilian Grumbach, Coco Chanel's
closest colleague, who was left the dresses and jewellery.

Jo Floyd and Guy Hannen with Gainsborough's *Portrait of James Christie*, which the Getty Museum kindly lent for the opening in 1977 of Christie's New York saleroom.

'Perkins, you call my lawyer and I'll call Christie's.'
Cartoon by Charles Addams.

The Dickin Medal, the "Animal VC", which was awarded to Mercury, a pigeon, for her 480-mile flight across the North Sea with a message from the Danish Resistance. The medal fetched £5,000 ($7,750).

Jo Floyd taking a jewellery sale in Geneva with the help
of Miss Judy Runick, now Mrs Alfred Taubman.

Elizabeth Flach in 1984 modelling jewellery belonging to
the late Florence Gould. Following the Press view there
was an armed break-in. But for the presence of mind of
one of Christie's jewellery experts, the sapphire and
diamond necklace Miss Flach is wearing would have been
stolen. Known as the Blue Princess, when the necklace
was sold with the rest of the jewels in New York it fetched
$1.3 million (£916,000). The whole of Florence Gould's
jewels sold for $8.1 million (£5.6 million).

delight, because it was the highest bid of the night – namely $880,000 (£517,647).

Before the sale he had been asked to produce some evidence of financial credibility. He had given as a banker's reference a Swiss bank account number which on being checked was confirmed "as being good for the sum envisaged". However, all Swiss banks are reluctant to give further information except in person and preferably with their client present. When asked for payment the young man said he didn't have any money. The extraordinary thing was that he had tricked Sotheby Parke-Bernet in exactly the same way only a few days before. The final insult was delivered to the girl who manned the desk in our lobby. The young man asked her out to dinner, and by some extraordinary chance had left his wallet behind, so the girl had to pay. The $880,000 had naturally to be deducted from the sum given to the Press as the sold total.

The sale of natural history books and autographs was on May 26th. Fortunately the Audubon was not at the end of the sale as often happens with the most important lot. When it came up it achieved $320,000 (£188,235), the highest price to date for a printed book. I phoned Stanley Johnson at his apartment immediately as arranged and sure enough he did a story which went out on the wire. There were two more sales after the books: of Chinese jades and Old Master paintings which made pathetic amounts compared to nowadays. They brought the total for the first series of sales in New York to $7.6 million (£4.4 million). As Anne and I were packing up the next day, I heard Jeanne-Marie coming down the passage talking to someone and as she passed the Press Office she said sotto voce (but I could still hear her), "I've never seen a man's face go green for a whole week." As far as I was concerned that was an accurate summing-up of Christie's New York debut.

On our return to King Street there was general depression about the bad publicity, and an immediate demand for a crash advertising campaign featuring our past successes: large advertisements in *The Times* and the *Daily Telegraph*. This may have been a natural reaction but it was the wrong one, as the advertisements were out of character with what the public normally saw in such papers, and if anything they provoked the thought that there must be some special reason for them, and it didn't take long to work out what it was. That, at least, was the reaction of many of my friends. Sotheby's of course made exactly the same mistake when they got into financial difficulties –

full-page advertisements which told a story, but not the one Sotheby's intended.

The proof that bad publicity on sales results, as opposed to expertise or management, should not be the arbiter of advertising policy, came in the form of business for the autumn which poured into Park Avenue later in the summer. To start with there was a house sale, and these always provided good publicity, at Newport, Rhode Island, of the contents of Bois Doré, the home of the late Elinor Dorrance Ingersoll, the daughter of the founder of the Campbell soup empire. The two-day house sale totalled $501,676 (£295,103), but this did not include some magnificent French furniture and works of art which Charles Beyer, our new American furniture expert, was able to cut his teeth on. This he did with great success, proving that a porcelain-mounted jewel casket thought to be nineteenth-century was actually made by Martin Carlin, Louis XVI's great ébéniste. Mrs Ingersoll also had some good Impressionists which like the French furniture were sold at Park Avenue. As a result of the success of this house sale, there was an even bigger one the following year of the contents of Ravenscliffe, the home of the late Mrs Charlotte Dorrance Wright, Mrs Ingersoll's sister. Ravenscliffe was one of the last "main line" houses to be kept with a large retinue of servants. Seven thousand people came to the view and there were well over 700 buyers for the 1,700 lots. The sale totalled $1.7 million (£961,325). That, however, was to be in 1978. In October 1977 there was a $1 million (£555,500) two-day sale of Sung ceramics; Nicholas Stogdon, who had been released by Noel Annesley, mounted a massive print sale in November which did well, while in financial terms François Curiel's jewellery sales made the most impact. These sales and others helped bring the total for Christie's first year in New York to just over $15 million (£9 million). Nobody at the end of May would have believed this to be possible.

"Sotheby's greatly under-estimated Christie's arrival in New York," according to Pollen, and not just because of what Peter Spira said about the effect of the buyer's premium. In December Guy Hannen returned to London, and David Bathurst became president of Christie's Park Avenue. Under his management and in spite of fierce competition Christie's sales in New York in 1983 were greater than those at King Street.

19

━━━━━━◦◯◦◯◦◯━━━

The Chanel Wardrobe Sale

While Christie's were preparing to open in New York, Sotheby's were embroiled in the furore which broke out when it was announced that they were to sell the contents of Mentmore Towers on behalf of the 7th Earl of Rosebery. Mentmore, in the Vale of Aylesbury, was designed in the Jacobean style in the 1850s for Baron Meyer Amschel de Rothschild to house one of the great family art collections. The 7th Earl of Rosebery inherited the vast pile on his father's death in 1974 and with it a demand for £4.5 million in death duties. Although by then many of the important works of art had been sold, the Earl fully realised the outcry there would be if the contents were auctioned. He tried therefore for two years to persuade the Government to buy the house and contents for £3.6 million, so that it could become a museum open to the public. The Government refused to be swayed by the considerable pressure from the conservationist lobby. Lord Clark, the foremost authority on works of art and well known for his books and lucid TV talks on art, advised that Mentmore, unlike Waddesdon, another of the great Rothschild houses, was not worth saving; but he refused to say so in public.

In January 1977 the Department of the Environment at last came off the fence and declared that it was "politically and economically impossible" for them to rescue Mentmore. This decision caused Mentmore to become a *cause célèbre* for the "Britain's heritage in danger" lobby, but for quite the wrong reasons. As is so often the case there was a tremendous lot of humbug about the outcry. Baron Meyer's collection was more one of sheer quantity than of quality. There were also many items such as the marble fireplace originally designed by Rubens for his own house in Antwerp which in no way could be described as part of the nation's heritage. However, the furore fuelled public interest in the sale, thousands flocking to the view. It is probable that many of the general public wondered what all the fuss was about and agreed with Peter Conrad of *The Times* who wrote of "the peeling paint and gilt tat of the guestrooms . . . It is difficult not to be exhilarated at this dispersal of geegaws and hideous rarities . . . coarse and unlovely embodiments of wealth."

There were of course still a large number of important pieces for which museums and collectors, at home and abroad, bid to their limits, so much so that the eighteen sale sessions totalled £6.3 million. It was left to David Carritt to show what an eye for a picture could achieve. The picture was incorrectly catalogued as *The Toilet of Venus* and attributed to Carle van Loo. David's interest in this huge picture, which measured 66 ins by 75.5 ins, was aroused purely by the black and white photograph in the catalogue. He quickly realised that the subject was *Psyche showing her Sisters her Gifts from Cupid* and not the toilet of Venus. For stylistic reasons he did not think it was by Carle van Loo, but he thought it might be by Boucher. However, on turning to all the literature on Boucher, he could find no mention of his ever having painted such a large picture of this subject. Fragonard was the next possibility, as he had worked in Boucher's studio as a pupil for five years. The Wildenstein catalogue on Fragonard, a very full work, actually mentioned that he had painted a picture of this subject when a pupil but that it was an "untraced work". That was enough for David. He and Colin Anson, a friend and colleague in Artemis, to whom I am grateful for these details, went to Mentmore to check that it wasn't a copy. Having satisfied himself that it wasn't, David bought the picture when it came up for sale for £8,800. After further research he proved to the satisfaction of the National Gallery, London, that it was by Fragonard and sold it to them for nearly £500,000 ($850,000). Brinsley Ford, the great connoisseur, expressed his admiration to me of David's identification and scholarship: "The picture must have been passed on the staircase many times by most of the art establishment in the world and not appreciated for what it was."

The furore over Mentmore did have one worthwhile result. Lady Birk, the Labour Government's junior minister at the Department of Environment, decided that something had to be done to protect Britain's national heritage. Finally after a departmental committee and then a parliamentary sub-committee had made their views felt, the Government in 1980 established the National Heritage Memorial Fund. It was granted what remained of Dalton's Land Fund, some £12.5 million, which was soon proved by auction prices to be peanuts;

but at least for the first time there were funds available to buy works of art which should not be allowed to leave the country, so that museums, the NACF, the National Trust and benefactors did not have the unenviable job of raising large sums in a short time.

The Mentmore sale was the biggest British collection that Sotheby's had ever had and also because of the Rothschild background it received a vast amount of publicity. Without exaggeration, however, the sale of the personal wardrobe and jewellery of the late "Coco" Chanel in December 1978 generated almost as much world-wide publicity as Mentmore, without the aggravation of the heritage lobby to give it extra hype. The production of the sale was up to C. B. Cochran standards and showed that Christie's could market a sale with show-manship equal to that of Sotheby's.

Coco Chanel's wardrobe was the property of Madame Lilian Grum-bach, who had been Coco's closest colleague during the last fourteen years of her life. The wardrobe consisted of forty suits and dresses and forty-four pieces of the costume jewellery which Coco had made famous. Some of the dresses had been cut for Chanel herself, while others were from her shows, including one of the celebrated "little black dresses" which became the rage on both sides of the Atlantic.

Christie's had been lucky. Madame Grumbach had approached Jeanne-Marie in Paris in May, although she might well have gone to Sotheby's which had a much bigger Paris office. Susie Mayor, being in charge of costume at CSK, was going to be responsible for the catalogue; she later persuaded Madge Garland, Professor of the School of Fashion and Design at the Royal College of Art, to write a foreword to it, stressing the revolutionary nature of Chanel's unconstricting clothes. Susie had already deservedly won a reputation from her costume sales and naturally wanted the Chanel sale for CSK, as indeed did all her colleagues. However, it wouldn't really have been practical. The King Street salerooms were not only bigger, but their layout – with interconnecting doors at the back – made them perfect for a fashion show, which was what Christie's would have to put on. In any case I doubt if Madame Grumbach would have been too pleased at not having her property sold by the main saleroom.

The dresses would have to be modelled professionally, so I asked a friend of mine, the late Joe Mattli, whose fashion house was well known, if he could recommend someone to select suitable mannequins. He suggested the minute Leni Tan, a delightful Malaysian girl, who was herself a designer. The choice was a very good one, but finding six models suitable to wear Chanel's clothes was not easy even for Leni who knew the fashion world. Madame Grumbach, moreover, had strong views on the matter; so strong in fact that on the day when the models who had been selected were trying on the dresses for the first time, relations became extremely strained between her and Leni. Fortunately it was just at that moment that I thought I'd better check on how things were going.

Leni had been given what was once the special viewing room in the basement so that the models could try on the clothes. I knocked discreetly. The door was flung open by Madame Grumbach who had a stern expression on her face; in the background I saw the models sitting or lying around scantily clad and looking very dejected. Edward Long's famous Pre-Raphaelite work *The Babylonian Marriage Market*, which Christie's had sold in 1878 for the then amazing price of 7,000 gns, immediately came to my mind; I remember Patrick pointing out a photograph of it in the Pre-Raphaelite section in the Bicentenary Exhibition and saying that the interest in such works was only just returning.

"Oh, Monsieur Herbert, regardez cette femme. Elle est trop grande," Madame Grumbach cried, grasping the jacket the girl nearest to her was wearing and opening it regardless of the fact that she was not wearing any bra. The poor girl had a perfect figure, but not in Madame Grumbach's eyes. "N'avez-vous pas une plus petite fille peut-être plus jeune?" I suddenly had a brainwave and grabbed the phone which was by the door and asked for Vicki at CSK. I told her to get up to King Street as quickly as possible but I didn't tell her why. When she arrived, rather breathless, she was stripped to her panties and bra and given a suit by Madame Grumbach. "Bravo, Monsieur Herbert, elle est magnifique." I went back to the Press Office and told Johnny van Haeften to get some champagne from the wine department and order a lot of smoked salmon and brown bread from Wilton's. To hell with expense. When I next went down everyone seemed much happier and Leni and Madame Grumbach were talking shop animatedly.

We had announced the sale some weeks before, but held a Press conference on October 9th with the models wearing the most attractive dresses. First Jeanne-Marie made a little speech about the significance of the clothes and introduced Madame Grumbach. There was a huge media turnout – reporters and photographers from newspapers, magazines and TV networks from America and virtually every country on the Continent, as well as our own Press. Thanks to getting the dresses so long in advance of the sale – which was to be December 2nd – it was a good story for the colour magazines which had long deadlines. The champagne flowed, the models looked lovely – Elizabeth Flach, who was Lord Mayor of Westminster in 1988, and Sheena Cousins are the only two I can remember by name. It was all great fun. Madame Grumbach was beaming with pleasure at the interest of the world's Press. Thanks to her we were able to supply magazines with colour transparencies which a Parisian photographer had taken for Coco; at the same time, as a precaution Christie's own photographer took a large number, so that there would be no trouble about copyright, and also it was important to have transparencies of our models wearing the dresses. A vast amount of money was spent on getting sets of these, and also of those taken during the actual sale, but such was the demand that they all went; and nobody fulfilled their promise to return them.

The sale was to be held at 7 p.m. on Saturday, December 2nd, with a champagne reception beginning at 6 p.m. It had to be a Saturday because all the furniture and other works of art which would otherwise have been on view had to be stored away, leaving the Big Room, anteroom and West Room available for seats, with the East Room for the models to dress and do their faces. It was a perfect arrangement, as the models could go out of the door at the back of the East Room and enter the Big Room behind the auctioneer's rostrum. They would stand on a small dais for a few moments, and proceed with the necessary swirl of skirt and pirouette down the aisle into the anteroom and then the West Room, and retrace their steps to the East Room. To ensure the proper timing and other details a full-scale rehearsal was held the day before. This went off without any rows or hysterics, but the next night was different.

The great staircase up to the saleroom had been garlanded with white flowers of which there was also a huge vase high up to the left of Jo's rostrum. These represented the flowers Coco always had for the presentation of her collections. The cat-walk down the Big Room, into the anteroom and then the West Room had been cordoned off; the champagne was on ice with waiters already filling glasses and Christie's staff were all in dinner jackets; the decor seemed perfect. It was the crowd which was the problem. Those with reserved seat tickets were allowed up first but that didn't mean they arrived first. Those with standing tickets were asked to remain in the hall. It was December. We couldn't ask them to stay outside in the cold, and yet inside, when they had left their coats with the cloakroom girls, the hall quickly became a seething mass of people, many of whom were soon protesting at having to wait. Eventually, to ease the pressure in the hall, we allowed them to go up and hoped they would be mollified with a glass of champagne – if they could get to the bar.

Twenty minutes before the sale was due to start I went up more out of curiosity than to get a glass myself and saw that it would have been a physical impossibility to get to the bar. Jo appeared from his room and asked if everything was under control, but he could read my face. I told him I would use the microphone to try to get people to take their seats. A porter told me that he could hardly hear me, so I went into the anteroom and shouted at the top of my voice; eventually there was some semblance of silence and I asked everyone to take their seats. Slowly they began to drift in, very often towards the wrong room. There were two men on each doorway to direct people to their seats and stop the rooms getting filled with gatecrashers. Half the anteroom had been allocated for those with standing tickets. There were seats for 600 and sufficient room for 400 standing in the anteroom and also round the walls of the other two rooms. However, there must have been at least 1,500 people in our rooms that night.

Jo was already in the rostrum, completely unperturbed by the scene at the entrance to the Big Room. Peter Rose, Mark Wrey, three porters and myself formed something like a small rugger scrum to push those trying to get into the Big Room back into the anteroom and re-establish the aisle. Paul Whitfield and Charlie Allsopp, who were the closed circuit TV auctioneers, watched our efforts with some amusement. The physical force needed to restore order was considerable, because of the determination of all those with standing tickets, or no tickets at all, to get into the Big Room; they refused to realise that they were blocking the aisle and until they moved back the sale could not begin. Eventually at seven twenty – it took twenty minutes to move the crowd back – Jo rapped his gavel and apologised for the delay, but no one seemed to have minded having to wait; perhaps it added spice to their evening. Among the VIPs was Gunter Sachs, the Baroness David de Rothschild, Mrs Riva (representing Marlene Dietrich), His Excellency Faisal Alhegelan the Ambassador for Saudi Arabia, the Duchess of Argyll, Monsieur Ternon from the Musée de Costume, Paris, and many others.

From then on it was an evening which made saleroom history; altogether twelve TV networks recorded it. The first forty-four lots were of costume jewellery – earrings, necklaces, brooches, belts – many of them made of simulated precious stones, with sometimes a Byzantine influence. This costume jewellery had had almost as much impact on fashion as Chanel's suits. It was created to be worn "blatantly on tweeds during the day, not like real jewels of the aristocracy kept for gala evening wear". There was no doubt about its popularity on that night in 1978, only two pieces being bought in, the remainder going for up to £1,600 ($3,200) for a brooch comprising a square simulated emerald in a circular mount with three simulated baroque pearls suspended below. Then there were a number of Chanel's famous simulated pearl necklaces. Dior said of her: "With a black sweater and ten rows of pearls Chanel revolutionised fashion."

A nice gesture of Madame Grumbach's was that she had had a specially made silk label sewn by hand into each luxuriously simple suit and dress which read "Chanel vente chez Christie's 2 decembre 1978". She had insisted, however, on some fairly high reserves. Nevertheless museums entered the sale to compete with private buyers. The first lot was a suit of beige tweed bound with pink braid which Chanel wore at her last three collections. Maybe because of this association it fetched the highest price at £2,400 ($4,800), which was paid by the Oslo Museum. The Smithsonian Institution, Washington, bought a similar suit for £1,000 ($2,000) and the Jupiter Corporation of San Francisco paid £1,800 ($3,600) for a suit of brown printed velvet made in 1961. The Victoria and Albert Museum textile and dress department showed their recognition of Chanel and "La Pauvreté de Luxe" in Picasso's words by buying a black sleeveless dress which was made for Chanel herself. Lastly the famed "little black dress" was bought by the Baroness de Rothschild for £1,500 ($3,000). At the end of the two hours the sold total was £43,250 – not very much but the sale was worth a fortune in world-wide publicity. There has never been anything like the Chanel sale since. The whole of Christie's enjoyed it, not only those closely involved. Indeed, the satisfaction of working at Christie's, Sotheby's or any of the other fine art auction houses is a real fact – a fact which was undoubtedly taken into consideration when the wage scales of the staff were being assessed. Job satisfaction meant becoming involved with things which were not just of great beauty or value, but which had an interesting background or were even part of social history.

Financially 1977 was not a particularly good year – pre-tax profits were £4.1 million compared with £3.6 million for 1976 – but it was an important year for a number of reasons. First there was the growth of interest in pictures by Victorian artists. This had begun in the autumn of 1976 but increased with every sale. The same trend applied to works by continental artists and pictures of Middle Eastern interest. Then, part of the increase in the 1977 profits, small as it was, was undoubtedly due to the success of Christie's South Kensington whose sales during the whole year totalled £6 million ($10.2 million) compared with £1 million ($1.7 million) when Christie's acquired Debenham and Coe in 1974. The policy behind CSK had initially been to provide a quick-sale service for works of art up to about £1,000 which were not of international interest. This limited objective was quickly overtaken as CSK became recognised as the best market for new collectibles such as dolls, costume, fans, mechanical music, photographs and cameras as well as the normal range of works of art. As the prices for the latter at King Street rose, so CSK sales became more and more popular.

Part of CSK's success was due to marketing, which took the form of regular weekend probes to different parts of the country, these having been well advertised in advance. They normally not only resulted in a worth-while supply of all types of works of art being brought back to London, but were a good way of showing the flag. These led to the popular BBC TV *Antiques Roadshow* programme which was invaluable publicity, Hermione Waterfield and Hugo Morley-Fletcher making regular appearances. At the end of July Michael Broadbent was made executive chairman of CSK, although he was still responsible for wine sales and in September sold a bottle of 1806 Lafite for £8,300 ($14,525). To consolidate CSK's position and in line with the advice of Robinow to Peter Wilson, Guy in 1978 organised the acquisition of the lease of 53/81 Old Brompton Road, further strengthening the balance sheet.

Another important business-getting move was to increase the number of regional representatives, so that as well as York and Cornwall, anyone in Cumbria, Shropshire, the Isle of Man and Dundee could get advice on anything they wanted to sell. Sotheby's took a completely different course which must have cost them a lot of money at the time. This was to buy up provincial auction houses, the first being Bearne's of Torquay. During the next few years they added Beresford Adams in Chester, King and Chasemore in Pulborough (now Sotheby's are at Billingshurst) and finally Humbert's in Taunton.

There had also been some important Board Room appointments at Christie's. Paul Whitfield had been made managing director, while a most popular promotion to the Board was that of Doug Ralphs, company secretary. Apart from his responsibilities in that role which he had been carrying out for some years, Doug had already rendered valuable service as an homme des affaires to Peter Chance and later Jo. He had at the same time the trust of the whole staff. Other new directors were Francis Russell (Old Master drawings), Anthony Browne (English drawings and watercolours) and James Spencer (Oriental department).

From the beginning of 1978 the state of the market continued to improve – and nearly every department benefited. The book department was given a shot in the arm in March by the arrival of Sara Bradford (as she was then), and her soon-to-be husband William Ward. Among other sales Sara produced an outstanding one of autograph manuscripts, which was her particular forte. This included Hofmannsthal's autographed librettos of Richard Strauss's operas *Der Rosenkavalier* and *Arabella* which were bought by the Austrian National Library for £45,000 ($87,750) and £75,000 ($146,250) respectively. In 1912 Hofmannsthal had received 13,000 marks (then about £541) in royalties for the *Rosenkavalier* libretto and with this had bought a landscape by the Swiss artist Ferdinand Hodler and, believe it or not, Picasso's *Self-Portrait*, which Christie's had since sold twice; the Picasso at the time was by far the cheaper of the two.

Christie's book department has always been run on a shoestring of expertise. Sara, who was an author in her own right, and Will were just what the firm wanted in the way of young, energetic, business-getting experts. Owing to a clash of personalities, an unwillingness by Jo and probably Guy to appreciate their intellectual value and a tactical error by Sara and Will, Christie's lost them to Sotheby's where they were greeted with open arms. However, Will is now firmly established as a book dealer and Sara is writing hard and successfully.

Meanwhile Stephen Massey, who was and still is responsible for the book department in New York, had been given a Gutenberg Bible to sell by the General Theological Seminary of New York. The Gutenberg Bible was the first substantial book to be printed with movable type and was produced in Mainz in 1456 by Johannes Gutenberg. It sold for $2.2 million (£1.1 million) and its sale resulted in many other books, manuscripts and letters being sent to Christie's New York.

The 1978 summer in King Street had seen the most important sale of English pictures to date which totalled £1.8 million ($3.3 million). It included Stubbs's *Labourers* which was painted in 1781 in enamel on Wedgwood biscuit earthenware and came from the collection of Sir John Wedgwood, Bt. It was bought by the Tate Gallery for £300,000 ($552,000), the highest price achieved to date for a work by the artist. In the same sale there were the splendid sporting pictures and portraits belonging to the late H. J. Joel, the diamond merchant, but more famous as a racehorse trainer and winner of the 1987 Grand National, among many other races. Among his pictures was Sir Thomas Lawrence's *The Woodland Maid: Portrait of Miss Emily de Visme* which made £120,000 ($220,000). Patrick's Old Master sale a fortnight later totalled £3 million ($5.7 million), no fewer than 160 of the 220 lots having come from abroad.

The 1978–9 season began in a completely different way from any other. Late in September, seventy students from all over the world assembled for the first term at Christie's Fine Arts Course. The original suggestion which was to provide education and training in all forms of the fine arts came from David Bathurst. Sotheby's had started something similar some years before which had resulted in tremendous publicity, as Caroline Kennedy became one of the students. There is no doubt, however, that those who were accepted for Christie's Fine Arts course received far more rigorous interviewing and had to be genuinely interested in becoming art historians. Situated close to CSK the fine arts course was in the words of its supervisor, Robert Cumming, previously a lecturer at the Tate, "the modern equivalent of the Grand Tour". And so over the years it has proved, the demand for places far exceeding the number it is possible to accept. Successful candidates might wish to join Christie's, although that wasn't the main reason for starting it, or get a job with a dealer or even a museum. They would all, however, be walking ambassadors for Christie's.

Taking a leaf out of Sotheby's book, it was decided to acquire Edmiston's the Glasgow auctioneers, with Sir Ilay Campbell who had been one of our Scottish representatives for some years as chairman. Michael Clayton who was based in Edinburgh would also be on the Board. Although the saleroom had to be redecorated, buying it made commercial sense in view of the distance from London. Christie's could now service Scotland in the best possible way, selling pictures and other works of Scottish interest or low value in Glasgow, but having a large enough team to see that really important works came south to King Street.

In New York Christie's Park Avenue was going from strength to strength, so much so that Jo was able to announce that in the first full year of trading it had made a contribution to group profits. It was particularly satisfying that John Marion, president of Parke-Bernet, had at long last had to eat his words and introduce the buyer's premium. Christie's New York had been given a tremendous boost in virtually every type of sale because they could quote better terms.

Because of its success Christie's New York was authorised to open a second saleroom. A six-storey garage on East 67th Street may sound unprepossessing as premises but it had a lift which would obviously be of considerable use and needed only to be smartened up. It would be called Christie's East and operate like CSK. Ray Perman was made responsible for converting it into a saleroom, for training attendants and for the first sales. It was an instant success.

In 1978 Christie's had been in Geneva for ten years. The November series consisted of seventeen sessions which totalled Sfr. 24 million (£7.4 million); 80 per cent of this huge figure was sold, which made it a remarkable success. The main jewellery sessions were made particularly glamorous by the presence of the then Miss Judy Runick, for some years now Mrs Alfred Taubman, who was later to take over Sotheby Parke-Bernet. With her shoulder-length blonde hair Judy – who had been Miss Israel some years before – showed off the jewellery to perfection and also helped me give out the results to the Press.

All in all 1978 had been a very good year for Christie's. The administrative changes and expansion had begun to pay for themselves and sales had been good. The pre-tax profits when announced in April 1979 were £5.6 million on a net sales figure of £98 million, while Sotheby's were only £7 million on a sales figure of £161 million, which included £18.4 million ($33.9 million) for the immensely successful collection of the late Robert von Hirsch, a German industrialist whose forebears had fortunately moved to Basle in the 1920s. Thus Christie's which had sold only 60 per cent as much as Sotheby's had made profits equal to 80 per cent of theirs. The gap was narrowing with a vengeance. (The Sotheby Parke-Bernet financial year went from August to July, while Christie's was January to December. This difference, however, is not relevant for comparing the profit trend.)

Sotheby's, or rather Peter Wilson's, policy of sales at any price, with little or no control on the number of staff, was beginning to tell. By 1975 his diabetes had begun to cloud his judgment. Any important decisions which needed his approval had to be timed when it was known he had had one of his regular insulin injections. Consequently he was more and more difficult to deal with. Equally significant was the lack of cohesion within the firm at Board level. There were rumours that Peter Wilson might be thinking of retiring as early as 1976, when he sold his house in Kent. Apart from his small flat in London he made Leeds Castle, of which he was a trustee, his base, and took frequent trips to Clavary, a small château he had bought some years earlier on the French Riviera, where he could really relax. All this resulted in a wave of politicking and back-biting as the Board was divided into different camps.

Many directors and senior staff had never had any liking for Peter Wilson's commercial hypes. Wilson himself aggravated the disharmony because he never wanted anyone around him who would challenge his authority. This was why he distanced himself more and more from Peregrine Pollen. Peter Spira found Wilson's attitude to his colleagues surprising because, with his ability as an auctioneer and knowledge of the art world in general, he had no need to have complexes about rivalry or plots or anything of that sort. "He was so distinctive in his own right, that there was absolutely no need for that. But he was not a manager in a professional sense. He never worried about providing for his succession, or having a strong management group around him."

The question of succession had never raised any problems at Christie's. There were obviously occasional differences of opinion at Board level, but it was generally accepted long before Peter Chance retired that Jo Floyd would become chairman, and Guy Hannen fully agreed to this. Equally, Patrick told me at lunch one day that he had no desire to be chairman, and didn't think he would be a very good one.

So fortunately for Christie's the question of succession solved itself without acrimony or ambition causing difficulties. Guy Hannen was much more suited to the role of deputy chairman and certainly was responsible for many important decisions. When problems arose Jo and Guy were generally able to talk them out without having a blazing row, even if they didn't always agree. There's no doubt that together their management of Christie's resulted in the continued advancement of the firm at a controlled pace.

One of the most important developments for Christie's in 1979 concerned the conversion of White Bros, Christie's printers, to litho printing in place of the traditional hot metal system. White's had outgrown its original Offley Works premises near the Oval, and had found an even more practical site near Vauxhall Bridge station. The technological and economic advantages of litho printing had been proved, but the new working practices entailed the firm's becoming a "union shop". No one at Christie's had any experience of negotiations with trade unions, so to ensure that the conversion to litho was carried out with the goodwill of the National Graphical Association and SOGAT, Christie's called on the help of Patrick Walker, chairman of Watmough's, the huge printing works at Idle, outside Bradford (and exactly opposite The Idle Working Men's Club).

Patrick had become a good friend as his firm had been responsible, and still is, for the printing of the monthly "forthcoming sales notice", which was enlarged later to *Christies International Magazine*. It was Guy who thought of seeking Patrick's help, and as a result Patrick took over the chairmanship of White Bros from him. Christopher Davidge became managing director. The changeover to litho, thanks to Patrick's wise counsel, went very smoothly both within White's and with the unions and had far-reaching effects. The demands on White's were going to increase considerably because of Park Avenue's catalogues.

Christopher Davidge went over to New York and saw a number of printers, coming to the conclusion that White's quality and speed of printing was not only better now with litho, but approximately 25 per cent cheaper than the Americans'. To begin with, White's were responsible just for printing Park Avenue's Impressionist and contemporary art catalogues, and two New York printers were employed to do all the other departments' catalogues. This avoided any danger of White's being over-stretched. However, with the strengthening of the dollar, the saving by printing in London became greater than ever. Christopher therefore reorganised White's, and by June 1980 the firm was equipped to carry out four-colour litho printing and could be responsible for virtually all Park Avenue's catalogues. This meant Christopher making forty flights to New York a year – each week of the season – to collect copy and transparencies and black and white photographs. It is amazing that he didn't get a duodenal ulcer from the worry of whether the departments would have all the material ready. No doubt this demonstration of the ability to organise and accept a tremendous workload was one of the reasons why he was made managing director of Christie's London in 1985.

The improved integration of White's within Christies International was of tremendous importance economically, strengthening the balance sheet and providing a better service to catalogue subscribers. Peter Wilson certainly would never have concerned himself with printing, but it's strange that other Sotheby directors did not recognise the advantages of having one's own printer, rather than using as many as thirteen as they do today.

The year 1979 began with a sale which had a special pleasure for Patrick Lindsay. This was a vintage car sale in Los Angeles, which included fourteen cars belonging to the late M. L. "Bud" Cohen, a successful "automotive parts" dealer who specialised in buying Mercedes-Benz cars when they were comparatively cheap. The fact that Christie's had been asked to carry out the sale was the result of the success of other such sales organised by Patrick at Beaulieu, in Geneva and in Amsterdam. The sale made motor car auction history because a 1936 Mercedes-Benz type 500K two-passenger Roadster sold for $400,000 (£210,526), while a 1929 Mercedes-Benz SS 38/250 hp two-passenger Roadster sold for $320,000 (£168,421). Mr Cohen's collection also included a 1967 Austin taxi which sold for $3,850 (£2,026). The total raised by his fourteen cars was $1.2 million (£631,578). Patrick's sale was the beginning of a very active and successful year for all departments whether in London, New York, Geneva, Amsterdam or Rome. The sale also inspired Mercedes-Benz to take full-page advertisements in the *Wall Street Journal* featuring Patrick and the car he had sold; they were so keen on Patrick looking as good as the car that they bought him a new suit – when Patrick went abroad he dressed in a typically relaxed aristocratic fashion. It was also a year when more provincial representatives were appointed: in Northern Ireland, Northumberland and Jersey and the Channel Islands. Likewise offices were opened in Vienna, Hamburg, Zürich, Oslo and Copenhagen, which meant that virtually the whole of Europe was covered.

Among the many important sales at King Street was the first part of the great library of Arthur Houghton Jnr, of New York, which can be numbered among the salient book auctions in history. Christie's had already sold his *Shahnameh* and Gutenberg Bible. A new high for a Victorian picture was established with the sale of John Frederick Lewis's *An Intercepted Correspondence* for £220,000 ($440,000). Sir John Figgess, who had taken over the Oriental department, went to see the Earl and Countess of Verulam in Hertfordshire. Before lunch he asked if he could wash his hands. When everyone was seated John said, "Do you realise you have a very valuable piece of Chinese porcelain in your washroom?" Needless to say the Earl and Countess didn't; in fact they had only recently brought it down from the loft. John told them that it was a fourteenth-century underglaze copper-red and white Ming wine jar. The Earl and his wife decided to send it for sale and it was bought by Mr Seijiro Matsuoka, a cheerful Japanese collector who has his own private museum in Tokyo, for £95,000 ($209,000).

John Lumley had a coup with twenty-eight Impressionists which had decorated the walls of a modest suburban house in St Gallen, Switzerland. Few people previously had known of their existence. They were the most important single collection sold to date by Christie's in London and the property of the late Hans Mettler, a Swiss textile merchant. They sold for "amazing" prices, although today these would not seem so remarkable; Toulouse-Lautrec's *La Grande Loge* achieved a record £370,000 ($810,300). A week before, Jan Brueghel the Elder's *Wooded River Landscape with Numerous Peasants and Travellers*, also from the Mettler collection, had sold for £400,000 ($840,000), having been bought in 1923 for only Sfr. 7,000 or £319.

The Mettler sale was only the beginning of a very exciting week of Impressionist and Contemporary pictures and sculpture. There were altogether five sessions which totalled £4.3 million ($9.4 million), Matisse's *Le Jeune Marin I* selling for £720,000 ($1.5 million), at the time a record auction price for a twentieth-century picture. Late in the year there was the superb collection of English watercolours formed by the late Norman D. Newall. This was catalogued by Anthony Browne, no doubt under Noel's eagle eye, and was of considerable interest. Many of the works although by English artists had been painted in France, so we were able to promote it in the influential *Connaissance des Arts* magazine, owned by Dimitri Jodidio, of whom in due course we will hear more.

Nevertheless, 1979 was not without its problems. In June the writ which the British Antique Dealers and Society of London Art Dealers had taken out against Sotheby's and Christie's regarding alleged collusion over the buyer's premium was heard in the Chancery division. In 1978 the VAT tribunal had decided that VAT would be chargeable on the aggregate of the hammer price and the buyer's premium as from the beginning of 1979 which was not welcome news for the auction houses, let alone the dealers, whose wrath was aroused once again. However, in June 1979, after considering what both firms had to say, the dealers decided not to pursue their claim for an injunction pending trial. The decision to charge the premium was made independently. Assurances to that effect had been given to the Department of Prices and Consumer Protection in 1975. But on July 9th the two dealers' associations applied to the High Court for an interlocutory injunction to prevent Christie's and Sotheby's from charging the buyer's premium; at a very late stage the application was withdrawn by the plaintiffs. The judge ruled that the subject was important and the case was to come forward for an early hearing. The Board was told that this would probably be in 1981.

Overseas sales were as successful as at King Street. In America the success applied to all departments; among the Impressionists, Monet's dreamy river view of Argenteuil, which had been Christie's first colour front cover of the forthcoming sale notice in 1964 when it was sold for Mrs Pamela Combemale for £39,900 ($111,720), made $350,000 (£171,568). François Curiel found jewellery sold just as well as in Geneva, while the most dramatic increase in interest in the whole art market was for art nouveau and art deco; a three-day sale totalled $2.3 million (£1 million). Alastair Duncan, who was responsible for these sales at Park Avenue, wrote: "The market escalated at an unprecedented rate, drawing more and more collectors and investors into the field as prices spiralled upwards towards and finally through the $100,000 barrier. Records were set throughout the year and promptly broken. The world record for Tiffany rose from $60,000 in September 1978 to $70,000 in December and finally to $160,000 (£75,000) in February 1979."

Geneva surpassed itself during the year with two magnificent series of sales, those in May totalling Sfr. 26.7 million (£7.6 million), which was exceeded in November by those totalling Sfr. 30.1 million (£8.6 million). The four sessions of jewellery in November achieved the highest total to date of Sfr. 23.7 million (£6.7 million), and created record prices per carat for an emerald, a ruby and a sapphire.

However, even before the November Geneva series, the interim figures had shown that pre-tax profits were £2.97 million compared with £2.68 million the year before. This showed a decline in margins due to increasingly high inflation rates and to the cost of the expansion in Europe, which would take time to produce results. In October, Guy said that sales in Britain should be rationalised as a matter of urgency. It was decided that lots worth £500 or less sold better at CSK. By transferring these works of art, King Street would handle only major sales which would be administered and marketed better. At the same time CSK would move up-market and King Street become an un-rivalled sales centre. Action was in fact taken against what was to prove to be the 1980–83 recession.

Sotheby Parke-Bernet on the other hand had finally agreed to John Marion's proposal to expand from the original Madison Avenue premises which were cramping his plans for the future. A friend of his had found what seemed perfect premises: the old Kodak building on York Avenue, a rather dreary area of Manhattan. To buy and convert the building would cost a great deal of money – in the end £8.4 million. Marion was a good auctioneer but an appalling manager. Infuriated by Spira's opposition, he had taken on his own finance director and together they said that by leaving Madison Avenue for picture and jewellery sales, they would be able to expand the number of applied art sales. Unfortunately they had chosen precisely the wrong moment. By the time conversion was under way, interest rates were climbing and art prices falling.

To add to Sotheby's difficulties, Peter Wilson on November 9th announced without prior warning that he was resigning the chairman-ship but would remain a director. Although it was a comparatively short time after he had told Geraldine that he would not retire at sixty-five, he had been persuaded by his tax lawyer that it would be advisable to do so, if he wanted to get his money out, retire to Clavary and avoid the danger of his sons inheriting massive death duties.

He announced that his successor would be his cousin David, Lord Westmorland, who had joined the firm in 1964 after being Master of the Queen's Horse. Peregrine Pollen, who was still favoured by some heads of departments, had lost out to the ex-courtier. The reason was quite obvious. Peter Wilson thought he would still be able to run Sotheby's from the south of France, by telling his cousin what to do, "as he had always done", in Geraldine's words. "It wasn't going to be a real retirement. It was a miscalculation because he couldn't run such an enormous empire from anywhere save his office in Bond Street."

Henry Ford's Impressionists

David Bathurst took over the position of president of Christie's New York early in 1978 after Guy had returned to London. Undoubtedly he was the right man for the job. He had already had valuable experience of business-getting in America. He was also less hide-bound than those directors who had been brought up in the Alec Martin or even the Peter Chance era, and had the self-confidence immediately to adopt a more commercial style of running the office.

The thing was, he told me in the course of a long interview in 1988, that Christie's prided themselves on being over 200 years old, but so far as Americans were concerned Christie's New York was only six months old. All the business about being an eighteenth-century house meant not one jot or tittle to the average American; we were just "a new kid on the block" and we would either make it or not make it in the next year or two.

"The initial issue was the premium. We had it and the opposition didn't. The opposition made some rather unwise comments about the premium which made our life a little bit easier, but there was a great conflict in those days about whether the premium from a business sense and even moral sense was the elixir of our existence or a poison which was going to kill us. The supporters of the first view finally won out. Sotheby's took the second view and thought they'd watch Christie's dig their own grave. Of course the premium allowed us to lower the vendor's commission and that's all the seller was concerned about.

"From my point of view the joy of working in America was that one didn't have to refer back to London. There were certain ground rules, such as not spending over $100,000 without reference to King Street, but there was a psychological understanding about 'don't keep bothering us with silly questions'. Frankly I was not at all keen to bother them, but was just anxious to get on with the job without being told you can or can't buy a threepenny stamp.

"We never ran into any problems over running the office as I thought best. We did some major things, such as doing deals and offering terms, which would probably have made the hair of those in King Street turn grey. But they understood that the way one did business in the States was entirely different from that in London. It wouldn't have been the same if it had been Paris or Geneva. The geographical distance made an enormous difference."

Otherwise, he found that it was not till one moved around the American continent that one realised the amount of business to be done there. SPB had become rather relaxed through having had a monopolistic position, but there was room for two fine art auction firms or even more. What is more, the dealers resented Sotheby's monopoly and strongly encouraged Christie's to come to New York, to provide some competition. Needless to say, once Park Avenue got going they resented Christie's success just as much. More important still, in America people were far more commercial and competitive-minded and less loyal than the British. "Over here most people are either Sotheby's people or Christie's people and you have to do something pretty ghastly in order to make them change. In America people looked for good points and bad points and because we were the new arrivals they might switch, either because our commission rates were lower or they liked the cut of our jib. So from that point of view Christie's New York didn't have to fight the ghastly fight they'd have to fight in England if they were a new auction house."

That did not mean that business fell into Christie's lap. Everyone had to travel, lecturing and appraising, and generally beating the drum, not only the technical staff but even Stephen Lash. Stephen toured the continent talking about a "balanced portfolio and tangible assets" and that went down very well with a precisely targeted audience of bankers and particularly trustees who were terrified of being sued for mismanagement.

It was not only that Christie's New York had to make their name known, but the interest in art even then was far more widespread than in Britain, and if they announced that an expert from Christie's was going to give a lecture on his subject people flocked to it. This meant haring round the country: California one moment, Texas the next. Everybody had to be much more mobile than in Britain and it was very hard work.

The decision to come into New York was made a long time before mid-1977; it was not the ideal moment, but Christie's were committed to it. "We didn't start with a bang, as you know. We were pegging along during 1978–9, doing OK, but not making the inroads into Sotheby Parke-Bernet that we would like to have done, until along came Henry Ford in 1980. That was a turning point."

Why Ford went to Christie's is a subject that fascinated and even mystified the New York art world. David said he didn't know, although Ford said, and David admitted this was flattering to him, that it was because of him. He had been to stay for a weekend with Ford. "It was a most remarkable weekend, because nearly everybody including our host was sloshed the entire time. During some of the moments one was sober one looked at the pictures and they were sensational." Henry took an interest in them, but they had largely been chosen by his wife Anne.

David and Ford talked about the pictures and David valued them for him, but there was no talk of a sale. Then Ford got divorced. He always claims that he didn't need to sell the pictures to pay off the alimony. "He moved into a smaller house and kept a lot of the good pictures so it wasn't as if he cleaned up. He sold only ten." Though Ford always said that the decision to sell through Christie's was because of David, the world at large thought it was because of Anne. She and Henry remained "good pals" and she had become one of Christie's representatives in Los Angeles. "It may well have been a combination of the two, but he never went to Sotheby's, ever."

The ten pictures in lot order were: Boudin's *La Plage*; Manet's *Portrait de Guillaudin au Cheval*; Cézanne's *Paysan en Blouse Bleue*; Renoir's idyllic garden scene *La Serre*; Van Gogh's *Le Jardin du Poète, Arles*; Gauguin's *La Plage au Pouldu*; Van Gogh's *Le Jardin Public*; Degas's *Etude du Nu*; Picasso's *Tête de Femme*; and Modigliani's *Nudo Seduto*. No group of Impressionist and Modern pictures of such remarkable and consistent quality had ever been auctioned before. Allowing for the small number of pictures this probably remains true even to this day, although SPB had sales such as Havemeyer and Gould with greater totals. The Ford pictures were the choicest.

From the earliest announcement of the sale in March it was clear the art world felt the same. They also thought, particularly the dealers, that Christie's could only have brought off such a coup by offering to sell the ten pictures for virtually no commission. But that was not the case. "I remember afterwards people saying, 'You give me the same terms as you gave Henry Ford,' assuming it was zero and being horrified to find it was 4 per cent. On one occasion I had to show a dealer the actual contract." In those days 4 per cent was "hellishly low, but today it's standard terms. At the time we gave him the best deal anyone had ever got, a specially designed catalogue and we shipped the pictures to London for exhibition. This is par for the course today, but then was completely new."

However, no auctioneer can ever be sure there are not going to be problems with highly important works. Four days before the sale the well-known New York dealer Acquavella came to David and Christopher Burge, who was responsible for the pictures and cataloguing them once the contract had been signed, and offered $5 million for the Van Gogh and the Cézanne. This created considerable soul-searching in Park Avenue. The reserves on the two pictures totalled $4 million so David and Christopher had a real problem. What to advise Henry Ford? "Christie's could have looked bloody stupid if the pictures had fetched $4.5 million and Henry Ford told the world, 'I could have had $5 million but I only got $4.5 million.'" David and Christopher decided, however, to advise Ford that "although that's a very fair offer on the two pictures you'd be ruining the sale by withdrawing the two plums". Henry Ford agreed and said he quite understood their reasoning. "It turned out to be brilliant advice because the Van Gogh alone fetched $5.4 million (£2.2 million); but one forgets that at the time there was no certainty of such a price."

By the time of the sale some 20,000 people had visited the five-day exhibition. Thousands more had telephoned with enquiries. Speculation regarding the total began with the highly conservative Press announcement of "more than $7 million", "which grew to $10 million, but there were more imaginative 'fantasies' of $11 million or even $12 million".

At 8.10 p.m. on May 13th, Lot 1, Boudin's *Plage*, an unusually large and good-quality view of crinolined ladies on Trouville beach, was held up in front of an audience of 1,300 people in four galleries. Those in the closed circuit TV galleries saw the pictures via transparencies flashed on a screen. There were bidders from all parts of the world on banks of telephones. For thirty electric minutes, battle was waged in front of an array of television cameras and lights, and when the dust had settled six world records had been resoundingly shattered for an extraordinary total of $18.30 million (just over £8 million). The firm's pre-sale estimate had been $10 million.

Van Gogh's *Le Jardin du Poète, Arles* achieved a new high for any nineteenth-century or Modern work of art by selling for $5.2 million (£2.2 million). Cézanne's *Paysan en Blouse Bleue*, a portrait of a ruddy-faced peasant (who incidentally had been one of the models for his *Card Players*) went to the Kimbell Art Museum, Fort Worth, for $3.9 million (£1.7 million); Gauguin's *La Plage au Pouldu* produced a record for the artist of $2.9 million (£1.2 million). The two nudes by Degas and Modigliani went for $900,000 (£393,000) and $600,000 (£262,000) respectively, while Boudin's *La Plage* made $480,000 (£209,606) – all three prices records for the artists. The second half of the evening's sale realised $7.1 million (£3.1 million), producing a grand total of $25.5 million (£11.1 million).

The success of the sale had a dénouement which is not without humour. Henry Ford had said first of all that he would come to the sale, but then told David that because of a strike in Detroit he wouldn't. In David's words, "It would look very bad if he was seen to have made $10 million or more while he was telling the automobile constructors to get stuffed for $1.5." So Ford gave David the telephone number of the restaurant where he would be dining and told him to call him with the results. "So I called him," David said. "'Hang on to your seat, Henry, because you're not going to believe this. Your pictures made $18.3 million,' and I ran through the catalogue. He was absolutely pie-eyed. 'Well done, David – Jesus, people are crazy, you couldn't have done me prouder, come round and have a bottle of the old champagne.'

"I didn't go, but in the morning when I got into the office I found a very cross Henry Ford on the phone saying, 'Why the hell didn't you phone me last night with the results of my sale?' 'Well Henry, I did.' 'You did?' Yes and you said this and you said that. 'I did? Well, quite possible, quite possible.' He didn't remember a damn thing so I had to go through the catalogue all over again. Lot 1 fetched such-and-such – 'That's a huge sum,' said Henry – and so I continued to the end. After that we got all the publicity in the world and Christie's New York was far more solidly on the map. We never really looked back from that moment onwards." The success of the Henry Ford sale was undoubtedly the most significant event in the art market in 1980. David deserves great credit for it.

The contemporary art sale three days later produced a record total for a sale of this kind of $2.6 million (£1.1 million) – nothing compared with future sales – Jackson Pollock's *Four Opposites* making $550,000

(£239,130). These sales were the responsibility of Martha Baer who had joined Christie's New York in 1978, and had quickly wrested from Sotheby Parke-Bernet their ascendancy in such sales, because of her association with the artists and collectors through having once been a dealer in such works. In view of the tremendous demand which developed over the next few years for Contemporary paintings and sculpture, Martha's sales became of immense importance.

Equally important were nineteenth-century pictures and sculpture, particularly those which reflected the aspirations and accomplishments of the new democracy. Artists had freed themselves from the tyranny of portraiture; likewise anything was popular that reflected America's frontiersman past, as were genre pictures of childhood scenes. The prices paid for such works within two or three years vied with Old Masters. Even in 1980 Thomas Moran's *Children of the Mountain* – a romantic projection of American scenery – achieved $650,000 (£280,172), while Frederic Remington's bronze *Apache Scout* sold for $320,000 (£138,000).

Back in London there was no shortage of important sales of all kinds. Rubens's great work, *Samson and Delilah*, which he had painted when he was about thirty-three, was bought by the National Gallery for £2.3 million ($5.4 million); the famed collection of Old Master drawings and other works of art belonging to the late Baron Hatvany sold for a total of £2.5 million ($5.8 million), which came as no surprise because of his superb taste; and the world-famous Castle Ashby Greek and Etruscan vases, the property of the Marquess of Northampton, went for £1.3 million ($3 million). The fifth and last portion of the Hooper Collection of Tribal Art brought the final total to £2.8 million ($6.5 million), an Austral Islands drum, 52.5 ins high – Captain Cook wrote of a similar drum being used to beat time during a human sacrifice in 1777 – selling for £190,000 ($444,600); and the second part of the famed library from New York of Arthur A. Houghton achieved just over £1 million ($2.5 million).

However, by far the most important work of art sold in London in 1980 by any auctioneer was the *Codex Leicester* of Leonardo da Vinci. The *Codex*, a manuscript notebook of some thirty-six pages, was the property of the 6th Earl of Leicester and the only remaining notebook of the thirty Leonardo wrote on different subjects that was in private hands. Compiled about 1508, the *Codex* is a collection of notes on water and cosmology, expanding into related topics such as astronomy.

It is undoubtedly one of the greatest manuscripts in existence. Written from right to left – *alla mancina* or in mirror-writing – and illustrated with drawings, the notebook shows Leonardo's probing mind exploring dams, drainage of swamps, lock gates, and pile driving. In a celebrated passage on submarine warfare, he mentions safety measures that can be adopted by a man swimming, including a snorkel. When he mentions his methods of remaining underwater, he dramatically states that he does not want to make them public because of "the evil nature of men, who would use them as a means of destruction at the bottom of the sea, by piercing a hole in the bottom of ships and sinking them with the men in them".

Dr Carlo Pedretti, Professor of Art History at the University of California and the foremost authority on Leonardo, wrote an introduction for the catalogue. Apart from dealing with the facts, he wrote: "It is hardly necessary to insist on the importance of the *Codex* in its conceptual relationship with the background of Leonardo's paintings . . . Indeed one may conclude that without it the *Mona Lisa* would not exist."

The *Codex* was bought originally by Thomas Coke, 1st Earl of Leicester, in 1717 and was offered for sale on behalf of the Trustees of the Holkham Estate, Norfolk, to help pay for large tax liabilities on the death of the 5th Earl. The sale naturally attracted world-wide interest, in particular that of the art authorities in Milan who offered Christie's exhibition facilities. They hoped thereby to persuade the twenty-nine private banks to bid for the *Codex*, having no confidence that the Italian Government would do so.

Naturally also there was a storm of protest from the national heritage lobby. Any criticism the Government might have made was settled amicably at a meeting Lord Coke and the Trustees had with Norman St John-Stevas, Minister for the Arts. So far as the heritage lobby was concerned Lord Coke's statement in a TV interview (conducted somewhat to my embarrassment by myself at the request of the Visnews team I had taken up to Holkham House) silenced their protests and underlined the problem facing the owners of so many great estates. When asked what his feelings were on losing one of his family's greatest treasures, Lord Coke said that the Leonardo manuscript had to be kept in a safe, not only for security, but also to lock it away from the dangerous effect of light. It seemed far more sensible "to keep all these lovely pictures that visitors to the house see, and get rid of something that is not seen. Of course people say,

'Aren't you ashamed that you are getting rid of our national heritage?' but . . . I don't regard this book by Leonardo as our national heritage. It is the Italians' if anyone's. In any case in 1949 on the death of the 4th Earl the British Museum came here and were given carte-blanche to take whatever they wished up to the rate of death duties including the Leonardo. They found it fascinating, but I think quite rightly they took English books printed before 1600 and manuscripts which illuminated our past history far more than the *Codex* could. If the *Codex* goes abroad it will ensure that this house remains intact for future visitors and the nation."

When it came to the sale on December 12th the price of £2.2 million – although a tribute to Leonardo's genius – was a slight disappointment to Lord Coke. Undoubtedly it had been affected by an earthquake disaster in Italy in which hundreds were killed. The Italian art and financial interests who wished to buy the *Codex* didn't think in the circumstances that such a vast sum of money could be spent. Instead the *Codex* was bought by Dr Armand Hammer.

Very different was the sale of the contents of Reddish House, the home of the late Sir Cecil Beaton. Because of the personality and artistic gifts of Beaton as a photographer and theatrical designer, this attracted as much world-wide Press interest as the *Codex*. Reddish House, built in the style of Wren, of delightfully mellowed brick, nestles in the tiny village of Broadchalke, near Salisbury, and was then filled with an amazing variety of pictures and works of art which reflected Beaton's taste, professional life and friends. This taste was demonstrated outside the house as well as inside. On the other side of the road, Beaton had created a water garden by diverting a stream, over which he built a bridge on to a small island on which there was a Giacometti bronze statue. Inside, the winter garden leading off from the drawing-room was reminiscent of the sets for *My Fair Lady*.

The sale obviously had tremendous PR potential so I decided on a reconnaissance for a Press trip. From the landlord of the local pub I found out that the village had a teenage brass band of international fame which would be delighted to play during the view days. In the end there had to be two Press visits, one for TV networks – British, American, French and Italian – and another one for newspaper and magazine journalists. The only thing that went wrong was that although I warned the TV electricians they had better check the fuseboxes and wiring, one fuse was blown which served not only certain lights but the deep freeze. So poor Miss Eileen Hose who had been Beaton's secretary for years and had given us much help had a most unpleasant job clearing it out.

Richard Buckle, one of Beaton's oldest friends, wrote in the 1980 *Review of the Season*: "In the week preceding the sales on 9th and 10th June, publicity reached such proportions that we Wiltshire yokels began to suspect we had been harbouring a Mentmore in our midst; but Beaton had made news for fifty years, and there were thousands who longed for a glimpse inside . . ."

For the view days the weather could not have been kinder. The sun shone, the band played tunes from *My Fair Lady* and other shows with which Beaton had been associated, and everyone lunched off champagne and smoked salmon. There was a real garden party atmosphere which I think Beaton would have appreciated. It was all summed up by one of Marc Boxer's cartoons for *The Times* which had the caption, "Mummy insists I do the whole season: the Royal Academy, Ascot and the Beaton sale."

Financially it was not a great sale, £400,000 ($936,000), but it was interesting to see what had taken Beaton's fancy. Among hundreds of items were Augustus John's portrait of *Dorelia in the Garden of Alderney Manor, Dorset*, £20,000 ($46,800); a set of eighteenth-century white marble medallions of the Four Seasons, £10,000 ($23,400); a pair of bronze lamps by Alberto and Diego Giacometti, £8,000 ($18,700); Rex Whistler's 1933 drawing of Cecil Beaton and, most nostalgic of all, the framed yellow rose given to Beaton by Greta Garbo on their first meeting in 1932, £750 ($1,755).

It was a great year also for negotiated sales of which there were many. The most outstanding, with which Christopher Ponter is rightly proud to be associated, was that of Albrecht Altdorfer's masterpiece *Christ Taking Leave of his Mother*, on behalf of the Trustees of the Wernher Estate, for a net price which represented an open market value considerably in excess of any other recorded in the world for any painting. A second great work, sold this time by private treaty, was Frans Hals's *Young Man Holding a Skull* from Elton House, near Peterborough. Both were bought by the National Gallery, London.

All in all, therefore, 1980 was a significant year, particularly as the world was still in a state of recession. The international art market remained conspicuously healthy, although increased costs, inflation and the strength of sterling had a depressing effect on margins. Nevertheless pre-tax profits were £7 million, and for the first time sales in Britain at £81.9 million were almost matched by those overseas of £79.9 million. The year 1980 was the 250th anniversary of the birth of James Christie and he would have been happy if not amazed at how his firm had expanded.

During the year Christie's had at last been able to buy Robson Lowe Ltd with whom for so long there had been a friendly association. The price was £750,000. Robbie Lowe is the most respected stamp auctioneer and philatelic author in the world; at the time of writing he is still hard at work. Back in 1968 when the association began Guy sent me down to see if I could help him with some PR. I asked Robbie if it was true that his interest in stamps was first aroused while he was confined to a wheel-chair as a young man, I presumed with polio. He said yes, but many years later he told me the real reason for his immobility. "It was all because of a dinner party trick. At the coffee stage I used to challenge anyone to run round the table balancing purely on the upright backs of the chairs. Normally I pulled it off, but on this occasion I fell and broke my leg." The integration of the Robson Lowe group into Christies International would now benefit philatelists all over the world.

Overseas there had been considerable activity. In Amsterdam what had once been the Maritime Museum had been acquired so that Christie's would have a purpose-built saleroom after it had been refurbished. This would be run by the amiable Harts Nystadt, a well-known Dutch art dealer whose family business was founded in 1832 and holds the royal warrant of the Queen of the Netherlands and Prince Bernhard. More representatives were appointed, so that there were now three salerooms and thirteen offices in Europe; very different from 1959 when Hans Backer was the sole representative of the firm on the Continent.

However, in New Bond Street morale in Sotheby's was not high. Peter Wilson was indeed trying to run the whole show from the south of France. It was an impossible task: he needed to be in his office every day to run such an enormous empire. Discussing this period with Geraldine, I suggested that Peter Wilson's colleagues wouldn't have stood for such an audacious scheme. "But they did," she said. "It was the year of maximum misery, of backbiting and so on."

Peter Spira confirms Sotheby's precarious position in a different way. In 1980 he had submitted a paper to the Board saying that the company should reconsider the whole of its capital expenditure. Spira warned that he feared an economic holocaust in 1981 and that the firm should retrench from its policy of spending huge amounts of money in the States. SPB was keen on keeping both Madison Avenue and York Avenue. Spira was trying to get that changed. Wilson seemed to believe that art prices would go up for ever and would protect Sotheby's from inflation.

21

"Just Say They Were Sold, John"

For David Bathurst, after his great success with the Henry Ford pictures the previous year, 1981 brought personal disaster. A catastrophic error of judgment led four years later to his and Christie's New York being involved in a $10 million lawsuit in the New York Supreme Court. The case, which was brought by Mr Dimitri Jodidio, chief agent of the Lausanne-based art investment group Cristallina, SA, was thrown out of court by Judge Eugene Wolin on July 2nd. However, in his affidavit David admitted telling the Press that two major Impressionist pictures in the sale on Tuesday, May 19th, 1981, had been sold, when in actual fact they had been bought in.

The news of the "erroneous" statement, as David's lawyer described it in 1985, shook the art market and the Stock Exchange – Christie's share price falling from 263p on July 8th to a low of 211p at the end of August, before recovering at the end of September. It also caused the New York Consumer Affairs Department to instigate an enquiry which was settled out of court; Christie's New York had to pay $80,000 costs, David had to surrender his auctioneer's licence and Christopher Burge, who admitted that he knew of David's "false statements" but did nothing to correct them, had to surrender his licence for four months. Announcing the terms of the settlement on July 19th in New York, Jo Floyd said, "It is with regret that I also announce that Mr Bathurst has resigned his directorship of Christies International plc and the chairmanship of Christie's in London", which he had taken over from Jo as from December 1984. An earlier statement issued by Jo in New York (July 12th) said that David accepted full responsibility for the false report. "The Board take the gravest view of this isolated lapse from the high standards of conduct that Christie's employ. This error was regretted by him and the Board. What had taken place was not Christie's policy and would certainly not happen in the future." If it had not been for a tragic momentary lapse of good sense, as well as a contravention of normal company policy, David would today probably be president of Christies International instead of Lord Carrington.

In his affidavit, David's explanation for his action was that it was for the benefit of the owner of the paintings and the art market in general. "It may be particularly difficult to sell a painting if the whole world knows you failed to sell it at auction . . . it doesn't help the art market to have banner headlines of seven out of eight paintings bought in." Few would dispute that bought-in paintings may be difficult to sell until a few years have passed, but that doesn't justify telling the Press that they were sold. As regards harming the art market, bad results are a commonplace and occur for many reasons, which are generally beyond the control of fine art auctioneers. The question which till now has never really been answered is why David, an intelligent and experienced auctioneer, reacted as he did.

In 1988 David gave me a long and frank interview in his new Jermyn Street offices where he operates as a dealer in Impressionist and Modern pictures and sculpture. For the first time, so far as I know, he explained his psychological reaction to Press questioning when he stepped out of the rostrum following the unsuccessful sale on the evening of Tuesday, May 19th, 1981.

The Jodidio–Bathurst affair began late in 1980 when Jodidio went to lunch at Christie's New York. As a result of this David went to see him in Lausanne the following February. A number of pictures had been taken out of a bank and Jodidio told David he wanted to raise $10 million. David selected eight pictures and gave Jodidio what he thought were realistic prices. There was some general discussion about these. "Jodidio had been an important client of Wildenstein's and knew a great deal about prices and the market generally. He could tell me as much as I could tell him." David told him he would have to discuss the prices he had suggested with Christopher Burge after his return to New York.

The pictures David selected were Van Gogh's *Mas à Saintes-Maries*, which was probably the most important work; Renoir's *Buste de Femme Croisée d'un Chapeau*; Monet's *La Seine à Rouen*; Van Gogh's *Deux Rats*; Berthe Morisot's *Apollon visitant Latone (after Boucher)*; Gauguin's *Nature Morte aux Mangues*; Cézanne's *La Maison Abandonnée au Tholonet* and lastly Degas's famous *Portrait of Eugène Manet*, the younger brother of Edouard Manet, the painter. The picture was a wedding present from the artist to Eugène and Berthe Morisot when they got married. The pictures selected by David were to be sold anonymously as "Eight Important Paintings from a Private Collection".

When Christopher had seen the pictures he made some adjustments to David's valuation – some up and some down – but then "we did a deal" with Jodidio on terms: it was a "pretty rough deal – a sliding scale with a little vendor's commission". After that David lunched with Jodidio regularly. When the catalogue came out in April Jodidio was effusive in his praise. The time came for adjustment of the reserves in the light of the public's reaction. This, according to Christopher, had been a bit slow. "It was then that the $10 million figure became a stumbling block, requiring some fine tuning."

In spite of this, David said, he went into the rostrum without any undue qualms. After all, the previous sale of this kind in November had gone very well and the one before that had been the Ford sale. They were good pictures and the room was packed with all the right people. "However, to my amazement and horror there was very little and in some cases no bidding. I'd never encountered anything like that before or since, to the extent that when we got to the eighth picture we hadn't sold a single one. To my surprise we sold it. Degas's *Portrait of Eugène Manet*, which I thought was going to be the most difficult one to sell, which was why I'd left it to the end, went for a record price for the artist of $2.2 million [£1 million]."

The sale then continued with works from other collections. There was *La Domaine Enchantée* – Eight Important Pictures by René Magritte – which had decorated a restaurant. The Belgian Government had insisted that they should be sold as one lot, and as each one was very large it was not altogether surprising that they were all bought in at $1.7 million (£809,523). Other pictures followed with equally dismal results ending in a 55–60 per cent sold figure. "Not good. Something seemed to have happened to the art market which we hadn't foreseen. In retrospect I thought and still think that as interest rates had gone up to 20 per cent by then, people felt it wiser to put their money on deposit and earn a sure-fire 20 per cent rather than risk their money on works of art, however good they were – and nobody had criticised the quality of these pictures."

I had watched the sale with increasing despondency. By sheer chance I had decided to take some overdue holiday and visit John Whittles, my old *Daily Telegraph* friend, and his wife in Los Angeles.

Knowing of the important two days of Impressionist and Modern picture sales I decided to stop off in New York. Apart from naturally being interested in seeing how they went, I always liked to keep in touch with Park Avenue, in particular with those in the Press Office. The results of the two sales seemed even worse than those of our opening sale in 1977.

I was sitting in the tiny Press Office disconsolately waiting for Elizabeth Shaw and her girls to check on the prices of what was sold, and the total. Elizabeth had joined Park Avenue after Tish had left and previously had been at the Museum of Modern Art, New York, for many years as Press Officer. Liz was a real pro and did a very good job. We hit it off together from the start. I was worrying not only about what the world Press was going to say, but about Souren Melikian whose Saturday article for the *International Herald Tribune* was widely read and regarded as authoritative because of his knowledge of art and the workings of the art market. I had learned when I first met him in the mid-1960s that one needed considerable patience in order to satisfy him. Although highly academic he was not without a sense of humour and over the years we had developed a friendship and, I think, a mutual respect. Before leaving London, Souren had called me from Paris to ask me to ring him immediately after the sale.

"It's all right, John. David says the Van Gogh of Saintes-Maries and Gauguin's mangoes were sold," Liz said interrupting my thoughts. "I don't believe it, Liz," I said and went in search of Chris Burge with whom the London Press Office had had a very close relationship before he went to New York. Christopher, who had hurt his leg while hanging the sale, was in a wheel-chair in the saleroom. I told him what Liz had told me and asked him if it was true, as there didn't seem to have been any bidding, or was there a big bid in the book? "You'll have to speak to David about those pictures," Chris said. That confirmed my suspicions. As Impressionist director, he would know, and it was part of his job to brief the Press Office.

I found David behind his desk. "Liz Shaw tells me that the most important Van Gogh and Gauguin's mangoes were sold. It didn't look like that to me, and Christopher says I've got to speak to you about it." "Just say they were sold, John; just say they were sold," David said. I looked at him. He looked at me. "Do you really want me to tell the Press that?" "Just say they were sold, John," David reiterated.

I left his room a worried man. I sensed disaster. I knew that David's instructions were wrong, but I had no authority in New York to argue further. So I returned to the Press Office and Liz and the girls got cracking ringing the New York papers and agencies, while I got on the phone to Melikian. "I gather all the pictures from the private collection were bought in save the Degas," Souren said; someone had obviously already phoned him. Four years later, after the truth came out in court, Souren told me that he remembered that there had been a momentary and unusual pause before I spoke to him and told him he was wrong and that the Van Gogh and Gauguin had sold. Souren reported our version of the results, although he thought "that pause" was strange.

According to my 1988 interview with David, the problem arose immediately he came out of the rostrum after a very unpleasant sale, not just the Jodidio section but also the main part of the sale. It had been a bad evening all round. In New York in those days, as soon as the auctioneer set foot on the floor he was besieged by reporters holding microphones to his mouth, asking all sorts of questions. (Things are better organised now.) David said, "In New York within two seconds you had to make some earth-shattering statement about what had happened. I distinctly remember this chap who wasn't an art correspondent – I knew most of them – with a pad in one hand and he said, 'The art market has collapsed, Mr Bathurst, hasn't it?' and I could see he had already written it on his pad. If I said yes he would probably have written 'confirmed Mr Bathurst'. I thought, 'Oh no, that's all we need, a headline saying, "Art market has collapsed".' So I said no, I don't think the art market has collapsed. Not a great sale, but not a collapse. He replied, 'Looked like a bit of a disaster to me. I call that a collapse.'"

David told the reporter that he had to speak to one of his colleagues but would be back in a few moments. He elbowed his way through the crowd to confer with Christopher Burge. David told him that for the good of the client he was going to say the important Van Gogh and Gauguin's mangoes had been sold. Christopher agreed with this suggestion. When David returned to the rostrum, the reporter "started banging on again about disaster on the art market and that 'one out of eight wasn't very good', to which David said, 'Three out of eight isn't too bad.' 'Oh three?' And this had the effect that the Press were marginally less rude than they might have been. It could have been worse."

David called up Jodidio and told him what he had done, and although unhappy about only one picture having sold, he understood and approved the reason for saying that three pictures had been sold. David also rang Jo with the results and told him what he had told the Press and why. "He seemed reasonably relaxed," and came to New York a week later.

But why hadn't the pictures sold? David may well have been right about the effect of interest rates. They had gone up, and it was the beginning of a period when buyers were more and more discriminating before paying vast prices. As Melikian wrote shortly afterwards and as Spira had prophesied to Peter Wilson in 1981–2, Sotheby's was in the red for the first time in decades.

However, it didn't look like that two days later after Sotheby's Impressionist sale – advertised by them as "the most important assemblage of Impressionist and Modern works from various owners to be offered in recent years". Even allowing for the fact that the sale had Picasso's (by now) well-known *Self-Portrait* which sold for $5.3 million (£2.4 million), the ninety-three lots brought $20 million (£9 million), only nineteen lots failing to sell. The New York Press naturally compared Sotheby's success with Christie's disappointing results at the beginning of the week. David Nash, Sotheby's senior vice-president, went as far as to say, "These seem to be the best of times."

Apart from interest rates Jodidio had an idea that Wildenstein, the most important picture dealer in the world, had influenced people against bidding. I asked David if it wasn't true that the two men had had a row. "Yes, they had, but Jodidio's theory was sheer paranoia. No one man can bitch a sale single-handed. No, I think it was the interest rates, plus the fact that the pictures were Jodidio's – his ownership was unearthed and published by the Press. People knew he had bought them partly for investment and he wasn't a popular man. But even so that doesn't stop people buying good pictures and I couldn't find anyone who didn't think the majority were good pictures."

I'd written to David long before the sale suggesting we should do some PR about "the eight pictures", and been told the owner was arranging for this himself. I didn't know and David didn't tell me that he'd arranged for Huon Mallalieu, who had worked with Noel for some time before turning to journalism, to write a eulogistic article about the pictures (although he'd only seen the colour transparencies) in *Connaissance des Arts* which Jodidio owned. David agreed that that wasn't very clever; it was all too obvious to those in the art market.

For a year nothing happened and then relations with Jodidio took a turn for the worse. Because Christie's had been so unsuccessful on his behalf, he made certain demands which they refused to agree to. The correspondence went on "for weeks, months, years", by which time, David said, the facts were pretty well known. It had even been said in certain art magazines that the Van Gogh and Gauguin had not been sold. No one seemed particularly excited about it. No one gained any money; no one lost any money; nobody was damaged in any way.

Eventually on July 2nd, 1985, Jodidio's claim against Christie's for negligence and other damages reached the Supreme Court. As I have said, the suit was thrown out of court, but David's admission of an "erroneous statement" was taken up by the Press "with great vigour". "I admit it was a silly thing to have done. Maybe I exaggerated the effect of those possible headlines about the art market collapsing. In retrospect, we should have let them write it and lived to fight another day, but at the time I thought a headline such as 'Collapse of the art market' was the last thing we needed and might unfairly damage the art market for the next year or two. So it seemed sensible to tone down the story a bit."

I said to David that it was surprising that Jo had made him chairman of Christie's King Street before the case came to court. Many members of the Press had mentioned this to me. David's reply was that when he was made chairman the case was in the air but not certain. It might be settled out of court and it wasn't going to be that serious even if it wasn't settled. If this was the real view of Jo, and presumably of Christie's legal advisers, it implies that they totally underestimated the reaction of the Press and indeed many of the general public.

Finally I asked David: "Do you agree now, with hindsight, that it was not the right solution?" "Of course it was the silliest thing of all in retrospect. I had about six seconds to decide how to react to this notional headline I'd seen about the art market collapsing and I decided to counter exaggeration with exaggeration. In retrospect I overestimated the seriousness of the situation. Even if they had written 'art market collapses', we'd have lived to fight another day. I would feel bad if I felt I'd cheated anybody." There I stopped him: "The people you cheated were the Press." David replied, "I did find the Press's moral indignation at my misleading them a bit rich coming from a profession which in my experience had never been too pernickety about the accuracy of what it printed or the damage it did when publishing untruths."

When the storm broke in the middle of July 1985, David suffered the worst excesses of being hounded by the Press, one reporter actually dressing up as an electrician and walking into his house where some genuine renovation work was being done. Fortunately David had a shrewd builder who knew there was no electrical work to be done and kicked the "electrician" out when, after being challenged, he admitted he was a reporter.

The 1985 Jodidio case was not the end of David's nightmare, because the next year Jodidio appealed against Judge Wolin's decision and five judges of the appeal court overturned it. Jodidio claimed that Christie's was guilty of negligence and fraudulent misrepresentation in the way it mounted the sale and withheld from him certain information regarding the state of the market at the time. Cristallina was claiming $5.5 million compensatory damages (the difference between what the pictures fetched eventually when sold later and what Christie's said they were worth), plus whatever punitive damages the jury saw fit; the figure of $11 million was being bandied about.

In view of Jodidio's close knowledge of how the art market worked and up-to-date prices his claim was not particularly convincing. Nevertheless there was the fear, and Christopher Burge admitted this, that if Cristallina won and Christie's was forced to pay compensatory damages, this would mean that from then on auction houses in New York would have to guarantee reserve prices, which would kill the auction business stone dead.

One wonders why Jodidio ever bothered, because on January 21st, 1987, there was an "amicable" out of court settlement. Prior to the settlement, Cristallina's attorneys dismissed all claims of fraud from the complaint and dropped all charges against David Bathurst personally, saying that they did not contest Christie's position that Mr Bathurst and Christie's had acted in good faith. Christie's press release said finally: "With the issues in the case narrowed to technical ones of auction practice, both sides concluded that it was better to settle the case between themselves rather than through the decision of a lay jury." Thus after six years ended a case which should never have happened.

Many ex-colleagues regret my writing this book because of this very chapter, while the art market – which takes such events in its stride – may well have forgotten about the incident. The Jodidio–Bathurst case is, however, part of Christie's post-war recovery story and cannot be swept under the carpet. Christie's, in any case, has since then gone from strength to strength, and David, although he would prefer to be at Christie's, will I'm sure have a great success as a dealer.

There were lessons to be learned from the scandal, not only by Christie's New York but also by the top management in King Street. As a result of David's lapse, Christie's credibility as a public company was damaged, and its future in New York was put in question if only for a short time. Christie's did in fact recover remarkably quickly from the setback.

The Press naturally had a field day, for auctions are public affairs, and the public as well as the Press can rightly expect to be given the truth. To do otherwise is not just morally and professionally wrong but madness, because the lie is bound in the end to become public knowledge. Sales at Christie's, Sotheby's and other fine art auctioneers are of considerable interest to the Press, as now must be obvious, and each auctioneer derives great benefit from such publicity, as does the London art market in general. Thus when things go badly auction houses cannot expect not to be targets for Press attention.

There are all sorts of ways of explaining why a sale went badly without infringing the truth, but if a sale has been a total disaster one has no alternative to giving the full facts. As Christie's learnt, the Press do not take kindly to attempts at manipulating them. To learn the truth of this in such a painful way should not have been necessary for David – particularly in America where the freedom of the Press is secured by the First Amendment to the Constitution, so misleading the Press receives short shrift.

As David Westmorland, chairman of Sotheby's, said a year or two later when his firm was in dire financial straits, "We lived by publicity and then we died from it." In Sotheby's case this was nothing to do with sales results – and, if anything, the Press are to be criticised for distorting Sotheby's financial situation – but Westmorland's words illustrate the voracious reaction of Fleet Street when things go wrong.

There was a gung-ho side to David's personality, which had served him and Christie's very well when it was a question of business-getting, but possibly led him astray in difficult situations which in turn resulted in unwelcome Press attention. Paradoxically there were times when he appeared really to enjoy talking to the Press, without any of the stiffness and prevarication of Peter Chance, Jo, Guy and Patrick. When David became chairman of Christie's King Street in January 1985, I organised a Press lunch for him, and it went splendidly. I will never forget Geraldine's words as she swept out of the front door: "A new wind blows through Christie's." How cruel and ironical life can be.

And she was not alone in being impressed by David. When the storm broke in July there was a petition to Jo Floyd which read: "We, the undersigned, feel it is in the best interest of Christie's that David Bathurst remains in his present position. In particular he should remain as chairman of Christie, Manson and Woods, Ltd." It was signed by a large number of directors – certainly the most senior – and allowing for others being away on business I am told only two declined.

There is no doubt David had great talents – imagination, intelligence, energy and personal attraction – which were recognised by his colleagues. Even so, some may be surprised by the support he received. The explanation, I think, is that an auction house is unlike any other business. Even today, when there is a Hertz–Avis-type competition between Christie's and Sotheby's, Christie's certainly still resembles a family whose members, recognising first and foremost the skill and expertise of a colleague, develop a natural loyalty to one another which may blind them to other considerations. The problem is whether clients, shareholders and the general public will feel the same way. Christies International Board evidently thought not.

By that time I had taken early retirement and I was not involved, but I think it would be wrong not to declare my own views. If I had been asked to sign the petition I would have refused, although I bear David no ill-will and our talks have been on the friendliest terms. The conclusion I came to at the end of our long interview was that although he thought it "a silly thing to have done" and he wouldn't do it again because of what it had done to his career, he still didn't say it was "wrong", just "silly"; he had no qualms about having misled the Press. Maybe because I had worked in Fleet Street and because it was a monumental public relations gaffe, I take his action more seriously than my ex-colleagues. In the world today I do not think anyone capable of making such a mistake should be chairman of a public company.

Some friends of mine after the furore scoffed at this attitude and said, "For goodness sake, everyone knows you've all been doing this [announcing BIs as sold] for years." Sotheby's certainly did do it and I often asked reporters, "Why do you take this treatment from Sotheby's?" Most of the misinformation concerned comparatively minor lots, and Stanley Clark, my opposite number who retired long before me, told me that he had advised Peter Wilson that Sotheby's shouldn't do it. However, Christie's London certainly did not do it; and I have quoted Geraldine as saying so.

Christie's New York, in spite of the disastrous sales in May of Impressionist and Modern pictures, managed to increase their sales total during the year by 17 per cent to £69.7 million, even though there had been no sale comparable to the Ford Impressionists. The buoyant market applied throughout the year to every department including the Impressionists sold in November. The only ones that went badly were in mid-May. Interest rates did go up, but there were buyers for works of top quality.

The prolonged recession throughout the Western world had a considerable effect on sales in London. Pre-tax profits declined to £5.3 million. Nevertheless it was a very active year at King Street, CSK and at the salerooms in Europe, with many successful sales so that those of us working at Christie's were not really conscious of the overall financial position.

The most important picture to be auctioned anywhere was Nicolas Poussin's intensely moving *The Holy Family with the Infant St John the Baptist and St Elizabeth with Six Putti* which was sold by order of the Council of Management of Chatsworth House Ltd, the proceeds going towards the charitable trust set up by the Duke of Devonshire and his family for the preservation of Chatsworth and its contents for the public. When the sale was announced the Duke himself, no stranger to the salerooms, took the Press conference, which both he and the Press enjoyed. The Government had not only been informed but had given the sale their blessing so altogether the Duke was able to defuse the inevitable cries of anguish from the heritage lobby. In spite of being asked some quite personal questions about the costs of running Chatsworth, the Duke was completely at his ease, handling the Press with humour and giving them sufficient facts to satisfy their curiosity.

However, when it came to the sale the result was a little disappointing for everyone concerned, as the last bid was £1,650,000 ($3.6 million) from Wildenstein of New York, which was not quite enough. The Duke, his advisers and Patrick discussed the matter and within minutes Patrick had the Duke's permission to accept Wildenstein's bid. But by that time Wildenstein had left. Patrick rushed out of the still crowded saleroom, while the Duke and I walked up and down the side passage where the pictures are stacked prior to a sale. The Duke was remarkably philosophical about not having got as much as he hoped, on which he had presumably been advised by Christie's. Much to everyone's relief Patrick returned to

say Wildenstein had agreed – most dealers don't in such circumstances. With buyer's premium the price was £1.8 million ($3.6
million). The picture was later bought jointly by the Norton Simon
Foundation and the J. Paul Getty Museum.

In the same sale, of considerable art-historical interest was a tiny
copper panel by the sixteenth-century German master Adam Elsheimer
which amazingly had turned up in Australia and been taken to Sue
Hewitt, Christie's Sydney representative, the owner having no knowledge of its importance. It was the seventh and final member of
Elsheimer's great tabernacle (see Chapter 13). The panel – *St Helena
Questions the Jew* – was the fourth panel from the altarpiece to be sold
by Christie's and it was bought by the Städelsches Kunstinstitut,
Frankfurt, for £110,000 ($243,100).

The other sale to make world headlines in 1981 was the Edward
James collection of Surrealist pictures, one of the most important
groups of such works ever to come up for auction. There were no
fewer than seventeen paintings by Salvador Dali, all dated between
1933 and 1939, and others by Magritte, Klee, Delvaux, Chirico,
Picasso and Leonor Fini. The sale had tremendous promotional potential, not only because of the importance of the pictures but because of
the bizarre nature of the owner, then aged seventy-three. (He has since
died.)

Edward James had been not only a collector but a patron of the
arts since the early 1930s. His father, William James, was born of
American parentage and his fortune came from copper mines and
railroads. His mother was a great society figure and friend of King
Edward VII, who frequently stayed at West Dean, the Jameses' West
Sussex home, and was Edward's godfather – there was a strong rumour
that he was in fact Edward's father.

Edward James was an eccentric collector to say the least, and also
a tax exile who lived most of the time in Mexico, where thirty years
before he had started building an architectural fantasy in what he
considered to be one of the last areas of unspoiled jungle. A few months
before the sale he was in Amsterdam helping to arrange an architectural
photographic exhibition which the Utrecht Bank wanted to mount.
James could not come to London because he had only two days left
from his Inland Revenue "allowance" of sixty days during one year in
Britain, and he was going to use them for the actual sale. However, I
needed background material about how he had met Dali and Magritte
– both of whom decorated parts of his Wimpole Street house which

was destroyed in the war – and his life in general. As he couldn't come to London I asked Harts Nystadt, our Amsterdam representative, to get a tape-recorded interview with him.

Harts was always game for anything but I doubt if he'll ever forget what was to come. He rang James who agreed but said Harts had to supply a dog – "Michael Schuyt [who was helping with the exhibition] says it's essential that I look eccentric." Harts arrived with a little dog and was there for hours – the transcript runs to nine pages. At times the interview was conducted in French which for some reason made the dog bark.

James bought his first painting when he was nineteen – it was a Brueghel; he also had several Picassos long before the artist became fashionable. However, he was most attracted by aspiring artists such as Dali, Magritte, Delvaux and Leonor Fini. He was so impressed by Dali that he engaged him to paint exclusively for him for a year in 1937/8. A little earlier, at the International Surrealist Exhibition in 1936, Dali had given a lecture dressed in a diving suit and helmet. Dali was inaudible in his helmet and signalled for it to be removed. Brute strength failed, so a box of workman's tools had to be sent for and he was freed with a wrench. Still wearing the rubber suit and very hot by this time, Dali gamely continued, but owing to his thick Spanish accent the audience found his French incomprehensible and left the lecture none the wiser.

By the end of the 1930s James had the largest Surrealist collection in the world. The most important work was *Le Sommeil*, painted in 1937, which was exhibited in the Dali retrospective exhibitions in Paris and London in 1979/80, the London one breaking all attendance records at the Tate Gallery. *Le Sommeil*, in which a melting head is seen propped up by crutches in an eerie landscape, is one of the best known of all Dali's Surrealist images. The major part of the sale was a series of small panels painted by Dali for James's dining-room.

An even weirder Dali work was *Téléphone – Homard*, a telephone in the form of a lobster, which the Tate Gallery bought for £19,000 ($42,940). James had a number of these telephones in his house, and at the beginning of the war Schiaparelli's niece, Bianca, was staying there. Schiaparelli warned James that her niece was a spy, but at first he didn't believe her. When Italy declared war Scotland Yard sent some men to arrest her. The police opened her purse and started reading her letters, when the telephone rang. Bianca lifted the "lobster", which was resting in something like a champagne bucket full of chunks of glass that looked like ice, and said "Hello." It was a boyfriend of hers. A conversation ensued which ended with her saying, "See you at Claridge's, darling." The police, seeing her talking to a lobster – they evidently didn't believe it was a real telephone – left, thinking her crazy. That is a typical incident from Edward James's life.

Edward James was coming over the day before the sale and staying at the Savoy. He promised on the phone to make himself available to the Press who were dying to meet him, their appetites having been whetted by a number of articles we had managed to land in the *Observer* colour supplement and other magazines, thanks to Harts's interview and to having transparencies of the pictures. I never thought he would remember the time agreed, but sure enough at 9.15 a.m. he entered Christie's and gave the Press the whole day, ending up at the BBC TV Centre and appearing to enjoy every moment of it. He was also pleased with the results of the sale.

When Christie's announced the sale an estimate was given of £1 million, but the eventual total was £1.7 million ($3.8 million), *Le Sommeil* selling for £360,000 ($813,000), while two of his small panels sold for £170,000 ($384,200) and £145,000 ($327,700). Later in the year his Picasso print (1935) *La Minotauromachie* was auctioned for £80,000 ($160,800) – then a record price for a print. James had bought this because the Minotaur had been chosen as the symbol and name of the Surrealist movement magazine sponsored by James for which Picasso had designed the cover. James flew off to his Mexican jungle home immediately after the sale, thus ending a short but fascinating association.

That year saw the publication of *Christie's Sales to the Nation*, produced by Patrick and Christopher Ponter, to demonstrate that ever since the Finance Act of 1956 Christie's had taken a lead in promoting negotiated sales and "private treaty" sales with the nation's museums. The National Heritage Memorial Fund played a key role in the private treaty sale of the great Altdorfer from Luton Hoo, making one of the highest grants to date, of £800,000, towards the sum needed by the National Gallery. The booklet demonstrated how Christie's auctioneering experience enabled sales of great works of art to be arranged for the benefit of the nation. It was an answer to the heritage lobby and MPs generally.

The year 1981 will be remembered also for a very different reason. At long last it brought an end to the threat by the dealers' associations of legal action over the buyer's premium. Jo reported to the Board late in September that on the previous evening there had been a meeting at Claridge's, finishing at 3 a.m., between Christie's and Sotheby's and the two main dealers' associations. As a result of the skilful mediation of Sir Patrick Neill, QC (since raised to be a Lord of Appeal), the dealers announced that "as a gesture of goodwill and in the interests of preserving London's position in the international art market" the plaintiffs had decided to withdraw their action, the differences in the pending action against the auctioneers having been composed.

As a reciprocal gesture Christie's and Sotheby's undertook within three months to conduct their own independent analysis of the premium, its rate and its relationship to the vendor's commission, with a view to considering independently the reduction of the premium. A joint committee of the trade and auction houses would be formed to consider matters of common interest in the art market, such as a common code of conduct, legislation regarding rings and harmonisation of VAT within the EEC. Both parties placed on record their intention to work together in a positive way and recognise their mutual interdependence. Christie's and Sotheby's agreed to contribute £37,500 each towards the dealers' legal costs, which were estimated at £150,000.

Just before Christmas, Jo called a Press conference and announced that the buyer's premium was to be reduced as from January 1st next year to 8 per cent, with the vendor's commission remaining at 10 per cent, except for lots realising less than £1,000 which would be charged at 12.5 per cent. This meant that Christie's would have to sell an extra £1 million worth of works of art in order to make up for the 2 per cent drop in premium. It was a brave decision of Jo's but the right one politically. Sotheby's had recently announced that they proposed to make no change in the premium – Spira's financial "holocaust" had become a fact – which was received badly by the dealers. Christie's decision, however, was appreciated by the fine art trade.

Jo had taken the decision in spite of there being no signs of an end to the recession. Pre-tax profits dropped again to £3.7 million, but Christie's managed to increase their market share and were able to control operating costs. What is more, the autumn results showed that the worst was over. The pre-tax profit for the second six months of the year was more than double that achieved in the first half. Moreover, it was the first improvement in a six-month period for three years.

Although as I have said the recession was still making life difficult, there were some outstanding items and sales.

At the Impressionist sale in March we had Dali's *L'Enigme du Désir* or *Ma Mère, Ma Mère*. This somewhat extraordinary picture even for Dali fans was bought in 1946 by Mr Oskar Schlag, a psychoanalyst and graphologist in Zürich. He had seen it in a local gallery and liked it immediately and bought it to hang in his waiting-room to gauge his patients' reactions, in the same way as Rorschach, another Swiss psychoanalyst of an earlier generation, used his famous ink-blot test. At the time of the sale Schlag had already retired, but claimed that on several occasions the picture helped him with his work, although he admitted that even after thirty-five years he didn't understand its meaning.

The puzzle has died with Dali, but there can be no dispute that *L'Enigme du Désir* is one of Dali's finest works. It was painted in 1929 at Cadaques where Dali lived virtually till his death. The picture was included in his first one-man exhibition which immediately established his reputation in avant-garde circles in France. When it came for sale at Christie's it found a permanent home in the Staatsgemalde-sammlungen, Munich, for the then record price of £453,600 ($816,480).

The Dali was really the only high-flier in the March sale, but there were a number of good Impressionists, Modern pictures and also German Expressionists, the most interesting of which was Conrad Felixmuller's somewhat macabre *Der Tod des Dichters Rheiner*. Felixmuller was a German Expressionist, but not one who so far had aroused any great interest. A photograph was sent to John Lumley from the owner who lived in West Berlin. It showed the poet Walter Rheiner committing suicide in Berlin in 1925 by throwing himself out of a window. "The photograph of the picture was marvellous," John Lumley remembers. "Jorg Bertz and I decided to go and see the picture." On the plane they discussed the maximum price they would be prepared to offer and decided on 150,000 marks, which was then about £40,000. However, when they saw the picture all those pre-arranged ideas vanished. The owner wanted a minimum of 200,000 marks and the picture was so fantastic that without any discussion John and Jorg agreed.

The picture had strong political overtones and reflected both the military and the economic defeat of the Weimar Republic, which had destroyed the hard core of solid Berliners, leaving the city at the mercy of speculators. The picture shows Rheiner's agony as he threw himself from a top-floor window into the darkness and down into the garishly lit streets below. Both Jorg and John had no doubts it would sell well, but they never expected it to achieve £145,000 ($232,960) or 543,750 marks.

Souren Melikian commented after a sale of English pictures: "If proof was needed that the art market does not follow the general pattern of economic evolution it came forth at Christie's auction on July 16th. The economic trends are never dramatically reversed overnight. But that is precisely what happened at Christie's. The sale was a stunning success in contrast to the depression that has been noticeable for the last few months in all sectors of the market and particularly so with works of British interest." It was not just the presence of Turner's *The Temple of Jupiter Penellenius Restored*, which sold for £648,000 ($1.1 million), but a number of large eighteenth-century portraits, four of which sold for record prices for the artists. The high prices were not confined to portraits – a wooded landscape with a ploughman at work near East Bergholt by Constable achieved another record at £324,000 ($560,520).

The autumn sale of English pictures was equally successful and of particular interest because it included four oil-sketches by Constable, two of which were preparatory studies for the last of his great six-footers, *Salisbury Cathedral from the Meadows*. Constable had given the four sketches to his daughter Isobel, who in turn in the 1830s gave them to her friend Alice Fenwick, the daughter of H. P. Ashby, a landscape painter who had known Constable. When they came up for auction one of the sketches of Salisbury Cathedral sold for £324,000 ($518,400), which equalled the Constable record achieved in July for the finished Constable landscape of East Bergholt.

There was an amazing sequel to the arrival of the four Constable sketches which had been brought to the Front Counter. As a result of the publicity before the sale, someone arrived with a study of Constable's famous *The Young Waltonians* who, although it was inscribed and dated 1811 on the reverse, had no idea of the importance of the picture. When it came up for sale it fetched £86,400 ($138,240). The finished picture had been sold at Christie's on June 20th, 1951 for 42,000 gns.

All departments benefited from the gradual improvement in the economic situation in the autumn, culminating in a French furniture sale which was the best of its type for a decade and totalled more than

£1.6 million ($2.5 million). In the 1960s a £100,000 French furniture sale was considered a great success. The December sale contained a number of old friends, including the Louis XVI black lacquer sec-retaire by Martin Carlin which had once belonged to the French opera singer Mademoiselle Laguerre. It had made £125,000 ($312,500) in June 1972 and now realised £626,400 ($1 million).

In New York it was Park Avenue's fifth year and the results can only be characterised by superlatives in all departments, jewellery, English and continental silver, French gold boxes, Oriental works of art, prints, sporting pictures, American "folklore" pictures, and Impressionist and Modern pictures which accounted for 70 per cent of all those auctioned in New York. Sales for the first time matched those in London.

The greatest rise was in contemporary art where Martha Baer's sales totals rose from $600,000 for the first one in 1978 to $7.5 million in 1982, the most successful sale ever held in this field to date. There were thirteen record prices for individual artists, one of them being $462,000 for *Reichstag*, one of Frank Stella's rare "black" paintings, painted in 1958. It was one of a series of twenty-three but most of the others were in museums. The taste for twentieth-century "conceptual" sculpture was just as great as for pictures, David Smith's *2 Doors* of polished steel selling in November for $572,000 (£357,500), naturally a record price; in 1979 the highest price for a work by David Smith was $99,000 (£45,000).

If Christie's were gritting their teeth financially at the beginning of 1982, Sotheby's were in considerable difficulties. John Marion had started sacking staff in 1981. Long before that David Westmorland, who with no business or even real fine art auction experience had been landed in a nightmarish situation not of his own making, called on Gordon Brunton's help.

Gordon Brunton (who was knighted in January 1985) had joined Sotheby's Board in 1978 as a non-executive director; he was still chief executive of the International Thomson Organisation. It was Peter Wilson who invited Brunton to join the Board after Michael Renshaw, a director of the *Sunday Times* and a friend of Wilson's, had rec-ommended him. Sir Mark Turner, a distinguished industrialist who was the only person Peter Wilson would listen to on management matters, had died in December 1980.

It was absolutely clear to David Westmorland that, if they didn't get some additional strength right at the top, Sotheby's would be in real trouble. When asked by Westmorland, Brunton agreed to investigate Sotheby's problems and make recommendations. He produced his report in March, having interviewed seventy of the staff on both sides of the Atlantic.

I asked him what he found: "No one was running anything. No one knew who was doing what. It was like a Byzantine empire with all kinds of little fiefdoms. A whole group of princes, each doing their own thing. No one knew who had authority to do what. Peter Spira had tried to create a financial structure and Graham Llewellyn was struggling hard, but there was absolutely no management structure at all. The company was totally out of control. This was compounded by the fact that most of the directors with the exception of Pollen had sold a lot of their shares."

Brunton's recommendations were forthright and hard-hitting. They involved slimming down the company at the top as well as the bottom, and closing Madison Avenue with the move to York Avenue. Westmorland as chairman read the report first and told Brunton that he agreed with his analysis and recommendations and asked him to present it to the Board. This he did and at a subsequent meeting, at which Brunton was not present, Sotheby's Board voted unanimously that Brunton should be asked to become non-executive chairman and carry through his proposals, including asking for the resignation of certain directors. Brunton then presented his report to the whole staff, and when he had finished Peregrine Pollen stood up and clapped and told the staff that he thought Brunton was absolutely right even though he was one of the directors to go. Peregrine Pollen and Marcus Linell in London and David Nash and Robert Woolley from New York left the Board.

Brunton set up a management structure with Julian Thompson as chairman of Sotheby's in London, Europe and Hong Kong. Graham Llewellyn became chief executive. It was made clear to Peter Wilson that his advice from Clavary was no longer required. In New York, John Marion was chairman and chief executive, but Brunton's main hope lay in Jim Lalley, who had been at the Columbia Business School prior to joining SPB. These changes and the quite obvious financial problems brought Sotheby's a hammering from the Press. Sotheby's refused, unlike Christie's, to give any figures for the 1981–2 season, and an article by Gwen Kincaed in the highly influential American *Fortune* magazine in May, under the headline *Sotheby's Lost Art: Management*, was virtually their death-knell.

Spira had given her all the relevant figures. The balance sheet showed borrowings of £13 million, and what used to drive Spira "absolutely crazy" was that the same balance sheet showed cash balances of £11 million, leaving a deficit of £2 million, which was neither here nor there because of Sotheby's assets in property. Following Kincaed's piece, article after article would refer to Sotheby's borrowings of £13 million. The loss of £8 million in September 1982 "made it quite clear that there was a need for radical surgery, and when we'd got rid of Madison Avenue and Belgravia we'd reduced the staff – which had climbed to over 2,000 – to 1,300. That was a very messy business."

Spira had promised Brunton he'd stay for a limited period. He was under no delusions: the business would have to be taken over. Sotheby's simply didn't have the management to do the things that needed to be done. "It's a bit like a bank, once you lose confidence, particularly with these articles being written about us – and we were pretty ham-fisted in the way we closed Belgravia – a customer would say, 'Why consign property to Sotheby's who have all these well-publicised problems when there's Christie's – lots of cash in the bank, reputation terrific, CSK, why take the risk?' Once you lose that confidence it's very difficult to see what to do." It was a question of either employing a very strong chief executive or getting someone else to do it for them. "So the irony of it was that we took £8 million out of the expenses by getting rid of 700 people. Did the dirty work and then Swid and Cogan and later Taubman came along."

This was a reference to the acrimonious takeover battle for Sotheby's which was to come. If ever there was a case of hubris it was in Sotheby's downfall, all due to Peter Wilson's insistence that art prices would go up for ever and be protected from inflation. In the view of many it was Gordon Brunton personally who saved Sotheby's from catastrophe before they were taken over by Taubman.

It was a sad summer also for Christie's and Artemis and all David Carritt's many friends. On August 5th, 1982 David died after a long battle with cancer which he fought with remarkable courage. St James's Church, Piccadilly, was packed with friends, rivals, museum officials, collectors and dealers from both sides of the Atlantic, for his memorial service. David would have appreciated an anecdote in *The Times*'s obituary quoting his reply to friends at Oxford who asked what he had been doing in the long vacation: "Up at I Tatti correcting a few attributions."

Downfall in New Bond Street

Brunton's surgery, as so often with human illness, was too late to have any real effect on the financial downfall of Sotheby's as a British company. By midsummer the share price had fallen dramatically. It wasn't surprising. The Parke-Bernet sales results were bound to be dreadful; the York Avenue building costs combined with the rise in interest rates made Spira's warning of a financial holocaust a certainty; the *Fortune* article in May and its emphasis on a £13 million overdraft underlined not only the firm's financial position but also its bad management; of far greater effect was the sale of shares, in many cases much earlier, by Sotheby directors anxious to get their money out before it was too late. Wilson had of course sold 250,000 when he retired in 1979 (leaving him with 400,000) and Pollen had sold 175,000 shares, but this still left him with 600,000 shares. He was the largest and last substantial shareholder to sell out, as he did in 1982. These sales naturally had a considerable effect on the price of the shares.

When Sotheby's went public the directors owned 53 per cent of the stock. By the end of 1982 the figure was down to 14 per cent. Not surprisingly, the City columns mentioned several names of those who might lend Sotheby's a "helping hand in their agony"; Warner Brothers, American Express, one British company, Sears Holdings, and a few private wheeler-dealers. To Sotheby's, American Express seemed to be the right sort of company, with a good reputation. Just before Christmas a Sotheby team was about to set off for New York for further talks with American Express when Brunton received a telephone call from Morgan Grenfell's Roger Seelig – whose name since then has become well known to the general public.

Seelig told Brunton that he represented Marshall Cogan and Stephen Swid. They would like an informal meeting with Sotheby's as they had become the largest single shareholder, having acquired

14.9 per cent of the shares for $12.8 million. Cogan and Swid were two New York investment brokers who in the mid-1970s had managed to buy General Felt Industries and later Knoll International, the leading manufacturer of modern furniture. Felt may not be the most prestigious product, but it has a large number of industrial uses, and it made Cogan and Swid financially independent. However, money isn't everything, particularly in the United States. Knoll furniture gained Cogan and Swid membership of museum committees. Socially they and their wives were on their way.

Brunton told Seelig he would see Cogan and Swid on his return from New York. Sotheby's was in a very dangerous position with the shares having plunged as low as 260p compared with a previous high of over £5. "We were beginning to move back into profitability because of the new structure, and that is when a company is most vulnerable, because it's too early for the share price to be affected and thus all the more attractive to predators."

Sotheby's were banking on their talks with Amex being successful, because Amex membership seemed to go with the lifestyle of Sotheby's customers. Everything seemed to be going well until Alers-Hankey, Sotheby's finance director, who had taken Peter Spira's place after he had left in August, announced that Christie's had overtaken Sotheby's. Brunton said, "The man conducting the negotiations went totally cold. It was like a curtain coming down. The most remarkable turn-up I've ever seen," and the talks broke up.

Takeovers are almost daily events and of interest only to the respective merchant banks, shareholders, stockbrokers and City journalists; but that of Sotheby's was very different. First, like Christie's, Sotheby's was a household name so the news in September of its being £8 million in the red, irrespective of assets, was a shock to the general public which made it the talk not only of the City but also of Belgravia and naturally of the Press. Secondly, Sotheby's reaction to what was quickly seen to be a hostile bid resulted in a six-month battle of intense ferocity.

It stemmed from the first meeting between the two sides on December 22nd, by which time Brunton and his colleagues had returned from New York. It took place at the International Thomson Organisation building where Brunton was still chief executive. As it was meant to be an informal meeting Brunton thought that there would be just Cogan, Swid and Seelig. He discovered at the last moment that the two predators were coming with a "whole cohort of advisers" – lawyers, accountants and PR men. He immediately summoned Warburg's, Sotheby's bank, and a comparable team.

According to Brunton, they went through the usual ritual of talks "without any unpleasantness whatever". Cogan and Swid had to catch the 6 p.m. Concorde back to the USA. According to Brunton, Marshall Cogan said to him, when it was time to go, "Thank you very much for the courteous way you have received us." Brunton then said that as it had been an informal meeting he presumed they would not be making any statement. Cogan and Swid looked at each other and Roger Seelig asked for a short adjournment. The Sotheby group left the room and were called back ten minutes later. Seelig looked straight across at Brunton and said, "Yes, it is informal and we shall not be making any public statement."

That evening Brunton had a Thomson dinner. At 9 p.m. he was telephoned by the editor of the *Financial Times* and asked if he had any comment to make on the statement which had been made by Mr Cogan and Mr Swid through Morgan Grenfell. Brunton said, "There must be a mistake, there's no statement." The *FT* editor said of course there was a statement. They'd received it at 7 p.m. and it ran to six pages; he'd send a copy round to Brunton. Brunton was understandably furious when he read it. Cogan and Swid, aided and abetted by Seelig, had not only made a statement about what went on at the meeting when they had promised not to, but had criticised Brunton's restructuring of Sotheby's. Much of it must have been prepared in advance as there would not have been time to draft the full statement after the meeting if Cogan and Swid were to catch the evening Concorde. Commenting on the statement, Brunton rejected the implication that Sotheby's financial standing was in any way in question. He also said that GFI/Knoll had "conceded that there was no synergy in the deal".

The next day David Scholey (now Sir David), the present chairman of Warburg's, on behalf of Brunton protested to the late William Mackworth-Young, then chairman of Morgan Grenfell, about "the total breach of trust". Seelig was summoned and apparently said, "No, no, there's a misunderstanding." David Scholey rejected the assertion of a misunderstanding. "From that time onwards," Brunton told me, "whatever might have happened we felt we were dealing with a very dirty, nasty situation. The only way of dealing with that situation is to be very tough yourself."

Early in January, Sotheby's had announced a pre-tax loss of £3.06

million for the year ended August 31st, 1982. Brunton and his Board feared a direct bid following these results and discussed what forces they could bring against Cogan and Swid. These were the possibility of finding a White Knight of their liking, the total determination of a united Board and staff and the use of whatever weapons they could wield, through the Establishment and politically, to stop the purchase of Sotheby's "in the public interest".

It was following this meeting that David Metcalfe, an insurance broker and son of Major Edward "Fruity" Metcalfe, ADC to the Duke of Windsor during the war, played an important part in Sotheby's future. Metcalfe, an old friend of Sotheby's, had followed their problems in the Press with concern. He also had a large number of rich contacts in America. One of them was the Michigan property tycoon Alfred Taubman, who had asked Metcalfe to look out for any interesting investment possibilities. Metcalfe phoned him and told him of Sotheby's desperate plight: "Why don't you buy them?" he suggested. "Tell them to call me," was the reply. Metcalfe found that his old friend David Westmorland was not in London. He tracked Westmorland down in Nassau where he was relaxing for the weekend, having been to New York on business regarding the hostile bid possibility. He gave him Taubman's number and the first vital contact was made. After meeting his lawyer, Westmorland some weeks later flew out to New York with the company's figures for his first meeting with Taubman. It was a fortunate moment because he could show Taubman that in spite of their vulnerability Sotheby Parke-Bernet had the famed Havemeyer pictures to sell.

Long before this meeting, however, and in spite of the animosity they had aroused, Cogan and Swid asked for another meeting with Sotheby's. This took place at Sotheby's on April 10th, a Sunday. Following the "breach of trust" after the first meeting, the second was not surprisingly frosty. The *New York Times* quoted Swid as saying they got a "chilling frightening reception". Cogan added: "We were treated as pariahs and they did everything possible to try to intimidate and frighten us." Brunton's version is different. "That's when it got rough. I told Cogan and Swid that the Board and staff were totally opposed to any takeover and that there was no synergy between GFI and Sotheby's. We were cold and incisive but not rude." Cogan and Swid requested the opportunity there and then to talk alone with Peter Wilson – who was revelling in being back on stage once again – and John Marion. Brunton refused this request but stated that he would agree to a short meeting with Wilson and Marion, if Julian Thompson and Jim Lalley were also present. A short meeting was held and the group returned to the Board Room. What was discussed at this private meeting is not known to me, but Brunton's basic premise that there was "no synergy" between the two bidders and Sotheby's was upheld and the meeting ended.

Cogan and Swid's reaction was swift and uncompromising. They instructed Morgan Grenfell the next day to make a £60.6 million bid for Sotheby's. They offered $7 (520p) per share for the remaining stock of Sotheby Parke-Bernet. This was nearly twice as much as the shares had been worth before the bidding battle had begun.

Brunton happened for once to be having a break in the South of France. While he was at dinner on the Saturday evening after the bid Scholey phoned to tell him of the bid and ask him to come back immediately. Brunton flew back the next morning and went straight to Sotheby's, where the directors were waiting. He found an air of panic and defeatism. Brunton called a Board meeting at the end of which he had managed to raise morale and there was general agreement that Sotheby's must fight the bid.

Graham Llewellyn, Brunton's chief executive, was appointed spokesman in dealing with the media. Llewellyn's line was that the GFI/Knoll bid was "totally unwelcome" because the two Americans were "simply the wrong people". Geraldine got the best quote, though. She rang Llewellyn in the afternoon and after receiving the firm's official line, asked him what he would do if Cogan and Swid succeeded with their bid. He laughed for a brief spell and repeated her question down the phone and then said: "I'll tell you what I'll do, I'll blow my brains out – that's what I'll do."

No journalist could wish for a better quote for such a story. This and another statement to a journalist – "there is no price at which we would recommend a bid from them" – caused considerable embarrassment to Sotheby's. John Hignett, head of the takeover panel, publicly censured Llewellyn. Llewellyn's statements to the Press in general had also suggested that Sotheby's disliked Cogan and Swid because they were felt manufacturers. Cogan and Swid's PR firm captured the interest of the *Mail on Sunday*, which on April 17th printed a long article headlined "Snobbery under the Hammer". This article caused great distress to Brunton because of the suggestion, printed in italics and without any substantiation, of "anti-Semitism". "That upset me personally very much because I have many friends who are Jews."

Before that Cogan and Swid had described their first meeting with Sotheby's as "disastrous", as opposed to Brunton's account of being thanked for his courtesy. "All we got was a barrage of insults thrown at us."

Perhaps Sotheby's were snobbish, but fine art auction houses like Sotheby's and Christie's, and many small firms, are different from huge manufacturing or industrial companies whose staff see little of their employers. Everyone in Christie's certainly, and I suspect it is the same in Sotheby's, is called by his or her Christian name. Porters work for years beside directors. I think the reaction of Sotheby's Board and staff was perfectly natural. If their firm was going to be taken over, the idea of being bought by a couple of felt manufacturers, compared with American Express, was abhorrent to them. The lack of synergy was the root of the directors' and staff's dislike – and I think Christie's would have felt the same.

It was not just the popular Press which Cogan and Swid's PR people were orchestrating. The City were far more sympathetic to them because they saw the takeover bid in purely financial terms. They had little sympathy for Sotheby's because their financial situation was obviously due to bad management, and their talk of "lack of synergy" reflected their dislike of Cogan and Swid's money coming mostly from felt. However, it wasn't just a lack of "synergy". Brunton had one arrow to his bow which the City could not dispute. This was Cogan's relationship with the New York Securities and Exchange Commission. In 1970 the SEC had accused Cogan of mismanaging a client's discretionary fund. Cogan accepted a ban on trading, although not admitting guilt. This was a damaging blow to the bidders' reputation and Brunton made the most of it, emphasising that Sotheby's was holding substantial sums of money and that total trust was essential.

But what was Sotheby's to do? The most hopeful line of defence was to produce a paper suggesting that such a takeover should be referred by the Office of Fair Trading to the Monopolies and Mergers Commission. This on the face of it was ridiculous, as there were Christie's, Phillips and Bonham's. Moreover Sotheby's, having bought Parke-Bernet, America's only real fine art auction house, were hardly in a position to moan about a monopoly, which they had had in New York for many years. In any case Sir Gordon Borrie, director of the Office of Fair Trading, knew all about fine art auctioneers after the buyer's premium rumpus, and took only a week to pass on his view to Lord Cockfield, Secretary of State for Trade – his political master – that there were no grounds for referring the takeover bid to the Monopolies and Mergers Commission.

Professional political lobbying was the next tactic. Michael Cudlipp, the International Thomson Organisation's public relations director, advised Brunton to call in GJW Government Relations. This organisation consisted of Andrew Gifford, Jenny Jeger and Wilf Weeks, all of whom in spite of being young had a lot of political experience. Brunton called them. Gifford's advice was that Julian Thompson, Peter Wilson and David Westmorland should act as the firm's front men, and that there should be an end to all contentious talk.

The GJW plan was to organise a referral to the MMC even though Gifford admitted there were no clear legal grounds for the argument. The only chance lay in demonstrating that the takeover would be "against the public interest" – the 1973 Fair Trading Act had a small but vital clause which empowered the Trade Secretary to block bids or mergers on that basis. It would be essential to obtain an interview with Lord Cockfield, who had a reputation for taking a line of his own whatever criticism it aroused.

Westmorland and Thompson sought and obtained an interview with Paul Channon, the Minister for the Arts. Almost more important, Patrick Cormack, the Conservative MP who was chairman of the All Party Heritage Committee, took up the cudgels for Sotheby's. Cormack, who lists his recreation in *Who's Who* as "fighting philistines", suggested to MPs of all parties, however far-fetched it sounds now, that Sotheby's was a national treasure which could not be lost to foreigners. One Tory, Anthony Beaumont-Dark, refused to be nobbled: "How can Sotheby's claim to be part of the national heritage when they have made so much money selling off bits of it?"

This did not stop Cormack, who put down a Commons question: "To ask the Minister of Trade whether he will take immediate steps to refer the proposed takeover of Sotheby's to the Monopolies and Mergers Commission." Even bigger political guns than Cormack were being brought to bear on Cockfield. Peter Wilson and Wilfred Weeks approached Edward Heath – he had stayed at Clavary, Weeks had been his personal assistant and he had been responsible for Cockfield's first appointment to high office. According to Weeks, Heath participated actively in the claim put to Paul Channon and Cockfield that Sotheby's takeover would be against the public interest. Andrew

Faulds, the ex-actor and Labour arts spokesman, needed little persuading to add his support, even though David Westmorland as Master of the Horse and Patrick Gibson of the *Financial Times* and Pearson Group seemed unusual company for him to keep.

Whether because of this groundswell of sympathy for Sotheby's or not, Cockfield on May 4th announced that he was going to refer the takeover bid to the MMC. Lord Cockfield naturally denied being pressurised and justified his course by quoting from the Director of Fair Trading's report: "the importance of London as the centre of the international art market and the position of Sotheby's in relation to that market". The decision aroused a cynical reaction from the Press as a typical example of Establishment manoeuvring. *The Times*'s view was that there was "no evidence" that "the public interest would be served if the bid were subject to closer examination". The *Financial Times* editorial went further:

> What is not desirable is for the Secretary of State for Industry to refer bids on the basis of nebulous and arbitrary criteria and to do the Director of Fair Trading out of a job by paying more attention to active lobbying on companies down on their luck . . . The art market has long been thoroughly international; and since Sotheby's under British ownership has taken itself wherever in the globe this business can be found, the xenophobic fears appear to be misplaced.

What was even more surprising was that GJW's astute PR campaign appeared in detail in the *Sunday Times*, for which presumably the lobbyists themselves were responsible, however embarrassing this might be for Sotheby's. Brunton took a philosophical view about this action, but even worldly members of the general public must have been amazed that such manoeuvrings could succeed, and that the Establishment was still so strong. The City was appalled by Cockfield's decision. For Cogan and Swid the referral was a tremendous shock, because they knew that not only was their fitness going to come under a microscope for the next six months but that this would give Sotheby's White Knight, who was already rumoured to be waiting in the wings, time to examine Sotheby's finances.

This potential rescuer was of course Alfred Taubman, whom Westmorland followed by Brunton had sounded out long before the referral. Brunton thought him a perfect White Knight. Taubman, an amateur boxer when young, had like Cogan and Swid come up the hard way, but was not only bigger physically but very much richer. In 1950 with a $5,000 bank loan he had formed a construction company, specialising in parking lots, from which he progressed to shopping centres for race-torn Detroit. By 1960 he was a millionaire and owned the Michigan Panthers, but like Cogan and Swid he wanted status and saw art as a way to get it.

It wasn't, however, until 1974 that Taubman got his chance and hit the jackpot. He realised the real value of a ranch of 80,000 acres, mostly growing orange trees, in the middle of Southern California, and organised an investor group which included Henry Ford II. The Ford Group, as it became known, eventually bought the ranch in 1977 for $337 million, and sold out early in 1983 to a developer for $1 billion. Taubman could easily take on Cogan and Swid.

Metcalfe explained the Sotheby takeover battle just before the referral to the MMC and introduced Taubman not only to Westmorland but also to Peter Wilson. Peter Spira meanwhile arranged for Taubman to get full details of Sotheby's financial prospects. On June 10th Alfred Taubman made public his interest in Sotheby's – he had in fact begun buying shares.

Those of us working at Christie's who were at Godmersham Park, near Canterbury, might have guessed that something was in the wind if we hadn't been so busy. Christie's had been asked to sell the superb collection of English and French furniture, tapestries, needlework and a large number of works by Arthur Devis and other English artists which decorated the house. Built in the eighteenth century, Godmersham stood in a superb position, almost surrounded by hills, with the River Stour meandering through the nearby water-meadows. It was bought in the nineteenth century by Edward Austen Knight, and his novelist sister Jane Austen often stayed there. Overlooking the house on one of the hills is a small pavilion to which she often walked and it may have been there that she first started work on *Mansfield Park*, the setting for which is reputed to be based on Godmersham.

The Godmersham whose contents Christie's had been asked to auction was the creation of Mrs Elsie Tritton, an old friend of Peter Chance's, who had died in February at the age of ninety-six. Born Elsie Richter of New York, she first married Sir Louis Barron, heir to the Carreras tobacco fortune. After his death she married Robert Tritton, an interior decorator. Her first husband's taste was reflected by the superb needlework and her second husband's by the French furniture. However, it was for the English furniture, for which Elsie had been chiefly responsible, that collectors and dealers came from America and Europe, as well as from all over England, by car, train and even helicopter.

The week-long sale was blessed with sunshine and was more like a garden party than a highly important commercial operation of Christie's. What is more, the sale total was £4 million ($6.3 million), instead of the estimated £2.5 million ($3.9 million). The Press were there in force, having been given a conducted tour weeks beforehand when the daffodils were still out. Like everyone else on the first day I was particularly busy in the marquee taking down prices, when suddenly the golden-haired Judy – Judy Runick who had helped me some years before in Geneva – got up from one of the front rows and came over. She'd worked on the Front Counter at Park Avenue for eighteen months after I'd met her. She was very friendly and we chatted and I asked her what was new: "Oh I got married again." I said the usual things like "lucky man", but never asked her her new name. It was of course Taubman. Judy was very active in the bidding, beating I think Mrs Seward Johnson, of baby powder riches, by paying £15,120 ($23,889) for a pair of George I petit-point cushion covers embroidered with flowers, fruit and a parrot. Ray Perman (who had been made a director two years before) was bidding on her behalf with Charles Beyer, furniture director at Park Avenue. Nobody could fail to notice her, and she was obviously enjoying her newfound wealth, but Geraldine missed a possible scoop when she interviewed her because, like most of Sotheby's staff, she hadn't heard of Taubman.

Judy, having known Ray well when working at Park Avenue, had rung him a week before the view started, and said she and her husband would like a private visit. So Ray and his wife Bev – who had worked in the filing department when she joined Christie's – took Judy and Alfred Taubman down to Godmersham on the Saturday before the view opened. On arrival Taubman asked where "the gents" was. Ray showed him to one just off the hall, then led the two women into the main drawing-room and started pointing out important pieces of furniture. Ten minutes went by, and no Alfred Taubman appeared. Suddenly there were muffled shouts and yells. Ray realised Taubman was in trouble. He'd pulled the door handle off and found himself locked in the lavatory. Ray's trip paid off because Judy bought other things besides the petit-point cushion covers. One of them was a superb George I walnut wing armchair upholstered in silk and wool petit-point floral needlework. Judy had to pay £81,000 ($127,980) for it, no doubt again bidding against Mrs Johnson.

The following week Cogan and Swid decided that they were going to make Taubman pay for all the trouble they'd been through. On June 13th GFI/Knoll raised its official bid for Sotheby's to 630p per share, close to $100 million. The bidding battle irritated Taubman. He hadn't expected to meet this kind of opposition. Eventually, having met Cogan and Swid in New York, Taubman on June 28th bid 700p a share for Sotheby Parke-Bernet, a bid which was approved by Sotheby's directors and by GFI/Knoll. It must also have come as a welcome surprise to Sotheby's shareholders and proof positive that the Board's tactics in opposing Cogan and Swid had been in their interests.

For nearly $120 million Taubman had bought a company with assets of about $20 million, a discontented staff and a record of mismanagement. As for Cogan and Swid, they had made a profit of nearly £7 million (about $10 million). So that was the end of Sotheby's as a British company, older than the United States of America. Sotheby's staff still didn't know what made Taubman, who was a Jew, different from Cogan and Swid, even if he was a Trustee of the Whitney Museum and the Smithsonian, to name only two cultural appointments. They were soon to learn.

In contrast to the final result of years of mismanagement and over-optimism at Sotheby's were the good sales Christie's were having in London and overseas, although the economy had still not completely recovered from the recession. The most significant feature of 1983 was that Park Avenue sales totalled $180 million (£120 million), for the first time more than those in London. This achievement showed not only the success of the New York office but the potential of the American market. Impressionist and Modern picture sales included works from the collections of Paul Mellon, the great philanthropist, Henry P. McIlhenny, the Philadelphia collector, and Mrs Edward G. Robinson. Such well-known American collectors demonstrated the confidence Park Avenue had won, and in 1983 this applied to all departments. There were successes with Contemporary paintings such as Willem De Kooning's *Two Women*, $1.2 million (£775,641); and with American "heritage" and genre paintings, such as *The Trap Sprung*. This, showing two little boys climbing a snowy hill to inspect their trap – albeit highly sentimental and some might even say "kitsch" – fetched an astonishing $880,000 (£611,111). In American furniture, a "Chippendale" kneehole bureau made in Newport sold for $627,000

(£396,835), compared with $385,000 (£215,085) for an identical one the previous year; and there were similar achievements with silver, jewellery, books, porcelain and art nouveau and art deco. Peter Wilson had been right in backing the hunch he had got while working for MI5 in Washington during the war, that Americans were going to be the collectors of the future. Geneva and Amsterdam had good sales, but nothing like those at Park Avenue.

Later in the year came the sale of the contents of Desmond Guinness's Dublin home, Luttrelstown Castle. And every department at King Street, Christie's South Kensington – its total for the year was £20 million compared with £1 million in 1975 – and Christie's Edmiston's in Glasgow was working flat out. Outstanding at King Street were the sales of Old Master drawings, prints and watercolours organised by Noel Annesley and his colleagues Francis Russell, James Roundell, David Llewellyn and the gallant Sue Wiseman – who unlike many secretaries of that time is still there and who always keeps her cool when the atmosphere in the department is getting tense and even quarrelsome: Rubens's *A Man in Korean Costume*, selling for £324,000 ($476,280), was one of a number of drawings bought by the J. Paul Getty Museum, as a result of the inspired policy of George R. Goldner and John Walsh, then the new director of the museum.

The prices for Victorian and Pre-Raphaelite pictures soared even further: Tissot's *The Garden Bench*, on which are sitting the artist's mistress, Mrs Kathleen Newton, and her children, sold for £561,000 ($842,400), while Millais's *The Proscribed Royalist* fetched a staggering £842,400 ($1.2 million). John Lumley had a coup with sixteen first class Modern pictures from the collection of Mr and Mrs Armand P. Bartos of New York. Perhaps somewhat surprisingly, they decided to sell them in London and they were not disappointed. The sale total was just over £4 million ($6.2 million), Piet Mondrian's *Composition with Red, Blue and Yellow* selling for what was then a record price for any abstract picture of £1.5 million ($2.3 million).

The buyer, a Japanese private collector, was so overcome by the bidding battle that he rushed out of the saleroom and relaxed perspiring on a sofa in the front hall. His name was Shigeki Kameyama, but only John Rydon of the *Daily Express* managed to speak to him. Being too idle to stand and watch the sale, he heard the price through the public address system in the Press office, and virtually ran into Kameyama as he came down the stairs.

One of the pictures which followed this success was Bonnard's

L'Indolente, painted in 1889, which raised eyebrows in certain quarters as it showed a young naked girl draped over a bed. Bonnard had painted two versions. In spite of this, the French authorities had refused initially to give it an export permit, so there was no doubt that they considered it an important work of art. When it came up for sale it fetched £302,400 ($471,744). I told Paul Whitfield, managing director, who like me was involved with the Phaidon Press production of the *Review of the Season*, that I had earmarked *L'Indolente* for the front cover. It was a little erotic, I admit, but it was also an important work of art and had a certain charm; I thought it would help sell the book. While I was on holiday, Jo and I believe Peter – "For God's sake, we're not a Soho porn shop" – learned of my plans and overruled me. Jo, however, left me a nice letter of explanation for my return.

Instead they chose Murillo's demure *Young Girl Raising Her Veil* which had fetched 5,600 gns in the Holford sale in 1928 compared with £378,000 ($582,120) that summer. That Christie's had sold this picture in 1983, the year of Sotheby's downfall, had a certain irony. The picture was one of the fourteen from the collection of Jakob Goldschmidt which his son Erwin discussed with Sir Alec Martin in the Savoy Hotel way back in 1956.

One of the real highlights of the year at King Street, outside the picture field, was the sale of French furniture on December 1st. It was a historic sale taken by Jo – although catalogued by Hugh Roberts – and totalled just over £2 million ($2.9 million), a record even to this day in spite of there being only fifty-four lots. There were many old friends, among them the writing-desk by Martin Carlin which originally decorated the bedroom of the Tzarina Maria Feodorovna at her Palace of Pavlovsk, outside St Petersburg as it then was. It remained at Pavlovsk until just after the Russian revolution, when together with other important pieces of furniture and tapestries it was sold to Lord Duveen. He sold it to Mrs Horace Dodge and it came to King Street with the rest of her collection in 1971. When I showed it to Souren Melikian in the special security viewing room he couldn't believe it was "right". The inside of the drawers looked as if the whole desk had been made yesterday – they were so clean and free of dust. In 1971 the desk fetched 165,000 gns ($415,800), a world record price at the time. On December 1st after twelve years in the Paris apartment of an Iranian, Mr H. Sabet, it became one of the most expensive pieces of furniture in the world, selling to the J. Paul Getty Museum for £918,000 ($1.3 million).

Another royal piece, whose provenance had been detected only by Hugh Roberts's initiative in seeking the help of Scotland Yard's forensic department, was a Louis XVI marquetry writing-desk by J. H. Riesener. The inventory number on the underside of the table had been almost obliterated by time, but was revealed with the pioneering use of laser photography. The resulting print made possible the identification of this long-lost piece of French royal furniture. Once the inventory number had been established, the Paris archives showed that the table was delivered by Riesener to Versailles on March 18th, 1779, for the use of Madame Sophie de France, sixth daughter of Louis XV.

Christie's continued to strengthen its base during the year in its own quiet way. An office was opened in the City to act for and advise those working there who might not have time even to telephone King Street for advice, let alone go there. Simon Birch, a delightfully rumbustious long-time friend of Peter's, recently retired from being a stockbroker, was a natural to run it.

Towards the end of the season there was official recognition of the London art market's contribution to the nation's economy. The recognition came from none other than Geraldine, who had been engaged by the Committee on Invisible Exports to write a report on *The Overseas Earnings of the UK Art Market*. In it she said:

> The British art trade is one of the many highly specialist sources of foreign currency earnings that are included in the United Kingdom's "invisible" exporting sector. The art market's contribution in overseas earnings to the UK balance of payments is noteworthy and in the 1980–81 period of this survey is estimated to have amounted to some £53 million.

Today it is probably twice as much. This is something which Members of Parliament and the lunatic fringe of the heritage lobby might remember when an important work of art is auctioned which has little if any connection with Britain and is by an artist/craftsman already well represented in our national museums.

On a very different note, one of the most memorable occasions of 1983 was when Her Majesty Queen Elizabeth the Queen Mother came to lunch in Christie's Board Room. Jo very kindly asked me to join him, Guy, Patrick and Noel to represent Christie's. The Queen Mother, accompanied by her equerry and lady-in-waiting, entered the room radiant in pale blue with that famous smile on her face. Noel had dug up a watercolour of one of the lodges in Windsor Great Park which was coming up for sale and which naturally interested her. We each had a few words with her over a pre-lunch drink and she was absolutely charming, making one feel completely at ease and expressing interest in what everyone did.

The meal proceeded happily and when it came to the liqueur stage the Queen Mother was asked what she would like. "Do you think I should?" said the Queen Mother and asked, I think, for a glass of port. Immediately afterwards a waiter put a plate of chocolate truffles in front of her – Patrick had told Jo that the Queen Mother had a particular liking for truffles (so do most of us) and Rosie Barnett, who in those days cooked all the Board Room lunches, was not to be defeated when asked if she could make some. "Oh truffles," said the Queen Mother, "I love them." The plate slowly circulated around the table and came to rest again in front of the Queen Mother. "Do you think I could have another?" she said. "Of course, Ma'am," said Jo. There was conversation about many things and it was altogether a delightful occasion.

Finally, with an instinct for the right moment, the Queen Mother's lady-in-waiting said, "I think, Ma'am, it's time to go." The Queen Mother smiled and nodded in agreement and then looked at the truffles which were once again sitting in front of her. Turning to Jo the Queen Mother said, "I suppose I couldn't take those with me?" "Of course, Ma'am," said Jo, showing not a flicker of surprise, "the waiter will get you a bag." The lady-in-waiting took the truffles and on the way out the Queen Mother was introduced to Rosie by Jo. In doing so he touched on a subject even closer to the Queen Mother's heart than truffles – horse-racing. Rosie at that time was a keen point-to-pointer, and there was a long discussion on equestrian technicalities which the Queen Mother obviously enjoyed. It was an unforgettable day for Rosie and for all of us.

23

The Chatsworth Drawings

The next year began noisily and violently. It was about 10 a.m. on January 20th, 1984, and in the Press Office everyone was busy with their individual chores. Suddenly there were loud, frenzied shouts of "Out, out, out," accompanied by the sound of people pounding down the stairs. I told the girls to get under their desks. Peter Rose peeped out of our frosted glass door which opened on to the Front Hall and closed it quickly. There stood with his back to us a man with a sawn-off shotgun and beyond him lying on the ground were the Front Counter staff, a security man and a member of the public. I rang for the police and they were in King Street fast, sirens wailing, but it was too late. Upstairs were £2.5 million worth of the late Florence Gould's jewels which had been on exhibition for three days.

After a few moments there was absolute silence, so we all went up to the anteroom. There we found a shaken Doug Ralphs, who'd walked into the anteroom just before two men in macintoshes had appeared. One had the sawn-off shotgun, previously hidden under his mac, and the other a sledge-hammer. Doug, the porters and security men were told to lie on the floor; the second man went to the Gould cabinets on the left and smashed the main showcase. Behind it, when we all arrived, was a white-faced Humphrey Butler, Albert Middlemiss's 27-year-old assistant. He had been showing the most important item, a huge sapphire and diamond necklace known as the Blue Princess, to Mr Peter Beaumont, Phillips's jewellery director, and his trainee assistant, Miss Andrea Macdonald. Seeing the two men walk in, Humphrey guessed what was going to happen and said to Andrea very quietly, "Please give me the necklace," and he slipped it into his pocket. Seconds later the showcase in front of him was smashed. Although the Blue Princess's absence should have been conspicuous because of the velvet stand on which it would have been hanging, the raider who'd smashed the showcase did not ask Humphrey for it. He and the rest of the gang must have known about it after the vast publicity which had followed a special Press view. Doug Ralphs said afterwards that he thought the raiders were just as nervous as him and Albert Watts, the porter lying on the floor beside him. The man just put his hand into the smashed showcase and grabbed indiscriminately at a diamond bracelet and some diamond earrings, dropping one of them in the shards of glass. He then crossed to the other side of the room where he had more luck. There in a showcase by itself was a magnificent diamond rivière, which had nothing to do with Florence Gould. This was due to be sold in Geneva in the spring, and had been brought to London specially for the exhibition. The sledge-hammer was wielded once more and the diamond necklace taken; it was worth at least £750,000 and was the only really valuable piece stolen. The raiders then turned and ran down the stairs shouting to the third man in the Front Hall to get out. Presumably there was a fourth man in a car nearby with engine running.

Christie's was soon swarming with police and also newspaper and TV reporters. Many of them had been to the special view we had held before the exhibition opened, with models wearing the jewellery. But for the success of the publicity campaign there probably wouldn't have been a raid. The irony was that the jewellery should have been on its way to New York, but the advertisement for the exhibition had mistakenly said that it would end on Friday, January 20th, instead of Thursday and so it had been extended. Needless to say, nothing was ever recovered. The jewels were probably flown out of the country within an hour of being snatched. However, the losses might have been far greater; nothing of any real consequence from the Gould collection was taken, thanks to Humphrey's coolness. Since then a sophisticated system of electronic doors has been installed at King Street.

Florence J. Gould was the daughter-in-law of the American railroad magnate Jay Gould (1836–92), dubbed by the Press as one of the original "robber barons". Since her marriage in 1923 to Frank Jay Gould, Jay's youngest son, she had lived in France, mostly at El Patio, their villa on the outskirts of Cannes. She died on February 28th, 1983, at the age of eighty-seven leaving an estate valued at $123 million. Most of this was left to foster "Franco-American amity" and for this purpose in the 1960s the Florence Gould Foundation had been set up. This reflected not only a lifetime's philanthropic contribution to medicine, but also patronage of the arts in all their forms.

Jay Gould had initially invested money in the Missouri Pacific railway, from the profits of which he gradually built up the "Gould System" of private railways in the south-western states. In addition he got control of the Western Union Telegraph Company and the elevated railways in New York.

Railways were not for Frank or Florence. Having settled on the Riviera, Frank put his money into real estate, building casinos all along the coast. He was responsible in particular for turning the fishing village of Juan les Pins into the appalling resort it has been for so long. Florence was a frequent visitor to the casinos, arriving in her Hispano-Suiza car. Wearing silk beach pyjamas, dripping with jewels, her eyes hidden always behind dark blue sunglasses, she wandered round the tables, gambling chips clacking away in her pockets.

However, it was her personality as much as her worldly goods which made Florence the American *grande dame* of France. Once an aspiring opera singer, she gave moral support and millions of francs to leading French literary figures. After the war her Paris salon on Thursdays in the Avenue Malakoff included such brilliant artists as Marie Laurencin and Jean Dubuffet, the musician Georges Auric and writers François Mauriac and Jean Cocteau. These *déjeuners littéraires* played an influential part in encouraging young talent. Florence Gould in this respect is best remembered for having taken over the Prix des Critiques in 1955 and for having founded the Prix Max Jacob for poetry. For her work in this respect she was made an Officier de la Legion d'Honneur and Correspondante Etrangère de l'Académie des Beaux-Arts in Paris.

Her intellectual life nevertheless took second place to her love of jewels, which she wore at any time of the day or night – even for breakfast – in her hair, on her shoes, round her neck, on her fingers and on whatever she was wearing. She was even seen disappearing into the Cambodian jungle to explore the ruins of Angkor Wat, shimmering in diamonds. Her collection was said to rival that of the Shah of Iran, although some might think some of the pieces a trifle vulgar. This could be said even of the Blue Princess necklace, which was designed by Florence herself, notwithstanding the quality of the four huge sapphires. She had a huge collection of cultured pearls. Vulgar or not, in the opinion of François Curiel, Christie's jewellery director in New

York, Florence's jewels were "one of the truly great collections of the century".

Then there were her Barbizon, Impressionist and post-Impressionist pictures, which she normally bought on the advice of Daniel Wildenstein: works by Monet, Courbet, Manet, Toulouse-Lautrec, Gauguin, Vuillard, Van Gogh and others. There was a particularly fine Van Gogh, *Paysage au Soleil Levant*, which Florence had bought off Robert Oppenheimer, the nuclear physicist. However, most of the pictures were not of that quality, for she did not have a real eye.

It's not surprising that Peter Wilson was a frequent visitor to El Patio. His château was only a thirty-minute drive away – though he realised years before he bought Clavary, indeed as early as 1958, the importance of cultivating a friendship with Florence and even asked her to the second Goldschmidt sale. So on the day her death was announced he called John Young, of the legal firm Cahill, Gordon and Reindel in New York, who was co-executor with the United States Trust Company of the Gould Foundation. He told Young that Florence had been a friend and neighbour of his for many years and that Sotheby's would be only too pleased to "help" if required. Young was non-committal. A few moments later Stephen Lash, from Christie's Park Avenue, called and as well as going through the same routine as Wilson suggested that perhaps the trustees would like François Curiel to value Florence's jewels.

It had been quite obvious to everyone at Christie's that when they opened in Park Avenue, François Curiel would not only run the jewellery department efficiently but would also capture sales. He had learned a great deal from Hans Nadelhoffer and had developed a very good eye for gems. Like Hans also he was always well dressed, had a good manner with customers and gave them immediate confidence that he knew what he was talking about. For the first season in New York (1977–8) Christie's jewellery sales totalled $1.1 million. By 1981–2 they rivalled Sotheby's total with one of $18.7 million. François's catalogues had also been made more interesting with footnotes about designers which were appreciated by clients and the trade. By 1984 François had rightly gained a reputation. Within four days of Florence's death John Young called Curiel and asked him if he would go to El Patio and value her jewels. François phoned Hans, who had taken a sabbatical, having been asked by the great house of Cartier to write their official history, and they met at Cannes. For François it was an automatic gesture of friendship apart from being good sense. The jewels were in a bank in Juan les Pins and François and Hans valued them at $5.5 million, which was later upgraded to $7 million.

There was then an agonising period of waiting. Sotheby's Graham Llewellyn had obviously been asked for his opinion. François and David Bathurst thought it time to show that Park Avenue had some marketing ideas. The executors received a detailed memorandum of the kind of sale envisaged by Christie's New York. It could be in Geneva, but in view of the Gould name, the glamour surrounding it and the cause of Franco-American amity, they favoured New York. Before the sale part of the collection would be exhibited in London and in seven centres right across America. The trustees queried the wisdom of a sale in New York because the jewellery would be subject to a 9.9 per cent duty. This applied to any goods imported by US citizens into America which were less than a hundred years old. Christie's American lawyers earned their fee when they found a law allowing the trustee of an estate of a deceased person who resided abroad to import into the USA all the personal belongings duty-free. The trustees were impressed. (Souren Melikian of the *International Herald Tribune* was, as far as I know, the only reporter to ferret out the legal niceties through which Christie's got the Gould sale.) Early in May, after two months' silence, the Gould Trustees called in David Bathurst, François Curiel and Stephen Lash and told them Christie's had the sale.

Christie's deserved to get the sale after François's and David's efforts, but there is no doubt that John Gould knew Sotheby's were in trouble. Secondly, York Avenue, even though the New York art market have got used to it now, was not as smart as Park Avenue. When Christie's announced on January 16th that they had been asked to sell the Gould jewels, Wilson was very disappointed. He had told his old colleagues and Taubman that he was sure his old friend Florence would have stipulated in her will that Sotheby's should be given the sale. David Bathurst must have had some anxious moments when the armed robbery at King Street made headlines all over America. However, he managed to reassure the trustees that security would be perfect when the Gould jewels toured San Francisco, Los Angeles, Fort Worth, Houston, Palm Beach and Chicago.

Nor were they disappointed by the results of the sale on the evening of April 11th, which was naturally a black tie affair. Jo went over to take it. The main saleroom and the closed circuit TV salerooms were not only packed but abuzz with excitement when he climbed into the rostrum to face an international audience. All the beautiful people – socialites and film stars – were there; more important, though, were the dealers and private buyers from all over the world. There was the usual scrimmage for everyone to reach their seats. Jo checked that the closed circuit TV telephones were working and that the red telephones for taking bids from outside were manned, and then he rapped his gavel for silence.

Jo beamed down on the crowd as he always did before going to work, smoothed back a rebellious lock of hair and, having made sure his bow tie was straight, welcomed everyone to Christie's Park Avenue "on this very special occasion". "We'll now have Lot 1," and the sale began. Compared with many sales in Geneva it was an easy sale to take. Most of the pieces had been made by Cartier, Van Cleef and Arpels, Bulgari, Chaumet, Alexandre Reza and other well-known jewellers. There were eighty-three lots and after one and a half hours of lively bidding, much of it from outside the building via the red phones, it was all over with a sold total of $8.1 million (£5.6 million), a record for a one-owner collection and far more than the trustees expected. Historically the most important gem was the Victory Diamond, a 31.35 carat rectangular flawless diamond, just one of thirty gems cut from a 770 carat "rough" diamond found in the swampy morasses of the Woyie River, Sierra Leone. It was christened the Victory Diamond to mark the end of the Second World War a few months after its discovery. A Saudi Arabian collector bought it for $880,000 (£611,111). The Blue Princess, the sapphire and diamond necklace which had been in Humphrey Butler's side pocket when its showcase was smashed, sold to a private bidder on the telephone for $1.3 million (£916,000).

The year 1984 was a special one for sales on the premises, not only by King Street, but also by CSK, Christie's Glasgow, Christie's Amsterdam and Park Avenue. The most memorable was that of the contents of Elveden Hall, the Suffolk seat of the 2nd Earl of Iveagh. Shortly after the raid on the Gould jewels Jo called me up to brief me on the history of the house and the importance of the sale. In the last century Elveden Hall was the property of the Maharajah Duleep Singh, a favourite of Queen Victoria, maybe out of pity because he was the deposed son of "the one-eyed Lion of the Punjab", Duleep Singh. Young Duleep remodelled the eighteenth-century house, enclosing an Indian interior in solid and respectable but unattractive red brick. On

Duleep's death in exile, the house and the estate was bought in 1894 by Lord Iveagh, then still Sir Edward Guinness, for £159,000. By 1919 when he was made 1st Earl of Iveagh he was generally regarded as the second richest man in England. Expense was no problem, therefore, when he more than doubled the size of the house and built the huge Indian Hall, of white Carrara marble, worthy of the Taj Mahal. The new house was furnished by Lord and Lady Iveagh in great style, and was one of King Edward VII's favourite places to relax.

His Majesty would arrive by the tiny local railway to be greeted by a Guard of Honour of the local yeomanry. Lord Iveagh would then take his royal guest by car to Elveden Hall, followed at a discreet distance by a horse and carriage in case the car broke down. To entertain the King there were many other guests, the women changing their ensembles at least three times a day. Each guest came with sufficient servants for their needs – there was a servants' wing of 180 rooms, which gives some idea of the size of the house. Heating such a large house in winter was a problem. The Indian Hall did have two huge fireplaces and even extensive underfloor heating but quickly gained a reputation as the coldest room in England. This was particularly true whenever King Edward VII was staying in the house. One of the tribulations the ladies had to put up with was His Majesty standing in front of one of the fires and owing to his bulk considerably reducing the temperature on one side of the hall.

In spite of the flat and rather bleak countryside, the attraction of Elveden to royalty and other guests was the shooting. Its efficient organisation – there were seventy keepers, underkeepers and others – and the sport it provided for his royal guests must have helped advance Lord Iveagh to the earldom he so desired. Apart from King Edward VII, the Prince of Wales, later King George V, and his son, the Duke of York, later King George VI, were regular guests. For twenty years up to 1914 and again after the war, more pheasants and partridges were shot at Elveden than on any other estate in England.

Having been briefed by Jo, I drove up on a cold drizzly day in February. From the outside the house could not have looked bleaker. There were no redeeming architectural features about the red brick building. Inside it seemed even colder than outside. Ray Perman, John Lynch and a gang of porters were beginning to refurnish the rooms as they thought they had originally been. The collection had been under dust-sheets since the wartime occupation of the house by the RAF and then the USAF, as the stencilled "Officers" and "Other Ranks" on certain doors indicated. The lifespan of the house, in spite of its rich furnishings, had been very short. It had been closed down just before the Second World War and only partially reopened since.

In the library Clive Aslet of *Country Life* was sitting at a table in his overcoat, doing some research for the history of the house which Christie's had commissioned him to write and from which I gleaned the social details of this bastion of Edwardianism. Aslet's history would accompany the six-volume catalogue. He showed me photographs of the house party guests with King Edward VII prominently in the centre, surrounded by women in huge hats and long dresses.

Elveden Hall obviously had a fascinating social history, but I could not then see any signs of works of art to match it, let alone a collection which would impress a specially transported bunch of hard-nosed reporters from Fleet Street. All the carpets were rolled up and piled on top of each other; hundreds of pieces of furniture were under dust-sheets, with tapes tied together at the base of each one. As for pictures, those I saw did not appear to be of any real value, the 1st Lord Iveagh having bequeathed his superb pictures to the nation with Kenwood House. I returned to London rather worried but began to make arrangements for a special Press view.

Anthony Coleridge and Hugh Roberts gave me a list of the most important works of art and I had gathered during my visit sufficient historical details from Clive Aslet to write a Press release. I just hoped the reporters would be impressed when they saw the inside of Elveden Hall. We didn't tell them where they were going until they were in the coaches. I needn't have worried about the first impression they were going to get. Ray, John Lynch and the porters had done a magnificent job matching up the sets of chairs, laying what turned out to be magnificent carpets and hanging the superb Gothic and Gobelins tapestries. It was this view which greeted the Press – warmed appropriately on arrival with Black Velvet. A video had also been made of the house's historical past. They were impressed and as a result of their reports, 18,000 people came to the view, some just to see inside the house but also dealers and collectors from all over the world, as at Godmersham, to see the contents. But the publicity plus the catalogue was of particular importance because it attracted the leading American dealers – Sotheby's had an important carpet sale in New York at the same time as Elveden's which was 52 per cent unsold – as well as others from the Continent.

Most of the furniture was sold as usual in a large marquee, but the tapestries and carpets were hung in turn over the balcony of the Indian Hall for the bidders below to see. It was a most effective form of presentation because the colours of the carpets and tapestries, which were in perfect condition, were shown to perfection thanks to the TV lights which were on for most of the sale. The "textile" section alone contributed £1.5 million ($2.1 million); three lavishly coloured Louis XVI Gobelins panels of the *Enfants Jardiniers* sold for £145,800 ($204,120). The carpets, all of which had been mothballed when the house was empty and in many cases had their original labels, went for astonishing prices: a large floral carpet catalogued as Ushak with an estimate of between £1,000 and £2,000 went for £48,600. The bidding for the furniture was equally keen, twelve early George III mahogany dining-chairs making £97,200 ($136,080). The final total, just to confound my fears and prove how wrong I was, came to £6.1 million ($8.6 million), nearly three times the estimate.

However, 1984 will be remembered for the sale of seventy-one Old Master drawings from the world-famous Chatsworth Collection. Somewhat ridiculously, though not from Christie's point of view, the drawings might never have come to auction if the Duke's original desire of a private treaty sale to the nation had not been thwarted. This was basically because of a difference of opinion between the British Museum, the Heritage Committee and their advisers and Christie's; the sum involved being a paltry £250,000.

The Chatsworth Old Master Drawings Collection had been formed for the most part by the 2nd Duke of Devonshire (1672–1729). With only three exceptions, the collection had remained undisturbed until the seventy-one works, carefully selected by Noel with the aim of expressing its character as a whole, came on the market. The negotiations began approximately nine months before the sale was announced. The Duke and his lawyer approached Paul Channon, Minister for the Arts, with the suggestion that the nation might like a representative group of drawings from the collection, for £5.5 million net. The drawings were the property of the Duke's trustees, but they agreed with the Duke's concern that extra funds were needed to endow the whole collection and preserve Chatsworth for the nation.

Like the sale of the Duke's Poussin, the Old Master drawings sale suggestion was for the best possible motives, and the approach to Paul Channon was an attempt to pre-empt the inevitable furore which had been aroused by the Poussin sale. Noel and Chris therefore decided that, having received instructions from the Duke and his trustees, secrecy was essential. No one should know of the negotiations which were proceeding. Jo knew only around Christmas, when Noel and Chris thought they should tell him as the longer the negotiations continued the more likelihood there was that word of them would leak out.

The Heritage Committee, on whom the British Museum depended for a major portion of the sum, insisted on a third party to advise them regarding Noel's prices. Agnew's were called in. The difference of opinion arose over what was a fair market price for a number of Rembrandt drawings and the "Vasari page". Agnew's disputed Noel's estimates and this led to the refusal of the British Museum to agree to the Duke's figure of £5.5 million net. They were willing to pay £5.25 million. In fairness some of the drawings, in spite of their quality, were not what the BM wanted, because the artists were already well represented in their collection. I would have thought, however, that some arrangement could have been made for other national or provincial museums to buy them from the BM. But on £250,000 the Duke's offer to the nation foundered.

There have been many sales described as "the sale of the century", but I doubt if there will ever be another sale such as that of the Chatsworth Old Master drawings on July 3rd. Even before the catalogue had appeared, the Press announcement had resulted in an unprecedented request for seats. By seven o'clock on the night of the sale Christie's was thronged as if in the rush hour, and crowds of excited bystanders spilled down the staircase into the street where contact with the auction was by association only. The heat generated by the television lights made everyone grateful that the spell of warm weather had been replaced by the cooler temperatures more characteristic of an English summer.

It was evident from the bidding for the first lot that unlike many major sales a high proportion of those present had come to bid. As Noel wrote in the *Review of the Season*, the drawings were "of somewhat cerebral appeal" and attracted a following of serious collectors, dealers and museum people. Since the war the drawings had been the subject of eight special exhibitions at home and abroad. They therefore not only had an unassailable provenance but were known to the cognoscenti all round the world. It was the unique opportunity to acquire drawings of such quality and rarity that caused prices to reach such dizzy heights. Of the thirty-nine artists represented only three failed to achieve a new "auction record price for the artist".

Raphael's *A Man's Head and Hand* was bought through a London dealer by Mrs Seward Johnson for £3.5 million ($4.7 million), herself outbidding the Getty Museum who employed a number of dealers to bid on their behalf (but of course for different lots). The museum also failed to buy a page from Vasari's *Lives of the Artists* with drawings by Filippino Lippi and his circle on one side and by Raffaellino del Garbo on the other. A very high price had been predicted for this, but even so the £3.2 million ($4.3 million) paid by the well-known New York private collector Ian Woodner confounded all expectations. However, the Getty were successful with Mantegna's *Saints Peter, Paul, John the Evangelist and Zeno* at £1.1 million ($1.5 million) and also with a second Raphael of *St Paul Rending His Garments* at £1.5 million ($2 million).

The prices for the Dutch and Flemish drawings were no less remarkable. There were a number of Rembrandt's views of the "undemonstrative countryside" on the Amstel outside Amsterdam, where he was in the habit of walking and sketching. It was these which were the bone of contention between Noel's estimates and those given to the BM by Agnew's. There was no doubt who was right. Noel's estimates were if anything conservative, but no one could have gauged the interest in these or any of the Chatsworth drawings. One of Rembrandt's drawings with pen and brown ink on brown-tinted paper sold for £648,000 ($868,320); it measured 5.5 ins by 8.5 ins. Then there was Rubens's magnificent *A Man Threshing beside a Waggon* in black chalk with touches of colour and pen, for £756,000 ($1 million); a second Rubens, *Three Groups of Apostles*, £604,800 ($812,700); Van Dyck's *Portrait of Hendrick van Balen*, £583,200 ($783,675) and lastly – there is no point in mentioning any more – Holbein's *Portrait of a Scholar or Cleric*, which measured 8.5 ins by 7.25 ins, for £1.5 million ($2 million), the fifth lot in the sale to exceed £1 million. All these five lots were bought by the Getty Museum, making seven drawings in all. It took Noel just under two hours to sell the seventy-one drawings, and at the end the total was £21.1 million ($28.3 million) compared with the £5.25 million the British Museum had been willing to pay. As Noel wrote: "It was an experience that no one is likely to forget."

The year 1984 was an exceptional one with prices moving ahead on all fronts: wine sales totalled £6 million; those of stamps – Robson

Lowe was fully integrated into Christie's by the end of the year – reached approximately £5 million, and Christopher Ponter's negotiated sales came to a gross valuation of £16.1 million. Among these, although by no means the most important, was Renoir's *La Pensée*. This exquisite picture, painted in 1877, was one of the seven Goldschmidt pictures which had blasted Sotheby's into orbit. In 1958 it fetched £72,000 ($203,000). In July 1984 it was accepted by the Government in lieu of tax from the Executors of the Jack Cotton Will Trust for a gross value in the region of £2 million ($2.8 million).

This year was the start of a boom and a period of mega-prices which at the time of writing still continues, in spite of the October 1987 economic crash. Such was the success of 1984 that pre-tax profits were £17.2 million compared with £9.7 million the year before. Apart however from Christie's having adopted an aggressive sales campaign, long before many of the sales took place talks had been going on about further expansion overseas. During 1984 an office had been opened in Monaco where sales would be organised. Even more important was the conclusion of Guy's negotiations during the past eighteen months which led to an announcement of the expansion of Park Avenue. Christie's saleroom in New York would be twice its original size and there would be extra offices and a warehouse. To be able to enlarge its saleroom (which would be ready by the next spring) while remaining in the prestigious area of Park Avenue was of the greatest importance. The cost was $7.7 million (£6.4 million), which came from Christie's resources. All very different from Sotheby's problems; but both firms were involved with the same market forces.

In June Geza von Hapsburg gave the Board a surprise by announcing that he wanted to resign and take up a position in America. This came to nothing and he has long since set up an auction house in opposition to Christie's in Geneva. "The Archduke" brought Christie's Geneva a lot of business, but I couldn't help remembering the lunch he gave me after the first sale in 1968 when he asked if his wife Monica could be paid for helping with PR. The man who was finding it difficult to afford to wear a different shirt every day had come a long way since then: shooting every year in Scotland and Europe and with sons at Eton. Hans Nadelhoffer (who, sadly, was to die in 1988) took his place. His series of jewellery sales that November must have been an encouragement to him in his new role as they totalled Sfr. 40.8 million (£13.1 million), which had been exceeded only once before. A fancy blue pear-shaped diamond of 42.91 carats was sold to a Jeddah dealer for Sfr. 11 million (£3.5 million). Another departure was that of Doug Ralphs, company secretary and a friend to everyone, who retired this year. He was succeeded by David Allison, who had been understudying him for some time, and was quickly made a director.

Finally just before Christmas there was a Board meeting at the end of which Jo, Guy and Patrick retired from the Board of Christie, Manson and Woods Ltd, and David Bathurst became chairman in Jo's place. The year ended on a sad note with the death on December 28th of Peter Chance. He had been ill for some time. Having joined Christie's in 1930, he was chairman from 1958 till 1976. As Jo said in the 1984 annual report: "It was primarily his leadership that was responsible in many ways for the present proud position of the company." The whole London art market as well as his ex-colleagues would agree with that. Even if he was at times irascible, the whole firm respected him. There was nobody else on the Board who had the imagination and determination to lead Christie's at a time when the odds were stacked against their very survival. Peter Wilson, his rival, who had taken Sotheby's into orbit in 1958, had died a somewhat lonely death in Paris on June 3rd the same year. In some ways an era had ended.

Meanwhile in New Bond Street just before Christmas Alfred Taubman gathered round him his new Board, which would have impressed even Peter Wilson. Wilson had always been a one-man band; but another way of impressing people if you didn't have Wilson's undoubtedly superlative knowledge about works of art was to get some of the richest collectors in the world behind you. Taubman had as his vice-chairman Henry Ford II, David Bathurst's friend; there were also Baron Heinrich Thyssen-Bornemisza, Mrs Anne Getty and a large number of other rich Americans. The Far East was represented by Mr Seiji Tsutsumi, chairman of the Seibu group, in one of whose stores Sotheby's had held their first Tokyo auction. Finally there was the Infanta Pilar, the sister of King Juan Carlos of Spain. In one swoop Taubman had gathered friends who if they did their job properly could influence collectors all over the world.

They arrived outside Sotheby's for the first time on December 15th and when gathered round the Board Room table were told that Sotheby's pre-tax profits were £5.1 million – the firm had earlier predicted £4 million. Ironically that had been at the time of Taubman's bid for the company. Trading conditions had indeed improved, but the profits were due to the steps taken by Brunton, who had refused point blank from the start to take any remuneration for trying to keep Sotheby's a British company. However, Brunton fully endorsed Taubman's initiative and, on his retirement from Sotheby's Board, was deeply moved when Alfred Taubman with the unanimous agreement of all the directors appointed him Chairman Emeritus of Sotheby's.

The End of an Innings

David Bathurst took over the chair of Christie's King Street for the first time at a Board meeting just before Christmas 1984. The appointment had been announced publicly as long ago as July. However, it came as a complete surprise to me that Patrick was retiring as well as Jo and Guy. (Jo and Guy remained chairman of Christies International and deputy chairman and managing director respectively, and retained their offices in King Street.)

David took the chair after their departure. He said, "I'm obviously not going to do anything immediately, but I'd like you over Christmas to fill in a questionnaire which I've prepared and which the company secretary will give you." The questionnaire was far-reaching, asking for personal facts about length of service, what one's job comprised, even what one thought one was good at, what ideas if any one had for one's personal future and that of the firm, and many other things. It was a good idea and from it David thought, I'm sure rightly, he would be able to get some idea of the potential of each director, apart from their specialist field. David may have been to Eton like Jo and Guy but he had a mind of his own and self-confidence. He would not be afraid to make changes and get rid of any "old wood", or to promote young executives who had proved their ability. And no doubt it was time for a few changes.

I wondered what it would be like to work closely with him, as I had done with Peter and Jo, and whether it would be possible. Regrettably there had never, at least up till then, been any of the camaraderie such as existed with Jo, Guy, Arthur, and even Peter, in spite of his position as chairman. David had done a tremendous job building up the Impressionist department in London and also running New York, but I didn't think we'd ever work well together.

By chance it had been announced at a Board meeting a few days before I was due to see David about my questionnaire that from now on there was optional retirement at sixty-two, the normal retirement age being sixty-five. In 1985 I was sixty-one so I wouldn't lose much by taking early retirement. My session with David went reasonably smoothly, but I told him at the end that I had decided to take early retirement. "I think twenty-six years is long enough in this job." He quite understood and thought he could get a replacement by the end of March. I doubted that and told him that the department had expanded so much compared with when I joined that it needed a total rethink, and that a "head-hunting" firm should be employed to analyse the problem. He said he'd had enough of head-hunting firms in New York when looking for a press officer.

After I had made my decision I was too busy to worry about the future. There was the annual report to be designed, its copy to be written, a dummy with illustrations to be produced and the whole thing to be got to the printers – I'm quite certain David didn't know this had been one of my chores for years, in conjunction with Doug Ralphs and now David Allison. More relevant still, it looked as if it was going to be not only a busy but a successful year.

Guy, who'd been the driving force behind the setting up of the Monaco office – Sotheby's had shown for too many years the advantage of having a foothold on the Riviera – had told all the European offices as well as King Street the previous autumn that the inaugural sales would be in December. There was nothing to sell at present, but unless a date was stipulated no one would make sufficient effort to set aside works of art; and for the opening sale they would have to be important. It wasn't until June that Christie's were instructed by the Trustees of the late Sir Charles Clore, who had died in 1979, to sell his fabulous French furniture and works of art. This would be perfect as a nucleus for the launching of the Monaco office which was to be run by Christine de Massy, niece of Prince Rainier. Sir Charles's superb collection of Fabergé would be sold in Geneva. At long last too an office was going to be opened in Hong Kong.

David had told the Board of my decision at a meeting on March 13th and paid tribute in a very nice way to my long service in "a somewhat thankless job". He said that I would be leaving directly a suitable successor had been found. But he wasn't able to find one by the end of March. This was quite fortunate as we were soon involved in the important sales and also in administrative improvements. It was a year which started with the sale of the Kofler-Truniger glass collection, the most famous in the world, which sold for £2.4 million ($2.64 million); in May Nelson and Napoleon memorabilia collected by a New York investment management tycoon, Mr Calvin Bullock, including the flag which was said to have covered Nelson's body after his death; and finally £3.6 million ($5.3 million) worth of prints from Chatsworth, the highlight being Rembrandt's *Christ Presented to the Temple*, £561,000 ($836,784) – over four times the highest previous price for an Old Master print.

There were many individual items of importance, ranging from the only surviving gold font made by Paul Storr in 1797 for the 3rd Duke of Portland, which sold for £950,400 ($1.3 million), to a new triumph for Michael Broadbent, who auctioned a bottle of 1787 Château Lafite bearing the initials of Thomas Jefferson, later President of the United States, for £105,000 ($155,453). The purchaser was Christopher Forbes, the third son of Malcolm Forbes, proprietor of the business journal *Forbes Magazine*, who immediately flew back to the USA in one of the Forbes private jets. He hoped to get back to New York in time to put the bottle on Thomas Jefferson's table which was on loan to the Forbes Museum from the Maryland Museum for the evening opening of an exhibition.

The year 1985 will be remembered for the sale of Andrea Mantegna's *Adoration of the Magi* from the collection of the Marquess of Northampton. Painted between 1495 and 1505, it was the most important Old Master to come up for auction since the sale of the Velazquez in 1970. The picture had been in the Splendours of the Gonzaga Exhibition at the Victoria and Albert Museum in 1981. Strangely, it was this that really first revealed it as a masterpiece. Moreover it was one of the last paintings by Mantegna in private hands. When announcing the sale, we attempted to defuse the inevitable cries of anguish by pointing out that Mantegna's art was well represented in Britain with the *Triumph of Caesar* series in the Royal Collection at Hampton Court and four major pictures in the National Gallery, London. Since the exhibition it had been on loan to the National Museum of Wales, in Cardiff, which quite naturally was very upset to see it go.

Mantegna's *Adoration of the Magi* is one of the most moving Old Master pictures I've ever seen, and the Press evidently agreed when we had a special viewing for them. It is comparatively small, measuring only 21.5 ins by 27.75 ins, and showed the Virgin and Child and St John with the Three Wise Men proffering gifts. Mantegna had painted it in tempera and oil on linen laid down on canvas. With the years the paint must have been drawn back into the canvas, so although the expressions on the faces concentrated in such a small area were breathtaking, the picture had to be specially lit. Also in the bottom right hand corner there was an area in need of restoration. However, nobody tried to crab the painting at the Press view and Patrick talked interestingly to TV networks, of which there were many, and journalists about the history and significance of the work.

David asked me to make arrangements to have the sale satellited to Park Avenue so that people in New York would be able to watch it live. The Press Office had never done this before but it did not prove such a challenge as I expected. In fact we all rather enjoyed arranging it. Although incredibly technical it was quite simple to get organised once I had found a firm which specialised in such work. The only difficulty was in getting the TV picture to Park Avenue from wherever it came down in New York. The firm we employed had to get similar companies in New York to solve the technical problems. The day before the sale a huge mobile TV production room, almost longer than an articulated lorry, appeared at the back door and put in the necessary wiring. It was a fascinating and most impressive example of modern technology which on the following night worked perfectly.

The firm we had employed was able to give us a video of the whole sale – there were only fourteen pictures – with the Mantegna being auctioned by Patrick for £8.1 million ($10.4 million), a world record price then for any picture, paid by Tim Bathurst, of Artemis, on behalf of the Getty Museum. The late Derek Hart and John Russell, the museum's London PR consultants, had a statement all ready from John Walsh, the Director of the Getty, which said that they were "overjoyed to have acquired the picture".

A fortnight before the Mantegna was sold there had been the annual general meeting when Jo was able to announce pre-tax profits of £17.2 million ($22.3 million) compared with £9.7 million ($12.6 million) the year before. World-wide sales had totalled £373 million, almost double the 1982 figure. Shareholders were pleased to hear that there was to be a "one for one" issue of new shares "in order to increase the marketability of the shares" which were standing at well over £6.

By this time Taubman had put his own special stamp on the New York art market as a financier, offering loans and special terms for those who had been proved credit-worthy, whether buyers or sellers. Naturally those taking advantage of such services had to pay 3 to 4 per cent above "prime". In 1984 Sotheby's lent $12 million against works of art to be auctioned in due course, while buyers once they had been checked out were to be given up to a year's bank credit. Taubman appeared to be turning Parke-Bernet into a kind of art supermarket. His prize line to a *Wall Street Journal* reporter was: "Selling art has much in common with selling root beer. People don't need root beer and they don't need to buy a painting, either. We provide them with a sense that it will give them a happier experience."

Jo in Christie's annual report made a point of saying, "We will resist the temptation to branch out into quasi-related financial services, lest they should provide an undue influence on demand and create an artificial price level for works of art." To a financial journalist he went even further and said that not only would there be no diversification of financial services while he was chairman but that Christie's "would stick to what we are good at". "If we lose business to Sotheby's because we will not play the financier, so be it." Leaving aside the question of using shareholders' money for such a policy, there was no doubt it could in time be highly inflationary and dangerous to the whole market.

Underlining this was the sale, shortly after that of the Mantegna, of Florence Gould's Impressionists – the sale which Peter Wilson had set his heart on getting for Sotheby's, even before Taubman's takeover. Florence's pictures may have been charming but were – with a few exceptions – of little significance. Nevertheless all the stops were pulled out and during the months beforehand $1 million was spent on promotion: the exhibition of a select number at the Royal Academy, London, and in Tokyo, Lausanne and America; parties galore and the transformation of York Avenue – nicknamed by the art trade "the people's palace" because of its initial drabness – into a miniature theatre with boxes, each with its own telephone for bidding, for all the smartest people. I'm sure it was just what Florence would have liked, but after months of what Souren Melikian of the *International Herald Tribune* described as "the heaviest hype campaign ever witnessed in art market annals", the Florence Gould pictures made $32 million (£26.5 million). Melikian summed up: "Sotheby's overstated its case. Too much was expected of too little."

Indeed apart from the promotional costs it was strongly rumoured that the canny Gould Trustees had driven a hard bargain by insisting on no vendor's commission. As if to confirm this Diana Brooks, executive vice-president of Sotheby's in America, was quoted in the *New York Times* as saying, in reference to the buyer-financing plan,

"We don't want to make money on this one. We just want to create activity in the saleroom."

One question was left after the Gould sale and that was the identity of the buyer of the one superb picture, Van Gogh's *Paysage au Soleil Levant* which Florence had purchased from Robert Oppenheimer in 1965 for $700,000; it sold on one of the fifty telephones in action for $9.9 million (£8.2 million). The buyer was anonymous, although there were strong rumours that Taubman himself had bought it, or else Mrs Amalita Fortabat, the South American cement millionairess.

In June David's new broom went to work. He had asked me whether I thought Paul Whitfield would be good for my job. Paul was a cultivated and intelligent man with whom I got on well, but I told David that on the whole I didn't think he would make a good press officer as he had no Fleet Street experience, although he was very suitable for such work as editing the annual *Review*. Paul had been managing director for a number of years and had had a fairly tough time with Jo and Guy. I suspect they were longing for a change. For some reason in the past Paul had rubbed Peter up the wrong way too because Peter had said some very harsh things to me about him.

In June it was announced that Paul would be taking my job. Even though it was almost a demotion, he seemed relieved and wrote his own Press release. It began with two lines saying I was taking early retirement, and then went into a lengthy description of "the newly created position of Group Public Relations and Marketing Director" which was to be his. I remember Patrick coming into the Press Office on his way home, when I was alone, and picking up a copy of the release and asking who wrote it. I told him Paul had done it. "Has Jo seen it?" I said that I thought he had, at which he raised his eyes, which spoke volumes. "The simple formula of Expertise and Publicity in the broadest sense make for a good sale, and that is what we are in business to provide. Our expertise is second to none; I am delighted to be able to get to work on the other part of the equation." Fleet Street is not impressed with such a release and probably threw it straight into the waste-paper basket. But the *Antique Collector* printed a large chunk of it out of sheer devilment.

Of even greater interest to the staff was the appointment of Christopher Davidge in Paul's place as managing director. Understandably this appointment came as a great shock to Ray Perman, his exact contemporary. Ray like Christopher had done yeoman service for Christie's, rising from catalogue boy to chief saleroom clerk;

helping Guy with all the preparations for Park Avenue and eventually being made director of administration on his return to London. There was no animosity between Ray and Christopher, but it was absurd to think that Ray, who'd done virtually everything at Christie's, would be happy working under Christopher. "We'd have been treading on each other's toes." In his new position Ray had made all kinds of improvements as regards the running of house sales and other matters. Apart from his self-confidence, initiative and willingness to take responsibility, Ray was no longer "the boy from Lambeth". He had become socially sophisticated and was at ease dining off gold plate in the Canaletto-decorated dining-room as a guest of the Duke of Bedford when he and his wife Bev went to Woburn with Jo for charity sales.

Christopher tried to get him to stay but Ray knew there wasn't room for both of them. "It was not a pleasant ending after a tremendous career." Ray was given three months' salary, having served the firm for twenty-five years. As he had resigned, Christie's could argue that it was all he was entitled to, but in my opinion it was a shameful way to treat any employee, let alone a director, who had taken on tremendous responsibilities at a young age. Sadly it was by no means an isolated instance. Tony du Boulay, having been denied a place in 1980 on Christie's European Board, felt quite naturally there was no alternative but to resign. This was another disgraceful episode as well as the loss of a valuable expert. I hope Lord Carrington will ensure that in future no director or member of the staff leaves in such unhappy circumstances.

It was in the middle of June that Patrick Lindsay was taken seriously ill and was operated on for what was obviously cancer. Jo told me two days later that Patrick had phoned him to say, "I decided today I wanted to live." The whole firm was naturally shocked by his illness, of which there had been no warning. I couldn't help thinking back to his enthusiasm exactly a year ago when to celebrate the seventy-fifth anniversary of Blériot's first flight across the Channel, Patrick borrowed a replica Blériot and flew it from Calais to a field above St Margaret's Bay. I helped him promote the flight which raised thousands of pounds for muscular dystrophy. It had been fun; and now . . . ?

My friends in Fleet Street were somewhat surprised by the news of my decision to retire, particularly Melikian who in a fit of excitement said, "John, it's a watershed. I must write a profile about you." I told him not to be so silly, but sure enough he did later. One day in the middle of June I got a ring from Donald Wintersgill of the *Guardian*, one of many saleroom correspondents I'd known for years, suggesting a drink the following evening if I was free. He'd come to Christie's. When he arrived he said he'd got a taxi outside and thought for a change we might go down to Fleet Street. He told the cabbie to stop at the Cheshire Cheese, and led me down to the basement which I knew could be hired out.

There I found over thirty reporters of many nationalities who at Donald's suggestion had agreed to give me a "goodbye party". What a nice gesture! After half an hour or so Geraldine called for silence and said everyone wished me well in my retirement and thanked me for my help to them. She then on behalf of everyone present handed me a glass goblet engraved with "John Herbert from the Press, 26.6.1985". I felt very honoured. I said a few words of thanks to them, not only for the party, but all their help in the past. Somebody then asked what my worst moment was, and I told them about the first sale at Park Avenue and having to announce its disastrous results, and what Jeanne-Marie had said about my "green face".

Almost the next day David Bathurst rang me saying he thought I should have a goodbye party, which was kind of him, and gave me free rein to organise it. Charlie, who is something of an amateur artist, drew the invitation card. I asked everyone from directors to telephonists, and art dealers and journalists as well. There were also friends such as Walter Goetz, Christian Carritt and Sue Rose, and my two sons Robin and Michael.

I've normally found that I have been too busy to enjoy my own parties, but this was the exception. For once I too wanted to say a few words, mainly a "thank you" to Christie's, because whatever the difficult times, being asked to run Christie's Press Office had led to a fascinating twenty-six years. Before I got into the rostrum to make my speech, Jo told the assembled company that Christie's, knowing my keenness on sailing, had given me an instrument which would show me the way home when I got lost: a satellite navigator. This had come about through a chance lunch with Guy who suddenly said, "We'd like to give you a present." I mumbled something about a silver mug, and Guy asked if there wasn't something I wanted for my yacht. Taking a deep breath, I said that a satellite navigator would be useful. He did ask the cost, which was in four figures, but then said, "OK, buy one." This was very kind, and very different from the way Ray had been treated.

Come and have a drink and wave
goodbye to John Herbert
on
Monday, July 8th at 6 p.m.
in the saleroom

However, there I was in the rostrum, holding the journalists' glass goblet full of whisky. I had taken the precaution of typing my speech out. Melikian in his threatened profile a month later when I was sailing off Brittany described it as "worthy of an Evelyn Waugh character". I don't know whether that's a compliment or not, but I wanted to get over three points and also to keep it light-hearted. First a "thank you" to Jo and Christie's and particularly to Peter Chance. Secondly, to point out mainly to the younger members of the staff that in 1958 the sales total was £2.3 million compared with well over £350 million for the current season. That had only been achieved by teamwork from everyone in the firm and the leadership first of Peter Chance and then of Jo Floyd. Thirdly, thanks to the leadership of both, the company had regained its rightful position. I liked to think at the same time that it was respected for its style by the general public, and I hoped by the fine art trade and even the Press. Having got over the heavy bit, I said a little about the problems of PR, and next managed to raise a laugh by imitating Jo taking a difficult lot at a big Geneva jewellery sale.

"Lot 527, a 44 carat marquise diamond ring." Jo would tighten his tie, run his finger round his collar, stretch his neck, rub his nose and then start: "500,000 francs, thank you . . . No? Well what about 400,000 francs. Thank you." He took it up slowly to 1.5 million francs – I could see over the clerk's shoulder the huge reserve. My heart was beating faster and faster as there appeared to be little interest. Then suddenly Jo went into top gear. It was rather like the pilot of a Phantom jet putting on what is known as the after-burner. He seemed like a man possessed, taking bids from both sides of the room thick and fast, creating such an atmosphere of competition that finally someone actually stuck their hand up and said, "3 million francs." It was an amazing effort.

Well, the speech seemed to go down all right, even with Jo who enjoyed my impersonation. That was on July 8th. The next day I cleared my desk and went sailing.

It appears from newspaper cuttings that roughly a week before my goodbye party Justice Eugene R. Wolin, of the State Supreme Court in Manhattan, dismissed Cristallina's $10 million case against Christie's regarding the sale of Dimitri Jodidio's Impressionist pictures in May 1981. However, it was not until the day after the party that what David had said about the sale of the Gauguin and Van Gogh appeared in the Press at large for the first time. This sad error of judgment, already described in Chapter 21, resulted in David's having to resign the chairmanship of Christie's King Street on July 19th and also his place on the Board of Christies International; he remained, however, a director of Christie's.

The "style" to which I referred in my speech did not now look so good. However, every company has problems some time or other. By the time the new season started the heat was off in both New York and King Street, but as a result of David's resignation Jo and Guy had to return to their former posts. Surprisingly, in spite of understandably hostile Press comment, Christie's credibility was not dented to the extent of losing business. In London the year finished well, while the sales total in New York was virtually the same as in 1984.

However, many of us were not thinking of sales totals but of Patrick. He'd come out of hospital after one operation in June, gone shooting and been to the USA. I happened to be in Christie's in October and had a chat with him and with his usual courage he was trying to pretend that all was well. In November he went into hospital for another operation which did not leave much hope, and on January 9th he died, aged fifty-seven. Lord "Johnnie" Oaksey, being an old friend, wrote a perfect obituary for *The Times*.

Patrick's funeral from all accounts, as regrettably I was abroad, was a most moving occasion. It was held at St Mary's Church, Chilton Foliat, near Patrick's country home, Folly Farm, Hungerford, on January 15th. The church overflowed with 300 to 400 friends from all walks of life. Amabel, his beautiful wife, had made all the arrangements with imagination, style and affection. She and her daughter Laura and her three sons – Ludovic, James and Valentine – were all wearing kilts of the rosy-red, dark blue and green Lindsay tartan. Amabel was determined not to have, and knew that Patrick wouldn't have wanted, a widow's weeds funeral. It was very much a family affair. At the end of the service the coffin was carried out by Patrick's sons and nephews, preceded by Kim Fraser, Amabel's cousin, playing the bagpipes.

Just before the committal in the churchyard – by split-second timing organised by Michael Cecil on top of the church tower with a walkie-talkie – there was a roar. Patrick's Spitfire came at 400 m.p.h. from behind some trees at a hundred feet, dipped over the cemetery and soared into the air doing a Victory Roll on the way and disappeared climbing as fast as it had arrived. It was flown by Tony Bianchi, an old friend of Patrick's.

What an emotional send-off! After the funeral, at the wake which

Patrick would certainly have expected, Amabel encouraged everyone to take their drinks and inspect Patrick's many interests apart from pictures. In the barns were the steam-engines, a working waterwheel, a showman's traction-engine and immaculate railway engine models; outside were his cars, polished and gleaming, all of which must have been a very moving display, fitting for a man of so many accomplishments.

As Charlie Allsopp wrote later in Christie's magazine: "In the final analysis it is the auctioneer's skill which is the vital element in every sale. Patrick gave us a style to live up to, but also he showed on a canvas far broader than Christie's that life could still be enormous fun."

25

The Art Market and Its Future

Without the support of the dealers, the fine art auctioneers could not survive and the London art market would not exist. The growth of the London art market in the last thirty years is one of Britain's post-war successes, earning today approximately £100 million annually in invisible exports. How does the fine art trade view the world-wide expansion of Christie's and Sotheby's particularly, and how does it see the future?

Few dealers are better placed to speak on this subject than Jack Baer, managing director of Hazlitt, Gooden and Fox, the picture gallery off St James's, and a past president of the Society of London Art Dealers. Having taken over the Hazlitt Gallery, opposite the back door of Christie's, at the age of twenty-three, Jack Baer has been selling pictures for longer than any other dealer in London. I have chosen a picture dealer; but it must not be forgotten that what gives London its strength is that there are more professional dealers in every kind of art in London than any other centre.

"Forty-two years ago when I started and today are two different worlds," Baer said. In 1946 it was extremely easy to buy, but very difficult for all sorts of obvious reasons to sell. Surviving was in the forefront of most people's minds. From 1946 until the mid-1950s the salerooms were still being conducted in the same manner as at the beginning of the nineteenth century. Pictures were gathered together; in general auctioneers waited until pictures came to them rather than going out to get them. When those pictures arrived, sales were made up; "little catalogues" were printed which gave the barest information to the buyer, and the buyers rolled along having viewed the pictures three days before, relying on their own knowledge to buy.

Now of course it is totally different. The auctioneers have broken out of their routine and become retailers. They go out to get beautiful things for sale and employ a large number of highly skilled art historians to catalogue the pictures. They leave no stone unturned: they are not aiming to sell only to the scholar-collector or scholar-dealer, but to the private individual as well – and he is going to rely on the information he reads in the catalogue. It is all a great sales promotion, aimed at a vast market.

As a result of this change of policy, starting probably with the first Goldschmidt sale at Sotheby's in 1956, the power of the auctioneers has been such as to diminish the success of the private dealer. It is not true to say that the private dealer was not necessarily very successful, but the breadth of his dealing has been diminished. In 1946, when Baer took over the Hazlitt Gallery, big galleries – the Leicester Gallery for instance – were used to disperse great collections. Nowadays of course those pictures would go straight to one of the auctioneers.

"The interesting thing is the interrelationship and interdependence between auctioneers and dealers and this is something I feel rather strongly about," Baer said. "I think that London as a world centre for the trade of works of art owes its position to expertise and a high standard of business ethics in the auction field and private dealing. Each side of the trade owes a great deal to the other."

In London, the capital of a country which had been a warehouse for works of art for a long time, the auctioneers played a very important part in sorting through a great mass of material and offering it to the public. The dealers, over a period of years which included slump and boom, had probably been the auctioneers' best clients – certainly their most loyal ones. In order to buy, the dealers had to be financially strong; they put their money where their mouths were; they took a chance perhaps and sat on pictures for a long time.

Auctioneers also needed to be very strong and to be able to afford through thick and thin to employ first-class people and to advertise to get what the dealers wanted. "If one or the other falls by the wayside, or if one or the other becomes so strong that they dominate the market; if the auctioneers were to carry their successes to a point where the dealers were left as only small people scratching a living, then when times got bad the auctioneers would find themselves with empty salerooms, empty of buyers, because in bad times it is the dealer who is usually the one to cushion the slump. So each needs the other. This is a fear that a lot of dealers have; that they might not always have the resources available in a recession.

"A particular difference between the art market today and forty years ago is in the type of buyer," Baer went on to say. "Even immediately after the war all buyers of pictures were serious collectors or people who found that the ownership of pictures on their walls was a human activity, similar to having chairs and curtains to decorate their homes. So people would go and buy pictures they liked. The idea of buying for investment or status symbols didn't really exist. Today there are a great number of people who have come in as dealers to make money, not because they found it an enjoyable way of making a living. There are people in the market to invest; there are people who bought pictures because it was the thing to do. There are people who want to be seen to spend money, whereas in the old days a gentleman wasn't seen spending money – he did spend money, but he did it rather quietly. Today there are some people in some parts of the world who think that if they are seen to be spending money they get into a higher social level. This applies to all countries, but principally to America where money has always played a part; you have always been an important man if you were rich, but totally unimportant and to be ignored if you were poor."

I asked Baer if he thought the advancing of credit to buyers and vendors, which Alfred Taubman initiated in America after he had taken over Sotheby Park-Bernet, was not introducing a supermarket approach to buying works of art and could be highly inflationary. Baer replied that advancing money to a man who was "on the up" in America, so that he could acquire expensive works of art before he might be ready to put the money down, was in his view "a very, very dangerous game".

"Works of art unlike stocks and shares can't be readily sold and the margin between buying and selling is a much wider one than in normal investment. Taking the auctioneer's commission and the buyer's premium, which together come to 20 per cent of the hammer price, you can work out very quickly that it is a wide margin between what a man is likely to pay on one day for a work of art and sell on another. It doesn't make for a ready market for investment." The danger in the future would be that when the people who had bought because of inducements or for investment suddenly found they had to sell a work of art for which they perhaps had still to complete payment, they might discover that the price they got was very much lower than they anticipated. "It's all very well for Mr Taubman of Sotheby's to offer these inducements to rich people to spend millions of dollars on works of art in a boom, but when the market turns, as all markets do, I can't think what will happen."

I next asked Baer how the average dealer regarded auctioneers such as Christie's and Sotheby Parke-Bernet, leaving aside the question of the premium. Baer did not wish to speak for people who were much younger than himself, but for the few left of his generation. These, he felt, looked upon the auctioneers as colleagues and friends since they had known them for many years, even though they were competitors, and very successful competitors at that. "The difference between Sotheby's and Christie's for me is quite considerable. Although I have great friends at Sotheby's and I had great admiration for Peter Wilson whom I knew personally quite well and who bought pictures from me as far back as 1947, I never really admired the way Sotheby's went about the enlargement of their business. The difference between Sotheby's in their struggle to achieve commercial success and Christie's in their fight for survival was that underneath it all Sotheby's and Peter Wilson particularly had a disregard for the well-being of dealers.

"Even though Wilson had a number of dealers whom he could count as his friends, he would do everything in his power to get the maximum amount of business out of dealers' hands. He would make direct approaches to my clients telling them how much better he could do for them and so on. And though one or two people at Christie's have stooped to that from time to time, in general I don't think that was the policy of Christie's. I don't think Christie's as a company would have allowed the head of their picture department to approach my clients and tell them that they could do very much better. And so in my time in the trade anyway there was a certain trust. I felt I could trust Christie's, and that feeling was not reciprocated with Sotheby's."

Baer then turned to another subject. He remembered the terrible feelings of let-down in the trade when it believed that there had been collusion between Christie's and Sotheby's in the introduction of the premium, which it felt was a blow to the auctioneers' relationship with the trade. The fact that the premium was brought in, and the way in which it was brought in, were regarded as striking at the jugular of the trade. It was very important later on that Christie's decided to reduce the premium from 10 to 8 per cent. He thought it showed that Christie's had some feeling towards the trade. A lot of the trade responded to this gesture and sent a number of works of art to Christie's which they might otherwise have sent to Sotheby's who had not reduced the premium. It was true that the premium had become an accepted fact. Christie's had in any case now increased their premium to 10 per cent and there had been no shouts and screams. The dispute was probably now a forgotten thing.

Baer thought that there was a lot the auctioneers could do to improve their image with the public. It was very important that the Art Trade Liaison Committee should be seen to be talking and trying to improve the public view of dealers and auctioneers alike. Some things were being altered. There was talk about changing the way bids could be taken "from the chandeliers"; there was talk about altering the whole system of reserves. One of the most unfortunate bits of legal mumbo-jumbo in this country was The Auction (Bidding Agreements) Act, 1969, which should be looked into. There were lots of improvements which could be made so that dealers could with equanimity buy jointly, because today most dealers didn't have the resources to buy on their own, and sometimes by joining together they paid more than each would have been able to do on their own.

Baer agreed that there must be reserves; but it was the relationship between the real bids and the unreal bids in order to protect and take the bidding up to a reserve which looked fishy to the public. The idea that a reserve could be £1 million and that there might be no real bidding in the room, but the auctioneer could still take the price up to just short of the reserve was wrong. This was one of the cosmetics, a sort of trickery which Baer didn't think should be allowed in the modern financial world. He did not have a solution for it, and could see that abandoning the practice could present problems for the auctioneer. However, it was wrong and misleading to suggest that a picture had had people interested up to the reserve figure when they hadn't been. He was quite certain that it was only a question of a few years for solutions to be found. There were also a lot of practices in the art trade which were not understood by the public, and gave the feeling that the trade were trying to pull the wool over their eyes and these should be discontinued.

Turning to the question of art expertise, Baer thought that the standard of expertise was now enormously high compared with what it had been, among both the dealers and the auctioneers. One of the great changes in the art market had been in the standard of cataloguing. It was totally different from the little flimsy white catalogues where the bare bones were put in and the buyer had to do his homework. It was even rather cross-making for a dealer who specialised in off-beat works to find that the auctioneer had done the catalogue so well that there was no discovery to be made. That must be a great deal better for the public.

Among dealers also, generally speaking, the level of knowledge was much higher. Forty years ago there was only one university with a history of art degree, and now there were courses all over the country, so that there were properly taught people coming into the trade. At the same time it was being realised that even with the highest level of scholarship mistakes could be made and that opinions could change from one generation to another.

I then asked Baer how he viewed the continual controversies over the British heritage. Did he think the Government should introduce tax incentive schemes on the lines of those in America? Baer thought that a lot of objects were considered to be part of Britain's heritage when they weren't. This was a mistake. Those concerned should be very careful to stick to the original Waverley criteria and these should be upheld. Britain should be very careful when it used the argument of national heritage in works of art.

On the other hand he thought it would be wonderful to keep in this country as many beautiful things as possible. When the country was rich it could keep these things, and when it was poor it couldn't. Where the lobby sometimes got itself over-excited was in the number of pictures or pieces of sculpture it wanted to save instead of the houses or bits of land which were just as much British heritage. "The gradual rape of the countryside is a disaster and the pulling down of a great number of houses with the loss of their contents is a greater disaster than the loss of a Canaletto, Rembrandt or even a Constable."

Regarding Government action the present "in lieu of tax" and private treaty sales were not enough. Too few people knew what the possibilities were. In America the idea that works of art could be given and attract tax relief of one sort or another had worked wonders for public collections; something could and should have been done in Britain particularly when taxation was at such a high level. "The Conservative Government haven't done anything at all to make it possible for the very rich in this country to give and for it not all to come out of their own 'net of tax' pocket. Some scheme should be invented whereby a firm or individual could make big contributions for the purchase of art for galleries and gain in some fiscal way." Museums, particularly in the provinces, would become lively places as they are in America. "In Britain on the whole provincial galleries and museums are not the centre of any sort of social or educational life, because very few people supported them, certainly up till the 1988 tax reforms, because nobody could afford to do so. There should be some arrangement where people could be seen to be supporting them as well as the Treasury."

Shortly after I talked to Mr Baer the furore broke over Hereford Cathedral's proposal, or that of the Dean and Chapter, to sell one of its greatest treasures, the Mappa Mundi. Hereford Cathedral needed £7 million for restoration and other purposes – and there are many other cathedrals in a similar plight. Curiously, there is no central agency to help cathedrals financially, even though they are just as much part of Britain's heritage as certain pictures; some people might think they were more important. Nevertheless cathedrals do not come under the aegis of the Heritage Fund.

Lastly I asked Baer how he saw the London art market's future with particular reference to the harmonisation of VAT. The London art market had lived with this threat for a long time, with Brussels advocating schemes which were totally alien to it. London had appealed without success to the French, the Italians, the Dutch and the Germans to consider the London art market's scheme so far as VAT was concerned and see how obviously better it was. "However it would appear that because Mrs Thatcher, God bless her, doesn't like certain people in the Commission or doesn't want certain things to happen in 1992, we may well be let off the worst excesses of the Brussels bureaucracy.

"The art trade would be terribly badly hurt by any restrictions on the import of works of art for sale in this country. Any imposition of VAT at the port of entry would immediately mean that auctioneers like Christie's and Sotheby's would conduct the sales of those objects abroad, either in America or Switzerland." As far as dealers were concerned, any scheme which involved a cascade of tax added to the total price each time the object was sold would mean that they would have to move their business to a country which did not have this scheme. The fact that at the moment the French who have very little international art trade, the Germans who have even less, and the Italians who have even less than that, and all the rest who have no trade at all object to London's scheme is simply jealousy. "When you get the Danes and the Belgians, who have a piffling little art trade, complaining about our scheme, it is because they really want us to suffer."

I must admit that when I first joined Christie's it seemed that a superior attitude was adopted towards dealers because they were in "trade" – with exceptions made for Agnew's and other public school firms. Now of course there is none of that nonsense. Generally speaking, in spite of competition there is a mutual respect of one for the other, and in many cases genuine friendship.

My colleagues who were responsible for individual departments obviously knew the dealers in their field very well, but I too got to know quite a few and established a close relationship which I valued. Competitors or not, it was interesting to hear the views of those who had dealt in one type of work of art for years, or had struck out when young and made a success. The variety of knowledge I was introduced to even in a small way was very wide, whether it was Old Masters, Impressionists, drawings and prints or the applied arts. Among those dealers I got to know were the late Sir Geoffrey Agnew, Evelyn Joll, the present chairman of Agnew's, and Dickie Kingzett, who have been immensely kind as well as informative; the always elegant and friendly Eddie Speelman, now retired but probably in his time the most successful one-man firm; Tim Bathurst and his colleagues in Artemis (David Carritt's old firm); Sir Hugh Leggatt; Godfrey Pilkington, Malcolm Waddingham, Lilian Browse, and Richard Green, who once sold me a picture for much less than he need have done because he knew I really loved it; and other picture dealers such as Leonard and David Koetser, the Sabins and Cohen Brothers. Then there were the Old Master drawings experts, such as John Baskett and Richard Day, and watercolour specialists, like Bill Thompson. This is not forgetting my ex-colleagues Christopher Wood, David Barclay, Simon Bull – who struck out on his own at an early age and has become one of the leading watch and clock experts – and David Messum.

I also got to know Ben How, the renowned silver expert, and likewise Martin Norton, who with his sons runs the great house of S. J. Phillips and used to have to bow and scrape to Madame Marcos, a particularly demanding collector; Kenneth Snowman, the greatest Fabergé expert in the world; John Partridge, George Levy, William Redford and Frank Berendt from the furniture world, and Roger Bluett and Eskenazi who know everything there is to know about Oriental art.

Some I knew well and some only because we were on the same charity committee or because they wanted some help, but talking to them gave me an insight into their world which, as Jack Baer said, was by no means an easy one. To know such people added an extra dimension to working at Christie's. What is more, now I have left Christie's their friendship remains as warm as before.

26

Christie's Great Surge Forward

Trading conditions improved in the autumn of 1983 and from 1984 a boom began which, to the amazement of all, continued till the end of 1988; whether it will still be with us by the time this book is printed is another matter. By the end of 1988 Christie's was in a position of supreme financial and professional strength. It would be quite wrong therefore to leave Christie's story in 1985 just because I retired, and not say something about the great surge forward the firm made in the three following years. Of particular importance was the change in management style and the mega-prices for Impressionist and Contemporary pictures.

The improvement in trading conditions was only one factor in the feeling of confidence from 1983 onwards. By that year – in some cases long before – heads of departments and technical staff had attained a high degree of expertise. Those who had joined in the 1960s and had not had their enthusiasm sapped by the "hangover" from Sir Alec Martin's reign had come of age. Another generation was fully qualified and experienced in business-getting. The Board had become a meritocracy and had been purged of nepotism.

But for his tragic error of judgment David Bathurst, Christie's first Impressionist and Modern picture director, would be chairman. It was David who brought so many important works to King Street from abroad at a time when Sotheby's was regarded almost as the only place to sell Impressionists. For seven years also he was president of Christie's New York, during which time sales surpassed those in London. It was also David who appointed Christopher Davidge managing director of Christie's King Street. This, I think, has provided Christie's with a managerial dynamic just when it was most needed and which has helped to yield such great results.

By 1985 the Board consisted mainly of what I have termed the second generation who are more liberal-minded and do not have the paralysing "upper crust" stance which was so apparent when I became a director. Good as they all are, I doubt if any of the heads of departments have as much energy and single-mindedness as Christopher and would be able to devote themselves to the whole firm rather than their department. From his position at White's, Christie's printers, and from being in and out of King Street every day, Christopher could see where the weaknesses lay; at the same time technical departments who relied on him for their catalogues could not help but recognise his drive and ability. Although he had not been to a public school he was accepted and in a position to introduce new ideas in order to make the company more efficient. Although younger than Charlie, Noel and many departmental directors and technical staff, he was the essential complement to the expertise of all of them. To improve and weld together the performance of a large number of sensitive and sometimes emotional art experts is a thankless task, but he quickly proved that he was more than equal to it.

A member of the staff who was at Christie's many years said, "Basically we all suddenly realised that there was an awareness at the top that Christie's was in the twentieth century – that it should be run as a business instead of some stuffy club. The jolly old boy network had gone for ever." This may be somewhat harsh criticism considering what Peter, Jo and the "old sweats" of 1958 had done for the firm, but when Christopher took over there was still a need for the management to be geared up.

There was nothing new about what seems to have been Davidge's essential premise – that communications needed to be improved throughout the whole firm. It is obvious that with forty or more directors it was impossible for there to be any real discussion at Board meetings, so they became more or less information-giving ceremonies. This may have been inevitable but it resulted in many directors feeling they were playing little part in the running of the firm, even if they were members of the Management Committee. Decisions were taken by Jo and Guy or by the whole Policy Committee and were then put to the Board for approval – not that any criticism was likely to be popular or successful.

Davidge saw to it that the disenchantment or feeling of near-futility at being a director was removed. Today there is a communications structure stretching from the Christies International Board through a whole series of committees down to individual departments. Through these committees guidelines for action are developed. This has not only improved efficiency but raised the morale of the whole company. For the first time people have felt that the firm has a sense of direction. The staff have responded to the chance of actually being able to say something.

Jo and Guy had of course organised the computerisation of records of vendors' property and sales results. Davidge took modern technology further, installing word processors in every department and also more photocopiers. Recognising the need for proper training, Davidge appointed a personnel director. A most important reform was establishing consistency in advertisements and stationery for use by all Christie's salerooms. I had been trying to do this for years, but it was an intractable problem and one which certain King Street directors refused to be reasonable about. The arguments had always come back to the Christie medallion; its position at the top of any page was sacrosanct, making any modern format impossible. Christopher Davidge recognised the difficulty and told Mark Wrey who succeeded me as public relations director to sort it out. With the help of modern designers a manual was produced which showed all Christie's salerooms and overseas representatives how advertisements should be designed so that they could be recognisable as a Christie advertisement, regardless of size.

Many of these new developments were nothing more than common sense, but to a firm like Christie's which in 1958 had to be dragged screaming into the twentieth century they didn't come easily; but they were all the more necessary for that.

At long last Christie's also decided to look after their staff. In some ways even in 1958 they were good employers, providing a non-contributory pension for those who stayed the course. A turkey and a bottle of wine were given at Christmas. Pay was abysmal, however, and I think it was just as bad at Sotheby's. Both firms adopted the policy that secretaries did not need a salary similar to those in an ordinary business because working in an auction house was something special. Some girls had fathers who could top up their daughter's salary; others made special arrangements with their bosses for time off, so that effectively they had part-time jobs. Others just had to lump it, and many in the end left. Male staff in technical departments and porters were equally badly paid. Those who had self-confidence often left when they had learned enough to set up on their own. In the mid-1970s a share-option scheme was introduced to make it easier for a select number of directors to buy shares, and this was provided for a larger number later on.

In the 1950s and 1960s, to be fair, Christie's probably could not have afforded to pay any more. Directors' salaries were just as far out of line. When I joined the Board my salary was £2,500, the same as I had been getting from my PR firm, and the same as that of Arthur, Patrick, Jo and Guy. In later years Peter and Jo made two attempts to introduce a proper wage scale according to the responsibility of the employee's position, by calling in Peat, Marwick and Mitchell. Directors had to report on the performance of their staff each year and suggest adjustments in salaries, but if there were increases they never kept pace with inflation or salaries outside, and could only be described as cheese-paring.

I raised the matter of junior staff salaries twice at Board meetings and got no support from anyone. I made the obvious point that the high turnover of secretaries was unenlightened and uneconomical, because just when a girl was beginning to be useful and to be able to spell the artists or craftsmen of her department, she decided she couldn't afford to stay even though she found the work interesting. I told the Board that at least four girls had worked in the Press Office for as long as eight years; that they were highly efficient and left only when they had married and a baby was coming along. Each one had become more and more valuable because she knew what to do in any situation. Paul Whitfield, managing director, broke in: "Oh John, they stayed just because they loved you." I was not amused or impressed that he should take such a frivolous line at a Board meeting when discussing a serious subject. The reason my secretaries stayed was partly because the Press Office was a particularly interesting place to work, partly because some worked only four days a week and, perhaps most important of all, because we worked as a team. I walked downstairs after the meeting with Jo who told me he was very worried about technical staff salaries – and well he might be because many had left and become successful dealers – but he didn't think secretaries' salaries were so important. As the years rolled by and the profits of the company became healthy, I thought that attitude apart from being unenlightened was appallingly unjust, because some staff were so loyal that they wouldn't leave in spite of their low pay. Today I'm glad to say salaries are virtually in line with junior and senior staff in business generally. This was mainly due once again to Davidge who called in consultants to bring salaries up to date.

In line with a realistic salary scale, Davidge decided to appoint a training officer who would be responsible for a proper career programme in Christie's for fine art graduates. This would replace the previous ad hoc system of promoting people from the Front Counter into a department which might well not relate to their main interest. All these management changes were carried out in three years. Basically they were all designed to make working at Christie's attractive and in particular to turn the staff into a team.

The most striking development of 1985–8 was that Christie's Impressionist, Modern and Contemporary picture sales certainly equalled those of Sotheby's; some people might go further and say that Christie's had actually captured from Sotheby's the market on which their original success in the late 1950s was founded. The year 1986 saw the beginning of the mega-price era when pictures selling for £1 million or more became a commonplace. In December Noel Annesley sold Manet's *La Rue Mosnier aux Paveurs* for £7.7 million ($10.9 million), then the highest auction price for a Modern picture. It showed the view from the studio Manet occupied from 1872 to 1878 and is mentioned by Emile Zola in *Nana*. Originally part of the great collection formed by Samuel Courtauld, most of which are on exhibition in the gallery which bears his name in Woburn Square, *La Rue Mosnier aux Paveurs* was one of a number inherited by his daughter Mrs Sydney Butler, "RAB's" first wife. When she died RAB was left a life interest in the pictures which hung either in his rooms at Trinity College, Cambridge, where he was Master, or in the Fitzwilliam Museum.

Apart from the record price, this was the first important sale which was organised in a sophisticated way. It is generally agreed by technical staff that Davidge, apart from having firm ideas of his own about improving Christie's performance, is a good listener. Mark Wrey must have suggested that big sales could be better organised. The Press Office had by now been relieved of the time-consuming responsibility of reserving seats. Davidge also arranged for a far larger number of staff to help with crowd control and with directing people to their seats in the different rooms. As a result there wasn't the last-minute feeling of panic as in my day, when those for whom there weren't seats poured into the main saleroom as the auctioneer was about to begin. Then it was taken for granted that the Press Office would make all the necessary pre-sale arrangements; and in a way we did. I should have gone to Jo, Guy or Paul and said, "We need help," but I doubt if they would have been very sympathetic. Another excellent idea was to improve the whole system of telephone bids by having a raised platform down one side of the main saleroom from which they could be taken; not only because of the different languages, but the number of such bids now demanded special treatment.

Even more radical and sensible was a gantry which for special sales could be put up on scaffolding at the back of the main room for TV cameras and photographers, instead of the normal fight for space. It all cost money but it was far more disciplined and professional. Davidge would listen to any new ideas and if he thought them good didn't mind the expense; if on the other hand they didn't work there would be trouble.

The importance of improving the style for major sales, advertisements, stationery and display windows was only part of a recognition of the need for marketing. There was nothing new about the idea, but before Davidge became managing director nobody cared enough about the end result to bring about agreement. A successful example of the new stress on marketing was the sale of the Nanking Cargo in Amsterdam. This was the highlight of 1986.

The Nanking Cargo consisted of approximately 160,000 pieces of mid-eighteenth-century Chinese porcelain together with 126 bars of gold brought up from the depths of the South China Sea by "Captain" Michael Hatcher, an ex-Barnardo boy with a delightfully buccaneering background. This was the second sunken cargo he'd asked Christie's to sell. In 1983, 20,000 pieces of mid-seventeenth-century blue and white porcelain had been sold successfully by Christie's Amsterdam.

However, the Nanking Cargo presented far greater problems. It seemed unlikely that the market would take such a vast quantity of porcelain which was "destined for the upper and middle classes of northern Europe, with few exceptional pieces to excite the committed collector" as Anthony Thorncroft wrote in Christie's *Review of the Season* for 1986. The only way to sell it was by widening the demand. This was where the marketing campaign came in. A video was made of diving sequences showing fish swimming amongst the tea bowls and dishes. The wreck was identified from marks on some of the porcelain as the Dutch East Indiaman, the *Geldermalsen*, which went down near Java in 1751. The wreck became living history because the names of the crew were known and it captured the interest not only of Holland but of every country.

The task of cataloguing this vast amount of porcelain, which included 40,000 tea bowls and saucers, fell on Colin Sheaf and James Spencer. It was not only the description which was the problem, but dividing such a vast amount into lots which would not be too big to deter potential buyers. However, the video campaign, lectures, special presentations, the Press release, even lunches in Christie's City office where some of the porcelain went on view, let alone the hardback catalogue which became a best-seller, stimulated interest not only from international dealers and collectors, but the general public; people were delighted to learn they could put the tea bowls or saucers in their dishwasher, because after being in the depths for so long the blue and white had proved it was impervious to a little water. On view days there were queues of 20,000 people outside Christie's saleroom in Amsterdam and by the time of the sale 125,000 commissions were in the auctioneer's book.

Christie's had been cautious with their initial estimate of a total of £3 million ($4.26 million), but by the end of the week it was £10 million ($14.2 million). This huge total was basically due to the marketing and the effect of a human story. Even hardened dealers paid many times more for a piece of "blue and white" from the Nanking Cargo than they would have done in a normal sale. The promotion of the sale impressed one Dutch newspaper so much it came out with a headline "Christie's deed een 'hell of a job'". A week after the sale there was a half-hour BBC documentary which kept the Christie flag flying.

In 1985 there had been a slight dip in the pre-tax profits to £12.2 million compared with £16.2 million the year before, when the Chatsworth Old Master drawings contributed £21.1 million to the total sales results. In 1986 the upward trend had returned because apart from the Manet and the Nanking Cargo the demand for pictures and works of art at the top end of the market was consistently strong. Pre-tax profits were £18.3 million, but in 1987 they leaped by 77 per cent to £32.4 million. This was mainly due to the supremacy of Christie's Impressionist sales, the particular star being Van Gogh's *Sunflowers* which came from the great Chester Beatty collection and was sold as a result of the death of his widow, Helen.

The sale of the *Sunflowers* dominated the 1986–7 season. Pictures of this importance do not just drop into the lap of any firm of fine art auctioneers, however well known they may be. To win them the correct strategy, timing and diplomacy are essential when making the first approach to an owner or to trustees. If there is not a long-standing association with the prospective vendor this is all the more important as the opposition may already have one. Sales have been lost by such small things as spelling mistakes. I remember well the anger years ago of Lord Scarbrough when Sotheby's spelt his name like the seaside resort. He never went to them again. Many years later Sotheby's were too quick in their approach to a widow about an Impressionist which her husband had owned, and although she had dealt with them for many years she did not forgive them, and sent it to Christie's.

In the case of the *Sunflowers* it was by good marketing that Christie's won the picture. In January, through an old connection, Christie's were invited to offer their services and moved very fast. First the Trustees were shown that Christie's could best promote and carry out the sale. A sample catalogue with the full history and provenance of the *Sunflowers* and a colour illustration was produced within a week – the Trustees were amazed when Chris Ponter showed it to them. The picture would be taken to Zürich, Tokyo and New York with receptions at each place. The appetite of private people who hadn't been interested in the picture before would be whetted by the use of a video; there would be a special presentation in Tokyo, where a picture of that quality had never been exhibited before. Then there would be the normal advertising and PR promotion in newspapers and magazines. The Trustees were evidently impressed because they gave Christie's the sale.

Van Gogh painted altogether seven studies of *Sunflowers* during a fourteen-month stay at Arles in 1888–9. Not only was the Chester Beatty study, measuring 39.5 ins by 30.25 ins, believed to be the last one he painted, but it was also one of the largest and the only one in a private collection. Having been instructed by the Trustees, Christie's had to market the picture through their "database and intelligence" system on collectors which is highly confidential. One thing was special about the sale of the *Sunflowers*. Jo was rightly determined that, having been instructed to sell the picture, it wasn't going to be whipped away from Christie's after the announcement of the sale by any dealers, as had happened with Van Gogh's *Portrait of a Peasant* from the same collection. A contract therefore was drawn up with the Trustees to prevent this.

The sale was on March 30th which by a quirk of fate was the anniversary of Van Gogh's birth in 1853. The cars and taxis disgorging people outside Christie's that evening marked a great occasion even to anyone not in the art world. Everyone had come early, so excited were collectors, dealers and socialites to witness the sale – everyone from Baron Heinrich Thyssen to Jeffrey Archer.

Charlie took the sale in his usual relaxed and cheerful way. Every auctioneer has his own style. Patrick had always appeared very serious and stern, only relaxing occasionally to coax an extra bid with a smile and twitch of his right eyebrow. Charlie has always taken sales in a completely different way; he has always been very active, leaning back and then forward and from side to side in the rostrum like an "over-enthusiastic evangelical preacher", as Geraldine reported once. However, like Patrick he always had control of the room and was able to draw bids out of people.

The atmosphere was electric when the *Sunflowers*, which was on a special easel, came up for sale. Charlie opened the bidding at £5 million. There was no shortage of bidders from the main saleroom, the three closed circuit TV rooms and on the telephone. The bidding went quickly up in £500,000 steps to £20 million, at which point the audience clapped with excitement. The bidding then developed into a nail-biting duel between James Roundell and John Lumley, both bidding on the telephone. Finally – after less than two minutes, although it had seemed much longer – Charlie knocked it down to James Roundell for £22,500,000, which with premium made the price £24,750,000 ($39.9 million); this was more than three times the previous world record auction price for a picture, for Mantegna's *Adoration of the Magi*.

Down below in the Press Office there was champagne for the journalists and the staff; there was also a huge birthday cake in honour of Van Gogh's anniversary with the *Sunflowers* reproduced in icing on the top. The buyer of this great picture was revealed two days later to be the Japanese corporation Yasuda Fire and Marine Insurance, which had assets totalling £7.75 billion to invest and like many other corporations and indeed private Japanese already had its own museum.

In June the Mantegna record was broken again by another, quite different painting by Van Gogh, and one which some connoisseurs consider to be a greater work than his *Sunflowers*. This was *Le Pont de Trinquetaille* which was bought by Maria Reinshagen, Christie's representative in Zürich, for a private collector for £12.6 million ($20.2 million), demonstrating that the art market in 1987 was able to contain the enormous growth, and that the *Sunflowers* was not just an isolated event.

In October readers of the *Independent* learned that it was almost a chance meeting that had brought the *Sunflowers* to Yasuda's attention. Geraldine had left *The Times* at the end of the summer season and spent a month in the Far East prior to joining the *Independent*. It must have been very satisfying for her to join her new paper with a world exclusive. While she was in Tokyo she decided to look up the Yasuda Corporation and visit their museum. Geraldine met Mr Hajime Goto, president of Yasuda, and Mr Hajime Abe, director of foreign relations. She was very lucky to meet Mr Goto because the presidents of Japanese corporations are very remote people, even from their staff. However, like the principals of other great Japanese corporations, Mr Goto and Mr Abe regarded it as their duty to contribute to the cultural refreshment of their staff which was why they had a museum. Also since the war the public popularity among the Japanese for art exhibitions has become far greater than in the West. Though there were also tax advantages, it was genuinely thought to improve a corporation's image and to be good for business.

Geraldine's article was fascinating, but it wasn't the whole story. James Roundell filled in a few details for me. By a lucky coincidence, in November 1976 Mr Abe was having dinner at the Imperial Hotel in Tokyo with Peter Roundell, a Lloyd's reinsurance broker with whom Yasuda did a lot of business. Because of this Roundell was trusted. Mr Abe told him that his chairman had given him the task of buying some pictures, particularly Impressionists. Peter Roundell naturally told Mr Abe that his brother, James Roundell of Christie's, was staying in the same hotel and had brought a number of Impressionists for exhibition which were going to be auctioned shortly in London. Mr Abe was immediately interested and arranged to meet James the next day and view the pictures.

James knew it was essential to get to see Mr Goto, the president, who was the only person who had the power to make a decision. Mr Abe was one of the very few men who had access to him. Thanks to the close relationship Mr Abe had with his brother Peter, James saw Mr Goto, not once but three times. It was the year of Manet's *Rue Mosnier*. James went through the whole catalogue with Mr Goto, taking care each time to be very respectful and not too pushy. James Roundell is all of six foot five, and Mr Goto was small like most Japanese, but he was decisive. He instructed Mr Abe to go to London for the sale and told him the pictures that interested him.

James realised it was most important to give him the best possible advice. Mr Goto had told Mr Abe that he was interested in two Renoirs as well as the Manet and to put bids in the book for all three. James told Mr Abe that he shouldn't pay so much for one of them, and that he should increase his bid on the other if he wanted to be sure of getting it. As regards the Manet, James said Mr Abe's bid might not be quite enough. James's advice was right on all three counts. Mr Abe got his two Renoirs at the price James said was the proper value, and was the underbidder for the Manet, at roughly the price James had said it would go for. As a result of this James won the trust of Yasuda.

In February 1987, James Roundell returned to Tokyo with the *Sunflowers* and other works. He had already been told by Mr Abe that Yasuda wanted a centrepiece for their museum. James told him in advance that the *Sunflowers* was the masterpiece they were looking for. It was a question of getting Mr Goto interested. When Mr Goto came to see it for the first time he brought a large entourage with him. One of Christie's staff told Geraldine that when Mr Goto saw it, "It was as if he was struck by lightning." After consultations with art experts who reassured him about it being a masterpiece, Mr Goto decided "to bring it to Japan". Mr Goto and Mr Abe decided to make £21 million their upper limit.

Mr Abe flew to London arriving at 6 a.m. on the day of the sale which began at 6.30 that evening. During the day he made enquiries and decided that there were no other Japanese dealers or collectors who were willing to pay £21 million, but that the price was going to go higher than that. An hour before the sale James Roundell gave Mr Abe a final estimate. Nothing had been heard from Alan Bond, the Australian tycoon and winner of the 1987 America's Cup, since the day before the sale. Mr Bond had commissioned a dealer to bid for him. When it came to the sale he gave up at £22 million and Mr Abe's bid of £22.5 million won Yasuda the picture.

Most Japanese couldn't believe that Yasuda had approached Christie's direct, as nearly all buying for private collectors is done through dealers or art advisers. After the sale there appeared in a number of British papers a story to the effect that Yasuda had embarrassed the Japanese Government by paying so much for the picture. This was quite untrue. More to the point, between October and December 1987 170,000 people paid to see the picture. Yasuda's museum is on the forty-second floor of the corporation's skyscraper headquarters and a special amphitheatre had been built to exhibit the *Sunflowers*. As many as 400 people a day are still paying to see the picture, and buy postcards and posters of it. The arrival and exhibition of the picture attracted massive TV, newspaper and magazine publicity for Yasuda which, Mr Abe told James Roundell when he next went to Japan, was worth £100 million. Many of the thousands of people who went to see the picture undoubtedly became clients of the corporation – so the *Sunflowers* may in the end pay for itself.

The whole operation was a triumph for James Roundell; but the last feature of the success of the *Sunflowers* sale was Christie's receipt of the British Sales and Marketing Award for Export from the Institute of Sales and Marketing Management. There are many awards nowadays, but this did show that Christie's had really established themselves as a highly professional and modern firm.

In July Charlie was made chairman of Christie's King Street and towards the end of the sales season called all the staff into the main saleroom. He made an excellent speech congratulating them on their efforts, in particular over the sale of the *Sunflowers* in which everyone had been concerned. In recognition of this, he said, every member of the staff would receive an extra £500.

Shortly after the beginning of the new sales season there was "Black Monday", October 19th. Wall Street prices had nose-dived the previous Friday but by that time the Stock Exchange had closed. On Monday the Stock Exchange dropped 300 points and the following day another 300, in the most catastrophic fall world financial markets had seen since 1929. Christie's shares fell from just over 700p to a low point of 293p on December 10th. However, the crash had very little effect on the art market. This was probably due to a combination of the weakness of the dollar and low world interest rates, which brought about a buoyant level of demand in New York and London.

By March 1988, Christie's shares had recovered to about 550p, and it was then that Christopher Weston, chairman of Phillips, announced that he had bought a 3 per cent holding in Christie's. The newspapers immediately got excited about a possible bid. Jo summoned him for a chat. Weston was quoted as saying that he had only bought the shares as an investment. Jo replied, "In that case you've made a very wise investment." In the autumn of 1988 Weston sold his shares to Caledonia Investment Trust and probably made quite a lot of money out of the exercise.

The continued resilience of the international art market was demonstrated on November 11th, 1987, when Sotheby Parke-Bernet sold Van Gogh's *Irises*, a lovely picture, to Alan Bond for $53.9 million (£30 million). It was obviously essential for SPB to be seen to beat the

Sunflowers price. On October 4th, 1989, the world learned that Sotheby's had advanced half the bid. Geraldine scooped her colleagues with the story. Mr Bond had been the underbidder on the *Sunflowers*, but in 1989 his financial empire was in disarray. He seemed to come into one of the categories of new collectors mentioned by Jack Baer in the previous chapter. Apart from the financial wisdom of accepting a loan of such a large amount, Sotheby's admission produced further rumblings in the fine art trade regarding a conflict of interests.

Other works of art which made 1987 such a record one for Christie's also demonstrated how little effect the financial crash had had on the prices for really first class works. They included the sale of another important Impressionist, Degas's *Les Blanchisseuses*, which was sold ten days after Black Monday for £7.4 million ($13.4 million). In New York, two days after the Wall Street crash, a D flawless 64.83 carat diamond was sold by Park Avenue for $6.38 million (£3.84 million) in a sale which generated the highest ever total to date for jewellery of $23.6 million (£13 million). Two days later a Gutenberg Bible from the famed Estelle Doheny library became the most expensive book at $5.9 million (£3.2 million).

The year 1988 proved to be the greatest so far in Christie's history. The market continued its upward trend in all manner of works of art. The Stock Exchange remained very much in the doldrums throughout the year. Christies International were one of the few shares to rise till early in 1989 they were back to 700p.

There seemed to be no shortage of money for works of art. Nigel Lawson's somewhat controversial budget of 1988 in which he reduced taxation considerably for those previously paying 60 per cent was quite likely to have suggested to those on top salaries that works of art might be better than stocks and shares. In March another of Degas's studies of laundry-maids was sold for £3.9 million ($7.2 million), compared with 2,300 gns in 1918.

In the spring Jo announced that he would be retiring at the end of June and Lord Carrington, previously Secretary-General of NATO, ex-Foreign Secretary and the first chairman of the Trustees of the Victoria and Albert Museum, would be taking his place. Jo had been chairman for twelve years and would remain a non-executive director of Christies International. Since joining the Stock Exchange in 1973, Christie's under Jo's direction had grown at a pace which outstripped inflation three times. Jo had had to take many difficult decisions and I think under his leadership Christie's was a far happier firm than

Sotheby's. I will always be grateful to Jo for his understanding of the problems of the Press Office. On PR matters we never had a cross word.

Jo left Christie's not only at the end of a record sales season, but able to announce that a 125-year lease had been acquired from the Crown Estates for the King Street premises and those owned in Bury Street and Ryder Street. This included the lease of the former premises of the Eccentric Club which would provide for extra salerooms and viewing rooms. The whole package cost £10 million and was paid for out of the firm's resources. This brought the total fixed (tangible) assets of the company to over £50 million, a remarkable sum considering those early days of 1958. Guy had been negotiating for nine months to ensure the firm's security for the future in King Street, and indeed the whole block.

The pre-tax profits for the first six months which Lord Carrington announced in September were £20.6 million compared with £18.3 million for the same period the year before. Considering the continuing uncertainty of the world's economy and that the *Sunflowers* had been sold in the same period in 1987 it was a highly satisfactory result, as financial journalists recognised. A small but significant part of the profits was due to owning a modern printing works. In June an Impressionist sale had included twelve important works from the collection of Alan Clore which were sold for a total of £6.1 million ($10.5 million). Mr Clore told Christie's and Sotheby's that he'd give the sale to the firm who produced a satisfactory catalogue first. Thanks to having White's, Christie's were able to produce a catalogue in one week, a tremendous achievement of cataloguing and printing.

There had been many good sales in all departments during the first six months, but it was the autumn season that proved really sensational. It was not only Impressionists and Modern pictures, but Contemporary works as well which accelerated in value to giddy heights. In New York, Christie's Park Avenue sold the famous Neuerburg Modern Print collection, which was a great success, followed by a Contemporary picture sale consisting of thirty-two works from the collection formed by Burton and Emily Tremaine – Burton had made a fortune in industrial lighting – which made £14.3 million ($25.7 million). Jasper Johns's *White Flag* became (for a short time) the most expensive painting by a living artist, selling for just over $7 million (£3.9 million). It was not only an incredible price, but an incredible picture, being the ghost of the American flag consisting of encaustic and newsprint and blown up to just over four feet by six feet. It is the most famous image created by the artist who pioneered New York's version of Pop Art.

The buyer was Hans Thulin, the owner of a Swedish real estate conglomerate. After the sale he announced that he intended to buy at least two major works of the ten most important artists of the period 1950–80. No doubt he went to Sotheby Parke-Bernet a few days later because another version of Jasper Johns's *White Flag* sold for $17 million (£9 million), over twice as much as the one Christie's had sold. Prices were going through the roof. People began to ask where and when it was all going to stop.

After their success with Jasper Johns, SPB had a disappointing Impressionist sale, while Christie's Park Avenue had the famed collection built up between the 1930s and 1950s by William and Edith Goetz, the husband a Hollywood producer, the wife the daughter of film mogul Louis B. Mayer. Every one of the twenty-nine pictures was sold, Picasso's blue period gem *Maternité* achieving $24.75 million (£13.7 million) and so becoming the most expensive twentieth-century picture sold at auction. It was bought by a Latin American collector – believed to be Mrs Amalita Fortabat, the cement millionairess – after a fierce duel with Shigeki Kameyama from Tokyo. There were seven new auction record prices and the total for the sale was $84.9 million (£47 million), a record for a single-owner sale.

But more was still to come, for King Street at the end of November had another Picasso, this time in gouache, which was regarded by many experts as being more important than *Maternité*. The title was *Jeune Arlequine*, a large work from Picasso's rose period which marked the crux of his development following the despair of his blue period. Picasso was moved to paint the picture following his visits, sometimes three or four times a week, with his mistress Fernande Olivier to the Cirque Medrano. This was in the Place Pigalle near where they lived in appalling conditions at Le Bateau Lavoir. The picture, one of twenty of circus performers, shows a famished-looking young harlequin looking at his companion, an exhausted acrobat. It is a haunting picture depicting the rigour of the daily performance, but there is a look of tenderness and companionship between the two figures.

The picture has a historic past. It was among the first Picasso rose period pictures to be exhibited in Paris in 1905. It was also the first Picasso to be illustrated in Guillaume Apollinaire's magazine *La Plume* later the same year, and the first Picasso to be sent to an international exhibition, the Venice Biennale of 1905. Finally, it was the first Picasso to enter a museum, the Stadtische Museum in Elberfeld in 1911. In 1937 it was confiscated by the Nazi Government as being "Entarte Kunst" – decadent art – and sold at the famous Entarte Kunst sale held by the Galerie Fischer, Lucerne, for Sfr. 80,000 to Roger Hanssen, a Brussels collector. Since then it had been the property of a number of private collectors.

Christie's estimate long before the sale was a conservative £10 million, but nobody took this very seriously after it had returned from its world tour. The Sunday before the sale 1,200 people came to see it and James Roundell agreed it might make £13 million. There were only six people in the world who could be buyers, and the Impressionist department knew each one of them.

The next evening nine TV networks were up in the gantry an hour before the sale was due to begin. I watched the sale with the mass of photographers who lined the right-hand wall. Charlie Allsopp mounted the rostrum at 7 p.m. and the sale began. The Picasso, one of sixty-eight works to be sold that evening, was Lot 19, which was unusual, as the most important lot is normally left till last.

There were murmurs of excitement and the clicking of cameras when the Picasso came up. Charlie started the bidding at £5 million and took it up briskly in bids of £500,000 to £12 million; it then soared past the previous record for a twentieth-century picture – achieved by Park Avenue only two weeks before with Picasso's blue period *Maternité* at £13.67 million ($24.74 million) – to £16 million, in bids of £1 million. The bidding then was between one of the large number of Japanese in the room and a member of Christie's staff on the telephone to America. Charlie finally called out £19 million "to the gentleman at the back on my left, any more, any more?" Down came the hammer and clapping broke out. It had taken just over two minutes.

The Japanese bidder then became the target of TV cameras and photographers, all jostling to get a proper photograph. I was standing by chance right behind them. Bedlam was not far away, as the photographers, frustrated at being unable to get near the Japanese, who had their heads down and were looking very worried, tried to push past those seated in the same row. A harassed Mark Wrey appeared and forced the photographers to withdraw, as they were disturbing the whole proceedings.

A little later the two Japanese got up and left before Mark could get to them. They went down the main stairs with the TV cameramen and most of the Press in hot pursuit, like a pack of wolves. Out into the street everyone went, with Mark Wrey, Christopher Davidge and security men trying to prevent the TV cameramen harassing the Japanese. Both were wide-eyed and just nodded their heads to the questions being fired at them, although as they didn't speak any English they didn't know what the Press were saying. At one moment the Japanese were pinned against a car. As no taxis were around, Mark helped by Christopher fought his way back, dragging the bewildered Japanese into the Press Office, and put a security guard outside.

An element of farce dispelled what was rapidly becoming a nightmare for Mark, when he took them into his personal sanctum only to find Geraldine and Donald Wintersgill writing their stories. As he gently pushed the Japanese back, both gasped, "Coca-Cola, Coca-Cola." By chance Mark had a secret store, and having grabbed three tins finally found sanctuary in the ground-floor Board Room. A taxi was called and the Japanese made their escape by a side door.

Meanwhile the sale continued for another hour and achieved five more auction record prices for works by Gauguin, £3.85 million, Giacometti, £3.74 million for one of his six-foot-high walking men; Klee £1.65 million, Signac £1.1 million and Kirchner £330,000. Although it did not achieve a record price, one of the loveliest pictures was Monet's *Le Pont Japonais*, one of the finest examples of his water-lily series of his garden at Giverny, which sold for £5.5 million.

Peter Rose announced the results in the Press Office – basically the drill was the same as in my day, but with modern technology and the ability to use it, the information came much quicker. With premium the Picasso had sold for £20.9 million ($38.4 million), not only a record price for a twentieth-century picture, but the third highest auction price for any picture. The total for the whole evening's sale was £55.4 million ($102 million), the highest ever total for any art auction in London. While Peter was talking to the Press, William Hanham and Marianne, both of whom had worked for me, were extracting any record prices from the computer and incorporating them in the after-sale Press release, the basis of which had been prepared before the sale began. By the time Peter had finished, Xerox copies of this were being run off in the office and given to every journalist. The Press release was then of course telexed to Christie's offices round the world.

While this was going on, Mark was preparing the nearby Board Room for the Press to discuss the sale over pink champagne with

Charlie, James Roundell and John Lumley. Picasso's *Jeune Arlequine* and the two top-priced Monets had been brought down long before and hung in a viewing room just off the Board Room so that the Press could see them at leisure. The anonymous Japanese buyer turned out to be Mr Akio Nishino, the art director of the Mitsubishi department store. A Mitsubishi spokesman in Tokyo said the next day that one of their customers had asked them to buy the picture.

Christie's had more than regained the prestige it had had in the 1920s. Quite properly, though, the firm was looking ahead to 1992 when in theory the art markets in Europe will be open to every member of the EEC, particularly France – Paris was the centre of the art market before the French Revolution. François Curiel had recently been made managing director of Christie's Europe. Aged forty and born in Paris, François is the perfect man to weld the European salerooms and offices together to prepare for holding sales in Paris.

Sensing that Christie's future lay more with Christopher Davidge's and François's generation, Guy Hannen just before Christmas decided that he would give up being managing director of Christies International, but remain deputy chairman. However, he was to retire from the firm in May 1989. This meant that Davidge was sole managing director of Christies International, as well as of Christie's King Street: no mean feat for a 43-year-old.

When they were announced, the 1988 results not surprisingly proved to be the highest in Christie's history. The sales total was £779 million with pre-tax profits of £42.5 million, compared to £32 million for the previous year. In addition there was a three-for-one scrip issue. Lord Carrington when announcing the results paid tribute to Guy Hannen's "unique contribution to the company's growth and international development".

Considering the inertia which existed in 1958 in spite of Peter's efforts to bring about changes, that none of the Board had any business experience and that the number of people in the firm with any real expertise could be counted on one hand, such figures and the recovery of Christie's generally was a staggering achievement. Peter Chance would have been pleased, I think, by the figures and happy that those who followed on after him were not found wanting.

Christie's today is a very different place from what it was in 1958 when Judy and I entered its doors for the first time. It is no longer an anonymous-looking building on which the name of the firm on the brass plates on the pillars each side was virtually invisible after years of Brasso. You have only to walk down King Street, St James's, and see the flags and look into the colourful display windows, which in 1958 didn't exist, to realise you are looking at an international business which is alive and forward-looking. I regard myself as very fortunate to have been asked by Peter Chance to join his team. There were times during my twenty-six years when being public relations director was like sitting in a "hot seat", but it was a very fulfilling one, now that I look back on it all. Like all of Peter's "old sweats", as Jo called us, I hope I can be forgiven if I confess to being proud to have played a part in the recovery of such a great firm and to have left it in such good hands that its continued success is assured.

Graphs

The "Tortoise and the Hare"

A comparison of Christie's and Sotheby's
Pre-tax profits, 1959–1988

This graph is only a guide illustrating the financial history of the two firms, although it is
based on official figures (where available). The financial years changed and at times
incorporated 15 or 18 month periods. Up till 1967, Christie's financial year ended on March
31 and since going public in 1973 it has been for the calendar year.

Christie's ————
Sotheby's ••••••••

Source: Teather and Greenwood

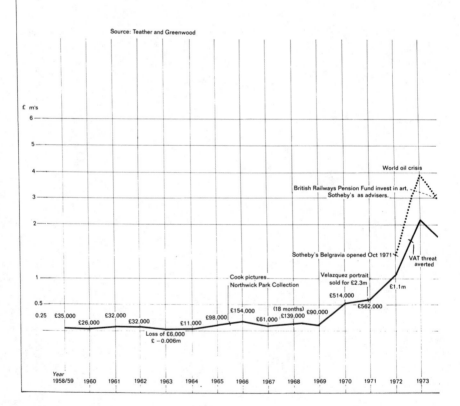

£ m's

6 —

5 —

4 —   World oil crisis

British Railways Pension Fund invest in art,
3 —   Sotheby's as advisers.

2 —

Sotheby's Belgravia opened Oct 1971   VAT threat
averted

1 —   Cook pictures   Velazquez portrait
Northwick Park Collection   sold for £2.3m   £1.1m
£514,000
0.5 —   £154,000   (18 months)   £90,000   £562,000
0.25   £35,000   £32,000   £98,000   £139,000
£26,000   £32,000   £11,000   £61,000
Loss of £6,000
£ −0.006m

Year
1958/59   1960   1961   1962   1963   1964   1965   1966   1967   1968   1969   1970   1971   1972   1973

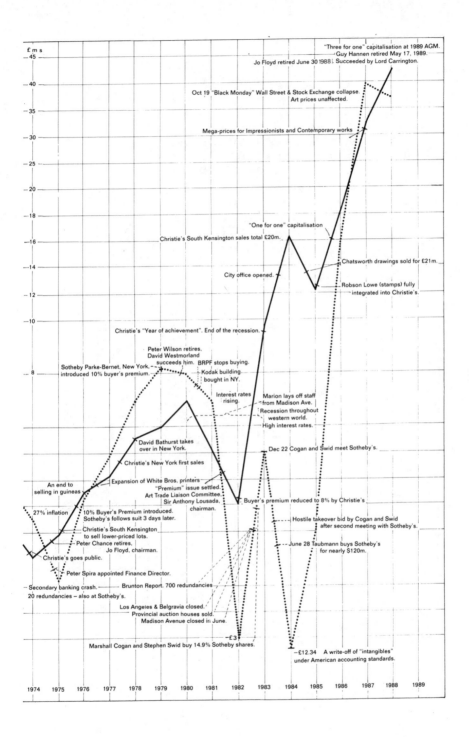

£ m s
— 45
— 40
— 35
— 30
— 25
— 20
— 18
— 16
— 14
— 12
— 10
— 8

"Three for one" capitalisation at 1989 AGM.
Guy Hannen retired May 17, 1989.
Jo Floyd retired June 30 1988. Succeeded by Lord Carrington.

Oct 19 "Black Monday" Wall Street & Stock Exchange collapse.
Art prices unaffected.

Mega-prices for Impressionists and Contemporary works

"One for one" capitalisation

Christie's South Kensington sales total £20m.

Chatsworth drawings sold for £21m.

City office opened.

Robson Lowe (stamps) fully
integrated into Christie's.

Christie's "Year of achievement". End of the recession.

Peter Wilson retires.
David Westmorland
succeeds him. BRPF stops buying.
Sotheby Parke-Bernet, New York,
introduced 10% buyer's premium.

Kodak building
bought in NY.

Marion lays off staff
Interest rates   from Madison Ave.
rising.   Recession throughout
western world.
High interest rates.

David Bathurst takes
over in New York.

Dec 22 Cogan and Swid meet Sotheby's.

Christie's New York first sales

An end to
selling in guineas

Expansion of White Bros. printers
"Premium" issue settled.
Art Trade Liaison Committee.
Sir Anthony Lousada,
chairman.

27% inflation

10% Buyer's Premium introduced.
Sotheby's follows suit 3 days later.

Buyer's premium reduced to 8% by Christie's

Hostile takeover bid by Cogan and Swid
after second meeting with Sotheby's.

Christie's South Kensington
to sell lower-priced lots.

Peter Chance retires.
Jo Floyd, chairman.

June 28 Taubmann buys Sotheby's
for nearly $120m.

Christie's goes public.

Peter Spira appointed Finance Director.

Secondary banking crash.   Brunton Report. 700 redundancies
20 redundancies – also at Sotheby's.

Los Angeles & Belgravia closed.
Provincial auction houses sold.
Madison Avenue closed in June.

—£3

—£12.34   A write-off of "intangibles"
under American accounting standards.

Marshall Cogan and Stephen Swid buy 14.9% Sotheby shares.

1974   1975   1976   1977   1978   1979   1980   1981   1982   1983   1984   1985   1986   1987   1988   1989

A COMPARISON OF CHRISTIE'S and SOTHEBY'S
ANNUAL SALES RESULTS –
1954–1989 in £m

Note: Until 1970 sales totals included "bought-in" lots.
Sales results for both firms are for the "auction
season" – October 1–July 31. As from 1973, when
Christie's went public, the results are for the
calendar year. Sotheby's total sales remain as
for the "auction season".

Christie's ——————

Sotheby's ••••••••••

Source: Teather and Greenwood

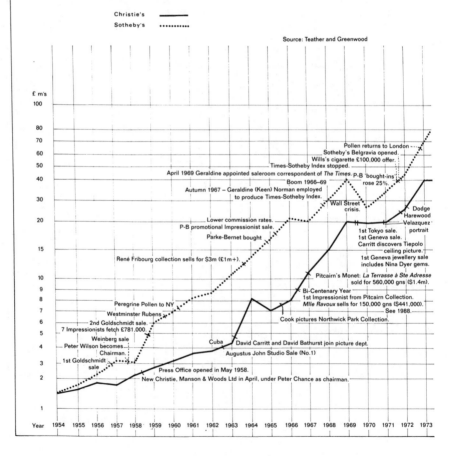

£ m's
100

80
70
60   Pollen returns to London - - - -
50   Sotheby's Belgravia opened.
                                               Wills's cigarette £100,000 offer.
                                        Times-Sotheby Index stopped.
40   April 1969 Geraldine appointed saleroom correspondent of *The Times*. P-B 'bought-ins'
                                          Boom 1966–69   rose 25%.
     Autumn 1967 – Geraldine (Keen) Norman employed
30   to produce Times-Sotheby Index.
                                                         Wall Street
                                                         crisis.   Dodge
20   Harewood
                              Lower commission rates.   Velazquez
     P-B promotional Impressionist sale.   1st Tokyo sale.   portrait
                              Parke-Bernet bought   1st Geneva sale.
15   Carritt discovers Tiepolo
                                                                     ceiling picture.
     René Fribourg collection sells for $3m (£1m+).   1st Geneva jewellery sale
                                                             includes Nina Dyer gems.
10   Pitcairn's Monet: *La Terrasse à Ste Adresse*
 9   sold for 560,000 gns ($1.4m).
 8   Bi-Centenary Year
                                             1st Impressionist from Pitcairn Collection.
 7   Peregrine Pollen to NY   *Mlle Ravoux* sells for 150,000 gns ($441,000).
     Westminster Rubens   See 1988.
 6   2nd Goldschmidt sale.   Cook pictures Northwick Park Collection.
 5   7 Impressionists fetch £781,000.
     Weinberg sale
 4   Peter Wilson becomes   Cuba   David Carritt and David Bathurst join picture dept.
     Chairman.
     1st Goldschmidt   Augustus John Studio Sale (No.1)
 3   sale.
             Press Office opened in May 1958.
 2   New Christie, Manson & Woods Ltd in April, under Peter Chance as chairman.

 1

Year 1954 1955 1956 1957 1958 1959 1960 1961 1962 1963 1964 1965 1966 1967 1968 1969 1970 1971 1972 1973

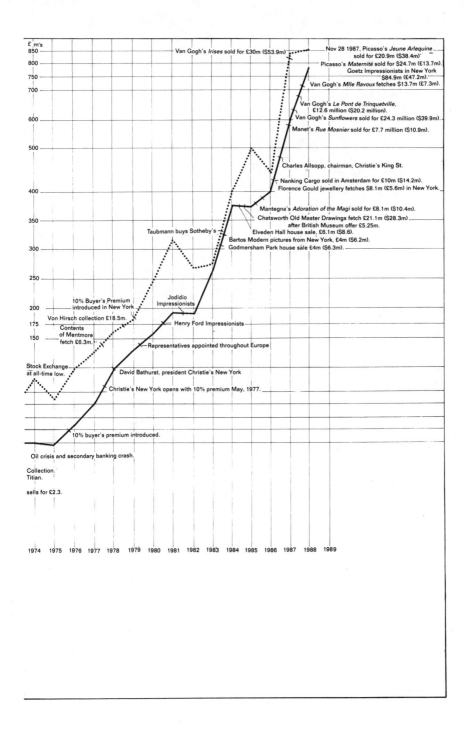

£ m's
850 — Van Gogh's *Irises* sold for £30m ($53.9m) — Nov 28 1987, Picasso's *Jeune Arlequine* sold for £20.9m ($38.4m)
800 — Picasso's *Maternité* sold for $24.7m (£13.7m).
Goetz Impressionists in New York
750 — $84.9m (£47.2m).
Van Gogh's *Mlle Ravoux* fetches $13.7m (£7.3m).
700 —

Van Gogh's *Le Pont de Trinquetville*, £12.6 million ($20.2 million).
600 — Van Gogh's *Sunflowers* sold for £24.3 million ($39.9m).
Manet's *Rue Mosnier* sold for £7.7 million ($10.9m).

500 —
Charles Allsopp, chairman, Christie's King St.
Nanking Cargo sold in Amsterdam for £10m ($14.2m).
400 — Florence Gould jewellery fetches $8.1m (£5.6m) in New York.

Mantegna's *Adoration of the Magi* sold for £8.1m ($10.4m).
350 — Chatsworth Old Master Drawings fetch £21.1m ($28.3m) after British Museum offer £5.25m.
Taubmann buys Sotheby's — Elveden Hall house sale, £6.1m ($8.6).
Bartos Modern pictures from New York, £4m ($6.2m).
300 — Godmersham Park house sale £4m ($6.3m).

250 —

Jodidio
Impressionists
200 — 10% Buyer's Premium introduced in New York
175 — Von Hirsch collection £18.5m. Henry Ford Impressionists
Contents
150 — of Mentmore fetch £6.3m. Representatives appointed throughout Europe

Stock Exchange at all-time low.
David Bathurst, president Christie's New York

Christie's New York opens with 10% premium May, 1977.

10% buyer's premium introduced.

Oil crisis and secondary banking crash.

Collection.
Titian.

sells for £2.3.

1974 1975 1976 1977 1978 1979 1980 1981 1982 1983 1984 1985 1986 1987 1988 1989

Index

Index

Index

Department of the Environment, 259, 260
Derby, Lord, 27, 179
Derby House, 27
Derham, Anthony, 149, 202, 206, 214
Des Graz, Charles, 38
Detroit, 171, 173, 176, 188, 189
Detroit Institute of Art, 183, 184
Deux Blanchisseuses Portant du Linge (Degas), 25
Deux Danseuses en Scène (Degas), 25
Deux Rats (Van Gogh), 288
Devis, Arthur, 315
Devonshire, Duke of, 297, 330, 331
Diamond, Father, 243
diamonds, 48, 50, 51, 52
Dick, Jack, 241
Dickin, Maria Elizabeth, 203
Dickin Medal, 202–3
Dictionary of Victorian Artists (Wood), 206
Dietrich, Marlene, 264
Dillman, Hugh, 175, 176
Dillon, Douglas, 170
Dior, Christian, 265
Director of Fair Trading, 314
Dodge, Anna Thomson, 171, 174–5, 176, 183, 188, 189, 190, 319
Dodge, Horace, 174, 190
Dodge, John, 174
Dodge Collection, 173, 174, 176–9, 182, 183, 184, 188, 198
Dodge Trustees, 173, 174, 178, 183
Doheny, Estelle, 369
Dolan, Patrick (PDA), 15, 16, 17, 42, 52, 53, 54, 201
Domaine Enchantée, La (Magritte), 289
Dorelia in the Garden of Alderney Manor, Dorset (John), 284
Doughty House, Richmond, 100
Drooglever, Debbie, 201
Du Boulay, Anthony, 17, 44–7, 86, 123, 130, 137, 148, 149, 150, 157, 167, 168, 173, 187, 228, 248, 342
Dubuffet, Jean, 324
Duccio di Buoninsegna, 97, 98, 226
Dufy, Raoul, 116
Duncan, Alastair, 274
Dunnally, Lord, 171
Durand-Ruel, 88
Dürer, Albrecht, 61, 101, 108, 112
Düsseldorf, 188, 207, 208, 221

Dutch art, 14, 24, 63, 332
Duveen, Lord Joseph, 31, 63, 171, 175–8, 205, 319
Dyck, Sir Anthony van, 22, 179, 332
Dyer, Nina, 155, 156

Eagle Star Insurance, 28
Earls Court motor show, 207
Eaton Hall, Cheshire, 52
Ecce Homo (Rembrandt), 206
Eccentric Club, 370
Eccles, Lord, 183
Edelstein, Annamaria, 220
Edinburgh, 268
Edmiston's, 268
Edward VII, King, 298, 328, 329
Edward G. Robinson collection, 163, 236
Edwards, Doreen, 118
Egypt, 89, 92, 159, 160
Egyptian sculpture, 208
Eliot, T. S., 65, 76
Elizabeth, Queen, the Queen Mother, 48, 49, 320–21
Elizabeth II, Queen, 48, 49, 85
Elsheimer, Adam, 178, 298
Elton House, 284
Elveden Hall, Norfolk, 327–30
Empire style, 41
Enfants Jardiniers tapestries, 330
Engelhard, Charles, 206
Enigme du Désir, L' (Dali), 302
Entarte Kunst sale, 372
Erickson, Alfred W., 112–13
Erroll, Lord, 137
Eskenazi, 355
Estate Duty, 168, 172, 173, 244
ethnographica, 46
Etruscan art, 281
Etude du Nu (Degas), 278
Eureka diamond, 49
European Board, 342
Evelyn Library, 227
Evening Standard, 49, 61, 73, 81, 129, 172, 225
Exeter, Lady, 45
Expressionists, 302
Eyck, Jan van, 172
Eyles, Reggie, 70–72, 130

Fabergé, Peter Carl, 45, 157, 167, 337, 355

391

Index

Index

Index